Psychoanalytic Perspectives
on the Rorschach

PSYCHOANALYTIC PERSPECTIVES

ON THE

RORSCHACH

Paul M. Lerner

THE ANALYTIC PRESS

1998   Hillsdale, NJ   London

Published by
The Analytic Press, Inc.
  Editorial Offices:
  101 West Street
  Hillsdale, New Jersey 07642

Index by Leonard S. Rosenbaum

Library of Congress Cataloging-in-Publication Data

Lerner, Paul M.
  Psychoanalytic perspectives on the Rorschach / Paul M. Lerner
p.   cm.
  Includes bibliographical references and index.
  ISBN 0-88163-234-1
1. Rorschach Test. 2. Psychoanalysis. I. Title.
  RC473.R6L468 1998
  155.2'842—dc21   97-51640
                                                          CIP

Printed in the United States of America
10 9 8 7 6 5 4 3 2 1

This book is dedicated to Caroline Rosalie and to the memory of Boca.

CONTENTS

Part 2
Research Applications

Introduction

In 1996 I was honored by the Society for Personality Assessment by being presented the Bruno Klopfer Award for distinguished contributions to personality assessment. Upon accepting the award, I admitted to an incurable affliction. My analyst, years ago, correctly described it as a romantic attachment to the past. I cry unabashedly when listening to the music of Gershwin, exploring the Baseball Hall of Fame Museum in Cooperstown, New York, or watching a small-town Fourth of July parade in Camden, Maine.

Professionally, my ailment finds expression in a reverence for tradition. Having trained at the Menninger Foundation, an institution itself steeped in history, it was inevitable I would follow in a tradition begun by David Rapaport and later extended by his students and his students' students, including Roy Schafer, Martin Mayman, Robert Holt, and Stephen Appelbaum. Being part of such a tradition affords one ties to the past, feelings of solidness and belonging, and a sense of place.

In this book, more so than in my earlier one, *Psychoanalytic Theory and the Rorschach*, I move away from several of Rapaport's thoughts and propositions regarding the Rorschach and Rorschach testing. Nonetheless, in body and in spirit, this book is an extension of his Rorschach vision and of the relationship he piloted between the Rorschach and psychoanalytic theory. Then too, embroidered into the fabric of this work are aspects of Rapaport's personhood.

Rapaport, according to Gill (1967), felt "an enormous debt to the past" (p. 7). Sharing in this obligation, for readers less familiar with Rapaport, I offer these cameo snapshots of his professional life.

Born in Hungary in 1911, Rapaport emigrated to the United States in 1938. After working briefly at Mt. Sinai Hospital in New York and Osawatomie State Hospital in Kansas, in 1940, at the bequest and urging of Karl Menninger, he moved to Topeka, Kansas and became, in

Margaret Brenman-Gibson's words, "the Menninger Clinic's first 'real psychologist'" (Gibson and Shapiro, 1993, p. 18).

It was Rapaport's intellectual rigor and passion together with Karl Menninger's foresight and charisma that helped establish the Menninger Clinic as the "Athens of psychoanalytic training and research" in the United States (Gibson and Shapiro, 1993, p. 18). For the eight years he remained at Menninger, Rapaport stimulated and directed a vast number of research projects beginning with his pioneering work on diagnostic psychological testing. Because he was instrumental in the elevation of psychologists in the 1940s from technicians giving IQ tests to clinicians employing full test batteries, he, according to Friedman (1990), was a national leader in transforming the role of psychologists outside academia.

When Robert Knight went to Austen Riggs in Stockbridge, Massachusetts in 1947, he persuaded Rapaport and his research group to join him. Rapaport left Menninger in 1948 and spent the final 12 years of his life at Riggs. It was at Riggs, following his years of immersion in psychological diagnostic testing, that Rapaport began his next project—integrating and systematizing psychoanalytic theory so as to establish psychoanalysis as a general psychology.

As part of this thrust, Rapaport conceived of the idea of a new journal *(Psychological Issues)* that would feature monographs all related to the theme of a general psychoanalytic theory of behavior. Erik Erikson's classic and seminal work, *Identity and the Life Cycle*, was selected for the first issue.

Rapaport agreed to write the introduction. In keeping with the journal's mission, he provided a systematic and brilliant overview of the conceptual evolution of psychoanalysis as a general psychology. He discussed Erikson, recognizing the remarkable step beyond Freud that Erikson had taken in his joining the inner with the outer world by according reality relations major significance across the entire life span. In response to Rapaport's characterizing his work as "an organic extension of Freud's theory," Erikson later confided to Gibson, "I suppose one might say that David was the only person who knew enough to put me in my place" (Gibson and Shapiro, 1993, p. 19).

Of his many and important contributions to the Rorschach literature, none was more significant than his wedding the procedure to a specific and comprehensive theory of personality. The marriage Rapaport brokered between the Rorschach and psychoanalytic theory has been a longstanding and productive one between method and theory.

Rapaport envisioned the relation between method and theory as a two-way street. It is this reciprocal thoroughfare that has provided the basic foundation upon which virtually all subsequent psychoanalytic contributions to Rorschach theory and usage rest. In one direction, he saw theory as offering the Rorschach examiner a vast array of clinical concepts and formulations that could serve to remarkably enliven, broaden, and deepen test-derived inferences. In the other direction, he saw the Rorschach as providing the psychoanalytic theorist and researcher a means for operationalizing concepts that were elusive and often overly abstract, and saw further how this process could allow the empirical investigation of important but untested formulations, and thus, in time, could add to the evolving scope of psychoanalytic theory.

This book, like *Psychoanalytic Theory and the Rorschach*, is organized in such a way as to reflect both sides of Rapaport's vision. In Part 1, total emphasis is accorded the clinical application of the Rorschach from a psychoanalytic perspective. In Part 2, emphasis shifts to research applications. Here, I review core psychoanalytic concepts and clinical syndromes, such as defense, object representation, narcissistic disturbances, and then present Rorschach scales and scoring systems that have sought to translate such concepts and disturbances into the language of the Rorschach.

Like the earlier book, this one too attempts to combine an introduction to a psychoanalytic approach to the Rorschach with an updated version of that approach by integrating recent theoretical, clinical, and research advances in both psychoanalytic theory and Rorschach theory and assessment.

This current work may and should be regarded as an extension of *Psychoanalytic Theory and the Rorschach*. Make no mistake, however; although both books are organized in a similar fashion and both share a common interest, this work differs from the earlier one in a number of important ways.

In Part 1, the previous structural orientation gives way here to a considerably more experiential one. Empathy, not only as a way of relating, but also as a way of coming to know another, is accorded major importance. This shift in orientation is reflected in the addition of several new chapters, including chapter 1, "An Experiential Psychoanalytic Approach"; chapter 5, "The Rorschach Assessment Frame"; and chapter 13, "Two Approaches to Interpretation." In accord with this shift in focus, several other chapters in this section have been significantly revised.

Based upon the very recent and ground-breaking work of Leichtman (1996), this book includes a chapter (chapter 2) on the nature of the Rorschach task. Scattered throughout the earlier book were more random thoughts and suggestions as to how the Rorschach assessment, including test findings, could be used for treatment planning. By comparison, and in line with contemporary interests and trends, these recommendations are systematically pulled together, updated, and presented in chapter 15.

Part 2, "Research Applications," has been significantly extended and revised as well. In order to reflect better current interests, chapters devoted to the concept and assessment of dissociation and to a systematic and integrated review of Rapaport's fifth scoring category (deviant verbalizations) have been added.

Chapter 16, "The Rorschach Assessment of Object Representations," has been significantly expanded, given the virtual explosion of interest and work in the area. Included in the current chapter are reviews of attempts to extend the assessment of object representations to groups of children and attempts to integrate the psychoanalytic concept of object representation with the concept of working models arising from attachment theory.

In the 1991 book, I furnished a progress report on a developmental object-relations scale, under construction, that was based upon an integration of Piaget's theory of early cognitive development with Mahler's theory of separation-individuation. The completed scale, together with preliminary findings, is presented in chapter 20.

Rapaport was generative. The debt he felt to the past was balanced by an equally weighty responsibility he felt to the future. I too feel a responsibility to the future and future generations. As I view the current Rorschach landscape, I am both pleased and disquieted by several contemporary trends. Quite heartening is the growing push to integrate two broad, different, yet not incompatible approaches to Rorschach assessment and interpretation—the empirical approach of John Exner and the psychoanalytic approach. Notwithstanding Smith's (1994) important reminder that the two approaches are based on very different epistemologies—a difference Smith characterizes, quoting from Bertrand Russell, as that between the "narrow minded" and the "fuzzy headed"—one need only review the recent contributions of Erdberg (1993), Gacono and Meloy (1994), Weiner (1994), and Acklin (1995) to appreciate this thrust.

Although I support and encourage such integrative efforts and devote chapter 26 in this book to it, I would like to sound a warning.

One should appreciate that psychoanalytic Rorschach testing is more than an application of a body of knowledge to test responses for interpretive purposes. It is that, but it also involves an attitude toward, a way of clinically assessing, and a way of thinking about individuals, psychic phenomena, and relationships. Involved too, is an obligation to constantly scrutinize what one does and why one does it.

The discomforting trend issues from biological psychiatry, with its attempt to deny human experience, and also from its counterpart, managed care, with its attempt to commercialize clinical work. Under the sway of these two forces, a language of diagnosis, behavioral description, and target symptoms is attempting to replace an earlier language of experience and dynamics; the clinical relationship, its meaning, value, and role as a vehicle of understanding and change is under siege; and genuine change is regarded as magical, quick, effortless, and painless.

To those intimidated and frightened by these forces, especially the young in our field, I suggest the following. Rapaport wrote his pioneering volumes (*Diagnostic Psychological Testing*, 2 vols.) more than 50 years ago, and Schafer wrote his Rorschach classic *(Psychoanalytic Interpretation in Rorschach Testing)* more than 40 years ago. This tradition has withstood the test of time. It also has not remained static. As psychoanalytic theory has shifted from an earlier interest in drives and structures, couched in the impersonal language of metapsychology, to its current emphasis on self and relationships, presented in a more experience-near language, this, in turn, has provided fresh and exciting opportunities for Rorschach theory and usage.

At the 1996 International Rorschach Congress held in Boston, I had the pleasure and honor of being interviewed with Marty Mayman. Mayman, a former student of Rapaport's and a Rorschach giant in his own right, had been a teacher and supervisor of mine at Menninger. We discussed a wide range of topics, including Mayman's experiences with Rapaport and my experiences with Mayman. Most poignant, however, was when the interviewer invited each of us to reflect back upon our careers and to select what felt most memorable and meaningful. Mayman spoke first. To my surprise and delight, independently, he mentioned exactly what I had intended to. He commented that his involvement with the Rorschach spanned almost 50 years. Yet, each time he is presented a new protocol, he still feels the same exhilaration, curiosity, and opportunity to be creative that he had five decades earlier. I enthusiastically echoed his remark.

This tradition calls for extended training, a strong commitment, discipline, hard work, preciseness of thought, and a willingness to make explicit what one does. The payback is in the surge of excitement, the feeling of clinical challenge, and the sense of being creative one experiences each time one administers and interprets a Rorschach anew. This too is a part of Rapaport's legacy.

Part 1

Clinical Applications

1

AN EXPERIENTIAL
PSYCHOANALYTIC
APPROACH

As noted in the introduction, psychoanalytic approaches to the Rorschach test are based on the pioneering work of David Rapaport. Yet, recent and significant shifts in psychoanalytic theory are leading Rorschach theorists (P. Lerner, 1992) away from Rapaport's virtually exclusive structural approach and toward an interest in experiential factors. In this chapter, I explain and discuss what is meant by an experiential psychoanalytic approach to the Rorschach. Although the emphasis here is experiential, this is not intended as a replacement of Rapaport's earlier structural focus. Rather, it should be regarded as an extension.

I begin by comparing psychoanalytic approaches to the Rorschach with empirical ones. Such a comparison is meant to serve two purposes. First, it is a way of introducing the reader to a way of thinking about and using the Rorschach that is based in psychoanalysis. Second, it will assist the reader in beginning to place an experiential approach within the broader scheme of Rorschach approaches in general. To locate an experiential psychoanalytic approach more finely, I then discuss the nature of psychoanalytic theory and the relationship between the theory and the Rorschach. Finally, I trace the roots of and outline a psychoanalytically based experiential Rorschach approach.

✦ ✦ ✦ Two Approaches to the Rorschach

The past two decades have witnessed an unparalleled interest in the Rorschach as a means of studying and understanding people. Two streams have contributed to this renewal of interest: an empirical one exemplified by the work of Exner (1974, 1993) and his Comprehensive System, and a conceptual one exemplified in attempts to apply psychoanalytic concepts and formulations to Rorschach theory (Leichtman, 1996) and interpretation (P. Lerner, 1991a).

Despite creative and relatively successful attempts to integrate these streams (Erdberg, 1993; Weiner, 1994; Kleiger, in press), the approaches are markedly different. Basic ways in which they differ include the following: (1) primary emphasis, including the role and value accorded the person of the examiner; (2) accepted sources of Rorschach data; (3) the importance of a testing rationale; (4) the issue of a test battery; and (5) the role accorded a theory of personality that is independent of the test itself.

Clinical Versus Psychometric Emphasis

Implicit in an empirical approach to the Rorschach is a primary psychometric orientation. It is the test that occupies center stage, issues of test reliability and validity are of paramount concern, the process is conceived of as one of measuring, and the examiner's essential task is to administer the test in the most unobtrusive and standardized way possible.

In contrast to a psychometric orientation, a psychoanalytic approach has a clinical orientation. Here, one is assessing, not measuring; the patient, rather than the test, is regarded as the centerpiece; and the assessment is conducted in a manner and style consistent with clinical purposes.

From a clinical perspective, the ultimate purpose of an assessment is not the achieving of a diagnosis and the assigning of a diagnostic label. Instead, one attempts to understand the testee in his or her totality, complexity, and uniqueness, and then use that understanding as a basis for making decisions and suggesting interventions that will be beneficial to that individual.

A clinical emphasis is especially reflected in the requisite capacities expected of the examiner and the expanded role and weighty responsibilities assigned to him or her. As with every clinical encounter with a patient, Rorschach testing requires that the examiner be sensitive, accepting, and nonjudgmental, and empathically attuned to the emotional nuances of the relationship. If, for example, a patient's heightened anxiety is creating undo distress and is interfering with his or her capacity to engage in the testing, then it is incumbent upon the examiner to deal with the distress and not insensitively push forward with the testing.

The clinical examiner, too, values standardized test administration; however, such adherence is balanced with tact, a sense of appropriateness, clinical judgment, and one's meaning-seeking orientation. For example, there are occasions when the examiner will depart from standardized test procedures. Slightly revising the precise wording of instructions, determining the patient's attitude toward an unusual response, or pursuing the meaning of an especially jarring response are three such instances. When the examiner does depart from standard procedures, the reason prompting the departure and its effect on subsequent responses need to be understood and taken into account.

The questions the examiner puts to himself or herself are, in Mayman's (1964a) terms, "person centered," not "test centered," and reflect his or her meaning-seeking stance. For example, rather than asking "Is this a schizophrenic sign?" or "How many texture responses are there?" one asks instead, "What use did the patient make of me in our testing encounter?" and "Is he or she likely to engage a therapist in a similar way?"

In clinical testing, then, the examiner is seen as vitally intrinsic to the process, and the role accorded is far broader and less prescribed. Underlying these differences in role and way of functioning, are contrasting attitudes toward the examiner. In psychometric testing, the examiner, like the research investigator, is seen as a potential source of bias and error. Efforts are made to minimize, if not altogether, eliminate his or her influence. Then too, little attention is paid to the transactions that occur between examiner and patient. In clinical testing, by contrast, the examiner is valued and trusted. He or she is regarded as a reliable and unique source of information. The variety of interactional reactions that inevitably and necessarily arise in the patient–examiner relationship are not avoided or disregarded. To the contrary, such reactions are observed, recorded, and then used as indispensable aids in bringing greater clarity and meaning to the patient's behavior and attitudes.

Sources of Information

A second difference between the two approaches involves sources of information. In general, those who approach the Rorschach from an empirical perspective tend to rely on one source—the scores and their interrelationships. For instance, even though Exner's Comprehensive system admits to three sources—the structural summary, the sequence of scores, and the patient's verbalizations—in reviewing illustrative case material, it is clear that the structural summary is the heart and soul of the system and that the other sources serve to refine and extend inferences derived from the summary.

The psychoanalytically oriented examiner recognizes that test scores and quantitative summaries are important, but that certain facets of the individual's experience are expressed on the Rorschach in ways not reflected by the scores. The psychoanalytic perspective, then, provides a number of sources of information about the patient that can serve as a springboard for developing clinical inferences. These include (1) the formal aspects of test responses, including test scores and their interrelations; (2) the content of the testee's specific responses, including his or her attitude toward the response; (3) the sequence of responses; (4) the patient's behavior in the assessment, including more spontaneous and offhand comments; and (5) the nature and vicissitudes of the patient–examiner relationship.

With respect to these various sources, the psychoanalytic examiner's task is to attend to each of these sources and to integrate the data of one with that of another. Each source must be given its due and be seen as having its own consistency with the other types of information. The art of psychological testing, as Schlesinger (1973) noted, consists of sensitively shifting attention from one to another of these sources, while developing and checking inferences throughout the assessment.

With respect to the empirical and psychoanalytic approaches to sources of information, there are two provisions to be added. First, with the movement toward integration has come a greater appreciation of the other approach's contribution. For example, those with an empirical bent (Exner, 1996) have begun to consider more seriously the inferential value of Rorschach content. At the same time, psychoanalytic examiners are coming to realize that more can be gleaned from a careful appraisal of the formal scores than they had allowed.

Second, beginning with Rorschach himself, a distinction has been drawn between the formal and structural features of a record and the substantative or content aspects. Some (Aronow, Reznikoff, and Moreland, 1995) have tended to associate the psychoanalytic approach with a primary if not exclusive concern with content. As I have indicated above, both historically and presently, this is not the case. Although several psychoanalytic theorists (P. Lerner, 1991b; Mayman, 1977) have suggested approaches to content that are thoughtful and systematic, this has not been to the exclusion or devaluation of structural features. Rapaport and those following in his tradition have insisted on complete and accurate scoring, together with a careful consideration of quantitative summaries.

Testing Rationale

The legitimacy of the Rorschach as a clinical diagnostic technique rests upon building bridges between test responses on the one hand, and personality, behavior, and the dynamic underpinnings of personality on the other hand.

Such connecting bridges, depending upon one's Rorschach orientation, have been based upon empirical findings, theory, or a combination of both. Empirically based approaches, as to be expected and in keeping with their psychometric focus, have established such links primarily on the basis of empirical findings. Assumed relationships between particular scores or combinations of scores and specific character traits have been subjected to more rigorous scientific investigation. As a result, what at one time was considered Rorschach lore is now a sound body of knowledge, which furnishes a sturdy basis for Rorschach interpretation.

Psychoanalytic theorists have taken a different route, a more theoretical or conceptual one, in which emphasis is placed on identifying mediating processes that connect test responses with personality structure and functioning. Representative of this approach is the work of Rapaport (Rapaport, Gill, and Schafer, 1945–1946). For Rapaport, the construct "thought processes" served this mediating function. It was from the organization of thought, including such subprocesses as concept formation, anticipation, memory, judgment, attention, and concentration, that he derived inferences related to other aspects of personality functioning.

This conceptualization of thinking as a conduit to personality structure and functioning, and of the inferential power of assessing thought processes, is especially well stated by Schafer (1954):

A person's distinctive style of thinking is indicative of ingrained features of his character make up. Character is here understood as the person's enduring modes of bringing into harmony internal demands and the press of external events; in other words, it refers to relatively constant adjustment efforts in the face of problem situations. The modes of achieving this harmony are understood to consist essentially of reliance on particular mechanisms of defense and related responsiveness to stimulation associated with these defenses [p. 17].

Rapaport did something else too. In addition to explaining how and why personality structure is reflected in Rorschach responses, he also established a rationale as to why psychological testing should be included in psychiatric examinations. Although offered almost 50 years ago (Rapaport, 1950), his argument is still as relevant and cogent today.

Rapaport (1950) began by noting that psychiatry, like other clinical disciplines, requires objectivity. That is, it requires procedures to complement its methods, which tend to be subjective and judgmental. For sources of information, psychiatrists rely on case histories and psychiatric examinations. Material gained from each, however, is manifold and requires selectivity. In taking a case history, the clinician must not only organize the data, but must also subjectively select those aspects thought to be most relevant. In providing a case history the patient, the informant, or both also introduce selective factors: an unconscious one, rooted in the organization of their memories; an involuntary one, rooted in the limitations of their knowledge; and a deliberate one, rooted partly in judgments based on their attitudes and partly in intentions to conceal. As a consequence, different case histories are likely to contain different categories of data. This means that no point-to-point comparison is possible between case histories. Furthermore, because one cannot quantify the data, organizing the material into a meaningful whole, so as to yield a diagnosis and treatment plan, also involves subjective judgment and selection.

By comparison with information elicited in a case history, psychological test responses are limited segments of behavior. Such behavior segments can be recorded relatively completely. In this regard, they are more objective.

The same categories of behavior of reaction are obtained from all individuals. Therefore, a second advantage of testing involves being able to make comparisons between recorded data. Comparisons are made interindividually and intraindividually—one compares both differences in performance between individuals and different aspects of a single individual's performance.

A core assumption to psychological testing is that every behavior segment bears the imprint of the organization of the behaving personality and, if properly chosen, permits a reconstruction of that personality. To be revealing of personality, the behavior segment must meet certain criteria: its meaning is unknown to, and not consciously manipulatable by, the subject, and the stimulus is unstructured enough so as to allow expression of the internal structuring principles of the individual. A relative lack of structure or multiple possibilities for structuring permit and encourage an expression of intrapsychic choices.

For Rapaport, then, psychiatric investigation constructs personality structure from observed or reported behavior, while psychological testing does so from the organization of thought as expressed in and inferred from psychological tests. The use of thought processes in this inferential way is predicated on the formulation that the development of thought organization is an integral part of and reflects the development of personality organization.

The Test Battery

The question of whether the Rorschach should be used as the sole assessment method or should rather be included as part of a test battery has interested both psychoanalytic and empirical writers. Exner (1993), from an empirical perspective, suggests an open-minded, flexible position. He argues that such a decision should be based on the nature of the referral question and practical considerations such as time and expense. His review of the literature yields mixed findings and different opinions. Those who challenge the use of a battery (Sarbin, 1943; Kelly and Fiske, 1950; Gage, 1953; Kostlan, 1954; Giedt, 1955) report that testers often do not use all the data, assign different weight to different pieces of data, and tend to reach a ceiling of predictive accuracy quickly. Others have found that a test battery does work well in the clinical situation (Vernon, 1950; MacKinnon, 1951; Luborsky and Holt, 1957; Holt, 1958). These authors report that validity is increased as data is added. Exner also argues against the use of a standard battery, suggesting instead that different referral questions may be best addressed with a different composite of tests.

Approaching the issue from a very different vantage point, psychoanalytic examiners insist upon using a test battery, usually a standard one, as opposed to relying exclusively on one test. The importance they assign to a test battery comes directly from Rapaport's formulations regarding the concepts of projection and levels of structure.

Historically, there has been a tendency to distinguish between projective and nonprojective tests. Accordingly, with nonprojective tests the questions asked (i.e., "At what temperature does water boil?") have a single, verifiable answer, and the tasks required, such as copying a design with blocks, have a confirmable solution. In projective tests, by contrast, there is no single, verifiable correct response. Instead, the individual's response is based on intrapsychic determinants and not on an external criterion of validity. Rapaport (1950) points out, however, that such a sharp distinction does not exist. Projective tests, he notes, also elicit responses that approach objective verifiability (i.e., popular responses on the Rorschach), and nonprojective tests do permit expressions of projective material. Indeed, Rapaport (1950) himself writes, "all the nonprojective tests, in so far as they reflect something about the personality, should be considered projective" (p. 348).

Finding the distinction "projective and unprojective tests" arbitrary and unhelpful, Rapaport replaces the distinction with the concept of "levels of structure." Here he suggests, "a hierarchy of structuring principles emerges; these principles not only organize unstructured material, but also bring structured material into an even more embracing organization. We are facing the issue of substructures" (p. 342).

Translated into a clinical context, Rapaport's notions suggest that a battery of tests, as opposed to any one test, permits the examiner to observe an individual in a variety of situations that differ in their relative degree of structure. For example, we are familiar with those patients who function smoothly and efficiently on the more structured Wechsler Adult Intelligence Scale (WAIS—III), yet experience serious difficulties, including regressive responses, on the less structured Rorschach test. Noting the quality of an individual's reaction to different levels of external structure often has major diagnostic and treatment implications.

For the psychoanalytic examiner, then, the matter of a test battery relates to conceptual and methodological concerns, and not to pragmatic ones.

Place of Personality Theory

In a recent and thoughtful article, Weiner (1994) draws a sharp distinction between the Rorschach as a method of generating data and the theories of personality that have been brought forward to interpret that data. He puts it this way:

> Because it does not measure anything, the Rorschach is not a test; rather, it is a method of generating data that describe personality functioning. Rorschach data can be interpreted from many different theoretical perspectives, but theory is not necessary to explain the utility of the Rorschach Inkblot Method [p. 498].

Weiner's last point, that the Rorschach is useful in its own right and is not dependent on personality theory, well captures the attitude toward personality theory held by those with an empirical perspective. For example, although the Comprehensive System was developed from a primarily perceptual cognitive perspective, Exner has consistently maintained that his approach is atheoretical. Theorists with an empirical bent view personality theory as constraining and argue that restricting the method to any one theory prohibits theoretical diversity.

Psychoanalytic theorists and examiners take a totally opposite position. Without theory, these proponents argue, Rorschach inferences would have little meaning, substance, or clinical relevance. In describing the enormous significance of Rapaport's wedding the Rorschach to psychoanalytic theory, Mayman (1976) notes:

> Rorschach inferences were transposed to a wholly new level of comprehension as Rapaport made a place for them in his psychoanalytic ego psychology and elevated psychological test findings from mundane, descriptive, pragmatically useful statements to a level of interpretation that achieved an incredible heuristic sweep [p. 200].

In a psychoanalytic approach, method and theory are inextricably interwoven. Therefore, in the next section I briefly comment about one aspect of the nature of psychoanalytic theory and then discuss the relationship between the theory and the Rorschach.

❖ ❖ ❖   Relationship Between Psychoanalytic Theory and the Rorschach

Before discussing the functions that theory serves and issues related to integration of theory with method, it should be noted that psychoanalysis is not a closed, tightly knit, fully integrated theory of personality. Rather, it is a loose-fitting mosaic of several complementary submodels, each of which furnishes concepts and formulations for observing and understanding important dimensions of personality development and functioning. These perspectives, separately and collectively, should be approached in terms of the function that theory serves in Rorschach assessment. The submodels most commonly identified include drive theory, structural theory, object-relations theory, and self psychology (Pine, 1990; P. Lerner, 1991a).

Building upon Rapaport's early work, later writers have attempted to outline the specific functions for Rorschach testing offered by psychoanalytic theory. Sugarman (1985, 1991) has identified four such functions: (1) organization, (2) integration, (3) clarification, and (4) prediction. For Sugarman, a theory of personality assists the Rorschach examiner in understanding and organizing data that are complex, often exceedingly rich, and at times inconsistent. In addition to organizing the mass of material, personality theory also enables the examiner to integrate seemingly disparate and unrelated pieces of data. The third function, clarification, means that personality theory can aid the clinician in filling in gaps in the data in an informed way. With respect to prediction, Sugarman notes that in the absence of personality theory, test-related predictions can only be based on test signs. Such data, he suggests, are useful in forecasting general trends but is limited in predicting the behavior of a single individual. Personality theory, then, enhances the prediction of an individual's behavior. To support this point, Sugarman cites findings from the Menninger Psychotherapy Research Project (Appelbaum, 1970) in which psychological testing yielded the best prediction of treatment outcomes.

In addition to the functions provided by a theory of personality, it is particularly important to review the nature of the integration of theory and testing. With specific regard to psychoanalytic theory and the Rorschach, I suggest the following points.

First, when theorists have integrated the Rorschach with psychoanalytic theory, it has not been with psychoanalytic theory as a whole, but instead, with one or several of the four most commonly identified submodels. For example, Rapaport's early integration involved exclusively drive theory and structural theory. Other early theorists (e.g., Holt, 1970; Schafer, 1954) also based their writings and thinking on these two submodels. In contrast, more recent authors, although not totally abandoning the earlier models, nonetheless have related the Rorschach to later submodels, including object-relations theory (Mayman, 1977; P. Lerner, 1991a; Smith, 1994) and self psychology (Arnow and Cooper, 1988).

Second, each of the psychoanalytic submodels includes a set of concepts and formulations that can be placed on a continuum based on their relative closeness to or distance from the patient's experience. Overall, the concepts issuing from drive theory and structural theory— such as libido, impulse-defense configuration, and apparatuses of primary and secondary autonomy—have been pitched at a more abstract, experience-distant level than have the concepts coming from object-relations theory and self psychology. It is ironic that part of the initial attraction to Freud's theory was that it spoke directly about sex and aggression and was not a "rose water" psychology. Only later, with theoretical elaborations, did it become more abstract. On the Rorschach one sees both relatively direct expressions of drives and more indirect and distant expressions that can only be seen as drive-related through the application of theory.

In any event, concepts arising from object-relations theory and self psychology, such as Winnicott's evocative notions of the "false self" and "good enough mothering" and Kohut's descriptive term "empathic failure," clearly have a more experience-near quality.

Third, implicit in each submodel is a particular view of psychopathology and the treatment process. For example, theories of treatment based on the drive and structural submodels stressed interpretation and insight, with therapy seen as a unique type of education and the therapeutic relationship as a special laboratory for exploring and experiencing the critical dynamic configurations as they emerged in the transference. In contrast, as Michaels (1983) has noted, conceptualizations of treatment based on object-relations theory and self psychology

> emphasize the psychological substrata and nutriments necessary for growth and development, with therapy being construed as a special kind of parenting, the interpretive process as a model of growth promoting interaction, and the therapeutic relationship as a substitute for the nuclear family as a matrix for individuation and growth [p. 5].

   Fourth, when applied specifically to the Rorschach and Rorschach interpretation, the submodel will affect the framework within which the interpretation is cast, the language at which the interpretation is pitched, the role accorded the psychological examiner, how relationships in general and the patient–examiner relationship in particular are conceptualized, and the mode of data observation and data gathering. To illustrate, on Card I a patient saw "a damaged moth with holes in its wings that was unable to fly." An examiner from a self-psychology perspective would likely focus on the "damaged moth" aspect of the response and infer an early narcissistic injury as experienced in a sense of self as "injured, damaged, and flawed." An examiner from an object-relations perspective might instead focus on the "unable to fly" part of the response, place the response within Mahler, Pine, and Bergman's (1975) developmental theory, and then infer "difficulties separating and individuating." A drive theorist would likely identify concerns with aggression, view "injured and damaged" as signs of turning aggression inward upon the self, and a structuralist would probably attune to the primitivity of the content. Even though the four inferences are compatible, they reflect differing points of emphasis and different ways of conceptualizing the core dynamic.

❖ ❖ ❖   A Psychoanalytic Experiential Approach

Background

The roots of a more experiential psychoanalytic approach to the Rorschach are to be found both in shifts in emphasis in psychoanalytic theory and in the early contributions of several psychoanalytically informed Rorschach theorists. Psychoanalytic theory has always been in a state of evolution and flux. From an early concern with identifying the instincts and their vicissitudes, and a subsequent emphasis on studying the ego, its functions and substructures, the focus—especially during the past several decades—has shifted to an exploration of the early mother-child relationship and its influence on the development of the self and the quality of later interpersonal relations. In concert with this evolution in theory has been movement away from an experience-distant metapsychology, couched in a mechanistic framework of impersonal structures, forces, and energies, to an experience-near clinical theory concerned primarily with experiences and subjective meanings.

With this changing emphasis in theory has also come, especially from self psychology, a significant and controversial call for a basic change in the mode of clinical observation and data collection. In his seminal (1959) paper, "Introspection, Empathy, and Psychoanalysis," Kohut argued that access to meaningful psychological depths could be obtained only through specific modes of observation: introspection into one's own subjective state, vicarious introspection, and empathy into that of another person. His position, which has gained increased currency, stands in marked contrast to earlier psychoanalytic stances that emphasized external (extrospective) observation and externally derived information.

Collectively, these conceptual and methodological changes in emphasis not only call for a reexamination of our traditional views of psychopathology and treatment, but they also invite models of Rorschach assessment that are more experientially oriented.

Within Rorschach parlance, one of the earliest and most comprehensive discussions of an experiential approach is found in the work of Schachtel (1966). Without dismissing the importance of earlier empirical and structural approaches, Schachtel's interest was in understanding what goes on in the test and in its interpretation. He put it this way: "The use of the test will be most fruitful if we understand fully the nature of the data we are studying in a Rorschach protocol and if we understand, furthermore, the nature of what we are doing when we score and interpret a protocol" (p. 2).

To provide such an understanding, Schachtel outlined a rationale for the test as a whole as well as for the scores, especially the determinants. Unlike Rapaport, who based his rationale on thought organization, Schachtel based his rationale on perception and its subprocesses, including various perceptual attitudes. By viewing perception as the mediator of experience, Schachtel was thus able to bring the Rorschach closer to more immediate, individual, actual "phenomenological" experience.

Each determinant, for Schachtel, represents a basic but different experiential-perceptual attitude. He (1966) noted that "each determinant usually represents a perceptual attitude that is characteristic for the visual experience resulting in a response based primarily on this determinant" (p. 78). For example, basic to the perception of color is what Schachtel referred to as an "autocentric attitude," that is, a mode of perceptual relatedness in which "there is little or no objectification; the emphasis is on how and what the person feels; there is a close relation, amounting to a fusion, between sensory quality and pleasure or unpleasure feelings (pleasure-unpleasure-boundedness), and the perceiver reacts primarily to something impinging on him" (p. 79). In suggesting that this same attitude also underlies the experience of affects, Schachtel could then relate color, not to the affect discharge process as had Rapaport, but rather to the affective experience itself, including responsiveness, tolerance, range, level of differentiation, and expression. In contrast to Rapaport, then, Schachtel suggested a set of test rationales that linked test responses more directly to the patient's actual experiences, thus offering a more experience-near understanding of the Rorschach task.

Finally, Schachtel (1966) addressed directly what he meant by an experiential approach to the Rorschach. He described it this way:

> I call the main approach I use . . . "experiential" because it consists mostly in the attempt to reconstruct, to understand, and to make more explicit the experiences that the testee underwent in taking the test and his reaction to these experiences, specifically his way of approaching or avoiding and of handling the experience of the inkblots in the context of the test task [p. 4].

A second major contributor to the experiential approach is Mayman (1967, 1977). Rorschach believed that his test could elicit conclusions about the individual's characteristic way of experiencing, but not about the content of the person's experience. Schachtel followed Rorschach's lead, and indeed his contribution relates to ways of experiencing defined in terms of basic perceptual attitudes. This approach directed Schachtel to consider the scores, the determinants, and the perceptual qualities of the inkblots. Mayman, however, directed his efforts toward an appraisal of the content of experience, toward the substance of the testee's phenomenological world.

It is in his discussion of the human movement response that Mayman (1977) lays the foundation for a more experiential approach to Rorschach content. He explicitly points out that human figures on the Rorschach may be taken as a representative sample of the testee's inner object world. Herein, he considers content, not from a symbolic perspective, but from an experiential one—that is, as a direct expression of the individual's interpersonal experience. Mayman likens his approach to one of dealing with the manifest content of a dream rather than the latent meaning.

Mayman (1963) also attempted to clarify the multileveled language of psychoanalysis and bring to the Rorschach a set of concepts and a level of language that were relatively experience-near. He distinguished three coordinated sets of concepts or language used in psychoanalysis. One set or level is the language used by the clinician in transaction with the patient, an everyday language more akin to poetry than science. Outside the clinical relationship, the clinician uses a "middle language" of "empirical constructs" that helps formulate clinical generalizations about an individual. A third, more abstract language consists of "hypothetical constructs," a system of impersonal concepts and formulations using more distant, third-person terms that comprise psychoanalytic metapsychology. Mayman has continually emphasized the need to apply the "middle level language" to Rorschach interpretation.

Lastly, Mayman (1964a) has consistently argued for a systematic but clinical-intuitive approach to Rorschach assessment and interpretation. His description of such an approach is strikingly similar to Schachtel's (1966) experiential approach. According to Mayman (1964a), "In testing a patient for clinical purposes, we are not simply measuring; we observe a person in action, try to reconstruct how he went about dealing with the task we set for him, and then try to make clinical sense of this behavior" (p. 2).

An Experiential Approach

Like earlier psychoanalytic approaches, an experiential approach such as I am advancing in this book involves a particular attitude, an essentially clinical one, toward the testing process and the nature of Rorschach data; a set of test rationales that apply to the test as a whole as well as to the scores, particularly the determinants; an appreciation of Rorschach content; and a specific view of the nature of the interpretive process. Furthermore, an experiential emphasis makes use of the same multiple sources of information and insists that the examiner make as exact and complete a record as possible of all that transpires between tester and testee, including the patient's verbatim responses, the direction of the examiner's own comments, and the patient's spontaneous and emotional expressions.

Rapaport had viewed the Rorschach as a means for exploring the deeper, more basic, and enduring structures that comprised the organization of personality. Without detracting from this goal, experiential theorists are equally interested in understanding the nature of the person's phenomenological experience.

To do so, to understand and reconstruct the testee's experience as expressed in Rorschach assessment, the examiner must first recognize that the testing experience takes place within the context of a specific "test task" and a particular "test situation" (Schachtel, 1966, p. 6). "Test task" is the term Schachtel uses to refer to the specific test directions, for example, "Tell me what you see" or "What might this be?" The experiential examiner pays close attention to the test directions and recognizes that Rorschach responses reflect, as well as are influenced by, the subjective meanings the patient ascribes to the directions. That is, Rorschach performance involves what the testee believes must be done to deal with the task.

The test situation and the subjective meanings it has for the patient also influence Rorschach performance. Of the various aspects of the test situation, the consideration that testing takes place in the context of an interpersonal relationship is of major importance.

From an experiential perspective, it is held that a Rorschach protocol cannot be fully understood without an awareness of its interpersonal aspects and implications. An intricate interpersonal relationship, replete with both realistic and unrealistic aspects, is intrinsic to testing, and this relationship not only has a significant influence on the patient's productions, but also can provide a wealth of information. Whereas earlier psychoanalytic approaches made exclusive use of the concept of transference (Schafer, 1954), an experiential approach considers other relational concepts as well, such as projective identification (P. Lerner, 1988) and selfobject transference (Arnow and Cooper, 1988).

As a psychoanalytic approach, the experiential one insists upon test rationales; however, it uses test rationales that are closer to the patient's experience and includes concepts and propositions that are experience-near. The shift from Rapaport's earlier emphasis on thought processes to Schachtel's emphasis on perception facilitates this and represents an early step in the movement toward a fully developed experiential approach.

An experiential focus views Rorschach content as an immensely rich and valuable source of information. Despite past abuses and misuses—for example, an earlier tendency to offer deep genetic interpretations to specific contents based solely on the examiner's own associations—it is held that content can be assessed in an informed and systematic way. The early work of Mayman (1977) and later contributions of P. Lerner (1991b) have resulted in an approach to content that represents a middle ground between those who approached it in terms of symbolism and those who have ignored it altogether. The perspective taken here consists of a theoretically informed clinical-intuitive approach to the raw Rorschach data, with a willingness to subject the derived inferences to standards of validity that fit the clinical situation. By viewing content, as Mayman (1977) suggests, as a sampling of the individual's representation world, the examiner can relate content more directly to the patient's phenomenological experience and at the same time derive inferences that are closer to the actual Rorschach data.

Finally, with an experiential perspective comes a particular view of the interpretive process. Both Schachtel and Mayman have described the process as an attempt to understand, reconstruct, and then make clinical sense of the testee's experience during the testing process. This attempt to understand can be based on external observation, as, for example, Mayman's (1964a) reference to "observing the person in action" (p. 2). In addition, following upon Kohut (1959), it can also be based on a more internal position in which the examiner uses his or her empathy to understand the patient's immediate experience. In terms of the latter, as in a psychotherapy session, the examiner views the patient's productions—in this instance, the response and the complete verbalizations—as a jumping-off point for attuning to the underlying subjective state. Herein, the examiner asks, "To have arrived at this response and said these things, what might the patient have been experiencing at that moment?" With an experiential approach, then, empathy as a way of coming to know the testee's inner experience plays a major role.

◆ ◆ ◆ **Conclusion**

In common with other psychoanalytic approaches to the Rorschach, but distinguishable from empirical ones, an experiential approach has a clinical emphasis, admits to several sources of information, insists upon test rationales, supports the use of a test battery, and views the Rorschach and personality theory as intimately related. In contrast to earlier psychoanalytic approaches, an experiential perspective makes greater conceptual use of object-relations theory and self psychology and attempts to balance an assessment of structure with an assessment of phenomenological experience. To embrace a phenomenological perspective, this approach uses several models to conceptualize the patient–examiner relationship, relies on perception rather than thought processes as the mediating link between test performance and personality, addresses Rorschach content in a particular way, and accords empathy a major role in the interpretive process.

2

THE NATURE OF THE RORSCHACH TASK

Despite the Rorschach's resurgent popularity, few who use the test, either for clinical or research purposes, fully appreciate the instrument's theoretical foundations. Many want to know how it works, but sparingly few have seriously considered why it works.

The need to push beyond the instrument's application and understand the nature of the Rorschach task itself has been echoed by virtually all the prominent Rorschach theorists, past and present (Rapaport et al., 1945–1946; Holt, 1954; Schachtel, 1966; Exner, 1974; Leichtman, 1996). The difficulty each has encountered, and the controversies stirred, all harken back to Rorschach himself, who never completed the theoretical foundations of his experiment (Rorschach, 1921).

In this chapter I first review those theorists who conceptualize the nature of the Rorschach task as one essentially involving perceptual process. This is then followed by a discussion of more recent efforts to shift the theoretical basis of the Rorschach from perception to representation. Finally, and in keeping with the applied clinical emphasis in this section of the book, I discuss the impact of the proposed theoretical shift upon the interpretation of Rorschach data. This chapter is intended as a summary rather than as a comprehensive review or penetrating critique. For such a review and critique, including a discussion of nonperceptual and nonrepresentational theories, refer to Leichtman (1996).

◆ ◆ ◆ Rorschach as a Perceptual Task

Rorschach (1921), in discussing the theoretical basis of his experiment, clearly noted that his diagnostic test was based on perception. He distinguished perception as recognition from perception as interpretation, and suggested that the test involved a complex form of perception together with other processes. Adopting Bleuler's concept of apperception, Rorschach conceived of perception as an interpretive process that included sensation, memory, and association. Accordingly, when showed an inkblot, the testee registers sensations, organizes them into images on the basis of past experiences, and then ascribes meaning to the images by associating them with analogous memory engrams.

Rapaport (Rapaport et al., 1945–1946) also accorded perception a key role, however; the principles he applied were derived from Gestalt psychology. In noting how relatively unstructured stimuli permit the expression of the form-giving nature of perception, he stated,

> These considerations may prompt the examiner to see in the subject's reaction to the Rorschach inkblots a perceptual organizing process which has a fundamental continuity with perception in everyday life. However, while everyday perceptions allow conventions, specific memories, and familiarities to obscure the active nature of the perceptual processes, the Rorschach inkblots bring the active-organizing aspects of perception into the foreground and provide the examiner with a treasure of insights into hidden aspects of an individual's adjustment or maladjustment [pp. 93–94].

Although accepting Rorschach's perceptual hypothesis, Rapaport also differed from Rorschach by assigning greater importance to associative processes. In contrast to Rorschach's concept of apperception, Rapaport argued that while perceptual features initiate associations, such ideas enter into the response process in a highly significant and far-reaching manner.

To account for the role and status of associative processes, Rapaport proposed an intricate "cogwheeling" model in which Rorschach responses represent an integration of both perceptual and associative processes. For Rapaport, according to Leichtman (1996), the interplay between these two processes works this way: "An initial process of perceptual organization gives rise to an associative process in which the organization is elaborated, which in turn leads to further perceptual judgments in which the potentialities and limitations of the inkblot act as a regulating reality for the associative process themselves" (p. 129).

Subsequent theorists have tended to accept Rorschach's proposition that his test fundamentally involves a complex form of perception; however, they highlight additional processes as well. Schachtel (1966), for instance, points out the importance in the response process of judgment and communication. His allegiance to perception, however, is clearly indicated in the following:

> Whether one agrees with Bleuler's and Rorschach's concept of perception or not, it is clear that the process of perceiving the inkblot, of associating remembered ideas and images, and trying to integrate them with inkblots (i.e., to restructure the perception of the inkblot in light of these images) and conversely, to try out these images for "fit" (congruence) with the inkblot play a decisive role in the typical "normal" Rorschach response. These are essentially the same processes that Rorschach had in mind when he came to the conclusion that the responses to his blots are based on perception [p. 13].

Exner (1991), too, conceives of the task as fundamentally perceptual. Basing himself, however, on a series of studies related to patterns of visual scanning of the blots, stimulus characteristics of the blots, response frequencies, set influences, and impact of personality and cognitive style differences on response, he subdivides the response process into three phases: encoding and classification, rank ordering and discarding, and final selection and articulation. During the first phase, the blot is scanned quickly and the products of the scan encoded. Evidence suggests that multiple potential responses are formed and then compared with information retrieved from long-term storage (Exner, Armbruster, and Mittman, 1978; Colligan and Exner, 1985). Research findings further indicate that critical stimulus properties or "bits" effect kinds of classifications (Exner, 1996). In the second phase, potential responses are compared with each other, judged, and weighed in terms of their fit with the blot stimulus, various sets, and censorship. Operations begun in phase two, including judging, rank ordering, and discarding, are continued into the third phase, in which final selections are made.

Exner, then, accepts Rorschach's assumption that the basic nature of the task is perceptual. Although he conceives of the Rorschach as a problem-solving task and describes the task in the language of information processing, he implicates several other processes, including cognition, judgment, and selection. Then too, he considers the role of task demands, or what Schachtel (1966) refers to as the "test situation."

◆ ◆ ◆ Rorschach as a Representational Task

One of the first of the more contemporary writers to draw attention to the importance of representational processes in the response process was Blatt (1990). Blatt argues that because Rorschach developed his method at a time when the scientific zeitgeist emphasized perceptual processes and behavioral response, it was inevitable he would consider his technique as "a test of perception."

Mindful of the "cognitive revolution" in psychology (Gardner, 1985), Blatt suggests that it is time to begin viewing the Rorschach "not so much as a perceptual test but rather as an experimental procedure that systematically presents an individual with ambiguity and allows us to observe and study how the individual constructs meaning from relative ambiguity" (p. 401).

Turning to Piaget (1937), Blatt notes that perception and representation are interrelated. Although representation is based on perception, it also extends beyond perception. When applied to the Rorschach, this means that:

> Interpretations of a Rorschach protocol as a perceptual test are still valid, but they are insufficient. The use of the Rorschach as a method of personality assessment can be greatly enhanced if we also consider responses not just as a perceptual experience but rather as [also] indicating cognitive-representational processes [p. 402].

Blatt proposes that aspects of Rorschach responses be viewed along a continuum from perception to representation. At the perceptual end of the continuum would be responses to form, color, and shading. Form level, the accuracy of fit of percept to a stimulus, would occupy a midpoint, reflecting a blend of perceptual and representational processes. And at the representational pole would be the movement response and content, Rorschach variables reflective of an individual's cognitive constructions and meaning systems.

It should be noted that Blatt does not call for a complete overhaul in how we view the Rorschach task. Rather, he contends that the Rorschach should be viewed not just from a perceptual perspective, but from a representational perspective as well.

Further contributions to a representational perspective on the nature of the Rorschach are found in the writings of Smith (1990) and Willock (1992) and their attempts, independently, to apply Winnicott's (1971) concept of "potential" or "transitional" space to Rorschach assessment. Winnicott used the terms "potential space" and "transitional space" to account for the space between the self and the object that facilitated and was also a result of separation: "I refer to the hypothetical area that exists (but cannot exist) between the baby and the mother (mother or part of the mother) during the phase of the repudiation of the object as not-me, that is, at the end of being merged with the object" (p. 107). This space can be conceived of as an intermediary area between one's inner world and one's outer world, between fantasy and reality if you will. It is the location of symbolic thought and cultural experiences, of creativity, and where work and play intermingle.

For Smith (1990), in the Rorschach situation, potential space may be found in the relationship between the testee (subject) and his or her Rorschach percept (the object). He notes: "Most studies of object representation in the Rorschach tend to focus on the nature of the object represented. I suggest that the nature of the subject's relationship to that object is a relevant dimension as well. How was the object created? At what distance from the self is the object experienced?" (p. 759). Importantly, Smith also points out that in the realm of potential space, objects, such as Rorschach responses, are simultaneously created and found.

Willock (1992) uses Winnicott's (1971) concept "transitional space" to describe the individual's encounter with the inkblots. As had Winnicott, he conceives of this domain as an arena for creativity and play. Willock describes the encounter between subject (testee) and object (inkblot) as follows:

The Rorschach presents ambiguous stimuli, asking subjects to make something out of them: "What might this be?" Inkblots are analogous to other expressive modalities, like modeling clay or the squiggle game in which the patient must find/make something out of the therapist's scribbling. With all these creative media, the challenge is to find/make something out of something amorphous [p. 102].

Neither Smith nor Willock had seemingly intended to address the nature of the Rorschach test. Their intent, instead, was to bring an object-relations perspective to Rorschach assessment by demonstrating the explanatory value of Winnicott's concept of potential or transitional space. Nevertheless, because of the concept itself, the authors, wittingly or unwittingly, were conceptualizing the Rorschach as more than, or other than, a perceptual test. By suggesting that in the Rorschach situation one creates, plays, and makes into, each is regarding the task as representational and not simply perceptual.

Although pointing in such a direction, none of the above authors was so bold as to call for a complete reconceptualization of our understanding of the nature of the Rorschach task. Leichtman (1996) has. In his recent book, *The Rorschach: A Developmental Perspective*, Leichtman proposes and argues for a new view of the Rorschach task in which representational processes, not perceptual ones, are given center stage.

Leichtman takes as his point of departure the Rorschach assessment of preschoolers, and asks the question, How do children come to master the task? On the basis of the observations of earlier writers (i.e., Klopfer and Margulies, 1941; Ford, 1946; Klopfer, Fox, and Troup, 1956), the developmental norms of Ames et al. (1974), and his own years of clinical diagnostic experience, he identifies three stages and two intermediate transitional periods preschoolers progress through in mastering the Rorschach.

The first and earliest stage is characterized by a pattern of pervasive perseveration. As described by Klopfer and Margulies (1941), "with utter disregard for the differences among the ten cards, the child simply repeats the same word as his reaction to each card" (p. 4). Because the response usually has little correspondence with blot characteristics, the examiner feels confused as to what led to the response.

By age two and a half, children begin to enter a transitional period in which there are changes in the pattern of perseverations. Instead of giving the same response to all cards, they offer new responses to a couple of them. In addition, the child now searches the blot for characteristics that justify the response.

In stage two, the perseverative tendencies noted in the previous stage abate and different responses are given to each card. These responses, however, reflect a confabulatory mode of concept formation characterized by confabulatory whole (DW) responses. As described by Leichtman (1996),

> instead of a balance being maintained between "perceptual" and "associative" aspects of the response process, the blot does little more than launch a subjective process that seems to take flight. Although some aspect of the card initiates the process, the subject is quickly caught up with ideas and fantasies that have little to do with stimuli [p. 52].

Between ages four and five, children enter a second transitional period, referred to by Klopfer, Spiegelman, and Fox (1956) as "confabulatory combinations." Although responses continue to bear little resemblance to the blot, two details rather than one are used. In this period as well there is an increase in number of responses and in the proportion of large-detail responses to whole ones.

A second major qualitative shift signals the child's entrance into stage three. As children reach the ages of six and seven, in Leichtman's (1996) terms, "the Rorschach becomes the 'Rorschach'" (p. 64). Here, the child demonstrates a reasonable understanding of the task and the examiner can trust his or her Rorschach scores. The confabulatory mode, pervasive in stage two, is transformed as "perceptual" and "associative" aspects of the response become better integrated.

In reviewing these stages, Leichtman offers several compelling reasons as to why theories of perception fail to adequately explain the developmental processes involved in mastering the task. First, early Rorschach responses by all accounts are not based on perception. Indeed, Klopfer, Spiegelman, and Fox (1956) suggest that responses in the early stages are based on different modes of concept formation. Second, the major qualitative shifts in Rorschach performance that distinguish the three stages do not correlate with, or are not explainable by, corresponding shifts in perceptual development.

Mindful of the shortcomings inherent in a view of the Rorschach task as essentially perceptual, Leichtman (1996) reconceptualizes the task as a representational one, and bases his new model on the earlier work of Werner and Kaplan (1963) on the formation of symbols. For

Werner and Kaplan, symbol formation is an intentional act in which a symbolic vehicle is employed to depict or stand for an object or concept. As Leichtman (1996) explains, "The situation in which symbolic activity occurs may basically be viewed in terms of four principal (generic) components: two persons—an addressor and an addressee, the object of reference or the referrant, and the symbolic vehicle employed in referential representation" (p. 40).

The relationship among these components is presented in Figure 2-1. The models consist of two dimensions. Along one axis is the addressor (the self) and the addressee (the other), and along the second axis is the symbolic vehicle and the referrant. Reflected by the vertical axis is the consideration that symbolic activity or representation is a type of communication, even an internal one at times. The horizontal axis indicates that communication assumes that there is something to communicate and a way of doing so.

Figure 1.

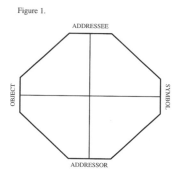

Figure 1. Components of the Symbol Situation.
(Taken from Leichtman, 1996, p. 160)

For Leichtman, viewing a Rorschach response from each of the four perspectives (components) explains why the task has been considered variously as perceptual, associative, creative, and communicative. Even more important, he suggests that a "consideration of the nature of these components and their relationship to one another reveals why each can be understood fully only as constituent parts of a representational act" (p. 160).

Leichtman argues that perception and the associative process each play a prominent role in the coming about of a Rorschach response, however, neither one, by itself nor in combination, totally explains the nature of the response process. He contends:

[S]omething more is involved, something that incorporates, but utterly transforms, perception and association. That something is an intention to use the stimulus to represent an object or a concept. Insofar as this intention is operative in approaching the Rorschach, perception becomes different from perception and association different from association. The processes are now components of a superordinate system that determines their functions and the manner in which they are coordinated—and they can be understood only as such [p. 163].

For Leichtman, then, in Rorschach testing perceptual processes are involved but are defined by representation; association, too, is involved but occurs in the context of a representational task; and the testee, knowingly, treats the inkblot as a symbolic vehicle.

Communication, too, is incorporated in this representational conception of the Rorschach response process. As Schafer (1954) and Schachtel (1966) have both stressed, testing occurs in the context of an interpersonal relationship and that relationship influences test responses (i.e., representations). In Leichtman's proposed model, the addressor-addressee axis accounts for this.

According to Leichtman, with a representational perspective, there is no need to change the standard Rorschach scoring categories. Each scoring category, as it was, is related to a component subsumed in the representational act. As had Blatt (1990), Leichtman suggests that a representational conception provides a sturdier rationale for certain scoring categories, such as form level ratings. Finally, a representational perspective broadens our view of the nature of the Rorschach stimuli. Whereas a perceptual conception highlighted the ambiguity of the stimuli, a representational conception emphasizes the stimuli's plasticity.

✦ ✦ ✦ Implications for Interpretation

As noted in chapter 1, implicit in conceptions of the Rorschach task as perceptual or perceptual-associative came the notion that perception or cognition could also be regarded as mediating processes that bridged test performance, on the one hand, with personality structure and functioning on the other. For Rapaport (1950) and Schachtel (1966), Rorschach interpretation rests on the assumption that Rorschach percepts reflect an individual's distinctive mode of thinking and perceiving, and as such, permit the reconstruction of the specific organizing principles of that personality.

This assumption has served psychoanalytic examiners well, and one is loath to relinquish it. Therefore, the question needs to be raised, does a representational conception of the Rorschach task change the rationale underlying interpretive practices? Leichtman assures us that it does not. Because he viewed representation as an overarching process that subsumes perception and cognition, Leichtman (1996) can then contend that it is "With only modest revisions, the assumptions underlying interpretive practices based on perceptual theories can be reformulated in representational terms that provide them with a more secure base" (p. 179). He further points out that in the test rationales that have been provided for specific determinants, the word "representation" can be substituted for the word "perception," with little change to the rationale.

Representational theory does introduce a change in the logic of the Rorschach inference process. In place of the earlier assumption that Rorschach percepts reflect characteristic ways of perceiving and representing, this new conceptualization holds that inferences from test responses "are based on the premises that there are consistencies in how individuals represent their experience across different symbolic modalities and different situations" (p. 180). Importantly, and in keeping with the experiential approach being taken in this book, this latter premise emphasizes ways in which an individual experiences and represents his or her world.

❖ ❖ ❖ Conclusion

In this chapter, I have reviewed various attempts to understand and conceptualize the nature of the Rorschach task. Beginning with Rorschach himself, earlier theorists emphasized perceptual processes with varying importance given to associative processes. More recent theorists have drawn attention to the role of representational processes. Blatt (1990), in a seminal article, placed representation alongside perception. Leichtman (1996) went much further. He proposed that the processes identified by earlier theorists—perception, association, communication, judgment—could and should be subsumed in a broadened representational conception. It is noteworthy that Leichtman's reconceptualization, with its emphasis on experience, representation, and interpersonal factors, comes at a time when others (Mayman, 1996; P. Lerner, 1992) are proposing more experiential approaches to Rorschach assessment and interpretation.

3

THE PSYCHOLOGICAL
TEST REPORT

In most settings and situations the vehicle for communicating assessment findings is the psychological test report. If the report is to lead to decisions and interventions helpful to the testee, then as Appelbaum (1970) has argued, it needs to be more than a technical or scientific document. As well, it ought to be political and diplomatic, strategic and persuasive.

On the basis of the distinctions Mayman (1963) drew among the different levels of language in psychoanalysis, and from an experiential perspective, a well-crafted report is conceptualized and organized at a "middle language" level, but is written at a descriptive, experiential level, free of psychological jargon and technical terms. In avoiding mechanistic phrases, explicating more abstract concepts, and remaining empathically close to the patient's subjective experience, one writes in the language of the consulting room.

For example, a patient who, in her report, could have been simply characterized as a narcissistic personality disorder with schizoid features, was instead described this way: "Like Holly Go Lightly, a main character in Truman Capote's *Breakfast at Tiffany's*, the patient blithely glides through life allowing little to touch or affect her. Her

31

seeming indifference, although both enticing and alienating, serves as protection against profound fears of loss and abandonment." Reports pitched at this descriptive level do more than breathe life into the assessee and convey useful information. They also create a portrait of an individual that the reader can recognize, understand, and relate to.

Mayman's (1963) conceptual schema serves another function in report writing. In alerting us to the various levels of abstraction in psychoanalytic theory, it emphasizes the importance of not confusing one level with another and of explicating the intervening steps that connect levels. We are all familiar with clinical reports in which the author mixes conceptual levels. In such a report, for example, a direct observation is immediately followed by a highly abstract formulation with little mention of the intervening inferential steps.

The organizing points of a report should be the clinical issues that prompted the request for the testing, as well as those issues that arose in the course of the assessment. Without such foci a report lacks purpose and direction. A report ought to have organization in another respect as well, the use of an internally consistent theory of personality and psychopathology. The theory must be understood in all of its complexity by the examiner-writer, so that he or she can explicate the layering and interconnections among the data and achieve a synthesis of initially disparate observations.

In what follows, one way in which a test report may be organized is presented. This example, beyond being useful in its own right, also illustrates the variety of inferences one can draw from tests and a way of organizing those inferences. In addition, the proposed testing report serves as an organizing and interpretive framework for the remainder of the clinical applications part of the book. That is, the subheadings in the report, while serving as organizational points of reference, also correspond to psychological structures and processes that I hold in mind in analyzing and interpreting test data.

✦ ✦ ✦ Introduction

The introduction should supply enough information regarding the clinical context to enable the reader to understand the report, even if little else is known about the patient. It should include a statement of the patient's major difficulties, the circumstances of the testing, and specific questions to which the testing is addressed. All questions raised in the introduction should be answered or acknowledged in the report. All the issues dealt with, however, need not be based on the referral question; there may be issues, based on the ongoing testing, that the examiner independently raises.

For example, a 20-year-old, single male was referred for psychological testing to assist in determining if paranoid thinking underlay his singular and inordinate interest in "space aliens." From the tests, the examiner confidently reported that even though the patient's thinking was idiosyncratic and nonconventional, it was not paranoid or in any respect psychotic. Despite not being asked, the examiner thought it clinically important to discuss the adaptive functions of the patient's preoccupation with aliens. To this issue he wrote, "Aliens and UFOs, the paranormal, is one of the only topics that engages the patient. More than an interest, it fulfills his yearnings for a sense of identity, and, ironically, affords him feelings of affiliation and a sense of belonging."

❖ ❖ ❖ Personality Structure

This section of the test report should include a description of the patient in terms of character traits, organized along the lines of distinct personality or character types. It should be noted that herein, the terms *personality* and *character* will be used interchangeably. Also, I refer to personality structures and types rather than psychopathological syndromes and clinical diagnoses. This particular emphasis is based, in part, on Rapaport's (1950) formulation that psychopathology always represents an exaggeration or decompensation of patterns already present in the personality structure. For Rapaport, diagnosis is always personality diagnosis.

For a theorist with a structural perspective, the concept of character has considerable importance. Character involves the notion of habitual modes of behavior and refers to constant, stereotyped modes of response the ego makes in mediating the demands of internal and external reality. Character traits are descriptive attributes ascribed to a person. They are necessarily an amalgam, a synthesis that expresses under one heading a combination of psychic factors that includes drive derivatives, defenses, identifications, superego aspects, modes of object relating, attitudes, values, and moods. Character structure refers to a cluster of character traits that typically go together to form a particular personality structure.

Character was slow to emerge as a central concern in psycho-analysis. It was first regarded by Freud as a unitary structure of minor import and peripheral to the major thrust of his theories. In his 1908 paper "Character and Anal Erotism," he noted empirically a relationship between a cluster of three character traits—parsimony, orderliness, and obstinacy—and the vicissitudes of the anal drive.

Reich (1933) focused on character as a defense. Character, for Reich, was an enemy of treatment, an armor against insight and cure. Defining character as the sum total of an individual's modes of reaction, he drew attention to such specific manifestations as posture, facial expression, and manner of speaking.

Several early authors, most notably Alexander (1930), focused on the pathology of character as a whole, highlighting the maladaptive aspects of large segments of typical behavior. Increasingly, writers have emphasized the adaptive function of character and have shifted their interest from the interplay between id and ego to that between ego and reality (Rapaport, 1957).

Contemporary interest in character stems from the observation that the concerns of patients now seeking treatment differs from the concerns described in the literature of 40 years ago. In the classical neurosis, an integrated personality was painfully disrupted by alien impulses, thoughts, and feelings. Currently, we seldom confront a uniform, coherent personality, but, rather, one that is disturbed and chaotic to such an extent that it is often difficult to distinguish between personality and symptoms. Many of us, for instance, have been referred patients who are reportedly in a crisis, only to discover, upon closer examination, that crisis for these individuals is a way of being in the world.

A psychoanalytic diagnostic scheme might include at minimum the following typical personality or character structures: the hysterical character, the obsessive-compulsive character, the depressed character, the masochistic character, the narcissistic personality, the infantile personality, the paranoid personality, and the schizoid personality. Each of these character structures will be described and discussed in the next chapter. Many clinicians will raise their eyebrows at the omission of the borderline personality disorder. Following Kernberg (1976), I conceive of borderline as a level of personality organization, rather than as a distinct type of personality. This issue will be discussed further throughout the text.

The various personality types just listed represent ideals based on the assumption that there is an intrinsic logic whereby certain traits tend to coalesce to form certain typical personalities. In clinical practice, one seldom confronts a pure personality type; rather, one more commonly encounters individuals with a mixture of character traits in which certain ones predominate while others are present but play a lesser role. Therefore, in offering a characterological diagnosis, instead of simply stating, "The patient presents as an obsessive-compulsive personality," clinicians are more apt to say, "The patient presents as an obsessive-compulsive personality with narcissistic and masochistic features." This statement would then be followed by a description of the obsessive-compulsive, narcissistic, and masochistic features observed in the patient, together with their respective roles within the overall personality.

Also included in this section of the test report, and reflective of an experiential emphasis, is the patient's array of self-experiences. By self-experiences I mean the variety of conscious and unconscious roles and identities, whole or fragmented, that determine the patient's experience of himself or herself and that direct the patient's behavior. This array constitutes the person's overall self-image and includes what he or she wishes or fears about himself or herself, the degree to which the self-image is accepted as part of the person, and its relative consciousness. Self-experience, as described here, involves both structural and thematic properties.

Closely related to one's self-experience is one's experience of others. I speak here of relational predispositions or transference paradigms. These are repetitive playlets in which the patient assumes a particular role and assigns to others roles that fit, in a complementary fashion, his or her ingrained expectations. These relational tendencies may themselves be described in structural terms entailing such considerations as the extent to which self and others are differentiated, as opposed to fused, and the extent to which relationships are seen as stable and enduring, as contrasted with conflict-laden and transitory. Such relational tendencies may also be described in thematic terms, as Mayman (1996) has recently done. For example, in describing the object relations of the oral character, Mayman notes, "This person . . . constructs his object attachments along almost exclusively 'oral' lines. . . . He feeds on them, he tries to fill himself up with the gratification he gets from them. People are his means of survival. And when they fail him, he may spit them out or regurgitate them just as quickly as he took them in" (p. 5).

◆ ◆ ◆ Thought Organization

Associated with each personality structure is a distinct style of thinking. In this section, that style is described and discussed. For instance, whereas the thinking of the obsessive-compulsive tends to be rigid, dogmatic, highly precise, factual, and laced with detail, the thinking of the hysterical personality is subjective, impressionistic, affect laden, nonspecific, and susceptible to that which is immediate, impressive, and obvious.

The most comprehensive and illuminating discussion of various styles of thinking and perceiving is represented in the work of David Shapiro (1965). With meticulous care, based on clinical and empirical observations, Shapiro outlines the ways of thinking and perceiving, the modes of subjective experience, and the modes of activity associated with the following styles: the obsessive-compulsive, the paranoid, the hysterical, and the impulsive. For Shapiro, these styles of thinking, which are more generally used to infer defense, character traits, and personality structure, are in themselves psychological structures of importance and are thus worthy of an independent appraisal.

Included in the description of thought style are the patient's approach to various tasks (i.e., systematic, deliberate, hesitant, impatient), the patient's reaction to his or her own performance, and the patient's capacity to reflect and think psychologically (psychological mindedness). In evaluating cognitive style, one also assesses ego functions, such as capacity for delay, capacity to attend and concentrate, tolerance for frustration, judgment, and quality of reality testing.

Intelligence clearly has a bearing on thought style. Despite the recognized dangers, providing a statement of the patient's IQ scores can be helpful. The IQ scores should not stand alone; they should instead be discussed in terms of whether such scores are an accurate reflection of the patient's capacities, and if not, why not. Factors interfering with performance should also be noted.

If relevant, in this section of the report I also address the issue of thought disorder. Too often, thought disorder is regarded as a unidimensional entity and is considered simply in terms of its presence or absence. This oversimplification ignores the consideration that different types of thought disorder are related to different forms of psychopathology. The fluidity and associative quality of thinking in the manic patient are distinct from the relational thinking of the paranoid patient or the fusion of thoughts in the schizophrenic. Therefore, one attempts to describe the thought disturbance quite specifically. In addition, and for completeness, one should also discuss the conditions, internal and external, within which it occurs; the patient's attitude toward the disturbance; and his or her capacity for control.

✦ ✦ ✦ Organization of Affects

Organization of affects refers to feelings and, more specifically, to the way in which they are experienced, expressed, and managed. For example, one may describe a patient variously as constricted, labile, explosive, or able to integrate various feeling states into the mainstream of his or her mental functioning. The organization of affects also includes the range of affects and the capacity to differentiate among affective states. The tester is also concerned here with predominant affects, be they fleeting or longstanding, as well as with the degree to which, and manner in which, they are experienced.

To label a feeling state is important, yet this is insufficient; the examiner should be able to go further and describe the state empathically and phenomenologically. For example, one can describe a depressed individual as "feeling tired, depleted, and dead inside," or as "perceiving the world as dark and barren and unable to meet one's needs." A phenomenological grasp of an affective state is useful in that it permits the examiner to infer to other areas, such as quality of object relations (P. Lerner, 1996a), treatment planning, and overall level of personality development (Blatt, 1974).

A concept that is gaining increased attention in the assessment literature is "affect capacity" (Thompson, 1986); by this is meant a person's openness, receptiveness, and capacity to experience various feeling states. With the integration of an object-relations perspective into psychoanalytic theory, the inferential and heuristic importance of assessing affect capacity has increased substantially. For instance, Melanie Klein (1935) proposed a developmental model consisting of two positions (paranoid-schizoid and depressive) distinguishable on the basis of the prevailing anxiety and the level of object relations. One feature distinguishing the two positions is the capacity to experience depressive feelings. For Klein, implicit in depression is a fear of loss, which in turn presupposes a capacity for concern and genuine care for another. From this perspective, then, depressive feelings are more than symptoms; they are also indications of a developmental achievement.

The phrase "managing affects" relates directly to the individual's defensive structure. Here too, one finds a correspondence between specific defenses and certain personality structures. Namely, the hysterical personality has been found to rely mainly on repression, the paranoid personality on projection or externalization, and the obsessive-compulsive on intellectualization, isolation of affect, and reaction formation. In a report, one not only identifies the defenses, but also discusses their effectiveness. Also, it is helpful to layer the defenses hierarchically, moving from those that are most characteristic and preferred to those that emerge only when others have failed.

Because of its close tie to specific affects, namely depression and anger, if suicide is an issue, it would be included in this section of the test report. When presented with the question of suicide, I attempt to address the following factors: the likelihood of occurrence and under what conditions; the structural, dynamic, and experiential features involved; and the patient's willingness to alert and make constructive use of others.

The following excerpt is taken from the test report of a young adolescent who was referred for testing in connection with an impending court hearing. The question of suicide had not been raised by the referrer, but was by the examiner, on the basis of test findings.

> To avoid experiencing depressive feelings, this young man tends to act out. One form of acting out, given his current circumstances, that others should be alert to is suicide. On several of his TAT cards death was in the air, and on one specific card with suicidal import, he blocked. He sees death as a way out, a viable alternative in situations in which he feels trapped and without options. Fueling the danger at this time is his sense that the alleged incident has permanently alienated him from others, especially those whom he loves and is dependent upon. He is in much pain and is accessible to therapeutic intervention. To judge from his willingness to discuss his fleeting suicidal thoughts with the examiner, the possibility of suicide would be appreciably reduced were he involved in treatment.

✦ ✦ ✦ Core Dynamics

Included under the heading "core dynamics" are the motives, urges, fears, desires, and conflicts that are prominent in the patient and underlie his or her actions, character traits, dysphoric affects, and symptoms. It is a truism that most conflicts can be found in most patients; certain conflicts, however, are considered dominant in that they inhibit solutions to other, often developmentally later conflicts and color much of present behavior. In this section of the test report one attempts to outline conflicts related to the vicissitudes of sexuality and aggression, disturbances in object relations, and impairments in self. Statements included here relate to both dynamic and genetic issues. The following is an example: "Underlying the patient's difficulties in establishing long-term, satisfactory relationships with men is a view of her father as overly exciting and seductive, highly dangerous, and as having violated essential and needed boundaries."

As noted in chapter 1, within psychoanalysis new models of personality development and psychopathology have appeared. Whereas earlier models were derived from theories of psychic conflict, these newer models issue from theories of structure and structure formation in development. In the newer models, development consists of the growth and differentiation of psychological functions that crystalize into more stable structures. Although conflict can occur among these structures, as conceptualized in earlier views, the structures themselves can be pathological as a result of faulty development.

I attempt in this section of the report to outline such structural impairments and their historic antecedents. If, as various theorists have suggested, structures arise from the gradual internalization of early object relations, then in these cases it is important that the examiner attempt to understand and describe the nature of the early object relations and the factors that may have interfered with the process of internalization. The following example illustrates these points.

> One is struck by the patient's inability to humanize her world. Her Rorschach percept of a "robot" nicely captures her sense of self as empty, mechanical, not totally human, and vulnerable to control by others. Developmentally, these more primitive feelings and concerns are rooted in a disrupted symbiotic relationship. Consequent to this disruption, she struggles with separation, dreads aloneness, and is unable to conceive of others as separate and complete.

❖ ❖ ❖ Treatment Planning

If in previous sections of the report inferences and findings have been couched in intervention-related terms, then in this section they are

summarized and integrated. Then too, there may be treatment issues
that warrant a more pointed discussion. I have found that therapists
are particularly interested in such topics as the following: specific problems that may interfere with the establishment of a therapeutic alliance;
the patient's capacity to think psychologically and to envision a role
for himself or herself in treatment; and potential therapeutic levers.
The following inference was found useful by the referring psychotherapist: "Treatment could be of benefit to this patient by assisting her to get in touch with that which is good in her and she values
. . . to help her define for herself an ego ideal, an ideal that could bring
greater order to her life and greater control over her chaotic and self-
harmful behavior."

With the emergence in psychoanalysis of new models of personality formation and psychopathology, there have also come new models of the psychotherapeutic process. This has implications for
Rorschach assessment. The psychological tester has long been called
upon to address the issue of the patient's treatability and to comment
upon the most appropriate type of treatment. In the past, treatment
was viewed rather narrowly and types of treatment were placed on a
continuum, ranging from intensive and insight-oriented at one end to
supportive at the other extreme. The level of external structure
required by the patient to maintain adaptive functioning was a critical factor underlying assignment within the spectrum. The evolving
scope of psychoanalytically informed treatment has changed this and,
as such, presents new challenges for the examiner. Now, the examiner
must redefine and broaden the limits of treatability. Commenting on
the degree of structure needed is not enough; the tester should also be
able to detail the quality and type of structure required.

The following is taken from the testing report of an older adolescent
who was initially considered untreatable by his referring psychiatrist.

> Despite his chaotic history and tendency to depreciate adults, I
> believe that this patient can benefit from treatment. He requires
> much support, structure, and containment, more than can be pro-
> vided on a once-per-week basis. Repeatedly confronting his ten-
> dency to depreciate will help provide the containment by
> demonstrating to him that his therapist can withstand his aggres-
> sion. This is to say that there is an object-seeking quality to his
> aggression, more specifically, an object he cannot destroy. He him-
> self recognizes that he has more potential than he can now real-
> ize, and this, for him, is a powerful motivation for treatment.

What he requires from therapy and has never had is a "good hold-ing environment."

◆ ◆ ◆ Summary

The summary consists of a concise restatement of the most relevant and salient aspects of the report. Like the body of the report, but in capsule form, the summary should provide an integrated, internally consistent, clinically relevant portrait of the patient. The following is such a summary.

In summary, the patient presents a mixed characterological pic-ture with narcissistic and depressive features most prominent and organized at a high borderline level. He is continually anxious and relentlessly restless and bored. Beneath a false-self facade, one sees a young man who feels empty, on the verge of fragmenting, vul-nerable, and aggressed against. Amid superior intelligence, his ego functions are relatively impaired. He has difficulty tolerating anx-iety and frustration and his impulse control is fragile. He is cur-rently being pressured by relatively intense feelings of anxiety and depression. Based on disturbances in his early maternal relation-ship, major difficulties are apparent in his object relations and in his sense of self. More specifically, there is little overall sense of personal identity and he has not achieved object constancy. He cannot tolerate being alone, and separations are experienced as abandonments. Intensive psychotherapy was suggested with the recommendation that contact with his subjective experience could be made around his fear of aloneness and his difficulties with sep-arations.

◆ ◆ ◆ Conclusion

Herein, I have outlined one particular type of psychological test report. Whatever the format used, it is suggested that the report address the major clinical issues, that it be guided by a theory of personality and psychopathology, and that it be written at as descriptive and experi-ential a level as possible. The report was presented at this point to provide an organizational framework for the remainder of the clinical section of the book. Two sample reports, using the proposed framework, follow.

The reports are presented here for illustrative purposes; however, they touch on issues that are sources of controversy in the current assessment literature. One such contentious issue is that of the borderline concept. As Sugarman and Lerner (1980) have noted, "Although the term borderline has become common and has stimulated a vast array of clinical data, theoretical formulations, and treatment variations, disagreement over its definition has never really subsided" (p. 11). The term has been used variously to describe a state, a personality disorder, a syndrome, a spectrum, and a level of personality organization. As noted previously, I herein use the term borderline, following upon Kernberg (1975, 1976), to refer to a level of personality organization intermediate between neurotic and psychotic organizations. Kernberg's entire diagnostic scheme will be presented in the next chapter, and the usefulness of this conceptualization for organizing and synthesizing the vast research data will be discussed in chapter 22.

The second issue involves the use of Rorschach data in making genetic reconstruction; that is, for drawing inferences about an individual's early psychological life. If theorists, such as Loewald (1973), are correct in asserting that psychic structures arise from the gradual internalization of early object relations, then, by inference, an assessment of present structures should provide information about the quality of those early object relations. Nonetheless, these inferences are many steps removed from the test data on hand. This issue, including rules of validity for judging the accuracy of Rorshach-based inferences, will be discussed in chapter 14 ("The Inference Process").

Psychological Evaluation

NAME:	Mary Smith	Tests Given:	Dates Tested:
AGE:	22 years	WAIS	4/12/88
		Rorschach	4/29/88
		TAT	5/02/88
REFERRER:	Dr. P. Jones		

The patient is a 23-year-old single female who is a recent college graduate with a major in elementary education. She is unclear as to her long-term career goals. Her parents have been divorced for 11 years. Her mother, whom she lives with, is a lawyer, and her father she describes as a "playboy." From the material presented, the referrer has noted struggles around separating and difficulties in establishing her own autonomous identity. To assist in determining her suitability for psychoanalysis, psychological testing was requested. This report is addressed to the issues of character structure, thought organization, organization of affects, core conflicts, and treatment planning.

In her approach to the examiner and the tests, the patient appeared as a youthful, warm, engaging individual whose relationship with the examiner was marked by particular fluctuations. She began each session in a rather tight, constricted way; as the session progressed, however, she was able to relax her tight controls and be freer and more spontaneous. Yet the relative looseness did not extend across sessions. That is, each time she tightened up again. She is youthful in the sense that she has a readiness and desire to idealize; she gives the impression of being an "unfinished product." Things have not yet come together or jelled for her. She is highly self-conscious, overly concerned with the views of others, hypervigilant, highly sensitive, and painfully thin skinned.

The patient at times adopts a false self and at other times actively defends against it. This awareness of, and upset with, her own false-self tendencies becomes evident in fluctuations between compliance and quiet rebelliousness and in a strong desire to declare a moratorium (take time out) and to genuinely find herself. Overall, the patient presents a mixed characterological picture with narcissistic, obsessive-compulsive, and hysteric features all in evidence.

The patient attained a full-scale IQ of 125 (verbal IQ 128, performance IQ 114), which places her in the superior range of intellectual functioning. One sees in her thinking, especially with structure, adaptive obsessive-compulsive controls. She approaches tasks in a deliberate, persistent, systematic way and places much emphasis on neatness and accuracy. As the structure is removed, she becomes tight and constricted and moves toward privacy. There was no evidence of thought disturbance, and in general her ego functions are well intact. I say in general, for at times she can be careless and at other times she has difficulty stepping back and maintaining perspective. That is, she is not always able to see the forest through the trees.

With respect to her affective life, she is open to various affective experiences but places great emphasis on control and regulation. Letting go is not easy or comfortable for her. She is currently being pressured by moderate feelings of anxiety and depression; however, neither feeling interferes with her functioning. Her depression becomes evident in an attunement to blackness and in long-standing feelings of low self-esteem.

With respect to her dynamic life, the referrer noted her difficulties surrounding identity. This is accurate, but her struggles take a particular form. On one hand, as noted previously, she is painfully aware of her false-self tendencies and defends against them. On the other hand, she is especially fearful of being controlled and of losing autonomy over her precariously established sense of self. At this point the patient is vitally interested in becoming her own person and gaining direction from within. This theme pervades her TAT stories, as evidenced by the following story: "This little boy is looking at the violin and he doesn't know how to play it. He's quite unhappy he can't play. Most people in his family, especially his father, were great violin players and he wants to be closer to his father by playing. Eventually he learns to play, but because the drive wasn't within himself but in the family, he doesn't play as well as others would like. Drive wasn't an appropriate drive."

Implicated in the story, and a source of extreme conflict for the patient, is her father. At one level, she idealizes him, viewing him as powerful and to be pleased. Beneath this, she sees him as malevolent, as someone who has excessive aspirations for her and yet robs and exploits her autonomy with these expectations. Currently, he is able to push her buttons, and she feels powerless to ward him off; thus a goal of hers in treatment is to free herself from his influence.

Finally, I believe that the patient is still responding to the breakup of her family. She has vague feelings of loss, which I feel are referable to the separation, and her desire to take time out to find herself, while legitimate, has an adolescent quality.

As to treatment, I strongly support the choice of analysis. She is highly suitable for this mode of treatment and would benefit from it. She is bright, reflective, determined, and persistent; most importantly, she senses herself as unfinished. Her problems may be viewed as interferences in development, and I believe the analytic situation will permit her the opportunity to resume growth.

In summary, the patient presents as an unfinished product; hence, one sees a mixed character structure with narcissistic, hysteric and obsessive-compulsive features all in evidence. She is of superior intelligence, and in her thinking one sees adaptive, obsessive-compulsive features. While she is open to affective experiences, control is especially important to her. She genuinely longs to be her own person. She aspires to be freer, more natural, and more spontaneous. Psychoanalysis is supported as the treatment of choice.

Psychological Evaluation

NAME: Janet Bell   Tests Given: Dates Tested:
  AGE: 33   WAIS   1/12/86
                           Rorschach   1/29/86
                           TAT   2/23/86

REFERRER: Dr. H. Fisk

The patient is a 33-year-old, single bookkeeper who lives with her mother. Because of the patient's complaints of agoraphobia, her "as if" features, and an unusual relationship with her father, the referrer suspected she might be borderline. He also wondered about her capacity to benefit from a more intensive, insight-oriented treatment. Those were the questions that prompted the testing. Setting up and maintaining appointments with this patient was not an easy matter. For example, she canceled one session in anticipation of a major sleet storm. To judge from her behavior around appointments, she constantly fears being overwhelmed and her behavior is marked by blatant inconsistencies. To answer the above referral questions, this report is addressed to the issues of character structure, thought organization, organization of affects, core conflicts, and treatment planning.

The patient appeared as a petite, attractive, striking woman with a "Barbie doll" quality. She dresses fashionably, is very heavily made up, and must spend considerable time making sure everything is in place. In her approach to the examiner and the tests, she appeared as highly anxious, tightly defended, and markedly superficial. Her superficiality is defensive in that she is terrified of being penetrated. I do not mean penetrated just in the sexual sense but more broadly, in the sense of being touched and rattled. She allows only so much in and closes issues off very quickly. Because of her heightened anxiety, which she has difficulty regulating, others are put in the position of containing her anxiety for her. Prominent in her character are narcissistic and masochistic features. She is self-absorbed, hypervigilant, and defensively sensitive. Sensing the environment as dangerous, like a mine field, she uses her sensitivity to alert herself to the always present dangers. Her stance is totally one of passivity. Unable to see herself as the initiator of activity, she feels herself as completely reactive. As noted by the referrer, "as if" features are prominent. Coincident with the passivity is an ease in feeling a victim. She tends to present as more helpless and inept than she is, and in part, she saw the tests as humiliating her—as making her feel "stupid." The overall diagnostic impression is of a narcissistic personality organized at a borderline level.

The patient attained a full scale IQ of 114 (Verbal IQ 111, Performance IQ 116), which places her in the bright normal range of intellectual functioning. Despite her heightened anxiety, she is able to pull herself together to attend. In addition, her abstraction capacities are excellent. By contrast, and in keeping with her self-absorption, her range of general information is limited. While there were no signs of thought disorder or impaired reality testing, there were impairments in several ego functions. She has difficulty concentrating; her persistence is limited; and when her anxiety is especially high, she behaves impulsively and uses poor judgment. In addition, her frustration tolerance is limited.

In general, the patient has difficulty containing and regulating affects; she is a leaky container. She is currently being pressured by strong feelings of anxiety that, although variable, at times reach the point of panic. Her anxiety becomes manifest in subjective feelings of restlessness, in a tendency to be impatient, and in an ease in becoming frazzled. She has a strong need for order and structure, and when either gives way, she becomes frantic. There is test evidence of depressive affect; however, her depressiveness is longstanding and not especially acute or intense. Central to the depression are lowered feelings of self-esteem and a basic sense of emptiness. With respect to her defensive structure, she relies heavily on avoidance and externalization. When the externalization is combined with displacement, it sets the stage for phobia formation, and one sees much evidence of a phobic tendency.

As to her dynamic life, the patient has considerable difficulty dealing with aggression, especially oral aggressive urges. The role of envy is particularly clear in the following TAT story. "I don't like this, I'm embarrassed. I can't do this. Looks like it is something he always wanted, and now that he has it, he doesn't know what to do with it. He's in awe of it." To judge from her more spontaneous comments, she is embarrassed by her envy, as she is by her greed. To ward off such urges, she externalizes them onto the outside world and sees her environment as hostile, dangerous, and exploitative. As well, such urges are turned inward upon the self, resulting in her masochism and sense of herself as victim. As to be expected, along with the oral rage are intense oral yearnings.

The patient also has major problems in the areas of self and object relations. I was somewhat struck by her inability to humanize her world. Her Rorschach percept of a "robot" nicely captures her own sense of self as empty, mechanical, less than totally human, and as vulnerable to control by others. She seems to both invite and fear such external control. Developmentally, such primitive feelings and concerns are rooted in a disrupted symbiotic relationship. As a consequence of this disruption, she struggles with separation, dreads aloneness, and is unable to conceive of others as complete objects.

Growing up has been a struggle for this patient; thus, one sees an infant in a woman's body. Father's role has been that of overprotecting and infantilizing her, whereas the mother has not furnished her with the nutrients necessary for growth.

With respect to treatment, the patient requires much structure. She does not have the resources to structure herself. She will view and use treatment as a container, to contain affects and desires she is unable to. While this is a legitimate and useful function, it is important that she not be infantilized. She should be taken seriously, and her therapist should ask and expect more of her than her family did. Her capacity to benefit from a more insight-oriented approach is limited. Nonetheless, being simply supportive is not enough, and therefore I would maintain a more insight-oriented stance.

In summary, the patient presents narcissistic and masochistic features organized at a borderline level. Highly defended and superficial, she is fearful of being significantly touched and possibly rattled. She assumes a totally passive stance and tends to present "as if" features. She is of bright normal intelligence and, with structure, functions acceptably. She is not thought disordered, but reveals impaired ego functions. Affects are poorly controlled and regulated. In her dynamic life are difficulties with aggression, impaired object relations, an estranged sense of self, and a longing for a symbiotic relationship.

4

PSYCHOANALYTIC DIAGNOSTIC SCHEME

There has been an ongoing and perhaps necessary tension between diagnosis for descriptive and research purposes and diagnosis for clinical and therapeutic ones. For example, attempts to make DSM-III (American Psychiatric Association, 1980) reflect what is observable, describable, and measurable—a reaction against the inconsistencies and subjectivities of its predecessors—pleased many researchers but frustrated many clinicians. In response to practitioners' complaints, the designers of DSM-IV tried to make that edition more sensitive to clinicians' needs (Frances, 1995). Nonetheless, the shortcomings of this edition further illustrate the inherent and insoluble problems in developing a taxonomy of psychiatric disorders that can serve both clinical and research purposes.

From both a clinical and psychoanalytic perspective, DSM-IV presents serious limitations. Like its immediate predecessors, DSM-III and DSM III-R, almost total emphasis is accorded that which is observable and describable, with little attention paid to underlying and more invisible structures, dynamics, and meanings. As one consequence, such an approach cannot conceptualize individuals who present marked contradictions between external and internal spheres of functioning.

49

Categories are included in the manual on the basis of empirical research findings and not on the basis of accumulated clinical experience. Thus, forms of psychopathology familiar to the psychoanalytic clinician, such as the "as if personality" (Deutsch, 1942) or the "oral character" (Abraham, 1921–1925), are excluded from this edition, as they have been from earlier ones.

In contrast to clinical thinking, each DSM edition has made use of a categorical schema rather than a dimensional or contextual one. By definition, different types of psychopathology are viewed as discrete and noncontinuous, and the distinction between normalcy and pathology is considered as one of kind, not as one of degree. To negotiate problems inherent in a categorical system consisting of discrete elements, users of the manual are encouraged to assign dual or multiple diagnoses. Such a practice, however, with the implicit premise that each diagnosis signifies a separate and distinct disturbance, is antithetical to the clinician who views various external expressions (e.g., symptoms, complaints) as arising from a common internal source, what McWilliams (in press) refers to as the "same overall sickness of soul" (p. 4).

Particularly disconcerting for the psychoanalytic clinician is the consideration that the DSM schema does little to inform a more dynamic form of treatment. The categories, in and of themselves, give no orientation to treatment nor do they assist practitioners in formulating a treatment plan. Assessment aimed at diagnosis, but unrelated to intervention and treatment, can come to be experienced by assessor and patient alike as academic and nothing more than a ritualistic exercise. Diagnostic practices that simply label an individual do not help the clinician in conveying an essentially therapeutic attitude (Schafer, 1983), an attitude considered necessary in promoting an optimal therapeutic outcome.

According to McWilliams (in press), for a diagnostic system to serve clinical purposes, especially therapeutic ones, it must address the following aspects of an individual: temperament and fixed attributes, maturational factors, defensive patterns, identifications, relational schemas, core affects, regulators of self-esteem, and pathogenic beliefs.

Although the diagnostic scheme proposed in this chapter does not meet all of these criteria, it does satisfy many of them. Emphasis is placed on the more fixed and enduring aspects of personality; there is an implicit developmental focus; and explicit attention is paid to defenses, relational schemas (i.e., internalized object relations), and self-esteem regulation.

As compared with DSM-IV, the proposed scheme goes beyond descriptive clarification by also calling for an analysis of personality structure. In addition, the scheme combines a categorical approach with a dimensional one. The proposed diagnostic scheme represents an integration of more classical psychoanalytic classifications of character structure with Kernberg's (1970) contributions regarding levels of personality organization.

Attempts to classify various character types go back to Freud (1908, 1931) and Abraham (1921–1925) and their understanding of different character structures on the basis of level of instinctual development. Fenichel (1945), dissatisfied with these earlier attempts, proposed a classification combining dynamic and structural considerations. From a dynamic perspective, he distinguished character traits that involved "sublimination" from those that were "reactive." In the former, instinctual energy was discharged freely, whereas in the latter, a defensive operation was evoked, and that operation became part of the character trait. Fenichel further subdivided reactive character traits into those that reflect an attitude of avoidance and those that reflect an attitude of opposition. From a structural perspective, he first defined character as "the ego's habitual modes of adjustment to the external world, the id, and the superego," and then classified character types on the basis of the modes involved. By combining the dynamic and structural points of view, he was able to classify the reactive character traits into those that reflect pathological behavior toward the id (the classical oral, anal, and phallic character traits), pathological behavior toward the superego, and pathological behavior toward external objects (e.g., pathological jealousy, social inhibitions) (p. 467). As late as 1964, Prelinger and associates (1964), in their review of psychoanalytic conceptions of character, noted that Fenichel's classification scheme was still the most widely accepted.

As part of an attempt to integrate the thinking of the British school of object relations theory with more classical formulations emerging from ego psychology, Kernberg (1970) has proposed a classification of character pathology based on an assessment of structural features. Using the concept of levels of personality organization, Kernberg's classification involves a systematic appraisal of level of instinctual development, manifestations of ego weakness, level of defensive organization, quality of internalized object relations, level of superego development, and attainment of ego identity. Kernberg's classification schema has received wide currency in the literature related to psychopathology, and the structural variables he has identified and described have proven especially useful in investigating more severe instances of character pathology, including borderline phenomena (Kwawer et al., 1980; H. Lerner and P. Lerner, 1988).

This diagnostic scheme involves assessing patients along two relatively independent dimensions. The first dimension consists of a descriptive characterological diagnosis in terms of character structure. As noted previously, because the character types represent ideals, it is important to clarify how much the patient approximates the ideal and how much he or she differs from it. The second dimension, based on Kernberg's system, involves an evaluation of the underlying level of personality organization. The dimensions are considered only relatively independent, because, as Kernberg has noted, specific character structures tend to be organized at certain levels. For example, whereas many hysterical characters are organized at a higher level, most infantile personalities are organized at a lower level.

Before discussing each of the more representative character structures, it should be noted that there are many possible characterologies. For instance, since classical times, people have drawn analogies between character and animals (e.g., the wolf, lion, sheep) and we are familiar with systems based on humors (e.g., sanguine, phlegmatic). Literature, too, has provided memorable examples (e.g., Don Juan, Hamlet, Scarlett O'Hara).

In general, systems of characterology are built upon two basic underlying assumptions. The first involves the iconographic value of the given types. That is, each type must be familiar enough so that it provides a vehicle for communicating. Here, there is a certain literary-artistic requirement: the character has to be convincingly drawn. New characters can be created and added to the list, whether taken from the theater (e.g., Willie Loman) or from the consulting room (e.g., the "as if" personality). In certain respects, the borderline concept began this way. That is, writers such as Reich (1933), Alexander (1930), and Stern (1938) described a type of patient that other clinicians could readily recognize.

The second aspect of characterology is the attempt to create a toxonomy or a systematic classification system. The history of psychiatry is replete with the hope of developing a truly adequate taxonomy that would capture something essential about the nature of man; for example, a basic biopsychosocial axis along which personality could be organized. Unfortunately, there are evolutionary considerations that suggest that such an a prori system cannot accurately reflect the kind of disjointed patchwork of novel structures one finds in nature.

Nevertheless, such a systmatic tendency retains its allure. Here, again, the borderline concept comes to mind. Beyond its iconographic value, the idea was appealing because it offered to fill a gap between neurotic and psychotic. This is to say, it seemed to make the system to classification more complete.

In addition to these two fundamental requirements, a psychoanalytic characterology ought to provide something more; namely, what might be referred to as a dynamic context. A psychoanalytic character type should be drawn in such a way that the internal relations between facets of character are identified, so that the significance of any specific feature can be understood in relation to the whole. For example, when an infantile character falls in love, this has different prognostic implications than it would if the patient were a schizoid personality; the former will cherish the experience until he or she is inevitably disappointed, whereas the latter may well fear he or she is going crazy.

In what follows, some well-known psychoanalytic character types are briefly described. In general, the approach taken in this book is to emphasize the iconographic value of utilizing these character types in assessment (i.e., their communicative value to other clinicians), while adopting a more agnostic, practical attitude regarding the possibility of a comprehensive system of classification. The list to be presented is by no means exhaustive, and the clinician should always be open to the possibility that the patient violates the expectations of this or any system in novel and even unique ways.

◆ ◆ ◆ Representative Character Structures

Hysterical Character

The hysterical character is described as subjective, highly energetic, buoyant, sprightly, and lively. Hysterics depict what may be characterized as "the emotional way of life." They manifest emotionality or, more accurately, emotional reactivity in an outward expression of the self as an involved emotional participant. Hysterics view their emotionality, as Easser and Lesser (1966) have noted, "as a jewel to be exhibited, fondled and cherished. Any attempt to move beyond it or remove it is viewed as an attack and is defended against with the total personality" (p. 72).

The emotionality lends a childlike cast to the patient and is used to sustain inhibitions and to avoid the acceptance of certain adult responsibilities. Feelings, rather than thoughts, are used in times of crisis and conflict. Hysterics, directly and actively, engage the human world. Their overt and covert need to be loved results in hypersensitivity toward others. They need to test love through interactions with others, and this accounts for the variety of emotional upheavals. There is often a pursuit of excitement, coupled with a defense against realization, with both deriving from a tendency to attribute sensual and sexual meaning to environmental stimuli. Whereas, historically, suggestibility has been considered the major trait of the hysteric, Easser and Lesser (1965) have proposed, more correctly, that "the hysteric receives (and acts on) the suggestion she has assiduously implanted" (p. 397). The hysteric dislikes and avoids the exact, the rote, and the mundane. A job is never done for a job's sake, yet superior performance is forthcoming when the task has sufficient scope to permit an expression of one's sense of drama. Finally, central to the hysteric's presentation is a sense of self as part child and part adult. For a more detailed description of the hysterical character structure, refer to Siegman (1954), Easser and Lesser (1965, 1966), and Krohn (1978).

Obsessive-Compulsive Character

Freud observed and described a cluster of character traits he found in individuals whose instinctual life was fixated and organized at the anal stage. He related these traits to early experiences centered around toilet training and to initial struggles over control with caretakers. Frugality, for Freud, represented a continuation of retention, prompted by the pleasure in holding onto and the fear of letting go. Obstinacy was seen in terms of holding one's position, and stubbornness was considered an elaboration of obstinacy. Orderliness he viewed as an extension of obedience. These character traits initially identified by Freud have been markedly extended; more current descriptions of the obsessive-compulsive include diligence, heightened conscientiousness, industriousness, punctuality, and thriftiness. The obsessive-compulsive is also considered to be perfectionistic, overly meticulous, scrupulous, rigid, dogmatic, self-critical, and pedantic. Whereas the hysteric lives in a world of feelings and avoids the mundane and commonplace, the obsessive-compulsive, by contrast, lives in a world of thoughts and ideas and welcomes that which is routine, familiar, and structured. For these individuals, preoccupied with issues of control, activity has a markedly driven quality. As Shapiro (1965) has noted, when the obsessive-compulsive announces an intent to play, what is actually meant is an intent to work at playing. Further and more detailed accounts of the obsessive-compulsive character are available in Fenichel (1945), Gardiner (1971), and Laughlin (1956).

Depressive Character Structure

Closely resembling the obsessive-compulsive character at a descriptive level is the depressive character. Like the obsessive-compulsive, the depressive character is somber, serious, hypercritical, conscientious, and tightly controlled. More specific to the depressive character, however, are chronic feelings of worthlessness, a pessimistic outlook, and an anticipation of disappointment.

Kernberg (1975) has suggested that the depressive character manifests three groups of character traits: vulnerability to loss of love; hypercritical attitude toward self and others; and pathological management of aggressive urges. Such patients, according to Kernberg, have an excessive need for love and approval from others. The continuous need for love makes them especially vulnerable to rejection and disappointment; repeated and accumulated experiences of disappointment eventuate in a pessimistic outlook, a sense that there isn't enough love available. The hypercritical attitude is considered a direct expression of superego pressures, a demand on oneself to be somber, serious, and reliable. In severe instances it is expressed in the conviction that "life is a fraud." Depressive patients struggle with aggression. Situations that typically evoke anger in others elicit depressive feelings in these individuals. To bolster their defenses against the expression and experience of anger, depressive characters are often ingratiating, subservient, and deferential. Comprehensive descriptions of the depressive character have been provided by Jacobson (1971) and Laughlin (1956).

Masochistic Character Structure

According to Reich (1933), masochistic features are present in most neurotic structures; however, only in the masochistic character do they converge and determine the basic tone of the personality and the person's reactions. For Reich, masochists present awkward, ataxic behavior, which is especially prominent in their mannerisms; they harbor intense feelings of suffering, which become manifest in their complaints; and they continually inflict pain upon themselves through self-debasement. Masochistic characters are provocative; they use their suffering to reproach and aggress against others. Masochists tend to provoke those by whom they feel disappointed; that is, behind the provocation is a disappointment in love—as well as an appeal for love. The masochistic character cannot tolerate praise and tends toward self-depreciation and self-abasement. Because praise represents an expression of exhibitionistic tendencies and, as such, a source of anxiety, it is minimized and avoided. A more complete description of the masochistic character has been provided by Reich (1933); for a more pointed discussion of the masochistic character in the testing situation, refer to Appelbaum (1963).

Infantile Personality

In many respects the infantile personality would appear to be a caricature of the hysteric, but there are important differences. Many of the same characteristics are demonstrated, but in sharper, dramatic relief. Bounds of social custom and propriety are violated and breached. The latent aggressivity of exhibitionism and competitiveness becomes blatant, insistent, and bizarre. In contrast to the hysterical character, adaptive functioning is erratic. Periods of attainment alternate with periods of serious dysfunction. Such ego weaknesses as poor impulse control, emotional immaturity, and childlike dependency are not circumscribed and limited to specific conflictual areas, but are evident in all aspects of life. The hysteric has difficulty *within* a relationship, the infantile personality *with* the relationship. The infantile patient begins relationships with great hopes and unrealistic expectations and feels bitter and resentful when the relationship fails and the expectations of rescue, nurturance, and unlimited care are not fulfilled. Emotional engagement embodies the desire to engulf and incorporate the other; this, in turn, is defensively experienced as a threat of self-depletion. Quite striking in the infantile personality is the tendency either to act on pregenital aims directly or to create a fantasy world and then live within it. Often, such fantasies and fantasized relationships substitute for real relationships. For a more complete description of the infantile personality, refer to Abraham (1921–25), Easser and Lesser (1965), and Sugarman (1979).

Narcissistic Personality

On the basis of Freud's 1914 paper "On Narcissism," two differing comprehensive descriptions of the narcissistic patient have emerged in the psychoanalytic literature. Kernberg (1975) reserves the designation for those patients "in whom the main problem appears to be the disturbance of their self-regard in connection with specific disturbances in their object relations" (p. 227). He describes such patients as manifesting a heightened degree of self-absorption, an inordinate need to be loved and admired, and an overinflated sense of themselves amid a desperate desire for adoration. He further suggests that their emotional life is shallow, they exhibit little empathy for the motives and feelings of others, and they feel restless and bored unless their self-regard is being nourished. In their relationships, potential providers of narcissistic supplies are idealized, whereas those from whom they expect little are depreciated and treated with contempt. Kernberg sees such individuals as cold, arrogant, ruthless, and exploitative beneath a veneer of charm.

Kohut (1971) too has described the narcissistic patient, but in ways different from Kernberg. Although he has identified a specific symptom complex (including lack of enthusiasm and zest, perverse activity, subjective feelings of deadness), he sees such a cluster of symptoms as insufficient for establishing the narcissistic diagnosis. Instead, he uses the concept of the "cohesive self" as the guiding principle for the differential diagnosis. The instability, or propensity for regression, of this psychic structure, for Kohut, is the most important diagnostic sign of a narcissistic personality disorder. In achieving a differential diagnosis, Kohut places major significance on treatment considerations, particularly on the nature of the emerging transference: he has identified and described a set of atypical transference patterns that unfold in the treatment of the narcissistic patient. Referred to overall as "selfobject" transferences, specific subtypes include the mirroring transference and the idealizing transference. Despite Kohut's reliance on process considerations rather than on descriptive features, it has been my experience that the type of narcissistic patient depicted typically presents as hypervigilant, hypersensitive, thin-skinned, and painfully vulnerable. Such patients attune to the cues and expectations of others and mold their actions and feelings accordingly. Their self-esteem is painfully low and the depressive affect they experience involves feelings of emptiness and hollowness.

Test scores, test responses, and test behavior characteristic of both types of narcissistic patients have been provided by Arnow and Cooper (1988), H. Lerner (1988), and P. Lerner (1988).

Schizoid Personality

With the increased currency being accorded the British school of object relations has come a renewed interest in more primitive personality structures, including the schizoid personality. Originally described by Fairbairn (1952), and elaborated by Guntrip (1961), the schizoid personality is characterized as detached, aloof, and emotionally apathetic. Beneath the facade of aloofness, however, is an intense need for a good love object, a hunger for love hidden from the outer world. Fairbairn (1952) noted that the schizoid individual keeps his love locked in because he feels that it is too dangerous to release upon his objects. He or she is afraid to want, seek, take from, or give to objects in the outer world. "Whereas the depressed person is afraid of harming and destroying his love-objects by his hate . . . the schizoid person is afraid of harming and destroying his love-objects by his love" (Guntrip, 1961, pp. 282–283). Out of a refusal to invest in objects in the outer world, the schizoid individual radically invests in his or her inner world. Hence, one finds an individual who, in addition to being detached from the outer world, is highly ideational and preoccupied with intricate fantasies and who tends to limit his object relations to the inner world. For a more detailed description of the schizoid individual, refer to Fairbairn (1952) and Guntrip (1952).

Paranoid Personality

In the paranoid personality, paranoid trends have reached a point of such intensity and a level of such pervasiveness that they themselves constitute the major descriptive element and determine the characterological diagnosis. Accordingly, such individuals are rigid, malignantly distrustful, highly suspicious, and continually embattled with persecutory objects. Central to their functioning is the process of externalization. They attribute causality idiosyncratically, assign malevolent intent, and perversely experience a sense of self-vindication and self-justification. Shapiro (1965) has compared the cognitive and perceptual style of the paranoid character with that of the obsessive-compulsive and concluded, "The paranoid is, in every instance, the more extreme, the less stable, the more tense and antagonistic, the more openly occupied with instinctual conflict, and, in a word, the more psychologically primitive" (p. 107). Although the paranoid personality has been a relatively neglected area of clinical inquiry and writing, descriptions have been offered by Shapiro (1965) and Blum (1981).

In the foregoing section I have presented a description of representative and commonly encountered character structures. The list, as noted, is by no means exhaustive; for example, one could add certain character structures from a descriptive perspective that stand out because of one salient feature (e.g., passive-aggressive personality) or because they represent a fit with a well-known literary or fairytale figure (e.g., Don Juan).

❖ ❖ ❖ Levels of Personality Organization

Insisting that a descriptive characterological diagnosis is necessary but not sufficient, Kernberg (1970) devised a system for classifying levels of personality organization based upon a systematic appraisal of underlying psychological structures. The system calls for placing each structure on a three-level continuum, ranging from higher level to intermediate level to lower level. The specific categories that are assessed include level of instinctual development, manifestations of ego weakness, level of defensive organization, level of internalized object relations, level of superego development, and the attainment of ego identity.

Level of Instinctual Development

The category of level of instinctual development involves the predominant level of instinctual attainment and fixation. In contrast to previous psychoanalytic classifications of character based on the stages of libidinal development (oral, anal, phallic), a major distinction is drawn here between genital and pregenital instinctual strivings.

At the higher level of personality organization genital primacy has been obtained: "Instinctual conflicts have reached the stage where the infantile genital phase and oedipal conflicts are clearly predominant and there is no pathological condensation of genital sexual strivings with pregenital, aggressively determined strivings in which the latter predominate" (Kernberg, 1976, p. 144).

At the intermediate level, pregenital, especially oral, regression and fixation points predominate. Although the genital level of libidinal development has been reached, oral conflicts predominate, reflective of regression from oedipal struggles. The aggressive aspect of the pre-genital conflicts is less intense and less pervasive than is found at the lower level of organization.

At the lower level there is a pathological condensation of genital and pregenital instinctual strivings with an emphasis on pregenital aggression. Oedipal strivings do appear; however, they are condensed with pregenital sadistic and masochistic urges. According to Kernberg (1976), the predominance of pregenital aggression is evidenced "by sadistically infiltrated, polymorphous perverse infantile drive deriva-tives which contaminate all the internalized and external object rela-tions" (p. 146).

Manifestations of Ego Weaknesses

Necessary for the category of manifestation of ego weaknesses is a careful evaluation of the patient's ego functions, including quality of impulse control, tolerance of frustration and anxiety, effectiveness of defenses, and quality of reality testing. Also involved here is an appraisal of the nature and extent of expressions of primary process thinking.

At the higher level of personality organization the patient's ego is somewhat constricted; however, defenses are effective and there is lit-tle instinctual infiltration of defensive character traits. At this level, one sees little evidence of ego weakness; rather, controls over primary process manifestations tend, if anything, to be overly excessive.

At the intermediate level the patient has fewer inhibitory charac-ter defenses available, and one begins to see character traits infiltrated by instinctual strivings. Ego weaknesses begin to appear, but in a more circumscribed manner, as reflected in Kernberg's (1976) term "struc-tured impulsivity."

Characteristic of the lower level of personality organization are severe ego weaknesses. Owing to the absence of ego organizers (e.g., integrated self-concept) and the lack of an integrated superego, patients at this level manifest poor impulse control, little anxiety tolerance, disruptions in their reality testing, and a lack of channels for sublimation. Primary process thinking infiltrates and interferes with their cognitive functioning, especially in more unstructured situations.

Level of Defensive Organization

Kernberg proposed two overall levels of defensive organization. At the lower level, primitive dissociation or splitting is the crucial defense, bolstered by the related defenses of denial, primitive idealization, primitive devaluation, and projective identification. At the higher level of defensive organization, repression supplants splitting as the major defense and is accompanied by the related defensive operations of intellectualization, rationalization, undoing, and higher forms of projection and denial.

At the higher level of personality organization, repression, characteristic of the advanced level of defense organization, predominates. Augmenting repression are various character defenses and defense mechanisms, such as intellectualization and rationalization.

At the intermediate level of personality organization, repression is still the major defensive operation; however, reaction formations are more predominant. In addition, patients at this level reveal some dissociative trends, some defensive splitting of the ego in certain areas, and a greater use of projection and denial.

At the lower level of personality organization, primitive dissociation or splitting predominates with a concomitant impairment of the ego's synthetic function. The patient's reliance on splitting becomes evident in contradictory and alternating ego states. As noted previously, splitting is supported by other defenses, including denial, primitive idealization, primitive devaluation, projective identification, and omnipotence.

Level of Internalized Object Relations

In keeping with formulations arising from the British school of object relations, Kernberg viewed the defensive organization and the level of internalized object relations as intimately related. More specifically, defenses both organize the inner object world and are reflected in external object relations.

Accordingly, at the higher level of personality organization there is no significant pathology of internalized object relations. Object constancy has been attained, object relations have a "whole" quality, and the inner representational world is stable and accessible. Object relations at this level are deep and stable, and the individual is capable of experiencing mourning, guilt, and a wide range of affective responses.

At the intermediate level of personality organization, internalized object relations are relatively nonpathological; however, external object relations tend to be conflictual. Even though pregenital urges enter into relational strivings, relationships are stable and lasting, and the individual is able to tolerate ambivalent and conflictual feelings toward the other.

Severe pathology of internalized object relations is evident at the lower level of personality organization. Object relations are on a "part-object" basis, object constancy is not firmly established, and there is an inability to integrate good and bad aspects of the object. Because of the lack of integration of libidinally determined and aggressively determined object images, object relations remain on a need-gratifying or threatening basis. At this level, ambivalence cannot be tolerated, there is a limited capacity to experience guilt and mourning, and relationships tend to be chaotic and transient.

Level of Superego Development

The internalization of object relations constitutes a major organizing factor for superego development. Failure to integrate all-good and all-bad self and object images interferes with superego integration by creating an excessively demanding ego ideal that insists upon ideals of power, greatness, and perfection. Sadistic superego forerunners, maintained through projective and introjective processes, are not toned down or integrated with idealized superego components. According to Kernberg (1976),

> the development of a level of integration within the ego creates the precondition for the integration of the sadistically determined superego forerunners with the ego ideal and the subsequent capacity to internalize the realistic, demanding, and prohibitive aspects of the parents [p. 150].

At the higher level of personality organization one sees a well-integrated but often relatively severe and punitive superego. Superego forerunners, based upon sadistic impulses, can be present and gain expression in a superego that may be overly demanding, relatively harsh, and perfectionistic.

At the intermediate level of personality organization the superego is more punitive and less integrated. Powerful ego ideal goals for greatness and powerfulness coexist with strict prohibitions and demands for moral perfection. At this level, there is partial blurring of superego-ego boundaries, some projection of superego prohibitions, contradictions in the value system, and severe mood swings.

At the lower level of personality organization there is minimal superego integration. There is little capacity for experiencing guilt and concern, paranoid trends are clearly evident, and sadistic superego components are externalized through more primitive forms of projection. The delineation between ego and superego is nonexistent, and primitive ego ideal goals are indistinguishable from narcissistic strivings for admiration and adoration.

Attainment of Ego Identity

The attainment of ego identity is also, related to the internalization of object relations. Only with the synthesis of good and bad self-images is the groundwork laid for the development of ego identity. Kernberg (1976) believed that "when 'good' and 'bad' internalized object relations (involving self-images, object-images, ideal self-images, ideal object-images) are so integrated that an integrated self concept and a related integrated 'representational world' develop, a stable ego identity is achieved" (p. 150).

At the higher level of personality organization, a firm and cohesive ego identity, including a stable self-concept and a stable representational world, has been established. Values are consistent, goals are realistic, and the sense of identity provides an organizing function by guiding and directing behavior.

At the intermediate level of personality development, ego identity has been attained; however, it is less stable and less firm. Values are less consistent and at times contradictory, ego ideal goals are more excessive and less realistic, and behavior is less guided by considerations of identity.

Because of the lack of integration of "all-good" and "all-bad" self and object representations, and the resultant absence of an integrated self-concept, at the lower level of personality organization one sees identity diffusion. The person's inner view of himself or herself is a contradictory, chaotic mixture of omnipotent, shameful, and threatened images.

In contrast with other classification schemes that place borderline disturbances along a descriptive, characterological dimension (e.g., DSM III), such disturbances in this scheme are placed on a structural dimension and regarded as a level of personality organization. More specifically, the lower level of personality organization comprises the borderline disorders. Conceptualizing borderline functioning and organization in this manner takes into account the clinical and research finding that patients with varying character structures can manifest borderline pathology. For a more complete discussion of the conceptual and clinical controversies surrounding the borderline concept, refer to chapter 22.

◆ ◆ ◆ Conclusion

In this chapter I have presented a broad, however incomplete, overview of one psychoanalytic diagnostic scheme. Based on contributions to the psychoanalytic literature on character formation and Kernberg's work on level of character organization, the system involves assessing patients along two dimensions. The first dimension involves a descriptive evaluation of the patient's character structure. The second dimension is level of personality organization, based on an assessment of the following underlying structures: instinctual development, ego intactness, nature of defenses, quality of internalized object relations, superego integration, and ego identity.

5

THE RORSCHACH ASSESSMENT FRAME

Aconcept that has received wide currency in the treatment literature but little attention in the assessment literature is "frame." Earlier terms, including the "analytic situation" (Greenson, 1967), the "contract" (Menninger and Holtzman, 1973), and the "psychoanalytic frame" (Bleger, 1967), have been used to describe what contemporary therapists now refer to as the "frame"; namely, the structural conditions that provide the framework for treatment to occur. It is widely agreed that the treatment process cannot proceed until the frame has been established (Chasseguet-Smirgel, 1992).

In this chapter I first apply the concept of a frame to the assessment process. I discuss its application both to the Rorschach and then to a broader assessment in which the Rorschach is part of a battery of tests. I then suggest ways of modifying the broader assessment frame so it more closely parallels the treatment frame, and thereby, increases the range and depth of inferences that can be drawn from assessment and applied to treatment.

❖ ❖ ❖   The Assessment Frame

An especially clear and comprehensive discussion of the treatment frame is found in the work of Chasseguet-Smirgel (1992). She begins her discussion by noting the role of the frame for the artist:

> In studying works of art, where the term "frame" is used, one understands that the basic condition for creation is the possibility of finding a place—a frame, a wall, a stage . . . , to serve as a container for the artist's psychic productions, his projective identification, in the shape of a painting, a drawing, a fresco, a play . . . for want of which there could only be hallucination. It follows, that in addition to giving precise form to his projective identifications, the artist must also contain these within defined limits. There must be a space between the artist and his work, for without this he would be psychotic [p. 22].

For the artist, then, the frame serves two vital functions. It not only provides a medium or vehicle for expression, but at the same time it allows for the containing of those expressions. In an analogous way, the treatment frame also allows for the emergence of certain psychic phenomena as well as for their containment. The treatment frame serves other purposes too. As noted by Chasseguet-Smirgel, its stability and permanence distinguish, spacially and temporally, the inside from the outside, regulate the physical and psychical attitudes of the two participants, and permit the appearance and observation of transference reactions.

Like treatment, assessment too has a frame. Indeed, if one were to consider the Rorschach alone, and then as part of a test battery, one could identify several types or levels of frames. With specific regard to the Rorschach, one type of frame, perhaps the narrowest, is that which is set by the inkblots themselves. Although authors have not used the term "frame," they have described functions provided by the cards which can be understood from the perspective of frame. Exner (1993), for example, argues on the basis of a series of studies that most Rorschach responses are based on critical stimulus properties of the blots and not on projections or personal attributions. Rapaport (Rapaport et al., 1945–1946), even though using a very different language, alludes to the same process when he suggests that the inkblots act as a regulatory reality for the associative processes. As viewed from the vantage point of frame, both authors here are referring to the inkblots' containing function. Willock (1992), by contrast, highlights the cards' expressive and shaping function. As pointed out in chapter 2, he likens the inkblots to other expressive modalities, such as modeling clay, and considers the Rorschach task as one of making something.

A second type of frame in Rorschach testing, one broader than the first, is that which is defined by the "test situation" (Schachtel, 1966)—the conditions within which testing occurs. Of particular importance in discussing the test situation is the consideration that Rorschach assessment takes place in an interpersonal context (Schachtel, 1966; Smith, 1990; Leichtman, 1996). Here too, even though the term "frame" has not been employed, authors have described both the expressive (Smith, 1990; Leichtman, 1996) and containing (Schafer, 1954; Levine, 1988; Exner, 1993) functions provided by the patient–examiner relationship.

A third frame, one most similar to the treatment frame, is that provided by an extended assessment in which the Rorschach is included as part of a battery of tests. Structurally, this frame and the treatment frame share several common features. Each consists of the place where sessions will be held, the number and duration of sessions, the agreed upon fee, the way in which missed appointments will be handled, and how the participants are to refer to each other (e.g., by last names, first names, titles). In addition, as part of each frame, roles, although subject to distortion, are relatively prescribed, orienting task directions are given, and confidentiality is safeguarded.

Like the treatment frame, the assessment frame also permits the expression and containment of certain psychic phenomena, regulates the attitudes and expectations of the participants, and allows for the activation and observation of an array of interpersonal transactions. Assessment, too, cannot proceed until the frame has been established. Despite this truism, this aspect of assessment tends to be neglected in assessment training. It is my experience that establishing and maintaining the assessment frame is often troublesome for younger psychologists and students.

A supervisee was asked to test a female patient to help determine her suitability for long-term treatment. He began the assessment by introducing himself by title and referring to the patient by her last name. The patient, an attractive and charming woman, several years older, immediately reacted. She noted that titles and surnames were formal and distancing, and suggested that they refer to each other by first names instead. He hesitantly agreed. Only later in supervision could the supervisee appreciate the patient's tendency to question and then redefine the assessment frame, his own readiness to bend, and the effect of this on the entire assessment.

As has been written about the patient–examiner relationship (Schafer, 1954, P. Lerner, 1991a), the patient's attitude toward and reactions to the assessment frame not only influence test performance, but can also be a valuable source of diagnostic information in their own right. A high-powered, 44-year-old real-estate developer was referred for psychological testing as part of a highly contentious custody evaluation. Setting up the first appointment proved formidable. Times offered by the examiner were immediately rejected and times suggested by the patient (late evening, weekends) were outside of the examiner's normal work hours. The patient virtually insisted that the examiner extend his schedule in order to accommodate to the patient's. Thus, even before having met the patient, the examiner already learned of the patient's inordinate need for control and compelling desire to be treated as special.

Because of the similarities between the assessment and treatment frames, the examiner who explicitly sets the assessment frame and then observes patient responses to it is in a unique position to predict patient reactions to the treatment frame.

As illustrated by the supervisee's female patient and the real estate developer, many of our patients seem bent on assaulting or at least altering the assessment frame. Various facets of the assessment structure, from arranging appointment times, to agreeing upon a fee, to negotiating what information will be conveyed to the referrer, become arenas for struggle. It is more than likely that such individuals will respond to the treatment frame in a similarly contentious way.

◆ ◆ ◆ Modifying the Assessment Frame

In addition to similarities, there are differences between the assessment and treatment frames. By thoughtfully altering the assessment frame, one can reduce these differences, and thereby broaden the range of inferences related to treatment.

One such structural difference involves time, meaning specifically the number of sessions involved in each undertaking. Recognizing that treatment is inevitably lengthier, one can, nonetheless, reduce this difference by extending the assessment over time. For example, instead of cramming the full assessment into one expanded session, at times lasting half a day, one can schedule three shorter hourly appointments spaced comfortably apart. Assessing in this way demonstrates a sensitivity to the patient's (and to one's own) physical and emotional stamina. Even more important, such a practice encourages a view of assessment as a process: a process with a beginning, a middle, and an ending, and in which change is possible and observable. It is not uncommon for patients to begin testing with considerable anxiety and an attendant defensive posture. Yet, often times such individuals are able to gradually relax and let up on their tight controls as testing progresses and the examiner, situation, and process become more familiar.

Treatment, too, can and has been subdivided into a beginning, a middle portion, and termination (Greenson, 1967). Therefore, by extending the assessment over time, the examiner is presented a telescoped view of how an individual enters a novel situation, maintains the situation, leaves it, and perhaps changes in the process.

A second modification involves the assessor including in his or her test battery instruments that differ in their degree of structure, regardless of referral question. As noted in chapter 1, by introducing levels of structure into the assessment, the examiner can then make treatment recommendations regarding structure based on the testee's reactions to the differing levels.

A 17-year-old male adolescent was referred for IQ testing because of repeated academic failures. Despite the specificity of the request, the psychologist, as was his customary practice, employed a full battery of tests in which an intelligence scale was only one instrument. On the WAIS-III the patient attained a full scale IQ of 84. While taking this more structured, school-like intelligence scale, the patient evidenced massive anxiety, crippling self-doubt, and a compelling need to undermine his own performance. His behavior and performance in taking the Rorschach was dramatically different. He not only experienced appreciably less anxiety with the more unstructured task, but, surprisingly, produced a rich protocol that included five accurately seen movement responses. The test findings clearly indicated the dynamic roots of his school difficulties. That, together with his very different responses to the more and less structured tasks, resulted in the examiner recommending a more expressive, unstructured type of treatment. If the examiner had not used a test battery and had not included in the battery tests varying in degree of structure, his understanding of the patient's difficulty would have been compromised and his recommendation far different.

A third type of modification is based on the premise that the examiner should attempt to secure the patient's active involvement in the assessment process. Too often, assessment is conceived of as a way of getting at the problem. With such a view, the patient is placed in a passive position, if not bypassed altogether. If, alternatively, the examiner repeatedly seeks the individual's active engagement in a cooperative relationship, then patient and examiner together are in a position to observe and assess the patient's functioning. The patient becomes a participating partner in his or her own assessment.

A specific way of gaining the patient's active involvement in the assessment involves modifying how one handles feedback—the communication to the patient of assessment findings. Typically, such findings are reported to the patient after the assessment has been completed and the assessor has had the opportunity to analyze and integrate the mass of data. Although this practice meets the professional needs of the examiner, it too contributes to the view of the patient as a passive participant.

To ensure the patient's more active participation, an alternative is to discuss findings with the patient, not after the assessment, but in an ongoing basis as they emerge during the assessment. In doing this, one attempts to be particularly sensitive to the patient's own understanding of his or her difficulties, to the dangers involved in premature insight, and to the effect of the shared information on the patient's self-esteem.

Others might argue that such a practice could affect a patient's subsequent test responses, as well as his or her attitude toward the testing. I too recognize this, but contend that a patient's reactions to the examiner's interventions may usefully be viewed as additional information, to be understood as would be any other type of information. What is important here is not that the patient's reaction may be altered, but that the examiner recognize the impact of his or her intervention and be prepared to understand later responses within that context. Herein, I am in agreement with Shevrin and Schectman (1973), who state the principle strongly: "If the diagnostician ignores his impact on the situation, he is ignoring the only instrument on which he can rely" (p. 494).

Modifying the assessment frame in this way provides the examiner with information upon which to make inferences in regard to several important, basically relational, aspects of the treatment situation. For instance, the level and quality of the patient's involvement in the assessment may be used as a barometer, indicating his or her capacity to invest and engage in treatment. By using himself or herself as an agent of change, the examiner is then able to observe the patient's capacity to make use of another to change, his or her attitude toward change, and resistances stirred by the possibility of change. Lastly, the patient's willingness and capacity to enter into a working relationship with the examiner—an assessment alliance, to use a more technical term—can be predictive of his or her capacity to form a treatment alliance with a therapist.

The practice of sharing findings during, not following, the assessment may be extended to the issue of recommendations. Several authors (Shevrin and Schectman, 1973; P. Lerner, 1991a) have observed that the same resistances evoked by and during the testing will also be evoked by the recommendations offered. This means that the examiner must consider how the recommendations should be broached and implemented. That is, one aspect of the assessment task is to subject the recommendations to the same kind of scrutiny, understanding, and planning that are involved in understanding the patient and his or her difficulties. Shevrin and Schectman (1973) propose that the patient should become gradually aware of what is needed by what has already taken place. By discussing findings as they emerge in the assessment, one is also preparing the way for accepting the recommendations.

The modifications in the assessment frame suggested here are essentially quite modest and are consistent with sound clinical technique. It is important that these suggestions be distinguished from those of other authors who propose more sweeping alterations in the assessment frame. For example, Aronow et al. (1995) have recently argued that one can integrate assessment with treatment by using the Rorschach as a psychotherapy tool—a device for stimulating patient productions, if you will. I see this not as an integration, but as a blurring or confusing of frames.

When done well, assessment can have a therapeutic effect. It assists individuals in understanding and gaining perspective on the nature of their difficulties and deciding what to do about them. Reciprocally, treatment includes a continuous reassessment of one's struggles and problems. Notwithstanding these mutual influences, I maintain that there are important differences between the assessment and treatment frames and structures, and between their respective objectives, and that these differences should be understood and respected.

◆ ◆ ◆ **Conclusion**

In this chapter I have applied the concept of frame to the Rorschach and to a broader assessment in which the Rorschach is included, but as part of a test battery. Viewing both the 10 inkblots and the patient–examiner relationship as types of frames has permitted a reconceptualization of the observations of others regarding these aspects of Rorschach assessment. Because of similarities between frames, a patient's attitude toward and reactions to the assessment frame may be used to infer how he or she will respond to the treatment frame. On the basis of differences between the frames, several ways of modifying the assessment frame to lessen these differences were suggested. The intent of the modifications is to increase the scope of assessment-based inferences one can make to the treatment situation. The alterations themselves are seen as part of good clinical technique and not as compromising the integrity of either the assessment or treatment frames.

6

ADMINISTRATION
AND SCORING

$\mathbf{I}$n this chapter, a method of administering the test is outlined, the need for recording as verbatim as possible is noted, and a scoring system is presented. Before discussing the specifics of administration, inquiry, and scoring, a few introductory remarks are in order.

As pointed out in chapter 1, from an experiential perspective, close attention must be paid to the directions. The directions not only define the task, but as Schachtel (1966) observed, they are imbued with various subjective meanings. These meanings, in turn, both influence and are reflected in subsequent responses. A 34-year-old, aspiring accounts executive produced a Rorschach record that consisted of 28 responses, all of which were accurately seen whole responses. Apart from the inferences that may be drawn from his high number and percent of whole responses, it is also likely that he read into the directions the additional requirement of having to account for all aspects of the blot.

In a similar way, inquiry too may have subjective meanings for the patient. Examiners typically view inquiry as a routine procedure meant solely to obtain more information for scoring. Testees, however, often experience inquiry altogether differently. H. Lerner (1996) recently suggested ways of gleaning meaningful clinical information from impoverished protocols that might otherwise be considered invalid. Records with fewer than 13 responses were drawn from the files of a community agency that evaluated, treated, and placed children and adolescents. Clients seen at the agency were characterized in general as abused, traumatized, neglected, and abandoned.

For these youthful testees with their coarctated records, Rorschach inquiry had quite special meanings. They experienced the examiner's demand to justify what they saw as a criticism, a reproach of their reality testing. Their sense was, they had not done it right. For this group, inquiring tapped their impairment in representing—holding onto what they saw and accounting for it—and evoked resistances against the implicit demand to reflect. Because inquiry spotlighted what they felt might be deficiencies in their representing and reflecting, they experienced the process as injurious to their self-esteem.

✦ ✦ ✦ Administration

With slight modifications, my method of administering the Rorschach test follows upon that originally developed by Rapaport et al. (1945–1946). I sit facing the patient, show the first card, and specifically ask: "Tell me, please, what do you see? What might this be?" These directions differ somewhat from those of other approaches in which the patient is encouraged to use fantasy: "Tell me what you imagine this to be." By making the task more reality oriented, I am attempting to establish a structure that will enable me to better understand excessive affective embellishments and more serious reality aberrations.

After the first response, and only on the first card, if the patient indicates that he or she thinks the first response is all that is required, then I ask, "Anything else?" The examiner should repeat this question after each response to Card I until the patient indicates that he or she sees nothing else. If the patient spontaneously offers more than one response, he or she should be allowed to continue until no further responses are forthcoming. Once the patient is finished and the card removed, the examiner points out, "This is how it goes, it will be the same with the rest of the cards."

If at any point the patient rejects the card and offers no response, he or she should be encouraged to keep trying for at least two minutes

before the card is taken back. In such cases, the examiner should repeat
the directions and even consider varying the instructions and adopting a more casual stance, as has been suggested by Appelbaum (1959).

✦ ✦ ✦ Inquiry

Other procedures described in the literature call for inquiry to be conducted only after all ten cards have been administered. Finding that
procedure burdensome, I follow Rapaport's suggestion of conducting
inquiry after each individual card is finished. I conduct inquiry as far
as possible, with the card removed from the sight of the subject, and
I do not restrict myself to one pat question, such as "What about the
card . . . suggested . . . ?" Rather, holding the principle of keeping questions general and nonspecific, I vary the queries and include such questions as "Why a . . . ?" or "Why . . . rather than . . . ?" or simply repeat
the response in a questioning manner.

Mindful of the potential suggestive influence of inquiry and the
added pressure it places on the examinee, Rapaport has suggested that
inquiry be minimal and that it be confined to clarifying the scoring of
a response. My experience has been otherwise. Too often, inexperienced
examiners underinquire and, as a consequence, determinants are missed
and scoring is unreliable. Administration, scoring, and interpretation
are all part of the same process; unless scoring is done accurately, with
ample information, the inferences derived are highly tenuous.

Inquiry should be aimed at securing information that would allow
the examiner to confidently answer the following questions: What
exactly did the patient see? Where did he or she see it? What in the
blot did the patient use in fashioning the response? With respect to
inquiry aimed at scoring determinants, I believe it is important that
the examiner familiarize herself or himself with the stimulus properties (e.g., color, blackness, shading) of each card, and that when a
response is given, the examiner consider the range of potential determinants that might have been involved. For example, if on Card V the
subject sees a "bat," the likelihood of blackness being one of the determinants is greater than if he or she sees a "butterfly." When inquiring
for scoring, it is important that the examiner hold these possibilities
in mind.

Although inquiry should be primarily directed to help clarify scoring, there are other occasions when inquiry is recommended. I find it

useful to inquire into affective elaborations. Thus, if a patient saw a "vampire bat," I would ask, "Why vampire?" Also, I believe it is important to assess through inquiry the subject's attitude toward obviously and blatantly deviant responses. One testee found the response "two bears climbing an ice cream cone" unrealistic but humorous, whereas another testee offered the same response but, during the inquiry, asked if the examiner could see it. Although each patient offered the same response, the meaning of the response for the patients differed because of marked differences in their attitudes.

◆ ◆ ◆   Recording

Ideally, all that transpires in the course of administering the Rorschach test, including the patient's complete verbalizations (not merely the response proper), the patient's off-handed remarks, and the direction of the examiner's questions, should be recorded as verbatim as possible. The time that elapses between the presentation of the card and the subject's first response should be recorded, as should be the time between the presentation of the card and the subject's returning it. The testee's rotation of the card and the position in which the card is held at the time of each response is indicated by a caret (Λ), with its top position in the same direction as the top of the card. The responses to each card should be numbered. Overall, recording should be so complete that if the examiner or someone else were to review the protocol at a later time, he or she would be able to accurately reconstruct all that occurred during the Rorschach testing.

◆ ◆ ◆   Scoring

Although several scoring systems are available in the Rorschach literature, I, in keeping with the theoretical slant of this book, use Rapaport's system, with selected extensions and modifications. Rapaport's system calls for the scoring of each response along five dimensions. Each dimension, or perspective, represents a set of abstractions about the formal aspects of the response offered.

The formal or more structural aspects of a response are accorded particular importance, for they provide information about the patient of which he or she is not consciously aware. The scores are considered to indicate "the function patterns of his awareness, rather than its content—that is, in what way he tends to become aware of situations, or experiences his affects, or avoids or elaborates on them" (Holt, 1968, p. 284). Formal characteristics are expression of perceptual organizing and associative processes that, because they tend not to be consciously experienced, are not subject to conscious control. The formal aspects are also important in that they permit the examiner to reduce the welter of response material into common denominators, each of which has psychological meaning.

Each of the five major categories will be described. Included within each category is a listing of the specific scores. All the scores will be summarized at the end of this section. In addition to the scored categories, there are additional scores that are not included under any specific heading. These too will be reviewed.

❖ ❖ ❖ Area Chosen

The area of a Rorschach card chosen for comment by the testee mainly reflects the perceptual organizing process; however, it also plays a guiding and supporting role in the associative process. As Holt (1968) has noted:

> The relative weight of the different scores in this category indicates to what extent the subject's perceptual organization is geared to hold together a total complex impression; to what extent it is limited to larger or smaller details in its integrative scope; to what extent the perceptional impression remains a global one or becomes articulated; and how well the associative process can supply appropriate content for each shift in the perceptual organization [p. 285].

The area chosen also reveals clues as to the flexibility and stability of the individual's perceptual organization. For example, rigid individuals with an excessive need for control have difficulty following the naturally articulated breaks in the blot; instead, they will arbitrarily impose their own cutoff boundaries. By contrast, subjects who are more flexible will move with the perceptual flow of the blot. Whole responses (defined below) are offered on those cards that lend themselves

to being seen as a total gestalt, while detail percepts are seen on the
more broken cards (Schachtel, 1966). The specific area scores include
the following.

W	Whole response—The area chosen is all or almost all of the inkblot (e.g., Card I: "a butterfly"; Card IV: "a monster"; Card VI: "an animal pelt"; Card VIII: "a state emblem").
D	Detail response—The area chosen is a part of the card that is conspicuous by its isolation, relative size, and frequency of response (e.g., center of Card I: "a woman with her arms outstretched"; side areas of Card II: "two playful bear cubs"; top orange areas in Card IX: "two wizards casting a spell").
Dd	Small detail response—The area chosen is a part of the card that is conspicuous by its isolation and relatively small size (e.g., upper extensions in the center of Card I: "two mittens"; peripheral spots on Card I: "islands"; red extensions at the bottom of Card II: "two spears").
Dr	Rare detail response—The area chosen is small, perceptually unbalanced, or arbitrarily delimited (e.g., cutting in half the side area of Card II and seeing the top half as "the head of a bear"). This area score is often accompanied by the determinant Fc (e.g., carving out of the heavily shaded central portion of Card IV an "angry face" and using the nuances of shading to delineate the outline and the facial features).
S	Space response—The area chosen is the white background rather than the inkblot proper (e.g., seeing in the white areas on Card I "four ghosts"). Exceptions here are large white areas that are frequently responded to because of their size and central location (e.g., center of Card II, center of Card VII). This score can be combined with another location score, W(S), as, for example, seeing on Card I "a spaceship and white spots are windows."

De   Edge detail response—The area chosen is not really an area but part of the contour line of the inkblot. Content usually accompanying this location score includes coastlines and faces in the profile (e.g., a right-hand edge of Card IV: "the coastline of New England").

Do   Oligophrenic detail—This does not specifically refer to an area chosen. It refers to the segregation of an area that is typically seen as part of a common W or D response of good form level (e.g., if a subject sees only the antennae of the bat on Card V and does not see the wings).

❖ ❖ ❖ Determinants

This category indicates which perceptual aspects, out of the mass of various stimuli, initiated and determined the response. The scores reflect the impact of each of the perceptual features of the inkblots on the testee. The individual's openness to various experiences is also reflected in the scores.

Because the determinants lie outside the subject's conscious experience and typically come into awareness only through the examiner's inquiry, for Holt (1968) they constitute the most important aspects of the response. An exception here is the hypervigilant, highly sensitive individual who quickly attunes to the purpose of the examiner's inquiry and defensively brings the determinants into conscious awareness. The determinants are as follows:

F   Form response—The response is determined solely by the outline, contour, and articulation of the area chosen (e.g., Card I: "a bird"; side D areas of Card VII: "two beavers").

M   Movement response—An entire human form is seen in motion or in some posture isolated out of a process of movement. An exception is on Card III in which simply identifying the forms as human figures warrants a movement score (e.g., Card III: "two people playing tug of war"; Card VII: "two women dancing").

FM	Animal movement response—This score is reserved for responses in which an animal is engaged in humanlike movement (e.g., "bears dancing"). It does not include animals engaged in movement inherent to their nature (e.g., "lions climbing"). Those responses are typically scored F.
FC	Form color response—Color contributes to the response but is contained within a definite form response and is only of equal or subordinate significance to the form determinant (e.g., center area of Card II: "a red butterfly"; center area of Card III: "a pretty ribbon, the red").
CF	Color form response—Color plays the predominant role but some form elements are included.
C	Color response—Color is the sole determinant.
FCarb	Form color arbitrary—The use of color is obviously incompatible with the content of the response, but the subject clings to its arbitrary inclusion (e.g., "red beavers," "blue monkeys").
FCc, Cfc, Cc	Color Shading—The texture or nuances of shading with color contribute to the response (e.g., "dried blood because in places the red is darkened and in other places lighter and transparent").
FCh	Form shading response—The light-dark (chiaroscuro) shadings of the area contribute to the response but are contained within a definite form response and are of only equal or subordinate significance to the form determinant (e.g., whole of Card IV: "an animal skin . . . its outline and it looks furry; [furry?] the shading"; large open area in Card II: "two lambs; [lambs?] shape of lambs and they appeared wooly").
ChF	Shading form response—Shading plays the

predominant role, but some form elements are included (e.g., whole of Card VII: "a group of clouds, they look fluffy and somewhat like the outline of clouds").

Ch — Shading response—Shading is the sole determinant (e.g., Card IV: "All I can think of is a fog. It's misty with all the shading").

FC' — Form blackness response—The blackness of the area contributes to the response but is contained within a definite form response and is of only equal or subordinate significance to the form determinant (e.g., Card I: "a bat"; [bat?] "the wings, its shape and the blackness"; Card V: "a large, black raven").

C'F — Blackness form response—Blackness plays the predominant role, but some form elements are included (e.g., Card VI: "an oil spill"; [spill?] "it's dark and goes off in different directions"; Card VII: "storm clouds"; [storm clouds?] "it's dark and they have the outline of clouds").

C' — Blackness response—Blackness is the sole determinant (e.g., Card IV: "black paint"; Card VI: "polluted water").

Fc — This score is used for responses that are form based and in which the nuances of shading are employed, not as shading per se, but to outline and articulate the response. The response is usually seen in a heavily shaded area, and the nuances of shading are used to delineate added features (e.g., "This is an angry face, the darker area here is the mouth, and these two lighter spots are the eyes").

✦ ✦ ✦ Form Level

Form level refers to the degree of perceptual fit between the response and the area chosen. It indicates the relative accuracy of fit, as well as how definite or vague is the response offered. The congruence of fit between response and the perceptual characteristics of the area chosen reflects a basic ego function—reality testing—and the initial control feature inherent to thinking. The following form level scores are employed and are based on Mayman's (1964b) extension of Rapaport's initial scoring categories:

F+	This score is given to the sharp, convincing, accurately perceived, well-articulated response that, when seen by the examiner, affords an empathic "aha" experience.
Fo	This score is given to obvious percepts that are commonly and easily seen. Little effort is required, but the response fits the location. All popular and near popular responses are included here.
Fw+	This score is given to weak but acceptable responses that are reasonable but not convincing. The examiner must stretch somewhat to see the response. Commonly, two or more features of correspondence between the percept and the area are articulated.
Fw−	These responses are weak and barely fit the chosen area. They are barely plausible, are quite difficult for the examiner to see, and hinge on only one feature of correspondence between the response and the location.
F−	These are totally unacceptable responses that bear no similarity to the area chosen. Such responses may be well articulated, but they are perceptually inaccurate.
Fv	The form intrinsic to the percept is vague (e.g., clouds, smoke, oil). This does not refer to the articulation of the response, but to its inherent vagueness.
Fs	Form spoil is scored when an acceptable response is distorted or lowered, either by introducing an inappropriate specification or by omitting a significant detail (e.g., a large man with a hairy tail).

◆ ◆ ◆ Content Categories

These scores do not convey the specific content of each response, but rather the conceptual category under which it may be subsumed. The scores reflect the final outcome of the perceptual and especially of the associative processes. The range of categories employed by an individual reflect the wealth, accessibility, and flexibility of conceptual realms from which he or she can draw responses.

H	Whole human figure
Hd	Part of a human figure (e.g., arm, leg, head)
A	Whole animal form
Ad	Part of an animal form
Obj	Inanimate object
Pl	Plants, including trees, flowers, and so forth
Anat	Anatomical responses (e.g., lungs, heart, stomach)
Geog	Geographical responses
Arch	Architectural responses, including buildings, domes, and so forth
Cl	Clouds
Bl	Blood
Sex	Sexual responses, typically involving sexual organs
Cloth	Clothing response (It is useful, if possible, to distinguish male from female clothing.)

◆ ◆ ◆ Fifth Scoring Category (Deviant Verbalizations

Analysis of deviant verbalizations stands out as a unique and distinctive contribution of Rapaport et al. (1945–1946) to Rorschach theory. Rapaport made explicit the notion that because verbalizations are a reflection of thought processes, they can convey indications of disturbance. More specifically, he noted, "From the verbalization, or from the verbalized reasoning usually elicited in inquiry, one can infer the presence of thinking which does not adhere to the reality of the testing situation as defined by attitudes, responses and verbalizations of the general normal population" (cited in Holt, 1968, p. 427).

Recognizing that the testee's thinking in the Rorschach situation must be judged in relation to the perceptual reality of the inkblot, Rapaport evoked the concept of "loss or increase of distance from the inkblot" to systematize the various forms of deviant verbalizations that may appear in the Rorschach situation.

To understand the concept of "distance," one must first understand the reality of the testing situation. On this point, Rapaport and associates noted:

> By and large normal subjects will understand the testing situation and the test instructions to mean that they are to give responses for which sufficient justification may be found in the perceptual qualities of the inkblot; that their responses must be completely acceptable to every day conventional logic; and that, just as they should not give responses they cannot confirm by reference to the inkblot, so their responses should not be so dominated by the perceptual configuration of the inkblot that they are no longer subject to critical control, and thus, become absurdly combined or absurdly integrated [cited in Holt, 1968, p. 429].

Given this context, a pathological "increase of distance" is evident when the testee's responses show little regard for the perceptual properties of the inkblot or when basically good responses are overly embellished with associative elaboration. If, on the other hand, the subject's responses reveal that he is taking the inkblots too seriously or, as Holt (1968) put it, "as an immutable reality, with its own real affective and logical propensities not admitting of critical control" (p. 429), then we have an indication of a pathological "loss of distance."

Rapaport et al. (1945–1946) identified 25 different types of deviant verbalizations. Because many had overlapping criteria, the interscorer reliability for some has been modest at best (Exner, 1993). Recognizing the value of these scores, but concerned as to their reliability, Exner (1993) included in his Comprehensive System only 14 of the indices.

Exner also subdivided several of the scores into two levels based upon the degree of bizarreness or primitiveness involved in the response. Level 1, for example, is assigned responses that reflect only mild or modest instances of illogical, fluid, peculiar, or circumstantial thinking. Responses involving severe lapses in logical, goal-directed thinking are assigned Level 2. The distinction drawn by Exner is quite similar to an earlier one made by Holt (1970); however, Holt's distinction applied to Rorschach content, not to the formal properties of a response.

The most commonly encountered deviant verbalization scores are described below. For a complete list of all deviant verbalizations, refer to Rapaport et al. (1945–1946), and for a revision of these original scores, including the Level 1/Level 2 distinction, refer to Exner (1993).

Fabulized Response (Fab)—A response with undo elaboration or too great a specificity. The elaborations are not unreasonable and the subject is usually aware of the fanciful nature of the interpretation (e.g., "an angry wolf's face").

Incongruous Combination (Incom)—Several blot details or images are inappropriately merged into a single object (e.g., "a two headed chicken").

Fabulized Combination (Fab-Comb)—Two accurately seen percepts are combined in an unrealistic, arbitrary way. The relationship is made on the basis of temporal or spatial contiguity (e.g., "two beavers dancing on top of an ice cream cone").

Confabulation (Confab)—A response that is so overly embellished with fantasy and affective elaboration that the subject loses the reality of the test and replaces it with the created fantasy (e.g., "a big, ugly, menacing man stomping around. He's coming to get me"). Confabulatory responses carry tendencies noted in the fabulized response to the extreme; in the latter, however, reality is not lost.

Contamination (Contam)—Two discrete concepts or ideas are fused together into one percept, so that the separate identities are ignored (e.g., "a bloody island," "a peppermint butterfly," "a bat rabbit"). Note how in the example the stimulus prompted two separate ideas and how the two ideas are fused into one.

Inappropriate Logic (Alog)—This score is similar to what Rapaport, et al. (1945–1946) referred to as autistic logic. A response is justified on a basis, often position, that shows little correspondence to conventional norms of thinking (e.g., "a stomach because it's in the middle"; "the north pole as it's on top").

Peculiar Verbalization (Pec)—An off-key, unusual verbalization that could conceivably pass as conventional and appropriate if used outside the testing situation, but within the confines of the testing it is jarring and out of tune (e.g., "part of a lady's vagina"; "two elephants on tippytoe").

Queer Verbalization (Queer)—Off key, unusual verbalization that would not be regarded as conventional or appropriate outside of the testing situation (e.g., "In response to Card IX, it still reminds me of female sex").

Vagueness (Vague)—This does not refer to vague form but to the subject's weak hold on a definite form percept (i.e., "I can almost get a bat from this, I don't know, these might be wings").

Confusion (Conf)—This refers to a confusion within the response itself or in the testee's experiencing and communication of the response (e.g., "These two animals look like mice. No, they are raccoons or even squirrels and they are about to step on this butterfly")

Incoherence (Incoh)—Extraneous and irrelevant material is brought into the response and is disruptive at times to the extent of rendering the response incomprehensible (e.g., "I think of an underwater scene. The red is like my brother's shirt after his accident. What a mess, perhaps the fish are all in battle with each other").

◆ ◆ ◆ Additional Scores

Not included within any of the five major scoring categories is a group of additional scores. Like the major scores, these scores were developed to bring to the examiner's attention meaningful aspects of the response process. As with the analysis of deviant verbalizations, many of the additional scores are based on the verbalization within which the response is embedded or on more spontaneous comments.

Inanimate movement "m"—This score is added to responses in which movement is ascribed to an inanimate figure (e.g., "a spinning top," "a volcano erupting," "flowing blood").

C denial, C' denial, Ch denial—The determinant is mentioned, but in the form of a negation or repudiation (e.g., "It wasn't the blackness"; "I didn't even think of the red").

C ref, C' ref, Ch ref—The determinant is referred to, but is not integrated into a response (e.g., "I like the colors. The blackness is foreboding. The red areas are sea horses").

C avoid, C' avoid, Ch avoid—In the examiner's judgment the determinant is implicit in the response; however, the determinant (e.g., blackness) is not explicitly expressed during inquiry (e.g., "two African women; [why African?] they are naked, have long necks and short hair").

C impot, C' impot, Ch impot—The subject comments upon his or her impotence or inability to use the determinant (e.g., "I can't make anything out of the red. I see the colors but I can't work them in").

C symbolism—Color is referred to, but rather than being integrated into the response, it is dealt with in a symbolic, intellectual way (e.g., "The red suggests they are angry"; "Because of the colors, I think of good and evil").

♦ ♦ ♦ Summary of Scores

Area Chosen

W	Whole Response—The area chosen is all or almost all of the inkblot.
D	Detail Response—The area chosen is a part of the card that is conspicuous by its isolation, relative size, and frequency of response.
Dd	Small Detail Response—The area chosen is a part of the card that is conspicuous by its isolation and relatively small size.
Dr	Rare Detail Response—The area chosen is small, perceptually unbalanced, or arbitrarily delimited.
S	Space Response—The area chosen is the white background rather than the inkblot proper.
De	Edge Detail Response—The area chosen is not really an area but part of a contour line.
Do	Oligophrenic Detail—This score refers to the segregation of an area that is typically seen as

part of a common W or D response of good
form level.

Determinants

F	Form Response—The response is determined solely by the outline, contour, and articulation of the area chosen.
M	Movement Response—An entire human form is seen in motion or in some posture isolated out of a process of movement.
FM	Animal Movement Response—An animal is seen as engaged in humanlike movement.
FC	Form Color Response—Color contributes to the response but is contained within a definite form response and is only of equal or subordinate significance to the form determinant.
CF	Color Form Response—Color plays the predominant role, but some form elements are included.
C	Color Response—Color is the sole determinant.
Fcarb	Form Color Arbitrary—The use of color is obviously incompatible with the content of the response, but the subject clings to its arbitrary inclusion.
FCc, CFc, Cc	Color Shading—The texture or nuances of shading with color contribute to the response.
FCh	Form Shading Response—The light-dark (chiaroscuro) shadings of the area contribute to the response and are of equal or subordinate significance to the form determinant.
ChF	Shading Form Response—Shading plays the predominant role, but some form elements are included.
Ch	Shading Response—Shading is the sole determinant.
FC'	Form Blackness Response—The blackness of the area contributes to the response but is contained within a definite form response and

	is of only equal or subordinate significance to the form determinant.
C'F	Blackness Form Response—Blackness plays the predominant role, but some form elements are included.
C'	Blackness Response—Blackness is the sole determinant.
Fc	Shading as Form—The response is based on form, and the nuances of shading are used to articulate and outline the response.

Form Level

F+	A sharp, convincing, accurately perceived, well-articulated response.
Fo	An accurate but easily seen response that requires little effort.
Fw+	A weak and acceptable response, but not convincing. The examiner must stretch to see the response; commonly, two or more features of correspondence between the percept and the area chosen are articulated.
Fw−	A response that is weak and barely fits the chosen area. These responses are difficult to see and hinge on one feature of correspondence between the response and the location.
F−	A totally unacceptable, perceptually inaccurate response that bears no similarity to the area chosen.
Fv	The form intrinsic to the percept is vague.
Fs	Form spoil is scored when an acceptable response is distorted or lowered by introducing an inappropriate specification or omitting a significant detail.

♦ ♦ ♦   Content Categories

H	Whole human figure
Hd	Part of a human figure

A	Whole animal form
Ad	Part of an animal form
Obj	An inanimate object
Pl	Plants, including trees, flowers, and so forth
Anat	Anatomical response
Geog	Geographical response
Arch	Architectural response
Cl	Clouds
Bl	Blood
Sex	Sexual response
Cloth	Clothing response

◆ ◆ ◆ Fifth Scoring Category (Deviant Verbalizations)

Fab	Fabulized Response—A response with undue but acceptable affective elaboration or too great a specificity.
Incom	Incongruous Combination—Blot details or images are inappropriately merged into a single object.
Fab-Comb	Fabulized Combination—Two or more accurately seen percepts are combined in an unrealistic, arbitrary, and illogical way.
Confab	Confabulation—A response that is so overly embellished with fantasy and affective elaboration that the subject loses the reality of the test and replaces it with the created fantasy.
Contam	Contamination—Two discrete concepts are fused without regard to their separate identities.
Alog	Inappropriate Logic—A response is justified on a basis that shows little correspondence to conventional norms of thinking.
Pec Verb	Peculiar Verbalizations—Off-key, unusual verbalizations that could pass as conventional or

	appropriate outside the testing situation.
Queer	Queer Verbalizations—Off Key, unusual verbalizations that would not be regarded as conventional or appropriate outside the testing situation.
Vague	Vagueness—The subject in his verbalizations conveys a weak hold on a definite form percept.
Conf	Confusion—Confusion within the response itself or in the testee's experiencing and communication of it.
Incoh	Incoherence—Extraneous and irrelevant material disrupts the response, at times to the point of rendering the response incomprehensible.

❖ ❖ ❖ Additional Scores

"m" inanimate Movement	Movement is added to an inanimate figure.
C denial	
C' denial	
Ch denial	The determinant is mentioned in the form of a negation or repudiation.
C ref	
C'ref	
Ch ref	The determinant is referred to but not integrated into the response.
C avoid	
C' avoid	
Ch avoid	The subject implicitly uses a determinant, but it is not explicitly mentioned.
C impot	
C' impot	
Ch impot	The subject comments upon his or her impotence in attempting to use the determinant.

C symbolism   Color is referred to, but rather than integrated
                 into the response, it is dealt with in a sym-
                 bolic, intellectual way.

◆ ◆ ◆ Scoring Questions

The following guidelines have been found useful in enhancing accuracy and ease of scoring.

1. In scoring determinants, begin by assuming the response is form based and maintain this assumption until the testee explicitly indicates otherwise. For example, if a subject sees "blood" in a red area but never, even in inquiry, mentions the color, then the response is scored form (F). The examiner here would likely assume color was used but not mentioned, and add the additional score C denial.

2. On all responses that have a definite shape, form is either the sole determinant or the dominant determinant; FC, FC', Fch, F(C). For another determinant to be dominant, the percept must be inherently shapeless (e.g., clouds, fire, blood).

3. The distinctions between CF-C, C'F-C', and ChF-Ch are based on the testee's explicit comments (e.g., "A storm cloud; [why storm cloud?] it is black and vaguely shaped like a cloud, mostly the blackness"). Based on the testee's remarks, this response would be scored C'F.

4. Movement responses are treated the same as form responses. Thus, "two black women dancing" would be scored (MC'), and additionally scored for form level.

5. Form level is scored only for those responses in which form or movement is the sole determinant or the dominant determinant. If another determinant is dominant, the form level is vague by definition and need not be scored.

6. In combinatory responses, in which percepts are first seen separately in separate areas and then combined, each percept should be scored and then bracketed. For example, if on Card VIII the subject sees "two bears climbing a mountain," the response would be scored:

D Fo A

D Fo Mountain

This differs from responses in which the subject has one overall impression and then comments upon the various details. An example here would be the following response to Card IV: "I see a large monster. He has huge legs, short arms, and a powerful tail." This response is scored W Fo Monster.

7. If the content of a response does not fit into one of the content categories, then simply write out the content.

8. If the testee refers to an area by its color, and then offers a response in which the color might be a determinant, clarify in inquiry if and how the color is being included. For example, if on Card III the subject responds, "The red area is a butterfly," then one might ask, "Why a butterfly?"

✦ ✦ ✦ Conclusion

Using the work of Rapaport et al. (1945–1946) as a basis, I have presented a method of administration, a type of inquiry, and a scoring system. I have also indicated a group of scoring guidelines. Administration and inquiry have to do with the mechanics of the test; however, they extend beyond this too. Both help to define the task and come to be associated with a host of different meanings. Such meanings influence and are reflected in test performance. Scoring attempts to account for the more formal aspects of a response. As such, it provides information about the patient of which he or she is not consciously aware.

7

THE PATIENT–EXAMINER
RELATIONSHIP

In chapter 1, I noted that the experiential psychoanalytically oriented examiner makes use of several sources of information about the patient in deriving clinical inferences. In this chapter I discuss one source—the patient–examiner relationship. Other sources will be discussed in subsequent chapters. Here, I begin by reviewing the seminal contributions of Schafer (1954) and Schachtel (1966). On the basis of contemporary trends in psychoanalysis, I then discuss the issue of countertransference. Finally, I survey more recent attempts to reconceptualize the patient–examiner relationship from the perspectives of object-relations theory and self psychology.

Please remember, all psychoanalytic theorists of assessment agree that regardless of how standardized or prescribed the examiner's role may be, an intricate interpersonal relationship with realistic and unrealistic aspects is intrinsic to psychological testing. It is further held that this relationship has a significant influence on a patient's test productions and can also provide a wealth of information in its own right.

◆ ◆ ◆ Contributions of
Schafer and Schachtel

The classic, and still most comprehensive, discussion of the patient–examiner relationship has been provided by Schafer (1954). The general dimensions of the relationship he has identified include the following: the professional pressures placed upon and experienced by the examiner; the examiner's personality, including his or her character makeup, defenses, needs, and problems; the psychological constraints built into the examiner's role; the constraints implicit in the patient's psychological position; and the variety of defensive reactions available to the patient, given his or her position.

Schafer reminds us of the following constraints in the patient's role that typically are not discussed, yet exert a powerful influence on the testing: intimate communication and violation of privacy without a basis in trust; the relinquishment of control of the relationship; exposure to the dangers of confrontation and premature self-awareness; regressive temptations and the dangers of freedom. He notes that under such challenging and anxiety-arousing conditions it is inevitable that defensive and transference reactions will be stimulated or exacerbated. Such reactions, he suggests, are not to be avoided, minimized, or ignored, but rather are to be scrutinized as one would any clinical experience, for they provide an important basis for understanding the patient.

Schachtel (1966) evokes the term "test situation" to emphasize that Rorschach testing takes place in an interpersonal context that consists of several common elements. The most important elements are the togetherness of two people, the presentation by one of a task to the other, the nature of the task, and the testee's awareness that his or her performance will provide the basis upon which the other will form judgments and make decisions that may affect his or her life.

How the testee experiences these elements, and then reacts to these experiences, constitutes his or her definition of the test situation. For Schachtel (1966), how individuals define experience and react to the test situation is particularly informative, because in doing so, testees "transfer to the test situation the attitudes, strivings, defenses, needs, fears, wishes, and interests which they characteristically show in other situations of their lives, which have been formed by their previous experiences, and which are part of the structure of their personalities" (p. 273).

Schachtel recognizes that individuals define the Rorschach situation in distinctive and idiosyncratic ways. Nonetheless, he describes three more general types of definitions based on formulations developed by Fromm and Sullivan and more readily elicited in situations, like the Rorschach, in which there is much freedom and an invitation to relax controls.

The authoritarian definition is characterized by a fear of, admiration for, and rebellion against, authority. The testee feels that the test results will render him vulnerable to external and internal (superego) approval and condemnation. He feels he must work to meet certain demands, yet finding an absence of imposed demands and deeply frightened of the freedom, he invents his own demands. The test is quickly transformed into a school examination. These self-imposed and ultimately self-limiting demands are then ascribed to the examiner, who is then viewed as the loved and feared authority.

The competitive definition is also oriented toward powerful parental figures; this definition, however, leads to competition with the imagined performance of others, in order to defeat all rivals and have the examiner's (i.e., parent's) love all to oneself.

The resistant definition is distinguished by a conscious or unconscious reluctance to see anything and may even include the desire to do the opposite of assumed expectations. If the patient feels especially weak and guilty, he may well react by conceiving of the test situation as a trial in which the best solution is to inhibit one's reactions, lest one be found out.

With meticulous care, Schafer and Schachtel have both attempted to outline the major dynamics involved in being tested, the transferential effect of these dynamics on the patient–examiner relationship, and the range of defensive reactions to be expected among different types of patients. Their emphasis, however, on "transference reactions" and "defensive reactions" reflects the prevailing drive theory and structural theory of the 1950s and 1960s. During the past decade, however, there have been shifts in psychoanalysis to a greater interest in object relations and the self. This, together with a growing concern with the difficult-to-treat patient, has prompted both a reexamination of the concept of countertransference and new conceptualizations of the patient–examiner relationship.

◆ ◆ ◆ Countertransference

Two strands, each rooted in the writings of Freud, have intertwined throughout the historical development of psychoanalytic conceptions of countertransference. In his 1910 paper, "The Future Prospects of

Psycho-Analytic Therapy," Freud speaks of countertransference as a hindrance or interference to treatment. Yet, barely two years later, he writes that the analyst "must turn his own unconscious like a receptive organ toward the transmitting unconscious of the patient . . . so the doctor's unconscious is able . . . to reconstruct [the patient's] unconscious" (Freud, 1912, pp. 115–116). Here, then, countertransference is not regarded as a hindrance, but instead as a source of understanding the patient.

While these two divergent attitudes toward countertransference have pervaded the psychoanalytic literature, treatment experiences with borderline and other more difficult patients has resulted in a third position. This position holds that such reactions are neither a hindrance nor a help, but rather, are intrinsic and inevitable components of the treatment, and that the understanding and working through of both countertransference reactions and the patient's transference reactions that induced them are at the heart of treating such patients.

The work of Gorney and Weinstock (1980) is representative of this line of theorizing. These authors take up the issue of therapeutic impasse, suggesting that the transference-countertransference stalemate is a necessary and inevitable development in the treatment of the borderline patient. Accordingly, "It is within stalemate that the original interactional pathology in object relating comes to be fully revealed and the seeds of its possible resolution germinated" (p. 169). In accord with the developmental distinction Winnicott (1969) drew between "object relating" and "object usage," the writers regard the impasse as a necessary intermediate phase of object relating in which the object (therapist) is recurrently destroyed and recreated. The therapist's capacity to survive the patient's efforts at destruction eventuates in the dissolution of omnipotent control and leads to resolution of stalemate through the gradual establishment of object usage.

The two contrasting attitudes toward countertransference found in the psychoanalytic literature on the theory of technique have pervaded, more quietly and implicitly, the Rorschach assessment literature as well. For the empirically oriented examiner, such reactions are regarded as an interference, a potential source of error. In his or her quest for psychometric purity, such reactions threaten to distract the examiner from the primary functions of administering and scoring the test, and then interpreting the uncontaminated data. The advent of computer-generated interpretations, and the call for automated administration, attests to efforts to all but eliminate the examiner and his or her reactions.

In stark contrast, psychoanalytically oriented examiners are increasingly viewing their own countertransference reactions to patients as a unique and valuable source of information. To more meaningfully explore this possible gold mine of information, examiners make use of the distinction Racker (1968) drew between indirect and direct countertransference.

As applied to Rorschach assessment, indirect countertransference refers to the examiner's response to a significant other who is external to the actual testing. An eight-year-old was referred for testing because of disruptive and aggressive behavior. Upon entering the waiting room to meet the patient, the examiner was stunned to see the youngster on the floor, atop his mother, literally pummeling her. After separating the two and taking the patient to his office, the examiner's initial shock gave way to feelings of anger toward the mother. He was anguished by her unwillingness to defend herself and to restrain her son. The examiner's anger subsequently entered into the assessment in two different ways. While with the patient, he found himself uncharacteristically restraining and limit-setting. Later, in reviewing the test data, the examiner used his own feelings of anger to better understand the patient's disruptive behavior. It seemed likely that the patient's aggressive outbursts were both an expression of anger at his mother's helplessness and an unspoken request for containment.

Direct countertransference consists of the examiner's reactions to the patient and to his or her test responses. A 42-year-old, experienced product manager was evaluated for a senior executive position. Mindful that several other candidates had been found unsuitable, both the psychologist and the company felt increasing pressure to fill the position. Pleased with the applicant's responses to the first several inkblots, the examiner was feeling growingly confident that here was a candidate he could recommend. On Card IV, however, the testee gave a distressing response. Not only was the form level weak and strained, but the content was blatant and primitive. The testee's subsequent responses were excellent; nonetheless, the examiner was nagged by the singularly poor percept. More than concerned with the testee's well-being, he felt disappointed and let down by the candidate. In a later feedback session, the examiner, informed by his own feelings of disappointment, discussed the response with the testee. The testee was able to recognize his unexplicable tendency to disappoint others and in what ways it adversely affected many areas of his life.

When attended to and considered, countertransference reactions can enrich test data and lead to a deeper and more meaningful understanding of the patient. In addition, these reactions also have important treatment implications. For example, in assessing more disturbed patients, the examiner, frequently and quickly, becomes the object for the patient's transference projections. In response, equally intense reactions, both conscious and unconscious, are stirred in the tester. Epstein (1979) has pointed out that such reactions are not unique to the assessor, but rather are representative of the types of reactions the patient's projective processes provoke in others. If this is the case, then the examiner can forewarn a therapist to the likely countertransference reactions the patient may arouse in treatment.

There is one further point to be made regarding countertransference. Even though I regard countertransference reactions as a potentially important source of information, I am also mindful of Freud's original view in which he considered such feelings and reactions as a hindrance. I treat his initial comments as a warning, as a necessary reminder that countertransference feelings can distort one's perceptions and judgments. Equally distorting, however, can be the defenses one uses to ward off these reactions.

In a provocative and challenging article, Karmel (1996) interprets the Rorschach protocol of Adolph Eichmann, applying Winnicott's (1935) concept of "manic defense." Concerned with the divergent findings reported by earlier investigators, Karmel makes this telling point:

> I began to wonder whether methodological refinements [referring to earlier studies] did not serve an unspoken function: (1) to preserve the mental intactness and rationality of the (Rorschach) clinician facing a most difficult task: judging the mental intactness and rationality of individuals whose behavior was beyond rational analysis and, in fact, incomprehensible. That is, in the final analysis, no diagnostic category nor psychopathological nosology could really be appended or affixed to their heinous crimes [pp. 2–3].

Karmel is suggesting here that when assessing an individual whose actions stir remarkably powerful feelings, the examiner unwittingly can use his or her methodology defensively to protect himself or herself from experiencing such feelings. Herein, what is advanced as objectivity is in the service of defense, and is, in itself, distorting.

❖ ❖ ❖ Newer Perspectives on the Patient–Examiner Relationship

As noted, shifts in psychoanalytic theory, together with a renewed interest in the concept of countertransference, are providing new perspectives for viewing the patient–examiner relationship.

Representative of these newer ways of thinking about the patient–examiner relationship is the work of P. Lerner (1988). In an attempt to find manifestations of projective identification in the testing situation, he applied Ogden's (1983) concepts of transference-countertransference to the patient–examiner relationship. Ogden has suggested that transference and countertransference can be viewed from the perspective of the interpersonal externalization of an internal object relation. Transference, he noted, can take one of two forms, depending on which role (i.e., self or self-identified with the internal object) in the internal object relation is assigned to the other person in the externalizing process. In one instance, when the role assigned is that of the internal object (i.e., the self-identified with the internal object), the patient experiences the other person as he had unconsciously experienced the internal object. Herein, countertransference involves the examiner unconsciously identifying with that part of the patient identified with the internal object. Projective identification comes into play in terms of the interpersonal pressure on the examiner to engage in the identification and to experience himself or herself in a way congruent with the representation of the object in the internal object relation.

A 28-year-old female patient was tested approximately four years after her father's death. Most striking in the testing was her hypervigilance, heightened sensitivity, and excessive vulnerability. Aware and respectful of her vulnerability, the examiner found himself relating to her at a distance in an overly cautious, at times measured, way. He made few spontaneous comments and did not confront her lateness. During the third testing session, the patient complained of his distance and formality. In retrospect, she had experienced the examiner consciously much as she had experienced her father unconsciously, that is, as aloof, remote, overcontrolled, and uninterested in her. In this example, the object component of the patient's internal relation with her father was projected onto the examiner, and he reacted in a way that was consciously constant with it.

The second form of transference involves the patient projecting the self component of the internal object relation onto the examiner and experiencing the examiner the way the internal object experienced the self. The countertransference in this instance consists of the examiner's identification with the self component of the patient's internal object relation. Projective identification here involves the interpersonal pressure on the examiner to identify with the projected self and to comply with the fantasy by experiencing himself or herself just as the self experienced the internal object.

A 38-year-old, single female patient sought treatment and was tested after the termination of an intense, conflict-laden, two-year relationship with a married man five years her junior. She quickly entered into an idealizing relationship with the examiner in which she regarded his interest in her and observations about her as precious gifts, which she rewarded with offerings of adoration and flattery. By contrast, when the examiner was nonresponsive and less giving, she withdrew, looked pained, and contemplated leaving the testing situation. Pleased by the patient's adoration, pained by the patient's withdrawal, and frightened by her threats to leave, the examiner found himself becoming more active, more giving, and more controlled by the patient's praise. In time, the examiner was able to understand this interaction in terms of the patient's early relationship with a depressed mother. More specifically, the patient was actively doing to the examiner what she had unconsciously experienced her mother as having done to her. Namely, in excessively rewarding closeness and depressively withdrawing in reaction to separateness and autonomy, the patient's mother had fostered within the patient an inordinate need for adoration and praise.

As Ogden has noted, projective identification is an inevitable aspect of the externalization of an internal object relation. When applied to the testing situation, it means that there is always a component in the examiner's countertransference that represents an induced identification with a part of the patient's ego that is enmeshed in a particular unconscious internal object relation. By attuning to these transactions and his or her own countertransference reactions, the examiner is in a unique position to understand these internal object relations and then to infer the earlier object-relational experiences from which they derive.

Arnow and Cooper (1988) have extended several of Kohut's formulations to the patient–examiner relationship, especially those regarding atypical transference patterns. In a series of publications, Kohut (1971, 1977) has identified and described a set of unique transference configurations that unfold in the treatment of patients with narcissistic personality disturbance. Referred to overall as "selfobject transference," specific subtypes include the mirroring transference and the idealizing transference. Each of these patterns has been found to have both regressive and progressive features, and the treatment of the narcissistic patient typically consists of movement along one or the other of these developmental lines, though it may involve shifts between these transference patterns.

Mindful that the testing situation does not permit the unfolding of a full narcissistic transference, Arnow and Cooper (1988) nonetheless point out that "the interpersonal aspects of the testing situation represent an opportunity for experiencing a patient's primary needs for self-objects and the feelings aroused when these needs are not met" (p. 54).

My own experience confirms Arnow and Cooper's assertion and supports the explanatory power of Kohut's observations. I have found that patients who need mirroring from the examiner typically enter testing with a compelling need to be treated as special, a craving to be admired, and a provocative sense of entitlement. As a consequence of such needs, these patients continuously assault the testing structure. Such routine mechanics as the setting up of appointments, adherence to session times, and ways of administering the tests become contentious and complicated. In reaction, the examiner often feels pressured to depart from standard testing procedures and to accord these patients "special" treatment. In a parallel fashion, their test responses are not offered to convey meaning, but rather to impress the examiner and to create a product that they feel is commensurate with their grandiose sense of self.

I was asked to assess the 19-year-old son of a high-profiled local attorney. On the verge of failing his second year at the university, he had been apprehended and charged with drug trafficking. Despite a filled schedule and a waiting list of other assessment cases, I found myself being harassed and pressured to begin the testing as quickly as possible. A cancellation arose and the patient was given that time. Although he reportedly was threatening suicide and was insisting upon his need to discuss his problems with someone, the patient missed the session, claiming that he had overslept. Only in a later testing session was he able to express his fury at the examiner for putting him on a waiting list and then offending him even further by fitting him into a time that had been slotted for someone else. For this patient, having to wait at a time of distress and having to comply with the needs of another (i.e., my schedule) constituted major blows to his overinflated sense of self.

In keeping with what Arnow and Cooper (1988) suggest, I too

have found that the testing situation permits the examiner to explore empathic failures. In these patients, canceling a session or reacting with a trace of irritation quickly stirs hurt and pain, emotional withdrawal, and a view of the examiner as cold, detached, and uncaring. This contrasts with an empathic responsiveness in which the patient feels coherent and whole and regards the examiner as an ally.

Arnow and Cooper (1988) also recognize manifestations of an idealized selfobject relationship as it presents in the testing situation. They note that these patients look to the examiner for soothing and calming and, if these needs are not satisfied, they typically react with panic and embarrassment. A second expression of the need for a powerful idealized object may take the form of using flattery or more subtle appeals to the examiner's narcissism.

◆ ◆ ◆ Conclusion

In this chapter, I have discussed the patient–examiner relationship as a major source of information for the inferential process. I began by reviewing the pioneering contributions of Schafer and Schachtel. This was followed by an exploration of the concept of countertransference and its application to Rorschach assessment. Finally, I sampled newer conceptualizations that are emerging from the expanding scope of psychoanalytic theory. Newer models in psychoanalytic theory, with their emphasis on the development of self and object relations, will increasingly inform our ways of understanding and formulating the patient–examiner relationship.

8

MAJOR SCORES:
THE DIMENSIONS
OF THE RORSCHACH

In the previous chapter I discussed the patient–examiner relationship as one source of information available to the psychologist who tests from a clinical perspective. A second source of information consists of the scores and their interrelationships. In this chapter I consider the major scores from a particular perspective. Rather than focusing on each score individually, I examine the basic dimensions underlying the scores. Therefore, this discussion is organized around the following basic topics: movement, form, form level, color, shading, and blackness. Certain other individual scores have been found especially helpful because of their capacity to reflect specific psychological processes; these are reviewed in chapters 9 and 10.

I am taking this perspective for several reasons. First, unlike those who use psychometric approaches, I do not view the scores as signs, nor do I believe there is a one-to-one correspondence between a specific score and a specific psychological process. Rather, in keeping with the psychoanalytic concept of multiple determination, I believe that any one score can reflect several underlying processes and that any one process can be expressed in various scores. Second, too often scores are viewed as ends in themselves and not as convenient, shorthand conventions for organizing, integrating, and representing aspects of the response process. It is the response process I wish to understand, and scores are chiefly meaningful as expressions of that process. Finally, it is my belief that if the examiner understands the basic dimensions of the test and the aspects of personality functioning they touch upon, he or she will be better able to view the scores from a broader perspective and appreciate the various psychological processes that might be at play.

✦ ✦ ✦ Human Movement Response

Beginning with Rorschach himself, many theorists have looked to the human movement response to assess some aspect of the interpersonal realm. Viewing the M response as a multidimensional concept, Rorschach (1942) advanced six interpretations for the response. Although Rorschach attributed meaning to the M response as a single variable, he based his analysis of personality on the comparison of movement with color. As such, those whose protocols revealed a predominance of movement were referred to as the "M-experience type," whereas those whose protocols emphasized color were referred to as the "C-experience type." Of the six interpretations Rorschach offered for the M response, two—rapport and empathy—are directly related to the interpersonal area.

Rorschach (1942) suggested that the M-experience type reflects "more intensive than extensive rapport" (p. 78). Intensive rapport is found in individuals whose relationships are few but are characterized by depth and closeness. This is in contrast to the extensive rapport found in the C-experience type. These people relate to others easily, but their relationships tend to be fleeting and superficial.

Following Rorschach's lead, other theorists as well have attributed interpersonal meaning to the M response. Piotrowski (1957) has suggested that from the M response one can infer an individual's conception of his or her "role in life." In a similar vein, Schachtel (1966) views the M response as reflecting an individual's basic orientation and attitudes toward himself, others, and the world around him—that is, the individual's self-concept and his or her relational anticipations. For example, if an individual were to see the central detail area of Card I as "a woman reaching out her arms and asking for help," Schachtel

(1966) might well interpret the response as expressing a sense of one-self as helpless and dependent, coupled with an expectant "oral" attitude (p. 208).

Dana (1968) concluded, on the basis of an extensive review of the experimental literature, that the M response expresses an interpersonal orientation. More specifically, he suggested that the M response represents a "syndrome of potentials, capacities for reaching out into the environment in a variety of ways" (p. 144).

The most extensive and sophisticated discussion of the M response, which goes beyond simple description and inference and is consistent with the thrust of this chapter, is represented in the work of Mayman (1977). On the basis of the writings of earlier theorists and of his own clinical experience, Mayman has identified five determinants of the movement response: (1) properties of the inkblot that help evoke movement percepts, (2) fantasy, (3) kinesthesia and its relation to the self-expressive character of the response, (4) object representations, and (5) empathy and identification.

The Perceptual Determinants of the Movement Response

It was Rapaport who first pointed out the purely perceptual determinants of the movement response. Basing his ideas in part on gestalt theory, he reserved the movement score for those responses in which the subject saw and associated to "an actual, demonstrable, perceptual imbalance in the inkblot" (Mayman, 1977, p. 231). Rapaport suggested that at an unconscious level the subject sees the gestalt in flux and is perturbed by the imbalance. Accordingly, without being conscious of it, the subject then sets matters right by ascribing to the image direction that gives the configuration better balance and stability.

This sensitivity to an imbalance, Mayman (1977) notes, "is no mean achievement. If nothing else, it requires that one be able to transcend an atomistic survey of a blot area and pay attention, rather, to its dynamic composition" (p. 231). Mayman is suggesting here that at a purely perceptual level, in order to see imbalance one must be able to take distance and gain perspective. Subjects who take hold of an area in a piecemeal manner, who tend to see simple and static forms and view details too discretely, will not be prompted to see the more subtle perceptual properties, including the dynamic composition.

Also derived from Rapaport's notion of the actual perceptual basis of the movement response is the suggestion that to perceive movement requires a certain level of ideational activity. Rapaport himself put it more strongly; he suggested that movement responses indicated ideational potential and covaried with the intensity and range of ideational activity.

The absence of movement in a protocol, however, does not necessarily imply intellectual limitations. To achieve an M response, one must also be able to tolerate imbalance. We are all familiar with those testees who, because of their own inner imbalance and instability, find comfort in external balance. For such patients, an imbalance in the inkblot cannot be tolerated, as it is too reminiscent of their inner feelings of flux. Here, then, the absence of M responses hints at inner fragility and turmoil rather than an intellectual deficit. For such individuals, inner unrest may, at the same time, place limits on their capacity to fully utilize their intellectual talents.

Mayman (1977) has also observed that "the sensitivity to dynamic composition and the sense of flowing interrelatedness of certain blot areas can go awry" (p. 232). For example, there are patients who are so compelled by the sense of intrinsic movement that they see relationships where none exist, or they brush reality considerations aside and abandon themselves to the single perceptual impression. It has been my experience that those patients who are overly sensitive to the intrinsic movement of the blots, who spontaneously comment upon it without integrating it into a response, tend to be hyperideational and overly suspicious and distrusting.

The Fantasy Component of the Movement Response

A second aspect of the movement response identified by Mayman involves the contribution of fantasy. For Mayman, requisite to the offering of an M response is the availability of a fantasy life one can dip into to help vivify the response. More than most other Rorschach responses, the M response is distinguishable by its aliveness and vividness.

Even though a movement response requires and draws upon one's capacity to fantasize, it should not be regarded as the sole, or necessarily the most, accurate indicator of access to a rich inner life. I agree with Mayman that the fabulized response, that is, any response that is imbued with affective or descriptive elaborations, is the best overall indicator of the wealth of an individual's fantasy life.

Because an individual's fantasy and his or her access to it are related to several adaptive functions, assessing them has important evaluative implications. Fantasy enriches and safeguards one's day-to-day life. It plays a role in reminding us who we are and helps make us feel alive.

Fantasy is also, as Singer (1975) has demonstrated, a component of well-being and control. It is a process we rely upon in steering a middle course between the two extremes of external and internal stimulation (Rapaport, 1957). Unimaginative people tend to be more vulnerable to boredom, restlessness, and impulsivity. Often it is more sensible and realistic to think and fantasize about an activity than to actually do it. A well-developed fantasy life, then, serves as a containment for aggressive and other urges.

Kinesthesia and Its Relationship to Self-Experience

In addition to its perceptual base and the requirement of the accessibility of fantasy, a third aspect of the movement response is kinesthesia, that is, the precise movement ascribed (e.g., fighting, dancing, clinging).

Rorschach (1921) considered the movement response broadly as an indication of one's capacity for "inner creation." Schachtel (1966) explicated as well as expanded this notion. He put it this way:

> When one disregards specific attitudes and pays attention only to the general process of enlivening the percept by looking at it, not detachedly, but by putting oneself inside of it in imagination, by feeling from inside how it moves and lives, then one is concerned with those general qualities of the movement response which make them representative of what Rorschach called the capacity for inner creation and what I believe to be a factor in man's capacity for creative experience [pp. 230–231].

By creative experience, Schachtel is referring to a process whereby one puts something of oneself into one's own experience—a type of empathic projection, if you will. Accordingly, to make an experience creative, one cannot be merely a mirror that reflects the image cast upon it; rather, one's own experiences must be aroused and then merge with the object of experience. Only at this point is something new experienced. Without this personal, subjective element, the object is reproduced, not experienced. For Schachtel, then, creative experience involves both an openness and sensitivity to the external world, as well as the capacity to bring one's own attitudes and previous experiences to that which is perceived. In this way, one is then able to understand and experience something in one's own unique way, claim it as one's own, and integrate it into one's life.

What is being described here is a way of understanding and relating to the world, including the world of interpersonal relationships. Whereas the process involves both projection and empathy, it also comes close to imagination as well as to what certain psychoanalytic writers refer to as "projective identification."

According to Schachtel, those attitudes that are available to the individual to use creatively in the act of experiencing are reflected in the kinesthetic aspect of the movement response. For example, a person whose repertoire of kinesthesias, as reflected in Rorschach imagery, is limited to more passive activities, such as resting, contemplating, reading, will either selectively empathize with this aspect of others or will ascribe it to them. Conversely, those whose movement responses include a broad and complex array of kinesthesias would be more able to empathize projectively with a fuller range of experiences.

Mayman (1977) extends Schachtel's formulation in a particular direction. He suggests that the attitudes reflected in the kinesthesias are more basic and central; that they "are drawn from a repertoire of kinesthetic memories which express some of his core experiences of selfhood" (p. 240). For Mayman, even though all movement responses may express some aspect of selfhood, there is an essential difference between self-feelings that derive from one's kinesthetic action potentials and those that are based on contact with familiar and warmly personal objects.

The value of taking stock of an individual's kinesthesias was vividly demonstrated in a protocol in which the testee saw "two people pulling something apart," "a person with shattered dreams and this is a symbol of the dream up here," "a baby being torn away," and "someone dropping a bottle that breaks into a thousand pieces." Viewing these kinesthesias as an expression of self-experience, the examiner took these responses as reflective of a damaged and fragile sense of self that was highly vulnerable to fears of fragmentation.

In keeping with the earlier clinical observation of Sharpe (1940), Mayman broadened his discussion of kinesthesia to suggest that kinesthesias are basic to all metaphors, not simply those conveyed in Rorschach responses. More specifically, in any metaphor a person is expressing a kinesthetic, quasi-conscious memory with important overtones related to early self-experience.

The following clinical example illustrates this point. While interviewing a 38-year-old university history professor, I commented on his exceptional and tasteful dress. Unlike the typical college professor, he was wearing a highly fashionable Italian suit, an expensive silk tie, and brightly polished spectator shoes. He chuckled at my comment, but then went on to say, "You know, that's the story of my life. It's like I am all dressed up and have nowhere to go." What he figuratively meant by this remark was that his friends and colleagues were being promoted and receiving raises, whereas he felt that his request for promotion and tenure was being delayed and not acknowledged. With mild prodding, he was then able to recapture a host of earlier memories related to his early latency years of sitting by the window, gazing out, and waiting for his parents to return from work. The experience at age seven was of a lonely, mildly depressed youngster who was "all dressed up" but had "no one to take him anywhere." Importantly, several of his Rorschach movement responses conveyed these same experiential themes of waiting, aloneness, and being left behind. For example, on Card VIII he saw "a beaver standing still next to a lake," and on Card I he noted "an orchestra conductor, arms in the air, but viewed from behind."

The Object Representational Aspect of the Movement Response

Mayman (1977) reminds us that "there is more to a movement response than kinesthesia; there is also the person carrying out the action" (p. 241). To understand this component of the M response he evokes the concept of "object representation." Herein, object representations are thought of as unconscious images of others that are rooted in early object relations and provide a substratum for all subsequent relationships. Given that a person brings to the Rorschach testing a large part of his or her repertoire of internalized representations of self and other, this component of the M response presents, for Mayman, a unique glimpse into the images that populate the person's inner life.

Taking note of these personal images is important but is only the first step; the examiner must push further and attempt to place these representations in the context of the person's self-system and object-relational organization. For example, the examiner must first determine the extent to which the figures represent an aspect of the self and the extent to which they reflect a sense of others. A helpful source of information in making this distinction is the testee's spontaneous comments offered throughout the testing, especially those remarks that express attitudes directly about the tests and indirectly about the examiner. It is my experience that in such comments the patient is unknowingly expressing core features of his or her relationship with the examiner, and that this relationship, in the here and now, parallels relationships expressed in Rorschach imagery. Thus, by paying careful attention to his or her ongoing relationship with the patient, the examiner is in a position to informatively locate those roles the patient assumes and those roles that are assigned to the other.

The Rorschach images referable to the self should be further evaluated in terms of whether they express what the testee feels about himself or herself or, alternatively, what he or she admires and would like to be. The inferential possibilities implied in these projected images are vast; only by sifting through them and being able to identify their role in the patient's experience can these possibilities be realized. A fuller discussion of the clinical aspects of the object-representational concept is presented in chapter 11.

Empathy and Identification in the Movement Response

The fifth and final aspect of the movement response involves the quality of the individual's object relations. Mayman (1977) draws a distinction between relationships that are on an empathic basis and those that are based on identification. Whereas the former includes two-way relationships in which separateness and self-other boundaries are maintained, in the latter self-other differences are blurred and there is little separateness.

The distinction Mayman draws between empathic relationships and identificatory relationships is quite similar to the earlier distinction Freud (1914) made between true object relations and narcissistic object relations. In a true object relationship, like Mayman's empathic relationship, the other is viewed as separate and distinct and as having motives and feelings distinct from one's own.

By contrast, in a narcissistic object relation, as in Mayman's relationship based on identification, the object is not regarded as separate and distinct, but as an extension of the self and as necessary in fulfilling functions that should, but cannot, be managed intrapsychically. In a narcissistic relationship the interest and investment is in the function being provided, or the supply being offered, and not in the person in the role of the provider or supplier. Typically, the individual in the provider role feels expendable, exploited, and used. One senses a tenuousness to the relationship and realizes that when the functions or supplies are withdrawn, one will be written off and then looked upon with contempt.

Mayman has identified several aspects of the movement response that distinguish these two modes of relating. Accordingly, individuals who are able to enter into true object relations, in which there is no dissolving of self-other boundaries, offer M responses characterized by the following: (1) there is a broad and complex array of images of others; (2) the responses take into account realistic properties of the blots themselves, that is, there is objectivity; and (3) from the description of the percept it is clear that the testee is describing someone else and not himself or herself.

By contrast, individuals who relate themselves to others on a narcissistic basis, and who thus blur self-other boundaries, produce M responses in which (1) the response is reported with undue vividness and conviction; (2) the action ascribed and the attributes expressed are largely fabulized rather than inherent to the percept itself; (3) there is an intense absorption and involvement in the behavior of the perceived figures; and (4) the testee seems to infuse himself or herself into the described figure and thereby vicariously share in the other's experience.

In essence, implicit in Mayman's indices is the assumption that the nature of the relationship between the testee and his or her movement responses, in terms of such dimensions as range, objectivity, and distance, reflects and parallels the quality of relationship the testee establishes with his or her objects.

Summary of the Movement Response

In summary, Mayman (1977) has identified five essential dimensions of the movement response. An appraisal of these various lines permits the examiner to infer a vast array of structural and dynamic aspects of personality, including the capacity for perspective, the intensity of ideational activity, the availability of fantasy, the role of early self-experiences, the nature of self and object representations, and the quality of object relations.

♦ ♦ ♦ Form Response

Because form is the most important aspect of the visual world, it is not surprising that in most Rorschach records at least two thirds of the responses involve pure form. Form has long been recognized as the ordering, structuring principle of the universe as perceived by man. However, form is adaptive, as Schachtel (1966) points out, only insofar as it allows for transformations. When it becomes fixed and rigid, it stunts and inhibits rather than structures life. So too on the Rorschach test, form can be adaptive by giving order and structure to the unfamiliar and unstructured inkblots; it can, however, be maladaptive when it becomes so overriding that it does not allow for flexibility and openness to other dimensions.

On the basis of an integration of perception, phenomenology, and psychoanalytic theory, Schachtel (1966) has identified six aspects of the form response. This section is organized on the basis of these six aspects: (1) the role of form perception in the human sense of sight, (2) the perceptual attitude underlying form response, (3) the concept of perceptual hold and its relation to the form response, (4) the meaning of dynamic form responses, (5) the place of delay in the form response, and (6) the development of form perception.

Role of Form Perception

It is the role of form perception to take hold of significant aspects of the environment. Such taking hold implies an active organization of the visual field. What is required here is an active perceptual attitude, a looking attentively at something as opposed to simply being struck passively by it. Form perception structures, orders, and objectifies the visual field and, as such, requires active focusing, attending, and structuring.

Schachtel (1966) has distinguished two modes of perceptual relatedness, and the distinction he has drawn rests on form perception:

> In the *autocentric mode* there is little or no objectification; the emphasis is on how and what the person feels; there is a close relation amounting to a fusion, between sensory quality and pleasure or unpleasure feelings; and the perceiver reacts primarily to something impinging on him. . . . In the *allocentric mode* there is objectification; the emphasis is on what the object is like; there is either

no relation or a less pronounced or less direct relation between sensory quality and pleasure-unpleasure feelings; the perceiver usually approaches or turns his attention to the object actively and in doing so opens himself toward it receptively or, figuratively or literally, takes hold of it, tries to grasp it [p. 79].

Viewed in this context, the grasp of form is essential for the allocentric mode of perceptual relatedness.

Perceptual Attitude Underlying the Form Response

Rorschach described the form response from two perspectives: the clarity of form visualization as expressed in the accuracy of fit between percept and area chosen (form level), and the level of personality organization from which the percept originated. As to the latter, he viewed form as a function of consciousness and hence as subject to improvement by conscious effort. Later Rorschach theorists extended these notions. Beck (1944–1945) considered form responses as reflecting intellectual, conscious control and a respect for reality, whereas Rapaport wrote of form responses as referable to the process of formal reasoning and as reflecting the person's adherence to the demands of reality.

Schachtel (1966), writing more phenomenologically, has described two perceptual attitudes that are involved in the form response—the "active attitude" and the "typical attitude." The active perceptual attitude, according to Schachtel, involves several steps, including an initial grasping of the inkblot features, comparing one's associations to the features of the inkblot, restructuring the inkblot features, and critically discerning the degree of likeness. Involved in these steps are various ego functions, including the processes of attention, reality testing, and critical judgment. Clearly, not all form responses are based on each of these steps; however, when the examiner notes an incompletely formulated response, it is important that he or she identify the missing step and attempt to understand the ego function impaired.

The second attitude identified by Schachtel, "the typical attitude," is "a neutral, impersonal, matter-of-fact, objective, detached quality in relation to the percept" (p. 95). Typically, not all form responses are offered with dispassionate objectivity and detachment. Were such an attitude to prevail throughout the test, it would likely reflect heightened resistance to the test and/or an individual who is inordinately and chronically inhibited, insulated, and restricted. Although the "typical attitude" represents one extreme and contrasts with the attitude under- lying the dynamic form response, what Schachtel is suggesting here is that the nature of the form response may reflect the testee's attitude toward the test.

Concept of Perceptual Hold

Schachtel (1966) evokes the concept of "perceptual hold" to designate the individual's taking hold perceptually of the object world. Herein, he is referring to an experiential dimension of perception that ranges from a firm, stable, enduring hold of the object perceived to one that is weak, tenuous, and vulnerable to interferences.

Schachtel views the form response as especially reflective of the degree of quality of the testee's perceptual hold. He notes that

> form perception can fulfill its abstractive, objectifying, identifying, orienting functions well only if the forms perceived are adequate; that is, if they correspond to the actual object seen and if the abstraction from the total object in the form perceived is valid and grasps the essential qualities of the objects [p. 109].

Thus, involved in perceptual hold is a recognition of familiarity, recep- tive openness, and a decisive grasp; such functions are reflected in the form response.

The concept of "perceptual hold" has much clinical utility. Beyond describing the patient's typical level of perceptual hold, the examiner is in a unique position to observe which factors disrupt the hold, the severity of the disruption, and under what conditions the disruption occurs. For example, diffuse anxiety can interfere with a firm percep- tual hold, resulting in percepts that are vague, indefinite, and amor- phous. Recognizing this, the examiner can then determine where in the record vagueness occurred, ask himself or herself why it appeared at that point, and then note if the vagueness continued or if the patient was able to recover.

Dynamic Form Responses

As noted previously, not all form responses are based on what Schachtel describes as the "typical attitude" of objectivity and detachment. Quite to the contrary, certain form responses can be rich, vivid, compelling, and lively. Schachtel refers to these responses as dynamic form, meaning that the percept is in a dynamic relation to the subject.

Schachtel's notion of dynamic form is quite similar to Mayman's (1977) concept of the fabulized response. Both writers are referring to responses that are embellished with affective and associative elaboration. For Schachtel, an important basis of the dynamic form response is emotion, whereas Mayman points to the availability of fantasy. Common to both theorists is the formulation that these types of responses speak to a rich inner life that is finding expression on the Rorschach test.

Dynamic form and the fabulized response are rich with meaning. For many individuals they reflect an interest and investment in the task, a willingness to go beyond merely what is called for. In contrast with a detached, intellectual stance, here one is playful and fanciful.

In addition to reflecting an attitude toward the test, such responses also express, more broadly, an openness to different types of experiences, a willingness, if you will, to relax tight controls and strict adherence to reality and to indulge in what Freud (1900) referred to as the "primary process." In judging this dimension, it is important that the examiner distinguish between adaptive regression and maladaptive regression. In the former, the excursions into primary process are under ego control; defenses are flexible but effective, and reality testing is maintained. In the latter there is minimal ego control; tenuous defenses give way under the pressure of unconscious forces and reality testing is lost. Rorschach expressions of maladaptive regression include a weakening of form level and a sliding from fabulations to confabulations.

As Schachtel has noted, in the dynamic form response there is an affective relationship between the testee and his or her percept. That is, something of dynamic importance for the subject is being expressed in the response. This means that it is incumbent upon the examiner to take careful note of the content of these responses. While the content tends to be charged with personal meaning and must be understood on an individual basis, Schachtel has identified certain contents that he suggests have more general applications. For example, he views references to size as reflective of one's sense of his or her own importance and power, references to enclosures as expressive of a need for or a fear of protection, aggressive content as indicative of a desire to hurt or a fear of hurt and injury, and references to solidness or fragility as reflective of the individual's sense of self.

Delay and the Form Response

The steps involved in the form or form-dominated responses and their underlying processes (attending, taking hold, comparing, fitting, judging) require a higher level of mental activity than do more immediate, less reflective responses, such as those involving pure color. Rapaport had this in mind when he asserted that form responses require and reflect a capacity for delay of discharge of impulses. Even when form was accompanied by another determinant, he suggested that it "indicated an ability to delay impulses until they can be integrated with the dictates of the formal rules of thinking" (Holt, 1968, p. 343). Holt amplified and refined Rapaport's initial postulation by noting that not all form responses indicate the capacity for delay. Furthermore, he noted, certain form responses indicate quite the opposite: an inability to effect delay and an absence of the critical attitude implied in formal reasoning. Holt pointed out that because of the wide variety of form responses, what might be involved here are different levels of delay, as well as different uses of delay.

Schachtel (1966), too, questions whether the form response is always expressive of an ability to delay. From a more adaptive perspective he points out that such responses can also represent "the enjoyable and fluctuating tension of exploratory play in contact with the world of the inkblots" (p. 148).

In accord with both Holt and Schachtel, it is my experience that simply producing a form response cannot be taken as an indication of a capacity for delay. Rather, one must judge each form response individually and take into account a number of factors, including the complexity of the response, the level of integrative activity, and the form level. For example, a young physician, after carefully studying Card IX, reported, "it looks like two musicians at a nightclub playing saxophones with a candle in the background." The physician's capacity to delay is clearly reflected in the accuracy, completeness, and complexity of this form-based response. By contrast, another individual quickly scanned Card V, tersely replied that it "might be a cloud," and handed the card back to the examiner. On inquiry, he added, "it somewhat resembled the shape of a cloud." This response too is form-determined; in comparison with the physician's response, however, it is cheap, simple, vague, and reflects no integrative activity. As such, although the response is form-based, one cannot infer from it a capacity for delay.

Development of Form Perception

With form, as with each of the other Rorschach dimensions (e.g., color, shading, blackness), it is important to maintain a developmental perspective. This is especially true when evaluating the records of children. For example, what in an adult record may be taken as an indication of disturbance might be regarded as normal in a child's protocol, given developmental considerations.

Ample evidence indicates that the perception of form is a relatively late developmental achievement that is based on a combination of maturational and experiential factors. Like other lines of development (e.g., cognition), changes in perception tend to proceed in an orderly, systematic, sequential manner, with certain built-in directions. Two such directions have relevance to the perception of form on the Rorschach test. Schachtel (1966) has emphasized the gradual shift from passivity and a state of being impinged upon by external and internal stimuli to greater activity and an expanding capacity to control such impingements. The second direction, based on the work of Werner (1940), involves a progression from relative globalness and lack of differentiation to increasing differentiation and hierarchic integration.

In analyzing a protocol it is often helpful for the examiner to keep these two developmental directions in mind. For example, noting the overall proportion of form responses in a record might offer an indication of the role of activity in the patient's mental life and his or her attitude toward more passive experiences. Also, assessing the relative preponderance of vague form responses may offer clues as to the level of perceptual maturity. Level of perceptual maturity has predictive import, in that P. Lerner (1975) has found that it is related to cognitive maturity, social maturity, and symptom expression.

Summary of Form Responses

Using Schachtel's (1966) work as a framework, I have discussed form from the perspectives of the role of form perception in general, the perceptual attitude underlying the form response, the concept of perceptual hold, the meaning of dynamic form responses, the role of delay of impulse, and the developmental aspects of form perception. Each perspective has much to contribute to our understanding of the production of a form response.

✦ ✦ ✦ Form Level

In the discussion of the form response, periodic reference was made to form level, the congruence of fit between the response and the area chosen. Historically, form level has been regarded as but one aspect of the form response; however, more recently—and especially with the contributions of Mayman (1964b)—form level has been elevated to a dimension in its own right and viewed as a source of useful inferences.

As previously noted, for Rorschach (1942) himself, an important aspect of the form response was its clarity of visualization (i.e., form level). Although he conceived of clarity of visualization as related to intelligence, he provided little more than a gross distinction between "acceptable" and "unacceptable" forms. Beck (1944–1945) accepted Rorschach's dichotomy but suggested that the distinction be based on normative data. Klopfer and associates (1954) introduced the notion of two cutoff points, one at each extreme of the form level continuum. Although this served to draw attention to especially good and especially poor percepts, it left almost 90% of all responses undiscussed in terms of the meaning of their form level. Rapaport et al. (1945–1946) distinguished good from poor form, as had Rorschach in his clinical work, and proposed two subcategories for each of the two major categories. Their criteria for scoring, however, were ambiguous and the meaning of the distinctions was unclear.

In his research, however, Rapaport did introduce a major innovation. To evaluate the quality of the perceptual-association integration of a response, he proposed a continuum with six discrete grades: F+ for a well-differentiated, well-perceived response; Fo for an acceptable response generalized from one or two crudely seen details; Fv (vague) for responses intrinsically amorphous; F− for inadequately justified responses; special F+ for an especially well-articulated F+ response; and special F− for responses that are well differentiated but arbitrarily interpreted. In spite of the innovativeness of this system, Rapaport limited its applicability to the whole response (W).

Friedman (1953) extended the work of Rapaport and applied the system to all responses, not just the whole response (W). Friedman also placed the scoring system in a different conceptual framework. Basing them on the developmental theory of Werner (1940), he defined the scores as representing different levels of perceptual functioning.

It remained for Mayman (1964b) to reconceptualize the scoring system in such a way as to make it useful for clinicians. Although the work of Friedman generated much research (see P. Lerner, 1975), it offered little to practitioners. Mayman not only offered specific refinements but, more important, provided a rationale for reinterpreting the scores as reflecting different levels of reality testing. He proposed a system consisting of seven scores, ranging from "reality adherence" at one extreme to "reality-abrogation" at the other extreme. The specific scores are as follows: F+ (good), Fo (ordinary), Fw+ (weak but acceptable), Fw− (weak and not acceptable), F− (arbitrary), Fv (vague), and Fs (spoiled). Because of its immense clinical value, each score will be discussed in terms of its meaning and scoring criteria.

F+ Response

A form good score (F+) is accorded those responses that are sharp, convincing, well articulated, and, once pointed out, clearly seen by the examiner. As Mayman (1964b) noted, "A good F+ response . . . may be hard to arrive at but is easy to grasp" (p. 8). Whereas one recognizes a Fo, one discovers an F+.

The F+ response represents a highly successful combination of imagination and reality adherence. Here the person goes beyond the ordinary but remains realistic. When embellishments and elaborations are offered, rather than detracting from the percept, they bring the response into an even sharper focus.

As with each of the form level ratings, the interpretive meanings of the F+ response lie in its relative proportion to the other scores. Ideally, one hopes to find in any record a sprinkling of F+, Fo, and Fw+ responses. When included with Fo and Fw+ responses, the F+ percept reflects a high investment in the task, an active perceptual attitude, a well-tuned sense of reality, and a willingness to depart from the commonplace.

The exclusive appearance of F+ responses in a record might indicate something altogether different. Reality testing is an ego function that involves a critical-evaluative attitude toward the external world. In some individuals this function may come under the sway of superego pressures, so that self-scrutiny becomes an end in itself and self-correction a form of self-castigation. In these instances, the individual feels considerable distress and guilt until he or she has reached the level of perfection supposedly implied in an F+ response. This is similar to patients with excessively demanding ego ideals, whose aspirations are so exalted that only in the F+ response are they able to attain a level that they feel will do justice to their overly inflated but precarious sense of self.

The significance of the absence of the F+ response in a protocol depends on the nature of the scores that have been employed. For example, from a record with a preponderance of Fo scores, one might infer a rather superficial quality of reality testing, in which the person was satisfied with what was obvious and most easily seen. In those records in which weaker forms prevail, one might be observing either impaired reality testing or a tendency to brush reality considerations aside under the impact of highly invested urges and desires.

Fo Response

A form ordinary score (Fo) is given to those responses that are well perceived but are so obvious and readily seen that they require little effort. One does not seek out these percepts; rather, they are there to be seen. Although all popular and near popular responses warrant the Fo score, not all Fo percepts are popular responses.

The Fo responses reflect an accurate but superficial level of reality testing; the testee was able to see the obvious. Protocols with a disproportionately high number of Fo scores indicate a preference for the conventional and safe; such individuals often appear as shallow and banal. Then too, those testees not involved in the test, or those who are rigidly defending against immersing themselves in the inkblots, will produce protocols with a high Fo percentage.

Rorschach records lacking in Fo responses may indicate impairments in reality testing; however, those individuals who have difficulty tolerating the obvious and conventional also tend to provide records devoid of the Fo score. It is not uncommon for such an individual to comment, "I know other people see a bat here, but I see other things."

A well-balanced protocol should include a high proportion of both Fo and F+ scores. This indicates an individual who sees and is comfortable with the conventional, yet at times can go beyond the obvious without losing his or her bearings in reality.

Fw+ Response

The form weak but acceptable score (Fw+) is applied to responses that are acceptable but require some stretching to see. The percept is not convincing, but it does fit. Although the percept is justified on the basis of few details, the overall idea does not clash with the chosen area.

For Mayman (1964b), the weak but acceptable form response represents a departure from the strict reality adherence implicit in the Fo and F+ responses. He suggests that these responses do not indicate a serious departure from reality, but rather that a permissiveness has entered the response process. The individual relaxes his or her more rigorous standards of reality adherence and lapses into a more lax and carefree state. Herein, fantasy is allowed to emerge without the need to maintain stringent reality testing. Optimally, records should have a few Fw+ responses, for not to allow such lapses is to have a too exacting standard of performance.

Fw– Response

Fw– responses are essentially unacceptable, but do have one or two redeeming features. Even though a detail may be offered to justify the fit between percept and location, overall there is little correspondence between the image and the blot area.

The distinction between the Fw+ response and the Fw– response may be viewed as a cutoff point between acceptable and nonacceptable levels of reality testing. In contrast with the Fw+ score, the Fw– score indicates a distinct lapse in reality testing. In this regard, the Fw– response shares commonalities with the F– and Fs responses. The Fw– response indicates not only a shift toward fantasy, but a significant departure from reality adherence as well; forays into fantasy and whim are at the expense of reality considerations.

F– Response

The form arbitrary score (F–) is assigned responses in which there is little or no fit between the percept and the area responded to. An idea is offered to an area with almost complete disregard for the configural features of that area. In essence, the perceptual reality of the blot is lost; thus, F– responses indicate an abandonment of reality. Even one F– response may be taken as an indication of severe disturbance. While there are some individuals who readily and cavalierly brush reality aside, more often the score is suggestive of a psychotic loss of reality. An example of a F – response was offered by a schizophrenic male who saw all of Card III as a "wounded crab."

Mayman (1970) is quite explicit in pointing out that the score refers to a perceptual disturbance and not a conceptual one. For example, an individual can see two percepts quite accurately, but then combine them in an illogical, unrealistic way (e.g., a child sitting on top of a pig's head). Even though this type of forged relationship is pathologic, the disturbance involved is qualitatively different from that underlying the F – response. As Mayman put it, "The F – is not a crazy thought; it is a crazy percept" (p. 14).

Fv Response

The form vague score (Fv) is reserved for those responses in which the idea applied to the blot area is intrinsically vague (e.g., clouds, abstract art, oil). Typically, vague responses are dictated mainly by determinants other than form (e.g., color, blackness, shading) and need not be scored. However, there are vague responses in which form is the sole determinant, and here the form vague score is applied.

The Fv score differs from those responses in which the person is vague regarding what is seen or why he or she saw it. In the latter instance, the confusion and perplexity are not reflected by the Fv score.

The Fv response is the cheapest response one can offer; it requires minimal effort. The score is not indicative of failures in reality testing. Rather, it either reflects a defensive stance toward the test, in which vagueness is evoked to ward off fears of self-exposure, or it indicates an impoverishment of associative processes.

Fs Response

The form spoil score (Fs) is applied when an acceptable response (i.e., F+, Fo) is distorted by either a significant omission or by the introduction of an inappropriate specification.

Mayman (1970) regards this response as indicative of a partial break with reality. As he puts it, "Something goes awry, and instead of an accurate perception of reality, the subject arrives at a surprisingly idiosyncratic misperception" (p. 12). In the Fs response, the properties of the blot are not strong enough to prevent the person from losing touch with reality, and as a consequence, a blatant distortion is incorporated into the organizing process. The Fs score is indicative of a reality abrogation; however, the departure is more transient and more contained than that reflected in the F− score. Illustrative of a Fs response was a female adolescent borderline's first percept on Card III—"Two women with chicken heads, especially huge beaks." As an aside, not unexpectedly, the patient experienced her mother as exceptionally biting and critical.

Summary of Form Level

Although various theorists have pointed to its importance, not until Mayman has there been available a graded, clinically relevant scoring system. Based on a scale developed by Rapaport and extended to the full range of Rorschach responses by Friedman, Mayman's work represents a refinement of the scale and a reinterpretation of the scores as representing various levels of reality testing. Seven scores are proposed, ranging from "reality-adherence" to "reality-abrogation." Conceptually, the distinctions between the scores are seen as qualitative rather than quantitative.

✦ ✦ ✦ Color

In the Rorschach literature, the color responses have been conceptually related to the individual's prevailing mode of affective responsiveness and expression; to the nature and degree of control over affects, impulses, and actions; and to the dimension of extroversion.

Rapaport et al. (1945–1946) viewed color and the relationship between color and form as indicative of the affect-discharge process and the concomitant capacity to effect delay. Thus, the pure color response reflected an absence of delay, the color-form response (CF) indicated greater delay but with minimal effectiveness, and the form color response (FC) suggested flexible control and adaptive delay. Rapaport further suggested that because the extent and modes of regulation over actions roughly parallel that of affects, one could also infer from the color response the capacity to effect delay before acting.

My own views of the color responses are more closely tied to those of Schachtel (1966), who related color more directly to affective experience, including responsiveness, range, level of differentiation, and expression. In keeping with Schachtel's more phenomenological perspective, in this section I discuss the Rorschach dimension of color in terms of the following: (1) the phenomenology of color perception, (2) the affective experience, (3) the concept of perceptual style, (4) the rationale for the relationship between color and affectivity, and (5) the role of color on the Rorschach. Finally, based on recent developments in psychoanalytic theory, I will draw relationships between the experience of affects and the experience of object relations.

Color Perception

In terms of Schachtel's (1966) notion of perceptual attitudes, the perception of color without form occurs with a passive *autocentric attitude*. This stands in marked contrast to the actively structuring and objectifying *allocentric perceptual attitude,* characteristic of the perception of form. Color impinges; one reacts to its impact rather than having to attentively seek it out. Whereas form invites active observation, color, if you will, takes hold. Schachtel (1966) put it this way: "Color seizes the eye, the eye grasps form" (p. 169).

The perception of color involves passivity, but other factors are also implicated. The color experience is immediate and is typically accompanied by a particular feeling tone or mood quality. Unlike the perception of form, colors are not just recognized but are felt, too. In this regard, the pleasure-unpleasure, comfort-discomfort dimension of the autocentric attitude is part of color perception.

The Affective Experience

The word *affect* derives from the Latin *afficere*, meaning "something done to" a person; something "affects" him. The word *emotion* comes from the Latin *emovere*, denoting a state in which one is "moved out of" a preceding state. Both words in derivation, then, reflect the passivity of the person.

Freud's view of affects also involved the notion of the essential passivity of the affective experience. Conceptualizing affects as drive derivatives, as a substitute form of discharge, he contrasted their passivity in relation to the active work of the ego in its attempts to maintain conscious control.

The affective experience is also characterized by an immediacy and directness between stimulus and response. Indeed, the stronger and more intense the affect, the less time there is for deliberation, reflection, and objectivity.

Perceptual Style

Basic to the relationship that Schachtel (1966) draws between the color experience and the affective experience is the concept of "perceptual style." This refers to enduring and pervasive perceptual attitudes that are characteristic of the person and find expression in his or her behavior and experience. The concept is akin to, and closely parallels Shapiro's (1965) notion of, "cognitive style."

Of the various attitudes that constitute one's perceptual style, of paramount importance, for Schachtel, is the tendency toward activity or passivity. Accordingly, the active-passive dimension is conceived of as cutting across all psychological domains. Thus, in the realm of affect discharge, extreme passivity becomes evident in being overwhelmed by affect, being swept up in it, and being unable to regulate it. Correspondingly, in the perceptual sphere, passivity is manifest in a tendency to be struck by the impact of sensory stimuli and thus to be unable to organize and take hold of it.

Rationale for the Relation Between Color and Affectivity

A brief review of the color experience and the affect experience reveals the following common features: both are experienced passively by the individual; in both, the individual is affected immediately and directly; both are closely bound to the dimension of pleasure-unpleasure. Because of these similarities, Schachtel sees the autocentric perceptual attitude underlying each experience.

Rapaport too recognized the relationship between color and affectivity; his acknowledgment, however, was more grudging and was argued on a more general and abstract basis. One sees his caution in the following statement: "Dependent upon their organization of affects and impulses and their modes of control over them, people have associative processes that allow for dealing with the color impression in a specific manner characteristic of their affective life" (Holt, 1968, p. 376).

Color and the Rorschach

In the context of the Rorschach test, color poses a challenge that can be tackled, avoided, denied, or solved in a variety of different ways. Its impact, the individual's general reaction, his or her reactivity, the extent to which color is integrated with form, the extent to which it interferes with perceptual articulation of form, and the ways in which its effects are limited, all are aspects of the color dimension that need to be considered.

Many of the above considerations are reflected in formal scores, but several others are not. Thus, more spontaneous, off-handed comments, such as "Oh, this one is colorful" or "I find the red distracting" provide candid glimpses into how the testee is experiencing the color and, in turn, how he or she experiences affects.

Between off-handed comments and the major scores are the additional scores. These too were devised to capture specific aspects of the color experience. Thus, simply referring to the color but not making use of it in a response (Cref) indicates a passing attunement to affects without integrating them into one's experience. Color denial speaks directly to the defense of denial in managing affects, whereas color avoidance indicates the tendency toward avoidance of affects. An investment in the idea and not the color, reflective of a tendency to intellectualize, is represented in the color symbolism response (Csym).

Virtually all Rorschach scoring systems provide for three major scores (FC, CF, C) to indicate the extent to which color is integrated with form. Using color as reflective of either affectivity or of a tendency to affect discharge, and using form as representing the ordering, structuring, controlling factor, the three scores are thought to reflect the role of integration of affects into the person's psychological life.

It is generally agreed that the most satisfactory solution of the problem posed by color to the testee is the form-color response (FC). For Rapaport, this response reflects flexible control and a capacity for delay. For Schachtel, the response expresses an openness and receptivity to affective experiences. Color, according to Schachtel, enriches perception, much as affectivity enriches life. Both make possible a more rapid recognition and grasp of external events and objects and thus enhance one's pleasure.

There is some disagreement as to the merits of the solution provided by the color-form response (CF). Whereas he notes that this response reflects greater control and capacity for delay than does the pure color response (C), Rapaport also suggests that the control is tenuous, the delay insufficient, and a tendency toward impulsivity remains. Schachtel differs; he believes the response reflects spontaneity and an even greater openness to affects.

The absence of form in the color response (C) is typically regarded as problematic. Rapaport views such responses as indicating an absence of delay, so that impulses are expressed directly and without regulation in action. For Schachtel, the response reflects heightened emotional reactivity coupled with extreme cognitive passivity, resulting in a proneness to emotional outbursts and a tendency to be overwhelmed and flooded by affects.

Several specific color responses (e.g., the form-color arbitrary response) are discussed in a following chapter; here, however, I would like to briefly mention those color responses in which shading and an attunement to the nuances of coloring play a role: FCc, CFc, Cc. These responses too will be reviewed in greater detail later, but let me note here that, in general, I have found these scores strongly indicative of the degree to which an individual is able to differentiate among various feeling states.

Affects and Object Relations

The relationships drawn by both Rapaport and Schachtel between the perception of color on the Rorschach and aspects of the organization of affects were based on Freud's view of affects as presented in his drive theory. In that theory, drives pressing for discharge are considered to be expressed and represented in consciousness by affects and ideas; thus, affects are regarded as drive derivatives.

More recent psychoanalytic conceptions of affects have tended to draw attention to their relation, not to drives, but rather to object relations. Representative of this line of theorizing is the work of Modell (1975, 1978) and his formulation that affects are object-seeking. He notes that whereas the sharing and communication of affects affords closeness and intimacy, defenses against affect are also defenses against object relations. We are all familiar with those individuals who are not only emotionally constricted, but self-sufficient as well. Believing that nothing is needed from others and that they alone can provide their own emotional sustenance, these people use self-sufficiency to ward off dangers associated with need and closeness. Winnicott (1960), in a similar conceptual vein, noted that individuals can keep themselves hidden by not sharing genuine feelings.

Only recently have these theoretical notions found their way into the Rorschach research and clinical literature. In one series of papers, P. Lerner (1979, 1981, 1986) has described the affect organization and quality of object relations of a subgroup of narcissistic patients and identified specific Rorschach indices reflective of both aspects of personality. In a second group of articles, P. Lerner (1994, 1996a) has provided clinical material demonstrating how a careful study of the testee's affective experience, as manifested in his or her ways of handling color on the Rorschach, can be used to infer aspects of the individual's object-relational experience. The following case illustrates this point.

The patient is a 31-year-old single bookkeeper who lives with her widowed mother. Because she complained of agoraphobia, presented herself as a "Barbie doll," and evidenced difficulty in separating from her family, the referrer questioned if there was an underlying borderline personality structure. He also asked for assistance in planning her treatment.

The patient's Rorschach included 24 responses, eight of which involved the use of color. Of these eight color responses, two were scored form-color (FC), four were scored color-form (CF), and two involved pure color (C). In addition, the patient referred to color on three other occasions but failed to integrate the color in her response (Cref).

Based largely on the number and distribution of color responses, the examiner's description of her affect experience was as follows: "Affects occupy a major place in the patient's mental life, however, they are poorly integrated. She has significant difficulty modulating and regulating feelings. She is vulnerable to affective sweeps, and in this regard, she is like an underequipped boat that can be thrown off course and cast about by a stormy sea."

Because several of her color-form and pure color responses involved aggressive content (i.e., explosion, forest fire, poisonous gas), the examiner explained further, "She is currently being pressured by intense and barely controlled feelings of anger. Her anger is likely to be expressed in episodic outbursts and explosions."

In part because of his understanding of her affective life, the examiner then described her object relations, suggesting that she would have significant difficulty establishing and maintaining long-term relationships. Consistent with his description of her affects, he characterized her relationships as "unpredictable, stormy, and chaotic." He added further, "Although she is pained by and struggles with her own feelings and fragile controls, she is oblivious to the impact of her feelings on others. Therefore, when others respond to her angry outbursts by counterattacking or withdrawing, she feels bewildered and misunderstood."

Affect and object-relational issues figured prominently in the examiner's treatment recommendations. Here he wrote, "The patient presents as a leaky container. Affects spill over and disrupt major aspects of her life. As a consequence, she needs, looks to, and relies on others to contain her feelings for her. Certainly at the beginning, but perhaps throughout, the holding aspects of treatment will be especially important."

Treatment progressed as the examiner had forecasted. It was difficult, at times thorny, and typically stormy. Nonetheless, the patient made good use of the containing aspects of treatment and the constancy of her therapist in effecting changes, which included beginning to separate from her family.

Recognizing the intimate relationship between affects and object relations has significant implications for Rorschach interpretation. One still explores the testee's use of color to infer aspects of the affect experience. In addition, however, one can now go further by attempting to tease out the object relations implications as well. Here, for example, one asks oneself a group of new questions, such as, "How would others tend to respond to the patient's affectivity?" and "Does the manner in which the patient expresses and defends against feelings serve to promote certain relational paradigms while discouraging others?"

Summary of Color Responses

Using Schachtel's phenomenological descriptions, I have related the testee's color experience in the Rorschach test situation to the experience of affects. Color poses a challenge to the testee; his or her attitude toward it and ways of dealing with it find parallels in attitudes toward and ways of experiencing affects. Basing my conclusions on the formulation that there is a close tie between affects and object relations, I have suggested that a careful appraisal of patients' color responses and references to color has inferential meaning in terms of their object relations.

◆ ◆ ◆ Shading

On his original inkblot cards, Rorschach had the dark areas uniformly grey or black. Because of the poor printing, however, differences in shading and the relatively vague forms appeared. When Rorschach saw the proofs of his cards, he quickly appreciated the possibilities of this accidental dimension. He wrote little of this determinant, however, although in his paper on Oberholzer's patient (Rorschach, 1942) he suggested that the response was related to an anxious, cautious type of affective adaption.

Binder (1933) extended several of Rorschach's initial impressions, and suggested a system for scoring chiaroscuro. As reported by Bohm (1959), Binder subdivided chiaroscuro responses into two broad categories: (1) responses based on the global and diffuse impression of light and dark qualities of the inkblots, designated Ch, and (2) responses in which shading is used like form to delineate and articulate the percept, designated Fc.

Following Binder, a great variety of shading responses were distinguished and their scoring refined. Leading Rorschach authors, such as Beck, Klopfer, and Hertz, differentiated a host of features, including textural quality, vista effect, and diffusion. Despite the refinements in scoring, the shading response remains shrouded in controversy and the meanings attributed have been the least validated of the scoring categories.

Exner (1986, 1993), following upon Beck, includes three separate types of shading responses in the Comprehensive System. Diffuse shading responses, scored FY, YF, and pure Y in his system, are considered as indicators of stress-related helplessness, passivity, and possibly the experience of anxiety. On the basis of research that has shown Y to be an unstable variable, Exner considers diffuse shading responses as reflective of a more situationally specific feeling of helplessness.

A second type of shading response included in the Comprehensive System involves texture, designated FT, TF, and pure T. There is some research evidence (Exner and Bryant, 1974; Leura and Exner, 1976) to support the formulation that texture responses reflect an emotional need for closeness. A third shading response, the vista response (FV, VF, and pure V), is understood as measuring a painful and ruminative introspection in which negative aspects of the self are prominent.

My scoring of shading is based on Rapaport (Holt, 1968) and Schachtel (1966) both of whom remained consistent with Binder by including only two shading scores—Ch and c. The Ch response subsumes all shading responses, including those based on the diffusion of light and darkness, the perception of texture, and the experience of vista or depth. Like Rapaport, I distinguish three levels of shading responses. When the shading impression is well integrated into a definite form response, the score is FCh; when the shading impression predominates, but vestiges of form are retrained, the score is ChF; and where shading is the sole determinant, the score is Ch. The second score c is reserved for responses that are based on form, and the nuances of shading are used to articulate and outline the response. Students of the Rorschach will note that I have changed the designation of this response from Rapaport's earlier F(C) to Fc.

Following Schachtel (1966) and Rapaport (Holt, 1968), I next describe the perceptual experience of shading and the perceptual attitudes underlying it, the rationale for relating shading to anxiety, and problems involved in assessing anxiety. This discussion applies to the Ch responses and not to the Fc response. A full discussion of the Fc response will be presented in chapter 10.

Perceptual Experience and Attitude

Schachtel (1966) refers to the shading or diffusion response as one in which the testee perceives the shading as more filmlike and in which there is a sense of pervasiveness and a loss of clear boundaries and structures: "The blot is no longer seen as a solid object but as diffuse which offers no hold; it seems to dissolve and to have no internal stability or solidity" (pp. 247–48).

Because shading, typically, is not sufficiently impressive to become a determinant, when it does it suggests a susceptibility or readiness to be moved by it. In other words, there is a vulnerability to the experience, and the underlying perceptual attitude presupposes that vulnerability.

Shading and Anxiety

According to Schachtel, the susceptibility to the shading experience on the Rorschach is the same as the susceptibility to the experience of diffuse anxiety. Like shading, the experience of diffuse anxiety is characterized by a lack of hold, a constant disruption of feeling secure, and a loss of clarity and stability. Schachtel (1966) put it this way: "The person prone to or actually experiencing diffuse anxiety . . . seems to be particularly susceptible to perceiving shading as diffusion, to be vulnerable to its objectless, nebulous, vague quality so similar to what he feels in himself when anxious" (p. 248). According to this rationale, then, the perception of shading and the experience of anxiety both issue from a common predisposition, and an impairment in the capacity to hold is involved in both. In addition, the individual attunes to the shading because its feeling tone resonates with a familiar internal feeling.

Rapaport also related shading to anxiety, but his rationale was quite different. He suggested that the diffuse shading and the relative lack of structure of the shaded cards contribute to the making of a response to these cards especially difficult. Because the anxious person already has difficulty integrating and articulating, the chances of failing on these cards are particularly high. Thus, the rationale he proposes focuses on the gross articulation of the cards and emphasizes the articulation difficulty rather than the similarities between shading and anxiety.

Despite differences in rationales, there is agreement that anxiety can interfere with the capacity to give well-perceived and articulated form responses and that the more intense the anxiety, the more likely the occurrence of ChF and Ch responses.

Problems in Assessing Anxiety

Assessing anxiety on the Rorschach or on any other test is difficult, complex, and beset with both conceptual and methodological problems. First, not only does anxiety take many forms (e.g., panic attacks, lingering free-floating anxiety, constant restlessness, subjective sensations of tension), but the form it takes can have important diagnostic meaning. Kernberg (1975) regarded chronic, diffuse, free-floating anxiety as a cardinal symptom associated with borderline pathology and the anxiety found in a neurotic patient as less relenting, more focused and circumscribed, and better regulated. Second, anxiety is not always assessed or observed directly. On occasion, one infers anxiety by the defensive activity observed. For example, if on a highly shaded card the testee uncharacteristically turns to the periphery and offers edge-detail percepts (De), then the examiner might infer anxiety on the basis of the avoidant behavior. Third, on the Rorschach test, shading is not regarded as the only expression of anxiety. The inanimate movement response (m) and the form vague percept (Fv) are also considered reflections of anxiety.

Because of the complexities surrounding anxiety and its crucial role in personality development and psychopathology, it is insufficient for the examiner to simply describe the patient as anxious. Rather, the examiner must strive to understand how the patient experiences and expresses his or her anxiety, the defenses the patient employs to regulate it, the effectiveness of those defenses, and the effect of the anxiety on various areas of functioning. For certain patients, such as impulsive characters, infantile personalities, and highly constricted individuals, the testing report is incomplete unless it also addresses the patient's openness to experiencing anxiety and his or her anxiety tolerance.

The following excerpt from a testing report illustrates the above points.

> The patient is currently being pressured by relatively intense feelings of anxiety. His anxiety, which is long-standing and constant, becomes evident in difficulties in attending, in an inability to tolerate frustration, in motor restlessness, in an inability to stick with tasks, and in an assortment of vague physical complaints. To ward off the feeling, he first relies on the obsessional defenses of intellectualization, isolation of affect, and reaction formation. When these fail, and they often do, he then uses denial and milder forms of projection. When these falter, as now, he then resorts to alcohol.

Summary of Shading Responses

In this section I have briefly reviewed differences in scoring and in meanings ascribed to the shading response. On the basis of Rapaport's system of scoring and Schachtel's experiential perspective, I have related the shading responses to the experience of diffuse, pervasive, free-floating feelings of anxiety. Recognizing that anxiety is experienced and expressed in various ways and that its assessment is complicated, I have attempted to identify structural and experiential aspects of anxiety that should be addressed in a testing report. Before ending this section, it should be noted that Kleiger (in press), in a timely and excellent article, attempted to integrate the shading categories from the Comprehensive System, including the meanings ascribed to the categories based upon empirical findings, with psychoanalytic theory. Kleiger's work is reviewed more fully in chapter 26.

✦ ✦ ✦ Blackness

Klopfer (1938) was the first Rorschach theorist to develop separate categories for scoring texture and achromatic color. Subsequently, with the exception of Beck, all other early Rorschach writers included in their respective systems a distinct category for scoring responses in which black, grey, or white is used as color. Achromatic color responses (FC',C'F, C') are included in Exner's Comprehensive System; they are not, however, just interpreted in the conventional manner as indicators of depressive affect, but are also regarded as expressions of emotional restraint. Rapaport too used the symbol C' to denote responses in which achromatic color was used. He also distinguished three levels of achromatic responses (FC', C'F, C') scored in terms of the degree to which form is integrated in the response. As Kleiger (in press) points out, "Only later did the meaning of achromatic color responses in Rapaport's system become associated primarily and directly with dysphoria and depressive mood (Allison, Blatt, and Zimet, 1968)" (p. 7).

As with the shading responses, here I again base my scoring on Rapaport's system and make use of a rationale proposed by Schachtel (1966) in which attunement to achromatic color is linked to depressive and dysphoric affect. It should be noted, however, that there have been major theoretical advances in the psychoanalytic understanding of depression. Unfortunately, with the exception of the work of Wilson (1988), these advances have not been extended to the achromatic responses, but instead have found expression solely in newer and more systematic ways of appraising Rorschach content (i.e., Blatt et al., 1976; P. Lerner, 1988).

Involved in Schachtel's (1966) rationale is the recognition that the response to darkness includes both an experiential reaction to diffusion and a perceptual attunement to colors. As in the experience of diffusion, Schachtel maintains that there is a predisposition or vulnerability to be moved by the darkness. As in the color responses, the testee is impinged upon by the stimulus, the experience is immediate and direct, and a feeling tone accompanies the perception. In this instance, however, it is the darkness that impinges and the feeling tone is dysphoric. Schachtel includes under dysphoria a range of depressive feelings, including sadness, mournfulness, despair, and barrenness. In comparing the color and darkness responses he notes that "responses to overall darkness usually convey a feeling, in varying degrees, as if the testee had been plunged into or enveloped by a darkling mood, and, as Binder has shown, point to pervasive dysphoric moods that are readily triggered" (p. 246). As with anxiety, dysphoric moods can interfere with the ability to give well-articulated form responses; thus, the more intense the feeling, the more likely the offering of C'F and C' responses. It is suggested that a loss of interest in the outer world and a sense of meaninglessness are involved in the depressive experience, and that these experiences interfere with the individual's perceptual hold and are reflected in a decrease of form-predominant responses. Schachtel's rationale for relating the perception of darkness to dysphoric feelings is sound, but it must be regarded only as a starting point. With more recent theoretical advances, we are now in a position to identify those more specific dysphoric feelings expressed in the C' responses.

There is a growing consensus (Blatt, 1974; Kohut, 1977) that there are two distinct forms of depression: a developmentally later, guilt-ridden form, characterized by the sense that something bad has occurred, and an earlier, empty form, characterized by feelings of depletion and helplessness, intense object seeking, and difficulties in self-regulation. Wilson (1988) has noted that with the dichotomizing of depressive affect into empty and guilt-ridden forms, the traditional equation between C' black and depressive affect is no longer adequate. The C' scores, he suggests, do not take into account the empty forms of depression. What is implied in the C' response, he notes, is a capacity for guilt, a time perspective, an ability to distinguish right from wrong, and a signaling capacity. Thus, according to Wilson, the dysphoric feelings expressed in the C' responses are at a higher developmental level and include conscious feelings of despair and guilt-tinged depressive affects.

Whereas Rorschach indices of the anaclitic forms of depression have been developed by Ludolph, Milden, and Lerner (1988) and by Wilson (1988), P. Lerner (1988) in particular has attempted to translate phenomenological aspects of these developmentally earlier types of depression into Rorschach-related terms. One feature common to these depressions is the feeling of emptiness. For Lerner, patients who feel empty provide enfeebled records in which there is a sparseness of responses. He suggests that in fashioning a response, few dimensions (such as movement, color, shading) are used, and even when such properties are employed, they lack vividness and impact. One's overall sense of the protocol is that it is muted, drab, and meaningless. A second feature described by Lerner is a sense of hollowness. Here he notes that when these patients attune to the white areas (space response), such attunement points to a sensitivity to themes of hollowness. Finally, Lerner notes that although these patients are reality bound, the contents they perceive typically have a quality of injury or deadness. Therefore, throughout their protocols, such percepts as skeletons, deserts, faceless creatures, and dead trees appear.

The assessment of depression on the Rorschach test is complicated, requires a familiarity with theory, and is fraught with many of the same difficulties as the assessment of anxiety.

Depression lacks a clear definition or reference point; it has alternately been used to refer to a basic affect, a more transient mood, a symptom, a syndrome, and a character style. Owing to the greater attention accorded to the writings of Melanie Klein, it has also been usefully conceptualized as a developmental achievement with important prognostic implications. Thus, not only does depression take various forms, the forms it takes are intimately related to level of object relations, cohesiveness of the sense of self, and the overall nature and level of psychopathology.

In assessing depressive affect, as with anxiety, it is imperative that the examiner attempt to understand the nature of the depressive experience, the defenses used to control it, the effectiveness of the defenses, and the effect of the depression on aspects of personality functioning. Not all patients present with depressive affect; nonetheless, for informed treatment planning, it is helpful that the therapist is apprised of the patient's capacity to experience depressive feelings.

The following excerpt from a testing report was found quite useful by the referring therapist.

> Amid affective constriction, the patient is now experiencing relatively severe feelings of depression. Her depression becomes manifest in a marked sense of loss, especially a loss in functioning, in a concern with her waning sexuality, and in an attunement to subjective feelings of coldness. As well, she is tired and depleted and stirs in others the sense that they are asking too much of her. She is concerned with death and abandonment. Finally, she has much difficulty concentrating and this contributes to her sense of lowered functioning.

Summary of Blackness Responses

In keeping with a rationale developed by Schachtel and others in the Rorschach tradition, I have related the perception of darkness to dysphoric affects. However, basing my beliefs on the recent formulations of Wilson, I suggest that the C' responses are related to developmentally later depressive feelings (i.e., despair, guilt-tinged depression) and not to the entire range of dysphoric affects. In assessing depressive feelings and their vicissitudes, it is especially important that the examiner be theoretically informed and cognizant of the role of depression in personality development.

◆ ◆ ◆ Conclusion

In this chapter I have discussed the major dimensions of the Rorschach test, including movement, form, form level, color, shading, and darkness. I have equated each dimension to an area of personality functioning and development and have attempted to provide a theoretical rationale for this. The rationales have relied extensively on the earlier contributions of Schachtel, Rapaport, and Mayman. When applicable, the rationales have been refined in the light of more recent developments in psychoanalytic theory. Ultimately, it is through a conceptual understanding of the basic test dimensions and the aspects of personality functioning they touch upon that the examiner is able to derive meaning from the scores.

9

THE FIFTH
SCORING CATEGORY

Ⅰn this chapter I review and discuss the major scores that comprise the fifth scoring category. Although they were initially, and still are, regarded as major indicators of disturbances in thinking, on the basis of more recent work of Athey (1986) and Leichtman (1996), I suggest that these scores may also be viewed more broadly as reflective of ways of experiencing. In chapter 21, I discuss several of these same scores in terms of the role they have played in Rorschach research.

As discussed in chapter 6, the analysis of the deviant aspects of the patient's verbal responses stands out as a unique, distinctive, and durable contribution of Rapaport's to Rorschach theory and practice. Following upon Rapaport, for decades clinicians have considered these scores as indicators of disturbed thinking in particular, and of psychological breakdown in general. They have proven useful to the practitioner in identifying aberrant thinking across a broad spectrum of clinical conditions, ranging from transient psychosis to schizophrenia to brain dysfunction. Their appearance in the Rorschach records of individuals who seemingly function well has become a reliable signal, alerting tester and therapist alike to the possibility of ego regression.

In laying the conceptual foundation for an understanding of these deviations, Rapaport and his colleagues emphasized the following basic points: verbalizations are a reflection of thought processes; a testee's thinking in the Rorschach situation needs to be judged in relationship to the perceptual reality of the inkblots; several of the deviations can be understood from the perspective of two types of autistically disturbed distancing problems (i.e., a pathological increase of distance and a pathological decrease of distance).

Rapaport et al. (1945–1946) identified 25 categories of unusual verbalizations. Although the categories were not formally organized, several were informally linked according to some underlying principle. For example, confabulations, fabulized combinations, and contaminations were all seen as expressions of the associative aspects of the response process overriding perceptual aspects. In addition, several of the categories were developed to parallel mechanisms Freud (1900) had identified as the processes that transform latent dream thoughts into manifest content. Here, Freud's description of condensation was translated into the Rorschach fabulized combination and contamination scores, and the process he referred to as "symbolism" found Rorschach representation in the confabulation response.

In Exner's Comprehensive System, this dimension of Rorschach analysis comes under the heading of Special Scores. Exner (1986a) devised 14 basic scores, 10 of which were adapted from Rapaport et al. (1945–1946). Of the 14 special scores, seven are arranged into the following subcategories of unusual verbalizations: (1) deviantly expressed responses (deviant verbalizations, or DV); (2) deviant response, or DR; (3) inappropriate combination of impressions and ideas; (4) incongruous combination, or Incom; (5) fabulized combination, or Fabcom; (6) contamination, or Contam; and (7) inappropriate logic, or Alog. The subcategory deviant verbalization is further subdivided into neologism and redundancy, and the subcategory deviant response is also subdivided into inappropriate responses and circumstantial responses. The confabulation response is included with perseveration in the category preservation and integrative failures. Exner (1986a) attempted also to provide a rationale for grouping these scores into conceptual categories according to a common underlying process. For example, incongruous combinations, fabulized combinations, and contaminations are all considered "inappropriate combinations" that consist of "condensation(s) of impressions and/or ideas into responses that violate realistic considerations" (p. 163).

In an attempt to integrate several of Exner's empirically based special scores with a greater conceptual understanding based on psychoanalytic formulations regarding the processes underlying the scores, Kleiger and Peebles-Kleiger (1993) suggested slight modifications to several of the special score categories.

Their first suggestion involved separating the three types of deviant response scores (inappropriate phrases and two subtypes of circumstantial responses) into different conceptual categories in order to capture the unique interpretive meaning of each. Within their new schema, inappropriate phrases, an instance of intrusive thoughts and derailment, are considered similar to Rapaport's "queer verbalizations"; one type of circumstantial response, personalized associations, is considered reflective of an egocentric approach to the test; and the other type of circumstantial response, the overly elaborate embellishment, is considered a form of confabulation.

The second suggestion involved refinements to the confabulation category. Unfortunately and confusingly, Rapaport included two very different types of responses in his category confabulation. One type involved overly elaborated, affect-drenched responses in which the embellishments could not be justified by the stimulus characteristics of the blot. The second type included responses in which one small detail served as the basis for an inaccurate perceptual impression of the entire blot (i.e., "This is a snout, therefore it is a pig"). Kleiger and Peebles-Kleiger suggest that the designation confabulation be used only for the overly embellished response, and, as in other scoring systems, the second type of response be scored and regarded as a DW response.

The authors' third recommendation involved first placing the more narrowly defined confabulation response on a continuum of varying degrees of elaboration, and then viewing the different degrees of embellishment in terms of perceptual accuracy (form level). Herein, they develop a 2 by 3 table in which two levels of embellishment (moderate and severe) are judged in terms of three levels of perceptual accuracy (ordinary, weak, and minus). The table developed by Kleiger and Peebles-Kleiger is reproduced herein (see Table 9-1).

Leichtman (1996), as part of his attempt to reconceptualize the Rorschach task as one of representation, contends that certain of the deviant responses may be viewed from the perspective of Werner and Kaplan's (1963) model of the symbol situation. As indicated in chapter 2, the symbol situation consists of four major components: two persons (i.e., the addressor and the addressee); the object of reference (i.e., the referent); and the symbolic vehicle. From this vantage point, certain disturbances (DW response) are viewed in terms of quality of

Table 9-1 Possible Diagnostic Implications of Different Levels of Excessive Embellishment

Form Level	Severity of Excessive Embellishment	
	Tendency	Extreme
Plus/ordinary (+/o)	Hypervigilant narcissism	Paranoid style
Unusual/weak (u)	Borderline	Delusional disorder
Minus (−)	Manic psychosis	Manic psychosis
	Schizoaffective	Schizoaffective
	Schizophrenia	

From Kleiger and Peebles-Kleiger, 1993, p. 86

referent, whereas others, such as fabulized combinations, incongruous combinations, contaminations, and confabulations, are considered disturbances in the coordination of vehicle and referent.

The addressor-addressee dimension of the symbol situation serves to remind us that Rorschach testing takes place in an interpersonal context. This means that deviant responses not only indicate disturbances in thinking and perceiving, but that such responses and how they are delivered also reflect matters of social judgment, capacity or willingness to censor, and how the testee experiences himself or herself and others.

Beginning with Rapaport, these responses have come to be considered indications of disturbances in thinking. In accord with the more recent work of Leichtman (1996) and Athey (1986), and in line with the major thrust of this book, I believe that these types of responses may be conceived of more broadly as reflecting the ways in which an individual experiences the world and as determining how self and others are represented. In regarding these responses as experiential modes, I attempt to encompass their perceptual, cognitive, and representational aspects.

I agree fully with Kleiger and Peebles-Kleiger (1993) that taking a sign approach to this data is highly insufficient. Instead, from a clinical perspective, one needs to study each of these responses, empathically and analytically, with the intent of understanding the underlying psychological process.

Then too, each time such a response appears on a record it should be viewed in terms of several contexts. One context, an interpersonal one, is the patient–examiner relationship. A second context is defined by the response itself, including such dimensions as form level, determinants used, location, content, and the testee's attitude toward the response. A third context is that of the entire protocol. Here, one considers where the responses appear in a record, along with the preceding responses and subsequent ones. Also, findings from the entire record can be used to enrich and deepen inferences drawn specifically from these responses.

In what follows, I group these responses in terms of a common underlying process. These groupings are not considered to be totally independent. For example, although confabulations and fabulized combinations are grouped separately, fabulized combinations, as Leichtman (1996) has pointed out, involve a confabulatory element. I then briefly discuss the major and most common responses.

Fabulations and Confabulations

Using the more restricted definition of confabulation as an overly embellished, affect-laden response, fabulations and confabulations are grouped together because both involve a subjective elaboration of the percept beyond the stimulus properties of the blot. As such, they reflect varying degrees of distance or departure from the perceptual reality of the card.

In fabulized responses there is a slight degree of departure, and this typically is not at the expense of perceptual accuracy. Indeed, in some instances the elaborations provide a better perceptual fit. As noted in the previous chapter, the fabulized response may be regarded as an indicator of the richness of an individual's fantasy life. The tendency to embellish, as reflected in the fabulized response, may also express an openness to different types of experiences and a capacity to relax tight controls and strict adherence to reality.

With the confabulation response, however, a line is crossed. Here, there is "an increase of distance from the card, so extreme, that one can no longer see any justification for the specificity and affect-loading; the intermediate steps in the associative-perceptual interplay are no longer apparent" (Holt, 1968, pp. 433–434). As Leichtman (1996) explains, in more severe instances the blot is "little more than a launching pad for flights of imagination" (p. 282). In these responses, the real properties of the blot are disregarded and replaced by fantasies and affects.

Athey (1974) has observed a parallel process in these individuals' object relations. He describes their object relations as "unalloyed affect-laden fantasy relationships" (p. 423), meaning that their relationships are affect-drenched and based more on fantasy than on reality. Leichtman (1996) extends this by pointing out that confabulatory responses may also reflect how individuals experience themselves and others. For instance, individuals who produce confabulatory responses on the Rorschach often see others on the basis of their own needs, fantasies, and projections, rather than on the basis of qualities and characteristics inherent to that other person. In treatment, a 32-year-old, single seamstress, whose Rorschach included three confabulatory responses, insisted that her physically abusive father was kind and loving. Only later in treatment could she acknowledge and accept her own need to have a kind and loving father and that these qualities that she had attributed to him were actually located within her.

Incongruous Combinations, Fabulized Combinations, Contaminations

These three types of responses are grouped together because each, in Exner's (1993) terms, represents an "inappropriate combination" (p. 168). They are responses in which the relationships seen and expressed between images, objects, or activities violate realistic considerations.

In the incongruous combination, blot details are inappropriately combined into a single object (e.g., "A woman with a duck's head"). Exner distinguishes two levels of incongruous combinations to indicate that such responses vary in the degree to which reality is transgressed.

Leichtman (1996) found that incongruously combined responses appear in the Rorschach protocols of young children in the transition from Stage II to Stage III. He understands the response as reflecting the child's difficulty in negotiating two competing realities—perceptual reality and conceptual reality—and of the child deciding upon perceptual reality. With adults, something altogether different occurs. As implied in Rapaport's concept "loss of distance," the individual loses perspective and takes the blot, in Holt's (1968) words, "as an immutable reality, with its own affective and logical propensities" (p. 429). In the process, ego functions, such as reality testing and judgment, are relinquished or lost.

Like incongruous combinations, in fabulized combinations there is also an unrealistic relationship; here, however, the relationship is drawn between two separate and discrete percepts (e.g., "two roosters hanging onto a space ship"). The relationship is illogical and is based upon temporal or spacial contiguity. These responses also vary in degree of severity and bizarreness.

Leichtman contends that there is a confabulatory quality in these responses, that they issue from a "fantasy-laden, reality-distorting thought process" (p. 282). I believe, differently from Leichtman, that these responses also reflect a "loss of distance" from the cards, in which the blots are taken too seriously. I would add, however, that the conceptual element Leichtman identifies involves a propensity to see relationships, be they realistic or unrealistic (relational thinking). This has clinical significance in that one of the elements of paranoid thinking is a strong tendency to see and draw relationships. In addition, one also sees in this response a loss of perspective and an abandonment of judgment.

It is unanimously agreed that contaminations are the most primitive and pathological of the inappropriate combinations. Such a response appears in protocols rarely; however, when it does occur it may be taken as a reliable indicator of psychosis. With the contamination, "the boundaries of concepts once formed are so fluid that separate abstractions from the same area cannot remain independent side by side, but fuse into a single idea. The final concept that integrates these two impressions represents a pathological increase of distance from the card, as well as from reality" (Holt, 1968, p. 437).

The fluidity and condensation of concepts seen in the individual's thinking forecasts and is paralleled by similar occurrences in the object-relations realm. According to Athey (1974):

> In his object relations the patient condenses fantasy shifts with changes in the reality of the relationship. As a result, the awareness of the other person becomes more dim and eventually the patient condenses the changing events in the relationship completely with alterations in his subjective state, resulting finally in alterations of only the experience of himself [p. 424].

Importantly, Leichtman (1996) rarely found contaminations in the Rorschach records of young children. He suggests that contaminations represent a disintegration of higher, more complex levels of thinking that children have not yet achieved. From his developmental perspective he regards the contamination as reflective of "syncretistic modes of experience in which visual forms, language, and concepts are intermixed and in which distinctions between self and objects collapse" (p. 284).

In sum, there is a consensus among theorists that contaminations reflect a way of experiencing in which there is a collapse in various structures, including conceptual, spatial, relational, linguistic, and a loss of self-other differentiations.

DW Response

In keeping with the recommendation offered by Kleiger and Peebles-Kleiger (1993), those responses Rapaport regarded as confabulations, in which the individual overgeneralizes from a detail to the whole, I treat as DW responses. Holt (1968) reports that these responses are quite rare and appear only in the records of schizophrenic patients.

In these responses, the level of perceptual accuracy is usually weak or arbitrary, the associative content is offered uncritically, and there appears to be some confusion between parts and wholes. Because the detail used is salient at the moment and is not well integrated, Leichtman concludes that such responses indicate an experiential mode that is labile and diffuse.

Inappropriate Logic, Queer Verbalizations, Peculiar Verbalizations, Fluidity

These scores are grouped together because they reflect disturbances in logic and language. They appear on a record in the ways in which the testee communicates his or her response or justifies and explains it during inquiry. Beyond their diagnostic import, these scores also are reminders to the examiner of the need to record responses as verbatim as possible, and during interpretation, to review a protocol response by response.

"Inappropriate logic," a term coined by Exner (1993), corresponds closely to Rapaport's earlier term "autistic logic." Both refer to instances when the testee reasons out his or her response with a type of logic that bears little relationship to reality or to conventional standards of reasoning. For example, with Card X turned upside down, the testee responds, "The south pole because of the shape and it is at the bottom." Here, there is a loss of distance from the card, in that a spatial relationship is taken for reality, the reasoning is strained and arbitrary, and the conclusion arrived at is farfetched. Such lapses in logic are typically regarded as indicators of a basic disturbance in thought processes. Exner (1993) views this score as an indicator of "loose thinking," Rapaport et al. (1945–1946) as an expression of "autistic thinking," and Leichtman (1996) as a reflection of a "collapse of the structures of logical thought."

In the verbalizations designated "queer" and "peculiar," the object of study is the verbalization itself, rather than the percept or the reasoning used to justify the percept. For Rapaport and colleagues (1945–1946), these two types of verbalizations differ in degree rather than kind. Whereas the score "peculiar" was used to denote verbalizations that could, outside of the testing situation, pass as conventional and acceptable, the ones scored "queer" could not. Kleiger and Peebles-Kleiger (1993) have pointed out that Exner's (1993) subcategory "inappropriate phrases" is similar to Rapaport's score "queer verbalization."

Rapaport and colleagues viewed these verbalizations through the lense of a pathological increase or distance from the blots. Although I find Rapaport's notion of increase or distance from the blot helpful in understanding the other types of deviant responses (e.g., confabulations, contaminations), when applied to queer and perculiar verbalizations, it seems overly broad and nonspecific. For example, verbalizations warranting either score may reflect the impact of an intrusive thought, a tendency to become lost in detail, an egocentric use of language, an unwitting attempt to confuse the examiner. Therefore, I regard these scores as signals directing the examiner to pay particular attention to the verbalization, with the intent of attempting to understand its unique meaning and the more specific underlying process it reflects.

I use the score "fluidity" to designate a series of verbalizations in which the individual expresses a sense of changing images. The examiner's own sense is that the change is occurring in the immediacy as the patient is struggling to fashion a percept. More than tentativeness, indecision, or an excessive striving for accuracy, here the emphasis is upon fleeting and shifting impressions. One patient conveyed the experience this way: "This is the profile of an angry person, no, now it looks like a coast line. As I look at it further, it's changing into a devil." Although three different impressions are presented, not one is held onto and developed fully, and one senses that the change is occurring in the moment, virtually in front of the patient's eyes. The fluidity is similar to the process Rapaport and colleagues (1945–1946) describe as preceding the delivery of a contamination: in this instance, however, the individual stops short of fusing the different ideas.

It is my understanding that such verbalizations are a direct expression of the individual's subjective experience. This is to say, these individuals experience both their inner and outer worlds as in an unending state of flux, so there is little stability and a marked absence of constancy.

✦ ✦ ✦ Conclusion

In this chapter I have reviewed the major scores that comprise Rapaport's fifth scoring category. These scores have been demonstrated to be especially useful to the clincian in evaluating disturbances in thinking, identifying ego weaknesses, and forecasting regressive tendencies. Viewing thought disorder as a unitary dimension and understanding it quantitatively is insufficient. Although these indices vary in level of severity, it is important to bear in mind that they reflect different underlying processes.

10

SPECIFIC SCORES AND THEIR MEANING

Although the determinant scores are based upon the basic dimensions outlined in the previous chapter, there are select scores that I have found especially useful and a rich source of data for drawing inferences. My understanding of these scores derives from clinical observation, the existent and growing Rorschach literature, more recent research, and newer formulations arising from psychoanalytic theory. In particular, Kohut's (1971, 1977) notions regarding the cohesive self, Winnicott's (1965) sensitively evocative concept of the "false self," Modell's (1975) careful description of narcissistic defenses, and Leichtman's (1996) development perspective on the Rorschach are all woven into the ensuing discussion.

◆ ◆ ◆ Fc Response

The Fc score was first identified by Binder (1933) as one of the two types of shading responses and was later incorporated by Rapaport into his scoring system. The score is given to those responses in which variations in shading are used like form to delineate and articulate the percept. For example, the testee might see a face in a heavily shaded area and then use the nuances of shading to outline the eyes, nose, mouth, and hairline. These variations in shading are subtle; therefore, to achieve a Fc response one must seek out, discover, and attune to fine nuances, as well as feel one's way into something potentially danger-ous and not readily apparent. To do this requires perceptual sensitiv-ity in addition to a searching, penetrating, and articulating type of activity. Schachtel (1966) has referred to this mode as a perceptual atti-tude "of a stretching out of feelers in order to explore nuances" (p. 251). Although such an attitude of heightened sensitivity and penetrating activity can reflect and underlie an adaptive capacity for achieving highly differentiated responses, attuning to subtleties of feeling, and empathizing with the nuances of another's experience, it can also go awry. We are all familiar with persons who have their antennae out, as it were, to feel out an assumedly hostile, cold, and unfriendly envi-ronment. In such persons, one observes a constant state of hypervigi-lance, heightened sensitivity, and excessive vulnerability.

In a large subgroup of narcissistic patients, I have found this state of unremitting hypervigilance, defensive sensitivity, and excessive vul-nerability to be related to an identifiable self-system, mode of object relatedness, defensive structure, manner of experiencing affects, line of cognitive regression, and manner of entering treatment.

Before these features are described in greater detail, it should be noted that, like Gabbard (1989), I believe the narcissistic personality disturbance can be conceptualized as occurring on a continuum between two extremes. At one end of the continuum is the more hypervigilant, vulnerable, narcissistic patient, characterized by a heightened sensitivity to the reactions of others, a tendency toward shyness and self-effacement, a painful self-consciousness, and a vul-nerability to feelings of shame and humiliation. At the other end of the continuum is what Gabbard refers to as the "oblivious narcissist." These individuals, by contrast, tend to be self-absorbed, arrogant, haughty, impervious to the needs and feelings of others, and exploitive in their relationships. Whereas the hypervigilant patient corresponds closely to those narcissistic patients described by Kohut (1971), the oblivious narcissist closely approximates the narcissistic patient described by Kernberg (1975). For a more detailed discussion of this conceptualization of narcissistic disturbances, refer to chapter 24. The patients described in the following paragraphs correspond to the hypervigilant type.

The hypervigilant narcissistic patient presents a passive attitude toward the environment, with an unspoken willingness to be influenced. Their vigilance and sensitivity, like radar, constantly scan the outer milieu in search of potential dangers or cues to guide and direct their desires, values, and behaviors. Like chameleons, they sensitively attune to the expectations of others and mold themselves and their behavior accordingly. This sensitivity and ready accommodation, however, is defensive and in the service of warding off threats to a rather fragile self-esteem. In this regard they differ from the "as if" character (Deutsch, 1942), whose compliance and imitative behavior are related more to a search for identity. The hypervigilant narcissist has attained a sense of identity but feels it must be kept private and hidden. Nonetheless, the accommodating is without investment; consequently, the other is left with a sense that something is amiss. In like manner, the patients themselves are painfully and helplessly aware of their compliance and are left feeling ungenuine and despairing. Intimately related to the compliance is a presentation of fragility and vulnerability. The fragility is disarming, for one quickly senses that the wrong word, the forgotten act, or the slightest hint of disapproval will strain an already strained relationship to a point beyond repair. Thus, relationships are tenuous and fleeting.

The affective life of the hypervigilant narcissist is characterized by feelings of low self-esteem, a particular type of anxiety, and an empty form of depression. Reich (1960) has suggested that because of the archaic nature of their ego ideal, these patients are especially prone to continuous feelings of low self-regard and little sense of self-worth. Their anxiety is similar to what Tolpin and Kohut (1978) refer to as "disintegration anxiety," meaning an intense fear associated with the potential loss of self. Associated with the anxiety is a subjectively experienced tension state that, when felt as intolerable, initiates a series of ego maneuvers directed toward lowering this state (Easser, 1974). The depressive affect of these patients is distinctive and involves unbearable feelings of deadness and nonexistence and a self-perception of emptiness, aloneness, and hopelessness.

Hypervigilance and hypersensitivity are used to ward off affects, especially those feelings that could lead to greater closeness and intimacy (Easser, 1974). With an increase in tension, minor forms of acting out become prominent, and if these escape outlets are cut off, then withdrawal, compliance, and suspiciousness ensue. There is a marked tendency to use projective identification.

These patients also reveal a particular line of cognitive regression.

They have a tendency to lapse into concrete, stimulus-bound thinking in which there is a loss of perspective. That is, there is a nearsighted clarity with an attendant loss of the backdrop.

As Easser (1974) has noted, these patients begin treatment under a cloak of vigilance, with a readiness to be distrustful. They are there, but with one foot out the door, so to speak. Upon beginning treatment, a rapid and at times massive regression occurs, involving feelings of terror and panic, outbursts of affect toward the therapist, and a rush of activity directed away from the treatment, but laden with meaning in regard to it. Easser offered an example of such activity involving a 20-year-old male who, upon agreeing to psychoanalysis, took out a large life insurance policy. In keeping with the hypersensitivity, all aspects of the therapist came under careful scrutiny. If the therapist recalled an incident or experience mentioned several sessions before, or responded in a particularly empathic way, the patient felt held together and considered the therapist an ally. If the therapist canceled a session, however, or responded with a trace of irritation in his voice, then the patient reacted with pain and regarded the therapist as hostile, distant, and uncaring.

The therapist's experience with the hypervigilant narcissistic patient is one of being viewed under a microscope. Not only is every movement of the therapist closely monitored, but his or her comments are carefully scrutinized and regarded as evidence to weigh before allowing the relationship to continue and possible deepen. This stance evokes a countervigilance and hypercaution on the part of the therapist. Realizing that interpretations will be met with an overreaction and taken as an attack, the therapist finds himself or herself less spontaneous, less relaxed, and more careful with his or her interventions.

The patient's heightened attunement to visual, gestural, and emotional aspects of the therapist may be likened to the young infant's early experience with the mother. Because of this reenactment, one can reconstruct that earlier experience. Genetically, the perception of emotional tones and of tension by the young child precedes the learning of language and the understanding of spoken content (Schachtel, 1966). It develops from the infant's perception of his or her own sense of comfort or discomfort with the mother, including her moods and tensions. As development progresses, with "good enough" mothering (Winnicott, 1960), attention to the obvious and to verbal content gradually overshadows the need for perceiving finer visual and emotional nuances of the outer world. In the absence of such mothering, this transition is tenuous and incomplete. While several authors (Kohut, 1971; Winnicott,

1960) have pointed to a defect in empathy in these mothers, I have been equally impressed with the extent and depth of their depression and how this has interfered with their capacity to freely and continuously attend and minister to their infants, as well as allow their offspring to fully separate.

The following case may be taken as representative of the type of patient who offers the Fc response. The patient, a 38-year-old divorcée and mother of three, produced a 24-response Rorschach protocol in which 4 of her responses were scored Fc. She was referred for treatment by her family physician amid a depressive episode precipitated by a psychiatric resident who had confronted her with his belief that she was psychosomatic. She took his comment as a severe moral condemnation, and soon thereafter became highly self-punitive and self-reproachful, felt inordinately ashamed, and was convinced, more than ever, that she was basically "bad."

Following her divorce some eight years earlier, she worked as an office manager for two years and then took a leave of absence because of a host of disabling symptoms, including vertigo, headaches, nausea, intense pain throughout her body, and continuous feelings of tiredness and depletion. At times her symptoms reached the point that she would be confined in bed for up to a week. While positive findings had been reported on various lab tests, a definitive diagnosis was not established because of the inconsistency of results. Lupus and encephalitis were considered but not conclusively substantiated.

Most vivid in her early memories was her sense of the family home. She recalled the house as grey, dingy, often in need of repair, and a place to which she felt embarrassed to bring friends. Her father, a real estate broker, suffered from a severe alcohol problem. Although he worked without interruption, on weekends, she recalled, he repeatedly drank himself into a stupor. Her mother worked full-time as a bookkeeper. With shame and disgust, she reported how each morning her mother would awake for work, eat breakfast, and then become nauseous and vomit until it was time to leave for work. Because both parents worked, the patient was expected to perform numerous household tasks. In general, she felt her parents robbed her of her childhood and that from an early age she was expected to mother her mother and ask for little caretaking in return.

During the two-week hiatus between the end of the psychological testing and the beginning of her analysis, and in anticipation of treatment, the patient devoted considerable time and effort to the preparation of a log that chronicled, in meticulous detail, the array of events and experiences in her life. She then began her analysis and spent each session of the next nine months reading from her log. Overtly, the patient appeared to be complying completely with the demands of the analytic situation, yet her analyst felt quite the opposite. He felt trapped and controlled by her behavior. On one hand, he felt like an ignored bystander, watching his patient conduct her own analysis; on the other hand, he also felt like a captive audience, continually being monitored (by the patient's hypervigilance) to ensure that his attention did not wander. Beneath the feeling of being controlled, the analyst also experienced himself and the treatment as a protective container into which the patient was pouring the hardships life had visited upon her.

◆ ◆ ◆ Variants of the Fc Score

Whereas Rapaport used the designation F(C), I use the designations FCc, CFc, and Cc to denote the use of shading in colored areas. Rapaport considered the response as indicating both a freer affective display and a mingling of anxiety with more highly charged affect. Mayman, according to Appelbaum (1975), attributed a similar meaning to this response as I have to the Fc score; namely, it may indicate an adaptive capacity for empathy or a thin-skinnedness and vulnerability to feel too much.

The meaning of the FCc response is not entirely clear. Nonetheless, it does suggest something unusual, such as affective responsiveness triggering hypervigilance. In any event, there is a line of research (Appelbaum and Holtzman, 1962; Appelbaum and Colson, 1968) which has found this score to be related to suicidal tendencies. Appelbaum and Holtzman offer a sensitive description of the experiential state of individuals who give these responses; however, they do not articulate precipitating motives or circumstances that might lead such individuals to attempt suicide. Among these patients I have found that precipitates leading to suicide typically relate to the nature of their self-experience and the quality of their object relations. More specifically, experiences that prompt fear of the loss of a sense of self, that involve a dramatic or cumulative loss in self-esteem, and that deny a yearned-for symbiotic attachment with a lost object are the types of events that trigger suicidal thoughts or behavior.

Finally, P. Lerner and H. Lerner (1980) found that the Fc determinant, when combined with the Dr location score (rare detail) and possessing content involving distorted part or full human forms, was a reliable and valid measure of projective identification. Lerner and Lerner reasoned that involved both in projective identification and in this combination of scores there is a sense of the environment as dangerous, an attempt to defensively empathize with the sources of danger, and a reliance on such preverbal modalities as putting parts of oneself into another in order to communicate with and control the other.

◆ ◆ ◆ Form–Color Arbitrary (FCarb) Response

The FCarb score is reserved for responses in which the use of color is obviously incompatible with the content (e.g., blue monkeys, pink beavers), but the testee clings to its arbitrary inclusion. Rapaport and colleagues (1945–1946) discussed the response as indicative of difficulties with integrating affects into one's mental life. While I agree with this formulation, I also find it narrow and overly restrictive. In reexamining this response, especially in light of the writings of Winnicott (1960), I believe the score also reflects compliance, cognitive passivity marked by a loss of perspective, fears of loss of selfhood, and the developmental of a particular defensive structure—the false self.

The FCarb score as an expression of compliance has been noted by Schachtel (1966). He suggests that one gets

> the impression that the testee had felt it incumbent on him to include the color in his response even though no natural combination occurred. . . . The color is not experienced as particularly striking or stimulating but it is noticed and then endowed by the testee with the same exaggerated demand quality that he attributes to the whole test situation [p. 181].

In addition to compliance, the response also involves a relinquishment of parts of the self (i.e., judgment, knowledge) and an acceptance as real of something the testee knows to be unreal. This aspect of the score touches on Winnicott's (1960) discussion of the relationship between self-development and symbol formation. According to Winnicott, with the mother's repeated success in greeting the infant's spontaneous gestures, experiences become imbued with realness, and an inchoate capacity to use symbols begins. Here Winnicott envisions two possible lines of development. In the first, with "good enough" mothering and empathic responsiveness to spontaneous gestures, reality is introduced almost magically and does not clash with the infant's omnipotence. With a belief in reality, omnipotence can be gradually relinquished: "The true self has a spontaneity, and this has been joined up with the world's events" (p. 146). An illusion of omnipotent creating and controlling can be enjoyed, and the illusory element can be gradually recognized through play and imagination. The basis for the symbol, then, is both the infant's spontaneity and the created and cathected external object. That is, symbol formation evolves from actions and sensations joining the infant and the mother. Conversely, when the infant's actions and sensations serve to separate rather than join subject and object, symbol formation is inhibited. In this second line of development, which involves mothering that is "not good enough," the mother's adaptation to the infant's spontaneous gestures is deficient, and symbol formation either fails to develop or "becomes broken up" (p. 147). In this case, the infant reacts to environmental demands *passively*, through imitation and with accompanying feelings of *unreality*. The passivity and the feelings of unreality observed by Winnicott are quite similar to what Rapaport conceptualized as a loss of ego autonomy with a resultant enslavement to environmental stimuli. Whereas Rapaport would conceive of this condition in terms of the ego and drive forces, and Winnicott in terms of the self and inner experience, what both theorists appear to be describing is a state of affairs in which the development of selfhood has been critically interfered with and in which the individual is therefore unable to maintain distance from the environment.

The color arbitrary response also reflects a loss of perspective and reflectiveness. It is as if in fashioning such a response the testee has suspended a more objective, critical, and judgmental attitude. For individuals in whom there is a loss of perspective, life events are not critically examined or placed in context, but rather are seen and experienced only in terms of their most obvious and immediate qualities. The present dominates and the significance of the past and of the future fades.

Involved in the color arbitrary response, then, is compliance, a relinquishment of parts of the self, cognitive passivity marked by a loss of perspective, and nagging feelings of unreality. These same processes that underlie the color arbitrary score are also involved in the "false self."

Winnicott (1965) conceived of the false self as a defensive structure, aimed at hiding and protecting the true self by means of compliance with external demands. Its origins are found in the infant's seduction into a compliant relationship with a nonempathic mother. When a mother substitutes something of herself for the infant's spontaneous gestures (e.g., her anxieties over separation in response to the infant's need to search and explore), the infant experiences traumatic disruptions of his developing sense of self. When such impingements are a core feature of the mother-child relationship, the infant will attempt to defend himself by developing a second reactive personality organization—the false self. The false self vigilantly monitors and adapts to the conscious and unconscious needs of the mother, and in so doing provides a protective exterior behind which the true self is afforded the privacy it requires to maintain its integrity. The false self, as such, thus becomes a core feature of the personality organization and functions as a caretaker, managing life so that an inner self might not experience the threat of annihilation resulting from excessive pressure on it to develop according to another's needs.

False-self features were especially prominent in the following case. A 37-year-old, married and childless woman was referred for an assessment and treatment following a relatively brief period of hospitalization. One month previously she had an intense and acute depressive episode, involving feelings of depersonalization and frightening suicidal ideation. Although the patient had been moderately depressed for several years, this acute episode followed a heated confrontation with her husband, in which he admitted his unwillingness to have a child but then refused to discuss the issue further. She experienced his reluctance as banishing her to a life of emptiness and meaninglessness.

The third oldest of four children, the patient described her childhood in terms of hardships, sufferings, and unhappiness, emphasizing her sense of herself as a large, ugly child, her sense of being saddled by family responsibilities, and her overriding fear of her father's violence.

She had graduated from teachers' college and accepted a position in a small community, teaching learning-disabled children. Although an accomplished and well-regarded teacher, she experienced her work as demanding and depleting. Unable to tolerate aloneness, she dated constantly but felt that male interest in her was exclusively sexual. In her sixth year of teaching she began to see her husband-to-be. He was a married, successful businessman, 23 years her senior, with three adolescent youngsters. They saw each other on a regular basis for several years, and in contrast to her previous relationships, she felt loved and

not used by him and genuinely loving toward him. One year following his wife's death from cancer, at his insistence, they were married.

She perceived her marriage as a new start in life and went about
disclaiming and disowning previous aspects of her life. Despite valu-
ing her job, she stopped working, converted to her husband's religion,
and broke off contact with old friends, electing instead to move
entirely into her husband's circle of relationships. In essence, she
attempted to forge a new identity, one totally different from and independent of her past.

Throughout the five years of marriage she found herself becoming
progressively more depressed and increasingly dissatisfied with her
husband. As her earlier feelings of loneliness returned, she experienced
a rekindling of her desire to have a baby and conceived of having a
child as her one salvation in life. As noted previously, her husband's
grudging refusal to have a child precipitated her hospitalization.

Psychological testing revealed a depressive personality organized
at a high borderline level. Her Rorschach consisted of 22 responses, 4
of which involved color. Of her 4 color responses, two were scored
FCarb—on Card III "a falling red monkey" and on Card VIII "a torn,
blue butterfly." In addition to the FCarb scores, and further to the
inferred false-self features, she identified the animals on Card VIII as
"chameleons," saw a "baby bear in hibernation," and reported on
Card IX, "two eyes peering out from behind a bush."

The opening phase of treatment was dominated by her depressive
affect and her unrelenting preoccupation with having a baby. Without
a baby or the hope of having one, she felt that life was meaningless,
she was worthless, and suicide was a viable alternative.

In time, the patient's depressiveness began to abate and give way
to more focused anger and disappointment with her husband.
Mobilized by the anger, she could then introduce changes into her life,
including the decision to pursue further training in music. Despite these
gains and her greater sense of control over his life, her singular insistence with having a baby persisted.

Seventeen months into treatment, an assignment in one of her
music classes had a profound impact on treatment and highlighted the
pervasiveness of her false self. She was asked to select an old photo
with important personal meaning and then compose a series of musi-
cal pieces that conveyed that meaning. She chose a photo of herself,
taken when she was four, in which she was sitting contentedly in a
rocking chair and gazing affectionately at a favorite doll. She brought
the photo to several sessions. While recalling earlier experiences and

feelings prompted by the picture, she mentioned, without affect and almost in passing, that when she was 21 years old, during her first year of teaching, she had a baby out of wedlock and soon after delivery had given the baby up for adoption.

As that experience was reviewed in depth it became clear that the loss, both of the baby and of parts of herself related to the baby, was intimately connected with her later preoccupation with wanting a child. Specific to the false self was the patient's need to maintain in privacy and not entrust to her therapist an intimate and meaningful experience—a part of her true self, if you will—that was dynamically related to her present behavior.

❖ ❖ ❖ Inanimate Movement Score (m)

An additional score I have found quite useful, especially as a reflection of subjectively felt distress, is the m score.

Piotrowski (1947) described the score as representing a role in life the testee desired but experienced as unattainable because of external difficulties and internal inhibitions. Piotrowski further suggested that the score reflects self-observation, intelligence, and an unwillingness to relinquish or alter goals originating in an earlier period of development. Piotrowski's interpretation of the m score comes from the high number of such responses he found in the test records of a group of immigrant professionals from Europe who were unable to pursue their careers in the United States. He reasoned that if their aspirations could have been realized and not blocked, they would have produced human movement responses (M) rather than inanimate movement responses (m).

Klopfer and Kelley (1942) attributed a very different meaning to the m score. They assert that the score expressed inner promptings that are experienced by the individual as dangerous and uncontrollable. Despite apparent differences as to the feeling tone of the urges, both authors agree that the response expresses drives that the subject feels incapable of doing anything about. Schachtel (1966) refers to this experiential state as that of the "impotent spectator."

An especially astute description of the m response, and one in keeping with my own clinical observations, is found in the work of Mayman (1977). According to Mayman, kinesthetic memories that contain core experiences of selfhood find their way into all movement responses, including inanimate movement. Although most tension states expressed in animate and inanimate movement are neither unfamiliar nor alien, there are some that are infantile, archaic, and linked to impulses that normally would be fully repressed. Of all the movement responses, the m score expresses those tensions that are the least ego syntonic. Thus, for Mayman (1977), "the little m is a metaphoric expression of forces which seem impersonal, not subject to personal control. These forces intrude on the self, they come at one from outside" (p. 240).

Viewing the m response as reflective of a failure in repression, with the unrepressed impulse spilling over into awareness in the form of subjective tension, has much inferential meaning. Because the testee offering the response to some degree feels out of control, he or she typically is accessible to therapeutic intervention. Further, contact with the individual's subjective experience can often be established around these feelings of inner tension; however, this needs to be done cautiously and tactfully so the individual does not feel even more out of control. The content within which the inanimate movement response is included usually reflects the sense of failing defenses or else depicts the nature of the impulse with which the individual struggles. Thus, there are references to "collapsing," "coming apart," and "breaking apart," which express faltering controls, and such responses as "dripping blood," "exploding flames," and "erupting lava," which may be taken as indicative of difficulties with aggression.

◆ ◆ ◆   Reflection and Mirror Responses

Although I have not included these types of responses under formal scoring, the reflection and mirror responses (e.g., a bear seeing its reflection in the water, a woman standing in front of a mirror) are an important source of information. With the increased attention accorded both the concept of narcissism and the narcissistic patient, Rorschach theorists are looking to these responses as expressions of some aspect of narcissism.

Exner (1993) discovered the reflection response somewhat by accident. In a study designated to investigate "acting out," it was noted that "psychopaths" offered a significantly greater number of reflection responses than did psychiatric subjects or nonpsychiatric subjects. Exner initially linked the response to narcissism, but subsequently to egocentricity, and included it as part of an index for assessing egocentricity. The index, which consists of the proportion of reflection and pair responses to the total number of responses, was found to relate to intense self-absorption and either overly high or excessively low self-esteem (Exner, Wylie, and Bryant, 1974).

Hilsenroth et al. (1996) recently investigated the efficacy of four Rorschach indices, including both the reflection response and Exner's egocentricity index, in identifying expressions of pathological narcissism. Two of these variables, the reflection response and a measure of idealization (P. Lerner and H. Lerner, 1980), proved especially effective in differentiating pathologically narcissistic patients from a nonclinical sample as well as from cluster A (paranoid, schizoid, schizotypal) and cluster C (avoidant, dependent, obsessive-compulsive, passive aggressive) personality disorders. In addition, the reflection response was found to be related to several DSM-IV diagnostic criteria for narcissistic personality disorder, including fantasies of unlimited success, sense of entitlement, a grandiose sense of self importance, and arrogant/haughty behavior.

Psychoanalytic authors (Urist, 1977; Smith, 1980; Kwawer, 1980; Coonerty, 1986; Ipp 1986; H. Lerner, 1988) have conceptualized reflection and mirroring responses as indicating a relatively early stage of relatedness, in which the other exists as an extension of the self for the sole intent of confirming and enhancing the self. The importance of this type of mirroring, particularly during the later symbiotic phase—a time in which the infant begins to differentiate self and object representations—has been stressed by Mahler et al. (1975).

These two conceptions of the reflection and mirror responses are conceptually compatible and represent the two sides—the self side and the object-relations side—of the narcissistic coin. Freud (1914) was the first to note the intimate relationship between level of self-esteem and nature of object relation. It is well documented that patients with compelling needs to be confirmed and validated, who relate themselves to others on a narcissistic basis, tend to establish in treatment what Kohut (1971) refers to as a "mirroring transference."

Research would suggest that the mirror response does tap into the narcissistic realm; however, whether that aspect is need, self-absorption, defensive grandiosity, narcissistic relating, or a combination of each, is not clear. Therefore, in evaluating these responses, two admonishments given by Gacono and Meloy (1994) should be heeded. First, rather than approach reflection responses with a fixed, global interpretive hypothesis with regard to meaning, it is preferable to hold in mind various meanings and to use the context within which the response is embedded (e.g., structural features, sequence, content) to determine specific meaning. Second, these authors further aver that the appearance of one reflection response, although not common, is not in itself pathonomic. Such single responses need to be evaluated within the framework of the entire protocol.

◆ ◆ ◆ Symmetry Reactions

Not to be confused with the reflection responses are those remarks directed toward the symmetry of the blots. These are not responses per se, but simply comments in which the testee expresses his or her attunement to the symmetry. In this instance, symmetry may be viewed as part of an overall feeling regarding a sense of balance or imbalance in the card. Noting symmetry introduces a sense of balance, but it is a premature balance. Possibilities generated by the imbalance or by providing balance through the response (e.g., the movement response) are excluded. Therefore, individuals who comment about the symmetry tend to have an excessive need for external order and clarity, struggle with ambiguity and unfamiliarity, and are characterologically inhibited and restricted.

A 29-year-old account executive with an MBA applied for a position as head of the advertising department in a newly formed electronics company. The position required an individual with much creativity who could work in a relatively unstructured situation. In part because of the testee's continued attunement to the symmetry of the cards and his concomitant tendency to become hypercritical unless he found perfect forms, the examiner questioned his having the requisite capacities for the position. The examiner further questioned as to whether he would be comfortable and satisfied in such a position.

◆ ◆ ◆ Perspective Reactions

On occasion, patients in describing a percept will introduce the notion of a perspective in which they assume a particular position in relation to their percept. Examples include the following: "Oh my goodness, what an ugly creature. He's standing over me and I'm looking up at him"; "From above, it looks like a bat in flight"; "An insect being looked at from a top view." In some instances, such as Card IV, introducing perspective makes for a better-fitting response; it accounts for slight incongruities and minor distortions in the stimulus. More often, however, it is my observation that perspective indicates a defensive maneuver and an object-relational stance. Thus, individuals who view their percepts from above tend not only to maintain others at a distance, but do so by placing themselves above others. Conversely, those patients who view their percepts from below tend to demean and degrade themselves and place themselves in a lesser, subservient position.

◆ ◆ ◆ Summary

In this chapter I have reviewed select scores and their meaning. The scores were selected because of their relevance to more recent formulations and concepts issuing from psychoanalytic theory. In addition to specific scores, I also discussed the testee's reaction to the symmetry of the cards and the introduction of perspective to a response.

11

THE ANALYSIS
OF CONTENT

There is no area of Rorschach analysis that has been more misused and more underused than content. For too many years Rorschach interpretation meant the interpretation of content, and so-called content analysis consisted of a poorly trained, beleaguered examiner who unsystematically offered his or her own associations to the patient's responses and then regarded the personal associations as meaningful inferences. The resultant testing report would thus consist of a series of loose-fitting, internally inconsistent impressions, presented as facts, from which one could not disentangle the examiner's preferences, values, and dynamics from those of the patient. Members of the academic and scientific communities, already distrustful of and antagonistic toward the Rorschach test, seized upon these practices and pronounced the instrument unreliable, invalid, and lacking in scientific respectability.

In an attempt to restore respectability to the Rorschach test, many theorists and investigators tended to shy away from assessing content of responses. With the Rorschach test viewed as an instrument best suited to assess formal variables (e.g., scores, ratios), content was either ignored or approached exclusively in terms of categories that could be scored. This counterreaction too was unfortunate. The content categories are important; their usefulness, however, is limited because they are abstractions that are a step removed from the response and the person offering the response.

To exclude content altogether, in the service of psychometric refinement, is to ignore an immensely rich and valuable source of information. Even though more structural approaches to the Rorschach test have clearly proven their mettle, this does not mean that the Rorschach test cannot be viewed from an experiential perspective too.

The rationale for a more experiential perspective has been well stated by Mayman (1977):

> When a person is asked to spend an hour immersing himself in a field of impressions where amorphousness prevails and where strange and even alien forms may appear, he will set in motion a reparative process the aim of which is to replace formlessness with reminders of the palpable real world. He primes himself to recall, recapture, reconstitute his world as he knows it, with people, animals and things which fit most naturally into the ingrained expectancies which he has learned to structure his phenomenal world [p. 17].

Schachtel (1966) has also written of the experiential dimensions of the Rorschach test; because of his interest in perception, however, he focused his attention exclusively on the various stimulus properties of the cards (color, form, wholeness of the card). To assess not only the structure but also the substance of the testee's phenomenological world, as Mayman has elucidated, requires a consideration of the content of the responses.

I was especially impressed with the potential richness of content as a vehicle for expressing meaningful experiential themes when I had the opportunity to review a set of Rorschach protocols obtained from a group of individuals who had immigrated to North America within the past five years. Although they had emigrated from various countries and represented different personality makeups, striking among this nonpatient group was a compelling need to create and then find in the blots images and percepts that conveyed a sense of familiarity. For this group, familiarity involved offering percepts that were clearly and explicitly linked to their country of origin. Representative responses included the following: "I can see the roof of a church like the church I attended as a child back home in Poland"; "A leaf I remember from Vietnam that has been eaten by some insect. It still has its basic shape"; "Back home in Pakistan I saw a volcano. This reminds me of the volcano and the lava is coming out."

A review of the structural qualities of these percepts (i.e., roof of a church, a leaf, a volcano) and their respective location indicates that each was of acceptable form level and that each, in part, was prompted by the particular configuration of the stimulus. Yet, to judge from the nature of the elaborations and embellishments, something of a more personal meaning and significance was also at play, and this added feature found expression in the contents of the responses.

If content is to be considered as a basic source of information and a viable springboard for the inferential process—and if we hope to avoid the plaguing misuses and abuses of the past—then it is imperative that it is approached in a thoughtful and systematic way. With content data, issues of reliability and validity cannot be disregarded; nonetheless, such issues need not exclude or minimize the clinical richness of the material.

Clearly, a middle path is needed, and groundwork for such a path is to be found in the work of Mayman (1977). Respecting empathic intuitiveness as a valid source of information, and insisting on theoretical soundness, Mayman has outlined a more systematic approach to content that combines an appreciation of the fruitfulness of the data with general principles of validity that fit the clinical situation. As noted in chapter 4, he has proposed a conceptual structure consisting of five dimensions, including content, for evaluating the human movement response. Three of these dimensions or components—the contribution of fantasy, kinesthesia and its relation to self experience, and object representation—can be extended to the content of nonmovement responses as well.

In addition to Mayman's contributions, a review of such well-established research scales as those of Holt (1977) and Blatt and associates (1976), as well as more recent ones, including those of Kwawer (1980), P. Lerner and H. Lerner (1980), Coonerty (1986), and Ipp (1986), reveals that investigators have employed content indices to operationalize more abstract and elusive theoretical concepts. Interestingly, these newer scales have been devised, in general, with the intent of investigating more experiential concepts. That content rather than formal scores has been used suggests that many theorists are viewing content as an especially sensitive expression of experiential themes.

The approach to content I outline here involves an integration of Mayman's work with that of the various researchers mentioned above.

More specifically, I use Mayman's three dimensions (noted earlier) as an organizational framework within which I place particular content indices that were found useful in research. I do not suggest that the research scales or even the specific indices be used for clinical testing; rather, I suggest that a familiarity with ways in which various contents have been conceptualized and used in the research literature provide the clinical tester with a way to think about content and to approach its analysis.

Inferences drawn from all Rorschach data essentially are tentative hypotheses that require validation and verification. The criteria applied to inferences drawn from content are no different from those applied to all other inferences; it is important, however, that the criteria be applied stringently. In the final section of this chapter I review rules of validity to be applied to test inferences, including those inferences derived from an analysis of content.

❖ ❖ ❖   General Guidelines

1. Although the content categories do yield important information, a complete analysis of content involves systematically scrutinizing a protocol, response by response. In using content, the entire verbalization, not just the response proper, constitutes the basic data; therefore, content analysis is particularly dependent on obtaining as complete a verbatim transcript as possible.

2. A particularly rich source of data and a useful place to begin content analysis are the elaborations and specifications added to a response that are not intrinsic to the blot. Such embellished responses are potentially rich with meaning. Exner (1996), making use of critical bits theory, arrived at a similar conclusion. He points out, "that some personal attributions will be manifest in any answer that is not conventional, including unusual as well as minus responses, plus conventional answers that have been embellished in ways that exceeds the distal properties of the stimulus field" (p. 476).

3. Content analysis calls for a complementary approach to interpretation to augment a more traditional structural approach. I refer to this approach as "experiential" to emphasize that it is more subjective and phenomenological, and is based upon the examiner's empathy. Both approaches to interpretation, the structural and the experiential, are discussed more fully in chapter 13.

4. A useful concept to hold in mind when approaching content analysis is "internal object relation." Increasingly, psychoanalytic theorists are emphasizing the distinction between internalized object relations and relations between the self and the objects in the external world. As implied in the term, an internal object relation refers to the inner representation of a relationship that had once existed in the outer world. While internal object relations derive from the internalization of early object relations, they exert, in turn, a considerable influence on current object relations. An internal object relation has three components: a self representation, a representation of the object (object representation), and a representation of the interaction between the two.

◆ ◆ ◆ Mayman's Three Dimensions Applied to All Contents

Contribution of Fantasy

Whereas the movement response requires the availability of a fantasy life one can dip into to help enliven the response, movement is not the only response that draws upon fantasy. Certain form responses can be equally rich, vivid, compelling, and lively. Common to these responses is a prevailing tendency to embellish a percept with affective and associative elaboration.

Embellished responses are potentially laden with meaning. For many people they reflect an interest and investment in the task, a willingness to go beyond merely what is called for. As well, in the embellishment or added specification something of dynamic importance for the subject is often being expressed. For example, to see the popular bat on Card V as a "huge vampire bat in full flight ready to descend upon a helpless victim" compellingly hints at significant trends in the personality.

While the content, as illustrated in this example, may be charged with personal meaning and should be understood and interpreted on an individual basis, Schachtel (1966) identified specific elaborations that he found to have more general application. He takes references to size (e.g., "large," "enormous," "tiny") as reflective of the testee's own sense of importance and power, to aggressive content as indicative of a desire to inflict, or a fear of, hurt and injury, and to solidness or fragility as suggestive of the individual's integrity of self.

The tendency to embellish responses may also express an openness to different types of experiences, a capacity to relax tight controls and strict adherence to reality, and a freedom to indulge in what Freud (1900) referred to as "primary process thinking." Holt's (1977) manual for assessing primary process manifestations and their controls is an excellent guide for conceptualizing and organizing particular contents. Holt outlines and details content reflective of and referable to the various stages of psychosexual development, draws important distinctions among various forms of aggression based on specific contents, and elaborates specific defensive operations inferable solely from content.

A descriptive overview of Holt's scoring system is presented here. I am not suggesting that Holt's scale—or even the specific indices—should be used for clinical testing; rather, I am suggesting that a familiarity with the ways in which Holt has conceptualized various contents can provide the clinical tester with a way of thinking about and approaching content analysis.

Holt's (1977) Measure of Primary Process Manifestations

Holt's system calls for the scoring of four sets of variables: content indices of primary process, formal indices of primary process, indices of control and defense, and overall ratings.

The content part of the manual is concerned with drive representations. A major distinction is drawn between responses reflecting drives with implied libidinal wishes and those with aggressive aims. The libidinal category is further subdivided into subcategories corresponding to the stages of psychosexual development. The aggressive category, which includes responses with hostile or destructive ideation, is likewise subdivided; these subcategories are established on the basis of whether it is the subject (aggressor), the object (victim), or the result (aftermath) that is emphasized in the destructive action or process mentioned in the response.

Cutting across the libidinal-aggressive division is a distinction representing two degrees of closeness to the primary process pole. Level 1 is accorded those responses that are primitive, blatantly drive-dominated, socially unacceptable, and focal to a drive-relevant organ. Responses reflecting a more civilized, contained, or socially acceptable content constitute level 2 responses.

The following categories from Holt's (1977) manual rely exclusively on content and are presented with representative examples.

Libidinal Content

Level 1 (crude, direct, primitive)

Oral receptive—mouth, breasts, sucking, famine

Oral aggressive—teeth, cannibalism, biting, parasites

Anal—buttocks, feces, hemorrhoids

Sexual—sexual organs, ejaculation, intercourse

Exhibitionistic-voyeuristic—nudity, exhibiting

Sexual ambiguity—same-sex kissing, person with breasts and a penis

Level 2 (indirect, controlled, socialized)

Oral receptive—stomach, kissing, drinking, drunks, food

Oral aggressive—animals feared because of their biting (crabs, spiders, alligators); verbal aggression (arguing)

Anal—intestines, toilet, disgust, dirt

Sexual—kissing, romance, sexual organs of flowers

Exhibitionistic-voyeuristic—undergarments, leering, peering, observing, prancing

Sexual ambiguity—transvestism, cross dressing

Aggressive Content

Level 1 (murderous or clearly sadomasochistic aggression)

Attack (sadistic aggression)—vivid sadistic fantasies, annihilation of person or animals, torture

Victim of aggression (masochistic)—extreme victimization, extreme helplessness, suicide

Results of aggression (aftermath)—decayed, putrefied, mutilated elements; catastrophe

Level 2 (more socially tolerated hostility or aggression)

Attack—explosions, fighting, fire, frightening figures, weapons, claws

Victim of aggression—person or animal in pain or wounded, frightened persons or animals, figures or objects in precarious balance

Results of aggression—injured or deformed persons or animals, parts missing, blood, aftermath of storms or fires

A second part of the scoring system in which content is evaluated is the section on control and defense. Holt conceptualizes these scores as indices of the manner in which primary process is managed. Here, what is important is not only the response, but also the way in which the response is delivered and any evaluative comments surrounding the response.

Remoteness

Remoteness conveys the notion of distancing. In this system the scores are considered ways of distancing impulses or wishes; a close look at the categories, however, would suggest that they also reflect a tendency to distance one's objects.

Ethnic	The figure seen is depicted as part of an ethnic group different from that of the testee (e.g., "Russian dancers," "Japanese wrestlers").
Geography	The figure seen is depicted as coming from a different and distant location (e.g., "African women," "a space man from Mars").
Time	The figure seen is distanced by placing him or her in the past or in the future (e.g., "A man from the 21st century," "a court jester").
Depiction	The main figure seen is depicted as in a painting, drawing, or sculpture (e.g., "a bust of two little girls," "a cartoon drawing of two men").

Context

The context or setting in which the response is presented is scored. The context seems to involve the subject's attempt to account for the primary process aspects of the response.

Cultural	The response is placed in the context of a ritual, custom, mythology, or other social reality (e.g., "naked women dancing who are performing a tribal ritual," "a man covered in black and red; he's a circus performer").
Intellectual	With the inclusion of scientific, professional, or technical facts or knowledge, the response has a strong intellectual flavor (e.g., "a dissection of the spinal cord," "a slightly inflamed tonsil").
Humorous	Some elaborations serve to place the response in a humorous or fanciful context (e.g., "Insects

at a convention," "two people with both male and female parts—I suppose a reunion of hermaphrodites").

Miscellaneous Defenses

Negation	This involves a denial of an impulse and is manifested in two ways. In one, the disavowal is smoothly blended into the response (e.g., "virgin," "angel") whereas in the other the response, or aspects of the response, are couched in negative terms (e.g., "two animals, but they are not dangerous," "these figures are not angry").
Minimization	Here, drive-laden material is included in the response, but in a reduced or nonthreatening way. This includes changing a human or animal figure into a caricature or cartoon figure (e.g., "the fist of a child," "a caricature of a man with a gun," "a cartoon lion").
Repudiation	A response is given and then retracted, or the individual denies having ever given the response (e.g., "Two angry people; no, no, wait a moment, they aren't angry but concerned").

Kinesthesia and Its Relation to Self-Experience

A second aspect of the movement response identified by Mayman yet applicable to a broad array of responses is kinesthesia, or the action component of a response. For Mayman, those kinesthesias that find their way into a movement response are drawn from a repertoire of kinesthetic memories, and involved in these memories are core self-experiences.

I believe that all kinesthesias on a record, not simply those expressed in human movement, are a potentially rich source of information and may provide clues to vital self-experiences, including subjective feelings of selfhood and of object relating.

In a recently obtained Rorschach record the following kinesthesias appeared: "pieces broken apart," "hanging on to," "split in the middle," "torn skin," "ripping away," "hands up," "struggling," "mouths open," and "still attached." A careful analysis of these kinesthesias indicates that they fall into two distinct clusters. One cluster (i.e., the first four kinesthesias listed), which convey a feeling state of heightened inner tension, painful distress, and excruciating discomfort, may be understood as reflecting a subjective sense of self that is experienced as split, torn, and fragmented. The other cluster (the last five kinesthesias listed) appears more object relational and seems to express a more oral mode of relating that involves issues of dependency, clinging, and symbiosis.

Several investigators, independently of Mayman, have recently devised content-based developmental object-relations scales and have employed specific kinesthesias, as expressed in all responses, to indicate stages in the unfolding of selfhood through differentiation from a primary mothering figure. In general, these scales represent attempts to systematically apply Mahler's (1968) theory of separation/individuation to Rorschach data.

To study early disturbances in the object relations of borderline patients, Kwawer (1980) developed a scale consisting of various points that represent early stages of levels of relatedness. An initial stage, which he calls "narcissistic mirroring," is represented by responses in which mirrors or reflections play a prominent role. Responses at this level are understood as expressing a state of self-absorption in which the other is experienced solely as an extension of the self and used for the exclusive purpose of mirroring or enhancing the self. A second stage, entitled "symbiotic merger," is represented by responses that indicate a powerful push toward merger, fusion, and reuniting (e.g., "Two women, like Siamese twins, *attached* to each other."). A third stage of interpersonal differentiation includes "separation and division" responses. The Rorschach imagery here is reminiscent of the sequence of cell division (e.g., "These two things were once connected but *broke apart*," "It's an animal going from one *dividing* into two. Like it's *breaking away* into two objects."). The fourth and final stage, "metamorphosis and transformation," is the level in which there is a very early and rudimentary sense of self. The incipient selfhood of this stage is manifest in such Rorschach responses as "fetuses" and "embryos" and in themes of transformation and change (e.g., "a caterpillar *turning* into a butterfly").

Another example of the creative use of kinesthesias to reflect levels of selfhood and object relating is represented in the work of Coonerty (1986). Using Mahler's descriptions as guidelines, Coonerty devised a measure for identifying and categorizing Rorschach responses that reflect concerns and issues associated with the prestage of separation and with each of the subphases of the separation/individuation process proper. Rather than review Coonerty's scale in its entirety, I will detail here only those indices that involve kinesthesias.

For Coonerty, concerns arising from the "early differentiation subphase" are reflected in Rorschach imagery of merging (e.g., "These are two girls, but they seem to be joined at the bottom"), engulfment (e.g., "A person, but he's being enveloped by the fog), and hatching (e.g., "a genie coming out of a bottle").

Responses indicative of rapprochement issues include figures, human or animal, that are seen in one of the following types of struggles: separating or coming together with resulting damage to one or both (e.g., "A person drowning with her hand up. This person is trying to save her but will be pulled under."), engaged in a push-pull struggle (e.g., "Two dogs facing each other but pointing in opposite directions"), and enmeshed or stuck and unable to separate (e.g., "Two rats stuck in the mud and they can't get their feet free."). Responses in which the form of the figure changes (e.g., "Two people talking, no, they look more like monkeys playing") are also indicative of rapproachement issues.

Ipp (1986) developed a scale, based on the earlier work of Urist (1977), for assessing the capacity to experience and conceive of one's self within one's own world and in relation to significant internal objects. The scale consists of five major categories and two subcategories; of particular relevance to this discussion of the use of kinesthesias is her category "catastrophic disintegration." Belonging in this category are responses in which there is a sense of annihilation by external forces greater than the self. Inanimate movement and strong agitation generally accompany these percepts (e.g., "planets exploding," "a swirling tornado destroying everything in its path").

Object Representation

A third component of the movement response, according to Mayman, is the figure carrying out the action, the object-representational aspect. This component too can be applied to all contents; when extended to nonhuman contents, however, such as animals or natural forces, one has to take into account the type of content used to express the internal object relation. For example, seeing an antagonistic or hostile relationship between two insects reflects a type of interaction; beyond this, however, it also reflects a quality and level of representation.

Understanding the nature of the interaction (e.g., antagonistic, competitive, helpful) is usually straightforward and can be inferred directly from the response. It is far more difficult and complex, however, to determine those characteristics referable to the self-representation and those to the object representation.

The following example illustrates this problem. On Card III the individual saw "A fragile, bent-over woman who had just been slapped around by a male space creature with the head of a bird." The interaction here can be characterized as sadomasochistic. If in this percept, however, the testee's self-representation is the "woman," then one could conjecture that the individual's sense of self involves being vulnerable, abused, defenseless, and at the mercy of others who are seen as hurtful, alienated, and less than fully human. On the other hand, if the self is represented in the "male space creature," then one might suggest that the testee sees himself or herself as estranged, harmful, and monstrous, and others as weak, helpless, vulnerable victims.

In distinguishing self-representations from object representations, the following may be used. Interactions seen on the Rorschach may involve helping, attacking, carrying. Correspondingly, one of the figures is seen as the helper, the attacker, the carrier; whereas the other is perceived as the one being helped, attacked, or carried. This is to say, cutting across these interactions and most others is a passive-active dimension. Determining if the testee tends to assume the passive or active role can be gleaned from his or her total test behavior, including other test responses and the nature of interaction with the examiner.

For instance, the patient who gave the above response ("fragile, bent over woman . . ."), in a variety of ways conveyed to the examiner that the tests made her feel "stupid" and "inept." Recognizing in her comments that the patient was presenting herself as a helpless victim and was placing the examiner in the role of the powerful victimizer, the examiner then inferred that in the Rorschach response the "woman" could be taken as a self-representation and the "male space creature" as a representation of the other.

Largely because of Mayman's (1967) pioneering attempts to apply the concept of object representation to Rorschach data, investigators have devised Rorschach measures aimed at evaluating personality variables theoretically related to object representation. Here again, these researchers have tended to look at content.

Representative of this line of research is the work of P. Lerner and

H. Lerner (1980) on the assessment of primitive defenses. Basing their work on the theoretical formulations of Kernberg (1975, 1976), Lerner and Lerner developed a scoring manual designated to evaluate the primitive defenses of the borderline patient. Their system calls for the human figure in a Rorschach response, either static or in motion, being evaluated in terms of the action ascribed, the way in which the figure is described, and the precise figure seen. Several of the defenses were operationalized exclusively in terms of content indices, and those will be reviewed here.

One defense defined in content-related terms is splitting. Because splitting involves a variety of separations, including a division of drives, affects, and object representations, Lerner and Lerner viewed the tendency to describe human figures in polar opposite ways as the Rorschach manifestation of this defense. Thus, the following are taken as Rorschach expressions of splitting: describing parts of a human figure in opposite terms (e.g., "A giant, his lower part is dangerous but his top part, his head, is benign"); including in a response two figures described in opposite ways (e.g., "Two figures. He's mean and shouting at her. She's angelic and just standing there and taking it"); and either tarnishing an implicitly idealized figure (e.g., "a headless angel") or enhancing an implicitly devalued one (e.g., "a devil with a warm smile").

A second defense indicated by and reflected in content is devaluation. This refers to a tendency to depreciate, tarnish, or lessen the importance of one's inner and outer objects. In assessing the Rorschach manifestation of this defense, three aspects of the human figure response are evaluated. The first involves the degree to which the humanness of the figure is retained. For example, waiters or clowns are considered more human than monsters, mythological figures, or robots. A second dimension involves a temporal-spacial consideration. Contemporary human percepts set in a current and close locale are scored higher than are those figures from either the past or the future and placed in a distant setting. The final aspect of a human figure response involves the severity of depreciation as conveyed in the affective description. Figures described in more primitive, blatant, socially unacceptable ways are scored lower than are those that are described in negatively tinged, but more civilized and socially acceptable ways.

To evaluate the use of the defense of idealization in a human figure response, the same dimensions used to assess devaluation are applied. In this instance, however, the investigators were concerned with the ways in which subjects enhanced or exalted their human figures. For example, distortion of human forms under the influence of this defense would involve seeing such enhanced figures as warriors, kings, or famous leaders (e.g., "Winston Churchill"). Similarly, affective descriptions are judged as to the degree to which the figure is inflated (e.g., "nice people," "the strongest warrior imaginable").

Although the scale developed by Lerner and Lerner was confined to an evaluation of the human figure, the criteria devised have been extended to all content by Cooper and Arnow (1986) and Collins (1983).

✦ ✦ ✦ Validity

Due to past abuse, it is especially important that inferences derived from content be subjected to considerations of validity. This is a thorny and challenging task. First, those standards of validity that are applied must fit and be consistent with the complexity and richness of the clinical situation. Second, inferences derived from content vary in their depth and in the degree to which they are removed from the actual test data; therefore, these inferences, particularly in contrast to those derived from the structural variables, pose special problems.

Weiner (1977) began to address these issued by drawing a useful distinction between two different types of interpretation of Rorschach data—representative and symbolic. In representative interpretation, Rorschach behavior is considered a sample or a direct representation of the actual behavior that the tester is attempting to assess or predict. There is a close tie between test behavior and actual behavior with minimal intermediate steps. In contrast, there is not a close tie in symbolic interpretation. In this instance, Rorschach responses are regarded as symbolic clues to the behavior under study and there is a chain of inferences that connect the interpretation with the test behavior. Concerning the latter, Weiner (1977) cogently argued "that a Rorschach interpretation based on multiple sequential inferences is subject to error at each step in the inferential process" (pp. 603–604).

At first glance, interpretations derived from content seem more closely to approximate symbolic interpretations. However, this is not necessarily the case. For example, Mayman (1977) was quite explicit in pointing out that he regarded human figures on the Rorschach as a representative sample of the testee's inner object world. In this regard, he views content not symbolically, but experientially, that is, as a direct expression of the individual's experience. Indeed, he likens his approach to one of dealing with the manifest content of a dream and not the latent meaning. Here, then, interpretations derived from human content seem to come closer to what Weiner (1977) referred to as representative interpretations.

In any event, recognizing that content-based interpretations vary enormously, perhaps what is called for is an approach to validity in which representative and symbolic interpretations are regarded as endpoints on an interpretive continuum, with the underlying dimension being the extent to which the interpretation is removed from the raw test data, thereby requiring more inferential steps.

It is also important to keep in mind that interpretations derived from content, whether they are representative or symbolic, typically are rooted in theory. That is, one tends to approach content analysis, including the intermediate inferential steps, with a theory of personality and psychopathology that lies outside of the test itself. Because of this, and in contrast with a more empirical approach, one looks to construct validity rather than criterion-related validity. The challenge then, as Weiner (1977) pointed out,

> is to formulate the theoretical relationships that adequately link the personality characteristics being measured with the condition being assessed or the behavior being predicted. These theoretical relationships can then guide appropriate clinical and research applications of the Rorschach, and, as an advantage for validity studies, they can be examined for the extent to which the bridge they provide between a Rorschach protocol and some aspect of behavior is firmly anchored at both ends [p. 597].

Apart from Weiner's general overview of validity issues and a unique study by Mayman (1967) in which he examined the scientific credibility of a clinical-intuitive approach to projective test data, comparatively little has been written on standards of validity that may be applied to the interpretive process. A noteworthy exception is found in the work of Schafer (1954). Although written more than four decades ago, criteria outlined by Schafer for judging "adequacy of interpretation" continue to have current relevance. Here I review several of Schafer's criteria, when necessary, introducing modifications suggested in more recent discussions of validity.

Schafer's first criteria is that of *sufficient evidence*. Herein, he suggested that as an initial step the examiner draw as many reasonable implications from a response as possible, but that the ultimately accepted interpretations be based on the convergence of several lines of evidence. By implication, the more an inference stands out in isolation from the mass of other test findings, the more it should be regarded with caution and tentativeness. For Schafer, the starting point for an inference should be the basic Rorschach data: images, scores, attitudes, and behavior.

By sufficient evidence, what Schafer referred to is convergent validity. That is, the interpretation arises from the coming together of several different lines of evidence. I extend this criterion and suggest that with each inference, especially those included in the testing report, the examiner should be able to identify the test data that prompted the inference and also should be able to explicate each of the theoretical formulations (i.e., chains in the inference process) used in constructing and connecting inferences. In this way, and in keeping with Weiner's (1977) discussion of construct validity, others can then evaluate the theoretical bridge between the Rorschach response and the inferred personality process.

The criterion of sufficient and converging lines of evidence is illustrated in the following. To Card IV the patient responded, "Its marshmallow man. Get the sense of you being small and it being large. Can see the body and what looks like a head." The response was understood by the examiner as a self-representation indicating the patient's sense of lacking an inner core and as experiencing his or her self as lacking coherence, firmness, inner direction, and solidness. Consistent with his interpretation, the patient offered responses in a tentative and noncommittal manner, looked to the examiner for guidance as to what was permissible in the Rorschach situation (i.e., turning the card), frequently asked if others saw what he saw, empathized with and accommodated to the examiner's need to write everything down, and often apologized to the examiner for his imagined lack of productivity (a projection of his exaggerated ideals).

The next several criteria relate to the interplay between the inference and psychoanalytic theory and, as such, touch on the issues of construct validity and face validity.

A second criterion elaborated by Schafer involves *hierarchy*, attempting to hierarchically place the inference in the overall personality structure. This criterion assumes that the examiner is employing a theory of personality that embraces the concept of hierarchical layers. For example, sets of concepts such as "drive-defense," "id-ego-superego," and "unconscious-preconscious-conscious" all involve the notion of hierarchy. The concept of hierarchy forces and calls upon the examiner to integrate his or her inferences into a clinically meaningful whole. To integrate findings and inferences, one applies well-established dynamic principles. In essence, Schafer described a methodology whereby findings are linked by dynamic formulations to form inferences, and then the inferences themselves are interrelated, again by dynamic principles, to form yet higher order inferences. Ultimately, this progressive interrelating of inferences results in an internally consistent, theoretically grounded psychological portrait of the patient.

With each step a more complete, refined, and individualized picture emerges. Bearing in mind Weiner's (1977) cautionary note that an error may appear at any step in this inference process, I found that the emergent picture at each progressive level may be used as an overall yardstick to judge the validity of any one inference.

Schafer's third criterion relates to the issue of particularizing the inference to the individual patient. Employing the term *intensity* of the inferred trend, he reminded us that the trends we infer are widespread and often apply to the majority of the population. Therefore, to individualize and differentiate the patient from others, it is important to specify the intensity of the inferred characteristic for the particular person.

Indeed, the more specifically and clearly an inference is stated, the more readily its accuracy may be assessed. However, there is another issue related to validity here. One can individualize or particularize an inference in several ways. One way I found useful is to couch the inference in terms and in language that remain close to the patient's experience. For example, if a patient were to respond to Card I with "That looks like a damaged bat," and if I were to regard the response as a self-representation, then I would rather infer that "the patient senses himself as damaged," rather than infer that "the patient has been narcissistically injured." The more the inference is pitched at an experiential level and the less one uses abstract concepts, the closer the inference is to the representative end of the interpretive continuum and the less chance there is of error.

A fourth criterion involves specifying, whenever possible, *manifest expressions* of the interpretation: How is the interpretation likely to be expressed in overt behavior? This is a difficult criterion, for as Holt (1970) noted, personality assessment and predicting behavior are not synonymous. Whereas the latter calls for an evaluation of situational variables in addition to personality factors, situational variables typically are not assessed in personality assessment. Nonetheless, in clinical testing the examiner often is called upon to predict to other situations (e.g., capacity to benefit from treatment, likely reoccurrence of criminal behavior, school placement), and the more he or she is able to frame inferences with behavioral referrants, the more helpful his or her report is regarded. Furthermore, inferences couched with behavioral referrants are more readily verifiable.

◆ ◆ ◆ Conclusion

A relatively neglected area of Rorschach inquiry has been the analysis of content. Historically, content was unsystematically approached from the point of view of symbolism, and this led to gross misuses and a subsequent distrust of content. An exception is represented in the work of Holt (1977). Employing psychoanalytic theory, Holt viewed content as an ideational expression of a drive, an outcome of the interplay between wish and defense. Although Holt's manual for the assessment of primary process manifestations and their controls spawned a great deal of research, the system for clinical testing is overly time-consuming and unwieldy.

A second approach to content, based on newer and more experience-near models in psychoanalysis, is found in the work of Mayman (1977). Viewing content as a sampling of an individual's representational world, Mayman identified five components of the M response that provide a conceptual structure for assessing self-relational and object-relational experiences. Three of these dimensions—the contribution of fantasy, kinesthesia and its relation to self-experience, and object representation—can be fruitfully applied to all content without compromising theoretical underpinnings.

Coincident with Mayman's work is the recent emergence of several Rorschach scales that use content to operationalize more abstract concepts. The approach to content taken here involves an integration of Mayman's work with that of current research. More specifically, three of Mayman's dimensions are used as an organizational framework within which research-derived content indices are placed.

Issues of validity cannot be ignored: They must be approached in a way that recognizes the uniqueness of the clinical situation. Herein, several criteria elaborated on by Schafer (1954) were applied and extended.

12

THE ANALYSIS
OF SEQUENCE

Many of the chapters in this book represent significant revisions from earlier ones that appeared in my 1991 book *Psychoanalytic Theory and the Rorschach*. That is not the case regarding this chapter on sequence analysis. That this chapter remains almost the same speaks directly to the degree to which this area of Rorschach inquiry has been neglected in the Rorschach literature. Virtually all Rorschach theorists agree that sequence is a meaningful source of information, however, few have provided a systematic and comprehensive way of conceptualizing or using it. Sequence does not lend itself to the careful analysis that the scores do, nor is it as compelling as content.

Schachtel (1966) regards the sequence of responses as an especially important dimension, noting that it is the aspect of the Rorschach test that is most reflective of the individual's understanding and subjective definition of the task. He suggests that sequence reflects the testee's approach, or lack of it, to the test and that the approach is based on how the person experiences, comprehends, and feels about the task. Schachtel places sequence on a continuum of rigid versus loose and then infers the attitude underlying various points on the continuum.

For example, a more rigid approach—one in which the same sequence is employed on each card—could be indicative of an attitude of heightened conscientiousness and obedience, in which excessive authority is ascribed to the tests and the examiner and in which the testee submits to this assumed authority. This approach contrasts with a looser one, as indicated by several sequences. In this latter instance, one could infer that the testee ascribes less authority to the test and is then able to approach the material in a more flexible and self-directed manner. Schachtel also attempts to determine, through an analysis of sequence, the testee's typical or preferred approach. He then uses this as a base from which to judge deviations. Despite the potential richness of Schachtel's view of sequence, it should be noted that he defines sequence exclusively in terms of the location scores; thus, his perspective is somewhat limited.

Klopfer et al. (1954) and Exner (1993) refer to sequence analysis too, however, like Schachtel's, I find their discussions restrictive. Klopfer and colleagues suggest that sequence reflects the individual's reactions to the world. Although they point out that sequence analysis consists of a card-by-card, response-by-response examination, they, like Schachtel, emphasize formal properties to the relative neglect of thematic content. Exner (1993) includes the Sequence of Scores in his structural summary; however, as implied in the term, he too limits his analysis to the formal scores. Interpretively, Exner includes the sequence of location scores in assessing an individual's approach to information processing.

A broader approach to the analysis of sequence, one which includes an appraisal of Rorschach content, is found in the work of Schafer (1954). In what follows, I offer general considerations regarding sequence analyses, weaving together Schafer's observations with my own clinical experience.

◆ ◆ ◆ General Considerations

1. I agree with Klopfer that sequence analysis does involve an evaluation of the entire protocol, card-by-card and response-by-response; however, it should also include test attitudes and test behavior, as manifested in the complete verbalization and off-handed comments. Thus, sequence analysis, like other data sources, is dependent on recording the administration as verbatim as possible.

2. An appreciation of the stimulus properties of each card, together with an expectation of likely content to be offered to a particular card or to a specific area in a card, enhances sequence analysis. For example, certain blots (I, IV, V, VI) lend themselves to being perceived as a whole, whereas others (II, III, VII, VIII, IX, X) are more "broken" and invite being seen in a more piecemeal fashion. Schachtel suggests viewing the sequence of location scores as reflective of the testee's approach to the task. For example, if a testee maintains the same approach on every card, this could well indicate rigidity; by contrast, altering the approach to reflect the differing properties of the cards would indicate flexibility.

3. Sequence analysis is especially helpful for observing progressive and regressive shifts in personality organization, and these shifts can be reflected in formal scores, content, or a combination of both. Two models of psychopathology are presented in psychoanalytic theory. The older "conflict model" emphasized impulses pressing for discharge, defenses evoked, and the interplay between the two. The more recent "developmental arrest" or "structural deficit" model focuses on impairments in the personality structure as a consequence of faulty development. Herein, the individual is thought to be vulnerable to marked fluctuations and disruptions in personality functioning.

From the perspective of the conflict model, sequence analysis provides a unique opportunity for observing the appearance of conflict, ways in which the individual attempts to resolve that conflict, and the relative degree of success or failure in the resolution. For example, if on Card II the testee first sees "two bears fighting," then in the same area sees "two lambs grazing," and finally turns to the center white area and sees a "delta-winged jet plane," then one might infer that unacceptable aggressive urges are dealt with by reaction formation and regression and that such efforts are relatively successful. By contrast, were a subject to respond to the whole of Card II with "a damaged face with blood," offer several other percepts, and then say, "I just can't get that face out of my mind, it bothers me," one, in this instance, might infer ineffective defensive efforts and a failure of resolution.

In terms of the structural deficit model, sequence analysis allows the examiner a close-up view of fluctuations in functioning; to be noted are the experiences that disrupt functioning, the areas of personality affected, and the individual's ways of attempting to deal with the disruption. If, for example, on Card III a testee were to say, "It's two women arguing, yelling at each other, no, wait a second. It's one woman looking at herself in a mirror, she's yawning, just woke up," one might infer that the testee tends to see relationships as hostile and malevolent and, in reaction, withdraws and retreats into self-absorption and self-isolation. Or, on Card IX, were a female patient to see the bottom reddish area as a "dead fetus with its umbilical cord wrapped around its neck," and then offer subsequent responses in which the form level is significantly poor, then one might infer that under the impact of highly charged, affect-laden material with possibly personal meaning, the patient's reality testing suffers.

As noted, shifts in personality functioning are reflected in the formal scores, the content, or in the interaction between them. Schachtel (1966) has emphasized the sequence of location scores, whereas Klopfer and colleagues (1954) have called attention to the sequence of all the scores, especially the determinants (e.g., the sequential use of color). Of the various formal scores, I have found the sequence of form-level scores and the sequence of responses involving a deviant verbalization of particular usefulness. Examining shifts in form-level ratings assists the examiner in assessing not only reality testing considerations, but also the integrity of the defensive structure. Thus, a progressive lowering of form-level ratings on several cards would indicate increasingly poor reality testing as well as a basic failure in defensive efforts. In contrast, marked but more random fluctuations in form level within a card would suggest weaknesses in the defensive structure with alternations between regression and recovery. The persistent instability, rapid vacillations in moods, circumscribed regressive bouts, and variations in reality testing associated with the borderline patient are reflected in their fluctuating form-level scores.

Deviant verbalizations (e.g., fabulized combinations, confabulations) constitute a major departure from the reality of the inkblot; therefore, when one is offered, it is often informative to consider the preceding responses and the subsequent responses. Whereas the former may provide clues as to what factors provoked the deviant response, the latter often reveals the patient's capacity to rebound from such lapses.

Schafer (1954) has suggested that the sequential analysis of imagery, especially when it includes test attitudes, often reveals a continuity of a theme from one response to another. Using the metaphor of the dream, he notes that in the continuity of theme the testee tells a story of conflict and then of the resolution of that conflict. He also points out that the sequential analysis of content is particularly illuminating when it focuses on responses that are dramatic and dynamically transparent.

A 27-year-old female patient offered the following responses to Card I: "two women, one's back is to the other," "an ugly insect," "a mask, perhaps a Halloween mask," and "a mannequin in the center." Applying the concept of internal object relations to the sequence of responses suggests the following possible inference: In reaction to a disruptive relationship with her mother, in which she felt rejected, the patient developed low feelings of self-esteem. To protect her precarious esteem and not let others observe her lowered feelings, she hid behind a false self. The false self has left her feeling empty, on display, ready to be defined from outside, and less than a total person.

4. It is often useful to begin sequence analysis with those responses that the examiner finds somewhat jarring or out of place. In reviewing a protocol, an examiner might find himself or herself moved by or drawn to a response, either because of formal considerations or of content. Sudden drops in form level, the appearance of deviant verbalizations, the unexpected rejection of a card, the offering of a pure color response amid form-based responses, and excessively long reaction times are all examples of appropriate starting points based upon more formal features. With regard to content, I agree with Schafer that the sequential analysis of imagery may begin with those responses in which the content is especially dramatic and compelling and dynamically transparent.

5. Sequence analysis is particularly dependent on a theory of personality and psychopathology that extends beyond and lies outside of test theory. In sequence analysis, one is attempting essentially to draw a dynamic relationship between separate observations that are offered in a temporally continuous manner. In this sense, one is regarding the stream of responses much as one views free associations. The connection drawn between the discrete observations is an inference, a hypothesis if you will. I believe that unless the hypothesis is based on theory, it is little more than common sense or, worse, is a projection from the examiner.

6. As with content analysis, it is vitally important that stringent rules of validity be applied to sequence analysis. The topic of rules of validity is discussed at greater length in the following chapter on the inferential process; however, it is important to note here that when drawing inferences from the sequence of responses, the examiner must be prepared to identify the Rorschach data that prompted the formulation and the theoretical postulates being employed.

◆ ◆ ◆ Conclusion

There is no greater need in the clinical Rorschach literature than for a systematic approach to the analysis of the sequence and content of responses. At one extreme, both areas have been abused and have contributed to the offering of inferences that were little more than wild interpretations. At the other extreme, theorists have either avoided sequence analysis and the analysis of content or have approached each in a highly cautious and tentative way. I have attempted to steer a middle ground, noting that both are immensely rich sources of information, but also suggesting that rigorous rules of validity be applied. More so than other aspects of the Rorschach test, the sequence of responses may reveal the dynamic interplay between various facets of the personality organization. Meaningful therapeutic intervention depends on a comprehensive and accurate understanding of the patient, including an appreciation of the latent, inference-based dynamics underlying more observable behavior. In contrast with more structured, static, clinically removed personality inventories and instruments, the Rorschach test potentially can provide a unique glimpse of these underlying forces.

13

TWO APPROACHES
TO INTERPRETATION

1n this chapter I first describe two different yet complementary approaches to Rorschach interpretation. One I refer to as structural and the other as experiential. I then discuss the role of empathy in an experiential approach.

Test interpretation for most theorists, starting with Rorschach himself, begins with the question of how and why the test works. To unravel the nature of the Rorschach task, some authors focus on the test and ask, "What is the Rorschach a test of?" Others attune more to the testee, and they ask, "What are the steps and processes involved in fashioning a Rorschach response?" Regardless of starting point and emphasis, all recognize that the final product, the actual response, represents an interaction of the 10 cards and their stimulus properties with those internal processes that together comprise the response process.

The next step in the interpretive process consists of bridging the test response, including one's understanding of how the response came about, with personality structure and functioning. That is, as described in chapter 1, one attempts to identify the mediating processes connecting test responses, on the one hand, with behavior

191

and personality, and the dynamic underpinnings of personality, on the other hand.

The connecting bridge between test response and personality is almost always based on a combination of theory, clinical experience, and empirical findings. For instance, one may first observe an empirical relation between a particular type of response and a specific character trait, and then offer an explanation for that relation. The explanation, regardless of level or complexity, in this context is taken as an instance of theory; or one may begin with a theory, derive a hypothesis from the theory, and then use empirical findings to support, dismiss, or refine the hypothesis.

The bridges linking test responses with personality, depending on their complexity, are conventionally referred to as test rationales. Such test rationales go beyond simply positing a relation between a test response and personality trait; they also attempt to provide an understanding and justification for that relation. For example, it was on the basis that the Rorschach is a test of perception and that each of the major determinants represented different but basic experiential perceptual attitudes that Schachtel (1966) related color on the Rorschach to the affective experience.

It should be noted that there is a reciprocal and mutually dependent relationship between empirical findings and test rationales. For instance, if an examiner feels comfortable and secure relying on a fixed meaning for a particular score based solely on research findings, it becomes far more difficult to always experience anew whether such meaning really applies to the actual concrete response, or whether other, even more important meanings may apply. An example is the white-space response. It has long been held (and supported by research) that such a response indicates negativism and oppositional trends in the personality. Yet, using a rationale developed by Schachtel (1966), I found that in a select group of narcissistic patients, the space response (in Schachtel's terms, the attunement to white or hollow spaces) reflected subjective feelings of emptiness and inner hollowness, not just negativism. In the other direction, years of test misuse and heated controversy has taught us that test rationales cannot just rest upon theory and lore; they need to be supported by empirical findings as well.

This approach to interpretation, with its emphasis on test responses, the response process, and test rationales, is based on Rorschach's belief that his test could elicit conclusions about the individual's characteristic way of experiencing, but not about the content of the person's experience. As such, the approach has led theorists to focus primarily on the more formal or structural features of a test record—the scores and their interrelations.

As one reviews this approach, whether it is the work of Rapaport et al. (1945–1946) or Exner (1993), it becomes apparent that interpretations drawn from the structural features of a Rorschach record tend, themselves, to have a primarily structural emphasis. Exner's structural summary, for instance, includes sections on ideation and processing and indexes for depression and schizophrenia. In a like manner, a test report written from a Rapaportian perspective emphasizes character structure, thought organization, and affect organization. For both, the emphasis is on the structural make-up and workings of the personality.

◆ ◆ ◆ Experiential Approach and Empathy

With utmost regard for this more structural approach and with full recognition of the lasting contributions that have issued from it, I would, nonetheless, point out that it is not without limitations. There is more to a Rorschach protocol than the scores and determinants, and there is more to a person than can be explained from just a structural perspective.

As discussed in chapter 1, an entire Rorschach record, in addition to the formal elements, also includes the content of the response, the complete verbalization within which the response is embedded, spontaneous and evaluative expressions, and the multileveled vicissitudes of the patient–examiner relationship.

Following upon Schachtel (1966), and for clarity, I refer to these features as the experiential aspects of a record. I use the term *experiential* to suggest that these data, including the response, alert us to the more subjective meanings that a particular response, the entire test, or being assessed have for an individual.

Although firm rules, especially by Exner (1993), have been established for interpreting the formal elements, comparatively looser guidelines have been offered regarding the experiential data (P. Lerner, 1992). Yet, when students and practionioners alike sense that there is more to be derived from a record than they are able to, I believe that they are unwittingly referring to this experiential dimension.

This aspect of the test record does not lend itself to the more formal and objective analyses one brings to the scores. Instead, it calls for a different approach with a more phenomenological orientation, an essentially subjective frame of reference. At the center of such a phenomenological approach, I would suggest, is the examiner's empathy.

Within current-day psychoanalytic theory, empathy is viewed in various ways. It is conceptualized as an important quality of a caretaker, a core feature of the therapeutic action of treatment, a powerful bond between people, and an information-gathering activity. Kohut (1959), in particular, drew attention to empathy as a mode of observation and data collection. In his paper "Introspection, Empathy, and Psychoanalysis" he argued that access to psychological depths could be obtained only through specific modes of observation: introspection into one's own subjective state, vicarious introspection, and empathy into that of another. Herein, I will refer to empathy as both a way of relating to another and as a way of coming to know another.

It is especially, although not exclusively, with the experiential data that empathy as an information-gathering activity has a vital role to play. For interpretive purposes, with this test data the examiner attempts to empathize with the testee's experience as he or she was taking the test. The examiner uses the individual's entire production—the response and the accompanying verbalizations—as a jumping-off point for attuning to the underlying subjective state. Herein, the examiner asks, "To have arrived at this response and said these things, what might the patient have been experiencing at the moment?" The following examples illustrate this process.

Holding the card sideways, to the middle green area of Card IX (D1), a 50-year-old physician responded, "An older black woman, like Aunt Jemima, bent over a stove stirring a pot of homemade soup." During inquiry he added, "Her hair is short and wrapped with a bandana. She also is wearing an apron that is tied at the back."

The examiner noted the patient's brightness and active mind, his sensitive attunement to detail, and his tendency to humanize his world. Turning to the content of the response, the examiner, empathically and intuitively, suggested that the patient tended to see "a black woman as nourishing." At the time, the examiner had little idea of the poignancy of this more empathic inference.

The patient sought treatment because of longstanding depressive feelings and concerns. He suffered from chronic feelings of tiredness; derived little pleasure from his work or play; felt a "panel of glass" came between himself and others; and was preoccupied with fears of loss. He sensed he had lost something, but was vague as to whom or what.

Early in the second year of his subsequent treatment he began to recapture memories of Emma, a black nanny who had cared for him in his first three years of life. Soon after his third birthday, Emma had mysteriously disappeared. He was told she had moved and he had not been given the opportunity to say goodbye to her.

In time, it became clear to him and his therapist that Emma, not his mother, was his primary caregiver, that his vague sense of loss as an adult was rooted in his early loss of Emma as a child, and that the barrier he felt between himself and others originated in his early relationship with his mother. The mystery of Emma's disappearance was solved too. Emma had not moved, as he had originally been told. Rather, she was abruptly dismissed when his mother sensed that he preferred Emma to her. This occurrence is not uncommon in families in which the mother is not the primary caregiver (Hardin, 1985).

This case also illustrates that in certain instances the validity of an inference is not always knowable at the conclusion of the testing. It is my experience that inferences drawn from the experiential, data based upon the examiner's empathy, can be of such depth and subtlety that their richness and accuracy do not become evident till long after the testing.

A second patient responded to Card I, "It's a frog swimming away from me. Eyes in front, round body, and large legs in the back." Here, the examiner empathically attuned to where the patient positioned herself in relation to her "frog" response. On this basis, he inferred her sense of herself as rejected and left behind.

A third patient offered three complex responses to Card I, two of which required extensive inquiries. As testing progressed, the examiner found himself having to inquire less and less as the patient herself volunteered the necessary information as part of her initial response. For example, on Card IX she responded, "I see a flower, an iris. The entire card. This area is the petals, the color, and the tones within the color make it appear velvety."

On the basis of the patient's heightened attunement to what he, the examiner, needed, her unasked-for willingness to provide it, and his own diminishing role, the examiner empathically noted the patient's hypersensitivity to the needs and expectations of others, her ease in complying with these expectations, and her subtle movement toward self-sufficiency.

I have provided three quite different examples to illustrate how this more phenomenological orientation, with the examiner's empathy as the centerpiece, is applicable to not only the content of a response, but

to many other features too. It can be applied to all aspects of a protocol, including obscure ones such as where the patient places himself
or herself vis-à-vis the response (i.e., "looking down on storm clouds"),
peculiar ways of expressing a response (i.e., "this looks batty to me"),
or a patient's tendency to conduct his or her own inquiry.

In chapter 14, I outline five distinct steps that comprise the inference process—data gathering, quantitative analysis, first-order inferences, transformation, and report writing. It is at the first-order
inferences stage that this experiential approach to interpretation, based
on empathy, is particularly useful.

I describe this stage as one in which the examiner carefully and
painstakingly reviews all the quantitative analyses and the Rorschach
record as a whole. With the protocol, the examiner combs through it
response by response, score by score, and phrase by phrase. Whenever
a reasonable implication can be drawn, that implication is written
adjacent to the quantitative summary, actual response, phrase, and so
forth, so that the examiner can keep track of data source.

The drawing of inferences can be done in several different ways.
One may draw on research findings, one may rely on external observation, or, as suggested here, one can adopt a more internal vantage
point and attempt to understand, through empathy, the person's subjective experience.

Empathy as an information-gathering activity, and its place in the
interpretive process, as conceptualized here, occupies a middle ground
between what is regarded as "wild interpretation," on the one hand,
and exclusive empiricism, on the other. Unlike the former, there is little reliance on symbolism, one does not offer his or her own associations to the individual's response, and one attempts to remain as close
to the data as possible. Empathy, not association, is employed in trying to sample, feel, understand, and reconstruct the person's experience. In contrast with strict empiricism, this approach admits sources
of data that would otherwise be excluded and makes use of a way of
knowing (empathy) that is viewed with skepticism.

The middle-ground position being suggested here is very similar to
the position advanced regarding the analysis of Rorschach content.
Furthermore, inferences derived from this more phenomenological,
interpretive approach must be subjected to the same standards of validity applied to content analysis—converging lines of evidence, hierarchically placing the inference in the overall personality, particularizing
the inference to the individual, and translating the inference into overt
behavior.

With respect to these two approaches to interpretation, there are several cautions to be sounded. First, there may be a tendency to apply the structural approach to the formal features of a protocol and the experiential approach to the content of responses. This is not what I am suggesting; it oversimplifies matters. The approaches are mutual and intertwined. For instance, the experiential approach can and ought to be applied to structural data. Reciprocally, more objective and systematic methods of analysis are increasingly being applied to what at first were regarded as experiential data (i.e., Rapaport's peculiar and queer verbalizations, Exner's morbid score). As I indicated with sources of information, each of these interpretive approaches must be given its due and integrated with interpretations drawn from the other.

Second, the approaches are mutual and intertwined in another way. Inferences derived from each approach should be either complementary or confirming, and in both instances, theoretically consistent. In the example of the physician who saw "an older black woman," the interpretive approaches yielded complementary information. From a structural analysis, the examiner was able to confirm the longstanding and disruptive aspects of his depressive affect as well as confirm that his personality was organized at a neurotic level. The experiential approach permitted him to specify the depression in terms of a vulnerability to loss and to point in the direction of the original lost object.

Inferences derived from the protocol of the woman who conducted her own inquiry were also confirmatory. The hypersensitivity, compliance, and self-sufficiency derived experientially, were confirmed by the structural analysis, which in terms of several FCarb responses, suggested a false self-organization.

❖ ❖ ❖ Conclusion

In this chapter I have described two different yet complementary approaches to the interpretation of Rorschach data—a more traditional structural approach and a more clinical experiential approach. Because a structural approach tends to yield inferences that are primarily related to the structural aspects of personality, such an approach is necessary but not sufficient.

Just as there is more to a Rorschach record than scores and ratios, there is also far more to an individual than can be explained from an exclusively structural perspective. A structural perspective has little room for the experiential themes that run through an individual's life or the meanings that individual ascribes to events, both in the present and from the past. Virtually 40 years ago, Mayman (1976), in a letter to Rapaport, made a similar point. He put it this way:

> I find myself missing a discussion of the subjective concepts and propositions in psychoanalytic theory, concepts like pleasure, unplesure, self, ego state, estrangement, self-feeling, and ego boundary. One almost gets the impression that subjective concepts have no relation to metapsychology, or are only epiphenomena. . . . I think it would be well to make some place for subjective concepts in a comprehensive treatment of metapsychology, if for no other reason than they serve as important links with the realm of discourse of the patient in the consulting room [p. 205].

There is little question that a theory of personality that claims to be comprehensive, including psychoanalysis, needs to account for structures. Such a perspective, however, should not nor need not exclude other vantage points.

Others well before me, including Schachtel and Mayman, have argued for a more phenomenlogical, clinical approach to Rorschach data; I have attempted, however, to emphasize the pivotal role of the examiner's empathy. Empathy, as a way of coming to know another, not only safeguards against wild interpretation on the one hand, and unnecessary restraint on the other, it also prompts one to remain close to the patient's experience as expressed in primary test data.

14

THE INFERENCE
PROCESS

T he inferential process consists of
the various interpretive steps the examiner takes in transforming the
raw material from the Rorschach test (and other tests) into a complete,
well-organized, clinically meaningful, informative testing report. It is
the most difficult and challenging aspect of the testing, requiring that
the examiner have an understanding of test theory, personality theory,
and psychopathology. Theory and practice converge at this point. It is
important that the examiner develop for himself or herself a testing-
report outline with implicit subheadings that can serve as reference
points for organizing the welter of test data. One possible report format was presented in chapter 3 and will be applied in this chapter.

In general, the inference process has been neglected in the
Rorschach literature. Much has been written of interpretation, but little of the systematic integration of interpretations. Exner, according
to a 1988 personal communication, has developed a computerized
decision-making program that details the sequence of steps to be taken
in systematically interpreting a protocol; his program, however, is
based on statistical and psychometric considerations, in contrast to
the theoretical perspective taken here.

Inferences drawn from test data are, essentially, tentative hypotheses requiring validation and verification. Accordingly, in the following paragraphs I first briefly review rules of validity that are to be applied to test inferences. I then outline the various steps that constitute the inference process. A Rorschach protocol will be used to illustrate each step.

◆ ◆ ◆ Rules of Validity

Schafer (1954) noted that the starting point for an inference should be the basic Rorschach data: images, scores, attitudes, and behavior. He then developed a set of criteria for judging what he refers to as "adequacy of interpretation." Those criteria, in general, are the same ones that were advanced in chapter 11 as standards to be used in evaluating inferences derived from content.

To briefly review, the first criterion is that of sufficient and converging lines of evidence. Here, the examiner develops as many reasonable implications from a response as possible, and then eventually accepts those interpretations supported by the convergence of different lines of evidence.

A second criterion involves attempting to place the inference hierarchically in the overall personality structure. This criterion applies when the examiner makes use of a personality theory that includes the concept of hierarchical layers. The concept of hierarchy encourages the examiner to integrate his or her findings into an integrated whole that is conceptually and internally consistent. As described in this chapter, findings and the inferences are integrated on the basis of well-established clinical formulations.

The intensity of the inferred trend is the third criterion. The trends we infer are general and often apply to the majority of our patients. Therefore, to individualize the patient from others, it is necessary to specify the intensity or importance of the inferred characteristic for the particular individual.

A fourth criterion involves outlining, if possible, behavioral and other overt expressions of the interpretation. Because behavior is highly complex and typically involves an amalgam of several motives and various defenses, together with situational factors, this criterion cannot always be met.

A fifth criterion is that of depth, or the level of personality to which the inference is addressed. Although Schafer suggests that the inference be as deep as the evidence permits, he also recognizes that the deeper the interpretation, the further removed it is from the test data.

The sixth, and final criterion relates to specifying both adaptive and pathological aspects of the inferred tendency. Too often, testing reports are directed toward demonstrating pathological tendencies, to the near exclusion of presenting adaptive strengths. If the examiner outlines the patient's difficulties, he or she should also include instances of how the patient attempts to resolve them. A complete report is a balanced report, one that includes both problems and assests.

✦ ✦ ✦ Steps in the Inference Process

Step One—Data Gathering

If test administration, test scoring, and interpretation are all part of the same process, then the inferential process begins with the administering of the Rorschach test and includes adequate inquiry, accurate scoring, and a recording of the proceedings that is complete and as verbatim as possible. As noted previously, the examiner has several potentially rich sources of information about the patient available. One source, the formal scores and their interrelationships, is dependent on accurate and careful scoring. The other sources—thematic content, sequence of responses, the patient–examiner relationship— can best be tapped if a relatively complete transcript is provided. An illustrative scored protocol is presented in Figure 14-1.

Step Two—Quantitative Analysis

Several highly sophisticated and richly elaborate Rorschach systems have been developed for quantifying the formal scores. Typically, scores are weighted, tabulated, and then compared with other scores in terms of prescribed ratios. The tabulated scores and the ratios become the basic data from which inferences are drawn. Because of its atheoretical roots, strong reliance on normative data, and emphasis on descriptive rather than dynamic inferences, I have tended, despite the richness of this approach, to avoid conducting more extensive quantitative analyses.

Nonetheless, there are several quite informal tabulations that I do make and have found useful. The first involves form level. Here, I first indicate if there are any F− or Fs scores, and then I simply note the number of responses at each level of form level (e.g., Fo, F+, Fw+). Second, I list all the kinesthesias. I include all kinesthesias, regardless of whether they appear in a human-movement response, an animal response, or an inanimate-movement response. Finally, I compile a list of all the human figure responses. The three more informal tabulations taken from the protocol presented in Figure 14-1 are presented in Figure 14-2.

Step Three—First Order Inferences

With the preparatory work completed, step three constitutes the beginning of the actual interpretive work. Here, I carefully review the lists of form-level ratings, kinesthesias, and human responses and note on the lists all possible implications (see Figure 14-3). For example, if two Fs scores are indicated, right next to them I would note, "The patient is vulnerable to severe disruptions in reality testing." Or, if the list of kinesthesias includes "yelling, arguing, screaming" I would write next to these "strong orally aggressive trends."

The Rorschach record is then reviewed in the same manner; I comb through the protocol response by response, score by score, phrase by phrase—literally word by word—and wherever a reasonable implication can be drawn, I write in that implication. The implication is indicated adjacent to the actual response, score, or phrase so that I can clearly keep track of my data sources. At this step I entertain as many reasonable inferences as possible.

This step constitutes a convergence of all sources of information, that is, the formal scores, analysis of content, sequence analysis, and indications of the patient–examiner relationship. I do not isolate one score from another or regard the score as totally independent of the content. For example, a pure color score might indicate a capacity for affective sweeps; however, if the content of the response was "blood" or "fire," then one could sharpen the inference by specifying the vulnerability involved in sweeps of anger. Likewise, if on Card I the patient saw "a damaged bat with holes in its wings that was unable to fly" and, during inquiry, indicated that the blackness of the card was implicated, then the examiner might make the following notations: adjacent to the FC' score would be written "depressive affect"; above

Response	Inquiry	
(Before beginning the testing he discussed an incident from the day before, and most striking was his vulnerability to narcissistic injury.)		
I. 8" 1. That looks like a spider. (else?)	(Spider?) Definiteness about it. Eeriness about it.	W Fw– A
2. Impression of two gargoyles or two angels.	(Gargoyles?) When facing away, gargoyles; when facing each other, angels.	D Fw+ (H)
II. As a whole, a spider 6" 1. Looks like a butterfly or a moth, like it's coming at me. A big thing, a moth.	(Moth?) Exactly what it looked like. A huge moth. The colorations. (Colorations?) The shades of blackness.	W FC' A o Confab
III. 7" 1. Two Africans making pots or something.	(Africans?) 'Cause they were black and figures, like people. (Sex?) I didn't notice	D MC' (H) P o

Figure 14-1

	Response	Inquiry	
2.	Looks like an insect's mouth and face. Very vicious mouth.		D Fw– Ad
3.	This way definitely an insect. This has a vicious mouth too.		D Fw– A
IV. 8"			
1.	A spaniel dog. It has long fur	(Fur?) Just looks furry. (Furry?) Not sure, I suppose the shading.	W Fw+ Ch A
2.	Also a microscopic organism.	(Organism?) Not much of a shape.	W Fv Org.
V. 9"			
1.	That looks like a flying insect.		W Fo A P
2.	I don't know. A kite, a bat kite. You want something else?	(Bat kite?) I had both ideas so a kite shaped like a bat.	W Fo Obj. contam.
3.	Maybe a cloud, no, yea, a cloud.	(Cloud) Just the shape of it.	W Fv Cloud
4.	A leaf eaten up by bugs and that's what is left.	(Eaten up?) Like silk worms eat a leaf. Rough edges.	F Fw+ Play
VI. 11"			
1.	Those things that stick to your clothes when you run through the bush. Spanish needles. They can stick you.		W Fw+ Pl.

Figure 14-1 (continued)

	Response	Inquiry	
VII.			
9" 1.	Now, this way, smoke or something. Nuclear bomb has been dropped and this is the dark cloud afterwards.	(Smoke?) Grey color and it puffs up. (Cloud?) Mushroom shape and it's grey and dark.	W C' F Smok W C' F Cloud
VIII.			
7" 1.	This way a reflection. A bobtail cat and its reflection down here. (Showed it to the examiner.)		D Fo A P reflection
2.	An abstract painting.	(Painting?) Different colors. Other cards were black with a bit of red; these have colors.	W C F Art
IX.			
14" 1.	I can use my imagination? This is a crystal ball with wizards. This is the base and magical smoke. See their hats. You don't see it, do you? One wizard is good and the other bad. He has control over a person's life.	(Smoke?) It goes with the wizards and looks a bit puffy. (Puffy?) I don't know, it just goes in different directions.	D Fo Obj D F+ (H) D Fv Smoke
X.			
8" 1.	One of those bags you have confetti in. This is the cork. Here's where you pull it and the confetti shoots out.	(Confetti) The different shapes and it's all over the place.	W Fv Obj
2.	Oh, a goat's head, like Satan worshipers would have. Horns, like an evil goat's head.		Dr Fw+ Ad

Figure 14-1 (continued)

Form Level

F+	− 1		Fw−
Fo	− 6		spider
Fw+	− 5		insect's mouth & face
Fw−	− 3		insect
F−	− 0		
Fv	− 4		
Fs	− 0		

Kinesthesias

making pots
leaf eaten up

Human Figure Response

gargoyles
angels
Africans
wizards

Figure 14-2

Form Level

		Variable Form Level	Fw-
F+	− 1	Form Level	spider
Fo	− 6	suffers around	insect's mouth
Fw+	− 5	oral aggression	& face
Fw-	−3 →	Too great	insect
F-	− 0	a capacity	
Fv	− 4	for laxness	
Fs	− 0		

Kinesthesias

making pots
leaf eaten up → oral aggression, identified with the victim

Human Figure Response

gargoyles
angels   distances and distorts
Africans
wizards   looking for the ideal object

Figure 14-3

the word "damaged" would be written "sense of injury, of being damaged and flawed"; and above the "unable to fly" would be written "difficulties separating and individuating." Through a series of arrows the examiner could then indicate that the three inferences were quite likely connected.

Inferences at this stage vary in their level of depth; nonetheless, I attempt to state the inference in as experience-near terms as possible. In the above example of the bat, even though the attribution of being "damaged" may indeed indicate the testee's sense of narcissistic injury, I prefer to employ the more descriptive term "damaged" that more closely approximates the testee's experience, rather than the abstract concept "narcissistic injury." In Figure 14-4 is the original protocol from Figure 14-1 after it has been reviewed in the manner outlined. Included is the array of possible inferences together with arrows to connect inferences that, at this step, appear to be related.

Step Four—Transformation

I refer to this step as "transformation" to indicate that here one is beginning to transfer the findings from the protocol into what ultimately will be the test report. I transpose the inferences from the protocols to work sheets, with headings that correspond to the same subheadings (e.g., character structure, thought organization) that implicitly constitute the testing report.

Inferences are placed under their appropriate headings; however, there is not always a convenient fit. In certain instances, the same inference may be placed under several headings. In the previous example of the damaged bat, one could include inferences from this response under several headings: under the section *character structure* in terms of a sense of self as "injured and damaged"; under the section *affect organization* as "lowered feelings of self-esteem"; and under the heading *core dynamics* as "consequent to difficulties in separating and individuating, the patient senses himself as damaged and less than a total person."

Within each section I attempt to group inferences based on the arrows indicated on the protocol and on theory. For example, if on various parts of the protocol the patient was described as "self-demeaning," "apologetic," "aggressively complaintive," and "provocative," then all would be grouped together because they indicate a masochistic streak in the patient's character structure.

	Response	Inquiry	

	(Before beginning the testing he discussed an incident from the day before, and most striking was his vulnerability to narcissistic injury.) *vulnerable to narcissistic injury*		
I. 8"	1. That looks like a spider. *bad, engulfing, devouring, mother* (else?)	(Spider?) Definiteness about it. Eeriness about it. *externalizes malevolence*	W Fw– A Reality testing suffers
	2. Impression of two gargoyles or two angles. As a whole, a spider *ineffective defenses*	(Gargoyles?) When facing away, gargoyles; when facing each other, angels. *splits his objects, push-pull type of relationship, rapprochement issues.*	D Fw+ (H) distances & distorts his objects
II. 6"	1. Looks like a butterfly or a moth, like it's coming at me. A big thing, a moth. *loses inner/outer boundary, loss of distance*	(Moth?) Exactly what it looked like. A huge moth. *his sense of smallness* The colorations. (Colorations?) The shades of blackness. *depressive affect*	W FC' A blackness o confab

Figure 14-4

	Response	Inquiry	
III.			
7"	1. Two *Africans* making pots or something. *distances objects (women)*	(Africans?) 'Cause they were black and figures, like people. (Sex?) I didn't notice	D MC' (H) P blackness o
	2. Looks like an insect's mouth and face. Very *vicious mouth.* → *intense oral aggression*	*reality testing suffers around oral aggression*	D Fw– Ad D Fw– A
	3. This way definitely an insect. This has a vicious mouth too.	*variable reality testing*	D Fw– A
IV.			
8"	1. A spaniel dog. It has *long fur. Underlying dependence & neediness*	(Fur?) Just looks furry. (Furry?) Not sure, I suppose the shading	W Fw+ Ch A
	2. Also a microscopic organism. *His sense of lack of firmness and cohesion. Also, sense of being examined*	(Organism?) *Not much of a shape* He has little *of an inner shape*	W Fv Org.
V.			
9"	1. That looks like a flying insect.	(Bat kite?) I had both ideas so a kite shaped like a bat (cloud) Just the shape of it.	W Fo A P
	2. I don't know. A kite, a bat kite *loss of boundary—very early boundary disturbance* You *want something else?*		W Fo Obj. contam.

Figure 14-4 (continued)

	Response	Inquiry	
3.	Maybe a cloud, no, yea, a cloud	(Cloud) Just the shape of it . . .	W Fv Cloud
4.	A leaf eaten up by bugs and that's what is left. *Projects his oral aggression and he feels ravaged, exploited & victimized by others. Feels less than total & complete.*	(Eaten up?) Like *silk worms* eat a leaf. Rough edges. *Depreciates others*	W Fw + Pl.
VII. 11"			
1.	Those things that stick to your clothes when you run through the bush. Spanish needles. They can stick you.	*He's constantly anxious, restless, & agitated; like there is something under his skin annoying him he can't get away from.*	W Fw+ Pl.
VII. 9"			
1.	Now, this way, smoke or something.	(Smoke?) Grey color & it puffs up *Strong depressive affect*	W C' F Smoke
2.	*Nuclear bomb has been dropped* and this is the dark cloud afterwards. *Potentially eruptive & explosive but the rage is basically turned inward & dealt with masochistically.*	(Cloud?) Mushroom shape & it's grey & dark. *His world, at times, is heavily grey & black.*	W C' F Cloud

Figure 14-4 (continued)

	Response	Inquiry	
VIII. 7"			
1.	This way a reflection. A bob-tail cat & its reflection down here. (Showed it to the examiner) *Self-centered, self-absorbed, relates on a narcissistic basis, early need to be mirrored.*	This way a reflection. A bob-tail cat & its reflection down here. (Showed it to the examiner)	D Fo A P reflection
2.	An abstract painting *Combined with the several vague responses suggests he can be elusive & use vagueness as a defense.*	(Painting?) Different colors. Other cards were black with a bit of red, these have colors.	W C F Art *difficulty integrating*
IX. 14"			
1.	I can use my imagination? *Asks for & needs external structure* This is a crystal ball with wizards. This is the base & magical smoke. See their hats. You don't see it, do you? One wizard is good & the other bad. He has control over a person's life.	(Smoke?) It goes with the wizards & looks a bit puffy. (Puffy?) I don't know, it just goes in different directions.	D Fo Obj D F+ (H) D Fv Smoke

Figure 14-4 (continued)

Response	Inquiry	
Capacity to split—fearful of being controlled		
Need for external, consensual validation		
X.		
8"		
1. One of those bags you have confetti in. This is the cork. Here's where you pull it & the confetti shoots out.	(Confetti?) The different shapes & it's all over the place.	W Fv Obj.
Inner chaos & fearful of fragmenting even further.		
Sense of barely holding it together		
2. Oh, a goat's head, like Satan worshipers would have. Horns, like an evil goat's head.		Dr Fw+ Ad
Externalized malevolence paranoid tendencies		

Figure 14-4 (continued)

After all inferences have been placed under their appropriate major headings and subheadings, I then review each of the sections separately to determine which of the inferences may be related and which specific inferences are so isolated and at a variance with the others that they are best disregarded. Arrows are again used to indicate interrelated inferences. Finally, inferences between sections are examined and these connections too are indicated by arrows. At this step the inferences are related on the basis of theoretical formulations. A completed work sheet based on the sample protocol is presented in Figure 14-5.

Step Five—The Psychological Report

The work sheets completed in Step Four furnish the outline and material from which the testing report is written. The headings may or may not be explicitly stated in the report; in either case, they serve as organizational points of reference. The report consists essentially of the inferences and the theoretical formulations tying them together. In general, in a testing report the inferences constitute the basic material, theory binds the material and provides tightness and cohesion, and the level of language used particularizes the report to the individual patient.

A report based on the sample protocol is shown in the psychological evaluation. I regard this report as somewhat incomplete, for, as noted previously, a complete assessment should be based on a test battery.

Psychological Evaluation

The patient is a 26-year-old divorced male who has been charged with three counts of selling cocaine to an undercover police officer. The patient admits that he sold the drugs knowingly; that he knew the person as a police officer. He further claims that he believed old friends and acquaintances were spreading rumors that he was an informer and that the only way he could disprove these rumors was by having himself arrested. Psychological testing was requested to assess the plausibility of his claims and his general psychological status. This report is addressed to the issues of character structure, thought organization, affect organization, treatment, and the genuineness of the patient's personal defense.

In his approach to the examiner and the tests, the patient

Worksheet

Character Structure

> Variable cohesion—falls apart & pulls himself together
>
> Anxious, restless, pressured
>
> Self-centered, self-absorbed, unpredictable, changeable, labile, fragile, vulnerable, hypervigilant, hypersensitive, relates on a need-satisfying basis—dependent
>
> Masochism—self-deprecatory, turns aggression inward
>
> Distrusting, suspicious, antennae are out
>
> Sense of self-impoverished, neglected, exploited, victimized

Thought Organization

> Impulsive, poor judgment, loses conceptual boundaries
>
> Variable reality testing—too lax
>
> Fragile defenses—looks for external validation
>
> Boundary disturbance—self/other, inner/outer
>
> Paranoid trends

Affect Organization

> Poor affect control, mood shifts, can be swept by feelings
>
> Anxiety—restless, agitated, free-floating, diffuse, something under his skin
>
> Depression—parts of himself as missing, empty, hopeless, low self-esteem, turns rage inward, world as black, vulnerable to narcissistic slight (abandonment depression)
>
> Defenses—splitting, devaluation, projection, omnipotence, vagueness, avoidance

Dynamics

> Core oral aggression—projects outward and senses the world as malevolent and himself as exploited and victimized.
>
> Early disturbance with mother—views her as engulfing and devouring, push-pull quality, rapprochement issues.
>
> Poor object relations—distances and depreciates
>
> Diffuse anxiety—fear of fragmenting further, masochism, annoyance under his skin

Treatment

> Looking for external control and structure
>
> He's aware that he loses control, this scares him and he looks for outside control
>
> Intense depressive affect

Figure 14-5

appeared as a highly anxious, pressured, restless, somewhat desperate individual who nonetheless related to the examiner in an
open and cooperative manner. Characteristically unstable, chaotic,
unpredictable, and emotionally labile, at this time he is especially
fragile and vulnerable. The patient is self-centered, self-absorbed,
and overly concerned with what others think of him. Hypersensitive, hypervigilant and thin-skinned, he has his antennae out,
feeling his way through an environment he senses as hostile and
dangerous. Needy and dependent, he relates himself to others on
the basis of their ability to satisfy his immediate needs. In his personality one sees a strong masochistic streak. He is self-deprecia-
tory and self-defeating, and he sets himself up to be hurt and taken
advantage of. Further, when he feels excessively anxious and restless, he is likely to abuse himself or set himself up to be abused.
Such abuse lessens the anxiety. He is vaguely aware of this, insofar as he feels himself impoverished, exploited, and victimized.
Although he feels this, he has little awareness of his role in engen-
dering hurt and pain. Despite his openness with the examiner, in
general he is suspicious and distrusting of others; in his own terms,
he trusts no one. The overall diagnostic impression is of a narcissistic personality disorder organized at a borderline level.

One sees in the patient's functioning marked ego weaknesses.
He is impatient and at times impulsive, his judgment is poor, his
sense of reality and reality testing are variable, and he is highly
arbitrary. Beyond these impairments, he is prone to circumscribed
and periodic psychotic bouts. At these times, paranoid trends inten-
sify, he loses the boundary between himself and others and between
fantasy and reality, and he sees malevolence everywhere and likely
feels persecuted.

Central to the patient's instability is his tendency to fall apart
and then quickly pull himself together. When he falls apart, he
senses himself as "out of control." In this context, his paranoid
thinking is an effort to regain control by bringing order and structure, as inaccurate as it may be, to his broken world. By contrast,
when stable, his thinking is logical, goal-directed, and reality-bound.
Of importance here are his rapidly shifting and variable levels of
functioning and his reliance on external structure for stability.

The patient has much difficulty controlling, modulating, and
integrating affects. He is vulnerable to intense mood shifts and
affective sweeps. He is currently being pressured by relatively
intense feelings of anxiety and depression. His anxiety, which is
longstanding and diffuse, becomes evident in feelings of agitation
and restlessness and in a sense of having a continuous annoyance

under his skin that he cannot get away from. As noted previously, when his anxiety mounts to an intolerable level, he discharges it by hurting or harming himself. His depression, which has the quality of an "abandonment depression," involves feelings of emptiness, aloneness, and hopelessness. As well, he suffers from low feelings of self-esteem. At times he feels the low self-esteem directly in terms of feeling himself to be bad, worthless, and less than totally human. At other times he defends against it and feels himself to be quite the opposite—all-powerful, psychic, visionary, and omnipotent. In any event, his self-esteem is fragile and subject to the least slight.

In line with his chaotic nature, he tends to polarize the world into either all good or all bad. There is little of a middle ground, and he is unable to tolerate different feelings toward the same individual. His feelings about himself have this same polarized good and bad quality. Bolstering this tendency toward splitting is his proclivity to either excessively depreciate or idealize both others and himself.

Basic to the patient's dynamic life are intense feelings of oral aggression. That is, he feels enraged and resentful over having been neglected and deprived. The rage is then projected outward onto the environment, leaving him with a view of the world as malevolent and dangerous—a veritable jungle, as it were. He feels he has been exploited and fears and anticipates further exploitation.

The patient's relationships are highly disturbed. Needful and dependent, he looks to others for sustenance and nurturance. At the same time, however, he distrusts others; thus, associated with desires for closeness are fears of being controlled, dominated, and used. Caught in the competing currents of desiring nurturance yet fearing the implied closeness, his relationships have a push-and-pull quality. In a similar way, mindful of his own inner disorganization, he looks for external control and structure; yet here too he distrusts and fears such control. Hence, he is likely to seek external structure and then respond to it with both obedience and rebelliousness. Further complicating his relationships is his tendency to view others exclusively as all good or all bad.

Finally, the patient is especially fearful of fragmenting and losing the limited sense of cohesion and precarious sense of self he has achieved.

The referrer specifically questioned the patient's claim that he knew he was selling drugs to an undercover policeman and wondered if such a claim were plausible and consistent with the patient's personality makeup. To judge from his tests, the claim is consistent with his personality. Behaving as he says he did is in keeping with his strong masochism, his feelings of omnipotence, his poor judgment, and his search for external authority. That he should assume others believed he was an informer is congruent with his paranoid tendencies, and that he should counter it as he did is consistent with his lapses into irrational thinking.

Because of his inner disorganization the patient is looking for external structure and control. As such, a long-term, highly structured inpatient treatment program is the intervention of choice. Contact with his subjective experience can be established around his strong depressive feelings, his feelings of restlessness, and his discomfort with being out of control.

In summary, the patient presents as a narcissistic personality organized at a borderline level. He is chaotic, unstable, vulnerable, and labile. There is a strong masochistic streak. In addition to having marked ego weaknesses, he is vulnerable to circumscribed psychotic episodes. In keeping with his diagnosis, he quickly "falls apart" and then pulls himself together. His mood shifts are rapid and he is prone to severe depressive bouts. In his dynamic life, one sees excessive oral aggression, disturbed object relations, and fears of fragmentation. His account of why he got into his current legal difficulties is consistent with aspects of his personality. He would most benefit from a long-term, well-structured inpatient treatment program.

❖ ❖ ❖ Conclusion

In this chapter I have discussed the inference process, including rules of validity that should be applied to inferences and the steps involved in moving from the Rorschach data to a testing report. One's understanding of the dynamics of testing, of the various aspects of the Rorschach testing situation, and of personality theory come together at this point. In my view, deriving accurate, meaningful, and clinically useful inferences constitutes the most challenging yet creative aspect of the testing process.

15

RORSCHACH ASSESSMENT AND TREATMENT PLANNING

$\mathbf{A}$s noted in chapter 1, from a psychoanalytic perspective, one assesses with the intent of understanding another person as distinctively and comprehensively as possible, so that such an understanding can be used to help make decisions and plan interventions that will be beneficial to that person. This basic intent informs all aspects of the assessment process.

The logic of first understanding the person and then using that understanding as a basis for developing recommendations, including those related to treatment, is not unique to a psychoanalytic approach. Exner (1993), from a different perspective, writes, "The finished interpretation should capture the uniqueness of the person, including both assets and liabilities. It should be a descriptive summary from which the intelligent professional can draw some logical conclusions and, when required, make some logical predictions" (p. 541).

Using Rorschach findings for the purpose of assisting in treatment planning is a daunting task. More than understanding the dynamics of testing and personality theory, the examiner must also be familiar with the structure and process of treatment.

The number and complexity of treatment-related variables to be taken into account are staggering. For example, in the Menninger Psychotherapy Research Project (Kernberg et al., 1972), the list of patient variables alone included ego strength, patterning of defenses, anxiety tolerance, quality of interpersonal relationships, severity of symptoms, level of psychosexual development, insight, motivation, level of anxiety, and self-directed aggression. Separate lists were developed for treatment variables and situational variables.

The Rorschach has been used to predict a vast number of treatment events, including the capacity to benefit from intensive psychotherapy (Hatcher and Krohn, 1980), prognosis for hospital treatment (Frieswyk and Colson, 1980), premature termination (Hilsenroth and Handler, 1995; Horner and Diamond, 1996), and treatment outcomes (Carlsson, Bihlár, and Nygren, 1996; Lindfors, 1996; Meyer and Handler, 1996).

Representative of the literature in predicting treatment outcome is the recent work of Meyer and Handler (1996). In a comprehensive project jointly sponsored by the Society for Personality Assessment and Rorschach Workshops, the authors conducted a meta-analysis of studies that have used the Rorschach Prognostic Rating Scale (Klopfer et al., 1951). Using outcome criteria obtained an average of one year after initial testing, the raw population correlation between the rating scale scores and outcome was found to be p = .43.

Despite the importance and necessity of the above studies, their value for the practicing clinician is limited. Unlike the researcher who often works in a laboratory setting, has considerable time to study findings, employs established rating scales, uses group data to uncover group trends, and engages in retrospective analyses, the Rorschach examiner works in a clinical setting, is often pressured by time constraints, relies on raw data, is concerned with one individual, and is asked to make prospective recommendations, not only with regard to the outcome, but also as to how the treatment itself should be fashioned.

Herein I identify and discuss specific aspects of the assessment process that the examiner may employ in assisting with treatment planning. I first review and summarize the earlier discussions of the assessment frame and the patient–examiner relationship. I then discuss the concept of object relations as an intervening variable linking test responses with treatment recommendations. Finally, I suggest that all Rorschach findings can be viewed through the additional lens of "implications for treatment."

◆ ◆ ◆ Assessment Frame

The assessment frame, as discussed in chapter 5, is the term used to describe the structural conditions that provide the framework for assessment to occur. It consists of the place where sessions will be held, the length and number of sessions, the fee, a stance regarding missed appointments, how the participants are to refer to each other, and the specific set of test directions.

The patient's attitude toward, and ways of reacting to, the assessment frame may be taken as a useful indication of how he or she is likely to respond to the treatment frame. There are those individuals who accept the frame without question, those who seem bent on opposing it, and those who find it necessary to negotiate a slightly altered frame as a way of asserting their autonomy.

From the patient's reaction, the examiner is in a unique position to inform the therapist as to how flexibly or rigidly the frame should be set and maintained. For example, a 38-year-old married woman coyly and subtly attempted to seduce the examiner into changing the frame. She suggested that the examiner refer to her by her first name while she referred to him by his title, sheepishly requested a hug at the end of each session, and offered the examiner a gift following their last appointment. In this instance, the examiner recommended that a clear and firm frame be set and then steadfastly adhered to. He noted the likelihood of the development of an erotic transference, but cautioned that such a transference would be fueled by aggressive urges, including a powerful need to break rules.

The composition of the treatment frame can also be addressed from a careful appraisal of the assessment frame. Therapists are often and appropriately concerned as to the optimal frequency with which a patient should be seen. It is conventionally held that treatment intensity and depth are directly related to frequency of sessions. Other factors too may enter into this decision.

A 42-year-old single male who lived with his widowed mother was described by the referrer as "interesting but detached and perplexing." Three testing sessions were scheduled; because of the examiner's schedule, however, there was a 10-day stretch between the first and second appointments. During the second session the examiner was struck by the lack of continuity between that session and the earlier one. The patient behaved as if he had not seen the examiner previously and was starting the testing anew. Seemingly, nothing about the examiner, his office, tests, or person, was held onto and carried over into the second session. The third session, which took place several days after the second one, was altogether different. The patient was less anxious, more present, and apparently comfortable in what he felt to be familiar surroundings. There was continuity between this session and the second one. Understanding the issue of continuity in terms of the patient's struggle to hold onto an internal representation of the other, the examiner suggested that the patient be seen on a several-days-a-week basis.

For certain patients, more important than their reactions to the assessment frame are the adaptive uses they make of it. Psychoanalysts are increasingly recognizing that the structure (i.e., the frame) of the treatment setting itself contains symbolic equivalents of the mother-child relationship. Modell (1978), borrowing from Winnicott (1960), has evoked the concept of the "holding environment" to conceptualize the caretaking functions, especially holding and containing, that are provided by both the therapist and the treatment structure. P. Lerner (1986) has observed that patients who use the treatment frame as a holder and container have previously used the assessment frame in a similar way.

In the previous discussion of the assessment frame it was noted that because of differences between the assessment and treatment frames, one can carefully alter the assessment frame and thus reduce the differences and increase the range of treatment-related inferences. One such adjustment involved the examiner's actively and thoughtfully attempting to secure the patient's full participation in the assessment process. To do this, several suggestions were offered, such as clarifying the patient's expectations, dealing directly with the patient's fears and apprehensions, encouraging the patient to reflect upon specific test responses, and sensitively sharing findings during rather than after the assessment.

The suggestion that the examiner use himself or herself as a vehicle of change, and then understand how and what the patient makes of it, is, in part, based on the consideration that treatment takes place in a relational context and consists of a multiplicity of different relationships. Greenson (1967) has identified and distinguished among three types of treatment relationships—the transference, the working alliance, and the real relationship. Transference, according to Greenson, is the "experiencing of feeling, drives, attitudes, fantasies, and defenses toward a person in the present which do not befit that person but is a repetition of reactions originating in regard to significant persons of early childhood, unconsciously displaced onto figures in the present" (p. 171). The working alliance, by contrast and as the term implies, involves the patient's capacity to work purposefully with the therapist in the therapeutic situation. The real relationship, in counter distinction to the other two, refers to the realistic and authentic relationship between patient and therapist. It is real in both senses of being undistorted and genuine.

From this perspective, in endeavoring to gain the patient's active involvement in the assessment, the examiner, in Greenson's terms, is attempting to establish a working alliance. How able and willing the patient is in entering the assessment alliance, and the resistances stirred, can than be used to infer his or her capacity to enter a treatment alliance.

✦ ✦ ✦ Patient–Examiner Relationship

A second source of assessment data for inferring treatment recommendations is the patient–examiner relationship. As noted in chapter 7, an interpersonal relationship is intrinsic to Rorschach testing and that relationship is infused with realistic and unrealistic elements. Schafer (1954), more so than others, has described how the structure of the relationship itself serves to promote transference reactions.

The concept of transference, however, is highly complex and has been used loosely to refer to a variety of interpersonal phenomena. Variously, authors used the concept to refer to, among other things, an individual's general interpersonal expectations, an individual's tendency to engage in certain types of interactions, and as Greenson (1967) employs the term, an individual's replacing a current figure with one from the past. Despite differences in usage, transference phenomena in general share several common characteristics: they involve repetitions, they are resistant to change, and they are defenses against memory, although they indirectly may lead in that direction (Greenson, 1967).

Because assessment is time-limited, one should not expect a testee to displace onto the examiner a specific significant figure from his or her past. Instead, what is expressed in the patient–examiner relationship are relational expectations, relational tendencies with certain classes of people (e.g., authorities, professionals), and relational proclivities more generally. These transference manifestations issue from internalized representations of the self and others, which, in turn, are based in part upon early relational experiences.

It is from a sampling of the patient's "representational world" (Sandler and Rosenblatt, 1962) as expressed in the patient–examiner interaction that the examiner infers relational paradigms to the treatment situation. Indications of an individual's representational world are not limited to the patient–examiner relationship. As discussed in chapter 11, such expressions may also be found in Rorschach content.

Owing to the work of Kohut (1971, 1977), the concept of transference has been meaningfully extended in a particular direction. On the basis of Freud's (1914) earlier distinction between narcissistic object relations and true object relations, Kohut described a set of atypical transference patterns that unfold in the treatment of patients with narcissistic personality disturbance. Arnow and Cooper (1988) (see chapter 7) have described expressions of two of these atypical patterns—mirroring transference and idealizing transference—as they are expressed in the patient–examiner relationship. Again, signs of the likelihood of a patient establishing a narcissistic transference in treatment may be inferred from other Rorschach data, such as the reflection response, the human movement response, and certain content.

The therapist who is forewarned to the possibility of the development of a narcissistic transference is far more able to treat these difficult and at times unlikeable individuals. In addition to having a set of technical recommendations provided by Kohut (1977), the therapist, with this understanding, is better equipped to tolerate the patient's provocative and alienating behavior.

Another type of interpersonal transaction, different from transference, that is sometimes experienced in the patient–examiner relationship is projective identification. The term was originally developed by Melanie Klein to describe a developmental and defensive process in which "parts of the self and internal object are split off and projected into the external object, which then becomes possessed by, controlled, and identified with the projected parts" (Segal, 1974, p. 27). Bion (1956) extended the concept by using the metaphor of a container and contained. Underlying this metaphor is the image of an infant emptying its bad contents into the mother, who accepts the unwanted projection, contains it, and alters it in such a way as to permit its reintrojection by the infant. For Bion,

> projective identification is an interpersonal process in which one finds oneself being manipulated so as to be playing a part, no matter how difficult to recognize, in somebody else's fantasy. In the interpersonal setting, the person projectively identifying engages in an unconscious fantasy of ejecting an unwanted or endangered aspect of himself and of depositing that part of himself in a controlled way [Ogden, 1983, p. 232].

Implicit in projective identification, then, are the following elements: the presence of an unconscious fantasy, pressure on the other to experience himself or herself in a way congruent with the unconscious fantasy, the defensive aspect of ridding oneself of unwanted parts, and the attempt to control the external object.

Levine (1988) has suggested that the examiner's countertransference reaction may be used to infer this defense in the assessment process. Mindful that more disturbed patients often provoke in the examiner intense feelings and fantasies, both aggressive and sexual, she has found it helpful to note her own thoughts, feelings, and fantasies as they arise during Rorschach testing. Levine further noted that at times her own subjective reactions paralleled the nature of object relationships as expressed in the content of responses, whereas at other times they did not. She points out, "Sometimes an emotional response which seemed discordant and contradictory to the patient's presentation and Rorschach responses have alerted me to an underlying emotional state of the patient" (p. 100).

Like Levine, I have found one's countertransference reaction to be a valuable source of information for inferring this defense. As an unsuspecting and at times an unwilling partner in the projective identificatory process, the examiner often finds himself or herself not only experiencing intense feelings and fantasies about the patient, but also being coerced or pressured into a role that seems to have little to do with the realistic aspects of the testing.

A 52-year-old hospitalized patient, unmarried, was referred for testing to assist in determining her suitability for long-term individual treatment. A high school teacher, she was hospitalized following a highly serious suicide attempt. Although it was standard practice for all newly admitted patients to be tested, the staff seemed particularly interested in her results. She had evoked in them strong feelings of concern, sympathy, and compassion. Uncharacteristically, they seemed to overempathize with her sense of herself as a tragic victim of life's harshness.

Quite rapidly, and in marked contrast with the other staff, the psychologist found himself enraged with the patient. The patient missed the first testing session, claiming she was too upset and distraught to "face being tested." The staff colluded with the patient in her decision and in her feeling that the examiner and his tests were a source of danger and fear. She then attended the three testing sessions and complied with the instructions in body, but with little spirit. Interspersed with her overly terse answers were snide, caustic remarks about the examiner's office, his attire, and his tests. Illustrative of the patient's provocative and alienating behavior was her reaction to the TAT. After telling the barest of stories and complaining of the ambiguity of the pictures, she noticed a picture on the wall as she was leaving. She commented on its evocativeness and proceeded to offer a detailed story that included various details asked for but not given with the TAT cards. Following the evaluation, as a result of a sense of himself as impotent, helpless, and incompetent, the examiner felt murderous rage toward the patient.

At a subsequent case conference, the projective identification was identified. On the basis of historical information, it was conjectured that the patient had projected into the examiner a disowned part of herself, namely, that part of her that felt helpless, ineffective, and constantly enraged at her cold, distant, unfeeling, and impenetrable father.

The therapist found this information especially useful. Instead of reacting to her provocativeness, he used his own reactions as a vantage point to empathize with her rage. In other words, knowing that his patient relied on projective identification enabled the therapist to maintain empathic contact with the patient.

To briefly recap, therapists are increasingly placing the therapeutic relationship at the center of the treatment process. They are recognizing that it is the arena in which change and growth take place. As McWilliams (in press) puts it, "The therapeutic relationship is . . . seen by most contemporary treaters not as the bottle in which the psychological medicine is stored, but as the medicine itself" (p. 7). The treatment relationship, as Greenson (1967) has observed, can be subdivided into several subrelationships. Information gleaned from the patient–examiner relationship, both with and without other test data, can be used to infer to different facets of the treatment relationship.

◆ ◆ ◆ Object Relations as an
         Intervening Variable

Basic psychoanalytic concepts and formulations that had been understood in exclusively structural and economic terms are being reformulated to take into account the decisive impact of early object relations. This conceptual shift has important implications for Rorschach interpretation. For instance, test scores and test responses, in addition to being understood in traditional ways, may also be viewed from the perspective of their object-relational meanings.

Furthermore, an object-relational perspective then allows the examiner to use the concept *object relations* as an intervening variable linking test responses with treatment planning. The following case illustrates the interplay among affect, object relations, and treatment.

A divorced woman with a history of numerous early losses was referred for psychological testing to assist in determining her suitability for psychoanalysis. Two earlier, more behaviorally oriented treatment experiences provided only limited help.

She produced a lengthy Rorschach record consisting of 35 responses; only one of her responses, however, included the use of color. The one color response—"red beavers" on Card VIII—involved an incompatible blend of color with content.

Based on the relative absence of color and the nature of her one color response (the incompatible blend), the examiner described her affect experience as follows: "Despite her seeming warmth and outward emotional displays, to judge from her tests, the patient is affectively insulated and places much emphasis on control. Her affects are neither spontaneous nor genuine; instead, they have a playacting quality and are based on what others expect her to feel and not on what she truly feels."

Making use of the conceptual relationship that Modell (1975) drew between affects and object relations, the examiner then suggested, "In keeping with her experience and expression of affects, her relationships as well are deceptive and disingenuous. She presents as cooperative but indeed is not. What passes for cooperation is an outward compliance which serves to hide and protect what she really wants and needs." The test inferences regarding the nature of her object relating were extended to treatment. Here, the examiner supported the choice of psychoanalysis, but cautioned that her fear of genuine openness with another and her investment in self-sufficiency would constitute formidable resistances.

The patient's behavior, particularly during the initial phase of her analysis, confirmed the examiner's inference. Before beginning treatment the patient prepared a photo album depicting many of the major events in her life. For the first several months of treatment she spent each session sharing and discussing individual photos.

The analyst appreciated the patient's dedication to her treatment and willingness to work at it. He also, however, felt little relatedness with the patient. Intimacy, closeness, and genuine trust were markedly absent. Rather than a real partner in her analysis, he sensed himself an observer relegated to watching a highly self-reliant individual conduct and control her own treatment.

In this case there was a striking parallel in the patient's attitude toward and way of defending both affect and object relations. More specifically, her emotional constriction and insulation paralleled, in the object-relations domain, her emphasis upon privacy and self-sufficiency. Affect and object relations may be related in any number of ways, not just in a parallel one. For example, in some instances what is most compelling is the impact of a person's affects and the position it places others in.

More broadly, not only affect, but other aspects of personality too, may be considered from an object-relations perspective. Winnicott (1956), for example, described a group of antisocial children who communicate not in words but in actions. For these children, their actions are unconsciously intended to elicit a particular response from the environment. H. Lerner and P. Lerner (1986) have discussed the role of object relations in cognitive development. More specifically, they outlined the stage-specific role of the caregiving object in facilitating cognitive development as well as in impeding such development. P. Lerner (1996c) extended their object-relations model of thinking to the Rorschach, and this is presented in chapter 20.

If object relations constitute a thread that weaves through the fabric of psychological development, then assessment of personality and psychopathology inevitably involves an assessment of object relations. With respect to Rorschach interpretation, this suggests that in addition to the traditional meanings we assign scores and determinants, one may also interpret these elements in terms of their object-relational meanings. Again, because treatment consists of various types of relationships, object relations may be used as an intervening variable linking various aspects of a Rorschach record with treatment planning.

✦ ✦ ✦ Conclusion

Psychoanalytically oriented examiners have traditionally been concerned with extending test findings to the treatment situation. Conceptual shifts in psychoanalytic theory are providing the opportunity to build additional bridges between assessment and treatment. Recognizing that a psychanalytic approach admits to more sources of data than do other approaches, I have herein, discussed two sources of information (assessment frame, patient–examiner relationship) and a conceptual perspective (object relation) for viewing Rorschach scores and content that are all ripe with meaning regarding treatment planning. Beyond these sources and perspective, all Rorschach findings may be viewed through the lens of possible treatment implications. To tease out such implications, the examiner needs to conceptually stretch by asking himself or herself, "What meaning might this finding have for treatment?"

Part 2
Research Applications

16

THE RORSCHACH
ASSESSMENT OF OBJECT
REPRESENTATIONS

1n psychoanalysis, with the increasing recognition of the distinction between internalized object relations and relations between the self and the object in the external world, there has been growing emphasis on the concept *internal object relations*, or on what Sandler and Rosenblatt (1962) refer to as the "representational world."

In proposing that we consider internal objects as the contents of the unconscious, Melanie Klein laid the conceptual groundwork for all further explorations of the inner relationship between self and object. Based on her early work in child analysis, Klein (1926, 1927) introduced the concept of internal objects, which she described as inner fantasy images of the parents which had a life of their own. In "Mourning and Melancholia," Freud (1917) explained how lost actual objects were transformed into inner presences. Klein extended this formulation by indicating that the "internal world of fantasy objects was a ubiquitous force in psychological life even when no actual loss had occurred" (Brown, 1996, p. 23).

Fairbairn (1952) broadened Klein's notions of the formation of internal objects in several important and unique ways. His "conception of endopsychic structures and their interrelationships imparted an anatomy and function to the internal world which is unparalleled in other theories, including Klein's, yet is congruent with her conceptions in other ways" (Grotstein, 1991, p. 37).

Since the pioneering writings of Klein and Fairbairn, a vast array of terms have appeared on the psychoanalytic landscape to describe the cast of characters that assumedly inhabit the internal object world. A partial list would include self and object representations, internal objects, introjects, identifications, selfobjects, autistic objects, symbiotic objects, good objects, and bad objects. In a recent article entitled "A Proposed Demography of the Representational World," Brown (1996) offers a map for organizing, interrelating, and locating these various concepts.

In what follows, I first review Brown's demographic analysis of the representational world, with the intent of defining the concept *object representation*. I then discuss the work of two research groups that have contributed to the study of object representations by means of the Rorschach.

❖ ❖ ❖ Internal Object Relations

Both Kernberg (1976) and Ogden (1983) agree that internal object-relations units, consisting of unconscious self-representations and object representations, are the essential units of psychic structure. Integrating the work of Kernberg and Ogden with the more recent writing of Hamilton (1995), Brown (1996) outlines five characteristics of internal object-relations units.

The first characteristic involves the degree of separateness between the representations of the self and the other. Here, one considers a continuum in which at one pole there is little if any differentiation between self and object, whereas at the other end there is a clear distinction between representations of the self and of the object. Mahler (1968; Mahler et al., 1975), in particular, has described the process through which self and object gradually and progressively become differentiated.

A second characteristic, one emphasized by Kernberg (1982), is the affective link between self and object representations. In internal object-relations units, the affective bind that links the self with the object may be positive or negative, clear or confused, somatized (Krystal, 1988), or even nonexistent.

A third aspect is the cognitive level of mental representations. Blatt (1974), on the basis of an integration of psychoanalytic object-relations theory with the developmental theories of Piaget and Werner, has discussed this dimension. He points out that representations begin as vague, diffuse sensorimotor experiences of pleasure and unpleasure, but they gradually expand and develop into well-differentiated, consistent, and relatively realistic representations of the self and object world. Earlier forms of representation are based on action sequences associated with need gratification; intermediate forms are based on specific perceptual and functional features; and higher forms are thought to be more symbolic and conceptual.

A fourth important aspect is the level of ego functioning associated with each internal object-relations unit. This aspect, in addition to drawing attention to defensive processes, also accounts for the way in which meaning is generated within each of these units and clarifies Ogden's (1983) contention that internal objects have, in a sense, a mind of their own.

The fifth and final dimension according to Brown (1996) is the functional aspects of the mental representations. This refers to the psychic functions the mental representations serve within the individual's personality. For example, such mental representations may provide self-soothing, bolster superego prohibitions, or enhance one's sense of identity.

In addition to specifying five dimensions along which object-relations units may be understood, Brown (1996), with a view to exploring the terrain of the representational world, further identifies four general classes of internal object-relations units.

Brown refers to one class as the "self in relation to autistic objects," a term he uses "to denote the primarily sensory experience of the object which is leaned up against, so to speak, in order to achieve the earliest definition of self as bounded by the skin surface" (p. 31). Grotstein (1987) points out that the autistic object provides a "sensory floor" upon which future development of the self is based. Brown's term "autistic object" subsumes other similar concepts, including sensation objects (Tustin, 1981), hard objects (Tustin, 1984), precursor objects (Gaddini, 1975), and confusional objects (Tustin, 1981).

A second class, more developmentally advanced, is the self in relation to symbiotic objects. According to Mahler et al. (1975), in the second month, with the beginning awareness of the need-satisfying object, the infant enters the symbiotic phase. The inborn stimulus barrier begins to crack, and with a cathectic shift toward the sensoriperceptive periphery, the infant behaves and functions as though infant and mother are merged in an omnipotent dual unity encircled by a common protective shield. Symbiotic objects provide "a background of safety" (Sandler, 1960) from which the child progressively separates and individuates. Kohut (1977) has described a type of selfobject relationship in which the object continues to be used later in development in a way similar to a symbiotic object. The relationship, according to Kohut, is one in which the self merges with the object so as to assure a sense of self-cohesion and ward off disintegration.

A third class for Brown (1996) is the self in relation to transitional internal objects. This describes "a manner of self in relation to an object in which they are both joined and separated simultaneously" (p. 37). This type of relatedness is similar to what Mahler et al. (1975) refer to as "hatching" from the earlier symbiotic relation, and Klein (1957) describes as occurring in the depressive position. Others have evoked the term "introject" to refer to the transitional internal object.

The final class, the self in relation to object representations, denotes the highest level of mental representation, the culmination of the formation of the representational world, as it were. Here, object representations are true symbols, in that they represent the external object at a conceptual level in a well-differentiated and realistic way. It is important to note that Brown (1996) is using the term "object representation" more narrowly than do other authors. For instance, Kernberg (1976), Blatt (1974), and Mayman (1967) all use the term in a far broader way to include all levels of mental representation.

Before concluding this review, it should be noted that increased attention is being accorded the relationship between the psychoanalytic concept of object representation and the attachment-theory concept of inner working models. As attachment theory has extended its emphasis from parent-infant interaction to include subjective experience and mental representations, authors have increasingly sought to integrate aspects of attachment theory with psychoanalytic object-relations theory (Bretherton, 1987; Main, Kaplan, and Cassidy, 1985; Pistole, 1995; Silverman, 1991; Slade and Aber, 1992; Wright, 1986; Zeanah et al., 1989; Zeanah and Barton, 1989).

Various writers (Bretherton, 1987; Levine and Tuber, 1993; Silverman, 1995) have also discussed similarities and differences between attachment theory and object-relations theory. For example, both theories are concerned with parent-child relationships, the ways in which mental relationships develop and are organized into schemas or structures, the internal and external affective link between self and object, and the process of internalization. At the same time, the approaches differ in the weight each assigns to factors that contribute to internalization. As Silverman (1995) points out:

> Attachment research, for the most part, relies on the repeated actual experiences that infants and caregivers share, that become internalized for the child as a working model of attachment. Psychoanalytic concepts of . . . self and object representations, while addressing real interactions as contributors, also consider the needs, fantasies, anxieties, guilt, and defensive reactions shaping perceptions and organizing internalizations [p. 155].

In a series of articles (Levine and Tuber, 1993; Levine et al., 1991), Levine and Tuber have reported on their attempt to compare measures of mental representation from attachment theory and object-relations theory. A group of pregnant adolescents was interviewed with the Adult Attachment Interview (AAI) (George, Kaplan, and Main, 1985) to assess mental modes of attachment, and then the Krohn Object Representation Scale (KORS) (Krohn and Mayman, 1974) was applied to the interviews to assess object representations. The infants were later videotaped at 15 months of age with their mothers in the Strange-Situation paradigm (Ainsworth et al., 1978). The authors found a high degree of overlap between the two measures of representation. In addition, the mothers' representations while pregnant predicted their infants' later attachment to them. In comparing the two measures, despite the overlap, the authors found, on the one hand, that the AAI did not sufficiently explicate less adaptive object representations, but on the other hand, the KORS relied more on clinical inference.

❖ ❖ ❖ Research Studies

Two primary research groups have contributed to the systematic study of the object-representation construct by means of the Rorschach test together with other projective techniques. The two groups represent different, but not mutually exclusive, approaches to the study of object representations. Mayman and his colleagues at the University of Michigan have focused on the thematic dimension of object representations. Employing early memories, manifest dreams, written autobiographies, and a variety of projective procedures, including the

Rorschach test, and developing innovative scoring systems, these investigators have studied the relationship between object representation and severity of psychopathology, type of character structure, quality of object relations, and capacity to benefit from psychotherapy. Informing their work and methods have been theoretical formulations rooted in ego psychology, including the more recent contributions of Mahler et al., (1975) and Kernberg (1975, 1976).

Blatt and his colleagues (1976) at Yale University, by contrast, have emphasized the structural dimension of object representations. While this group has also developed independent projective measures and scales (e.g., parental descriptions, Thematic Apperception Test scales), they have studied the developmental level of object representations across a wide spectrum of normal and clinical populations. The work of this group too is based on ego psychology and object-relations theory; in addition, and in keeping with their developmental thrust, these researchers also integrate the developmental cognitive theories of Piaget and Werner.

There is yet another well-regarded and widely employed method for assessing object relations that makes use of the construct object representation. The method, however, has not been applied to Rorschach data, therefore, I will not review it at length. Basing their work in psychoanalytic theory and using a social-cognitive developmental approach, beginning in the late 1980s Westen and his colleagues (Westen, 1991, 1993; Westen et al., 1989) have devised four scales for assessing different dimensions of object relations. The four dimensions include complexity of representations of people, affect-tone of relationship paradigms (the affective quality of the object world, from malevolent to benevolent), capacity for emotional investment in relationships and moral standards (need-gratifying orientation to the social world versus investment in values, ideals, and committed relationships), and understanding of social causality (tendency to attribute causes of behaviors, thoughts, and emotions in a complex, accurate, and psychologically minded way). Each dimension is evaluated along a 5-point Likert-type scale, and with the exception of affect-tone, the scales attempt to measure developmental dimensions (i.e., Level 1 is relatively primitive, and Level 5 is relatively mature). The scales have been primarily applied to T.A.T. data; four similar scales, however, were developed for interview data, including early memories, psychiatric interviews, and psychotherapy transcripts.

The Study of Object Representations
at the University of Michigan

Employing the specific theoretical contributions of Jacobson and Erickson, Mayman (1967) conceptualized object representations as templates or enduring internalized images of the self and of others around which the phenomenological world is structured and into which ongoing experiences of others are assimilated. Mayman asserted that Rorschach content, like the manifest content of dreams and early memories, was more than simply an embellished screen that concealed and hinted at deeper and more profound levels of unconscious meaning. He argued that manifest content in its own right could reflect levels of ego functioning, relative capacity for object relations, and the nature of interpersonal strivings. According to Mayman (1967):

> A person's most readily accessible object representations called up under such unstructured conditions tell much about his inner world of objects and about the quality of relationships with these inner objects toward which he is predisposed [p. 17].

Mayman (1967) identified several dimensions by which to assess the content of Rorschach responses in order to answer the following questions:

> What kind of world does each person recreate in the inkblot milieu? What kinds of animate and inanimate objects come most readily to mind? What manner of people and things is he prone to surround himself with? Does he put together, for example, a peopleless world of inanimate objects; if so, which objects have special valence for him? Do they hint at a certain preferred mode of acting upon the world or of being acted upon by it? Are they, for example, tooth-equipped objects? Or, phallically intrusive objects? Decaying or malformed objects? [p. 17].

In addition to psychosexual levels of the image and the degree of humanness in Rorschach responses, Mayman also considers both the extent to which conflict or rage permeates the portrayal of the other and the degree of the individual's vulnerability to separation and loss. For Mayman, the Rorschach human response is viewed as a vehicle for understanding "important personal meaning" about "a person's capacity to establish empathic contact with another human being" (1977, p. 244).

In an early study, Mayman (1967), equipped with these notions and with a commitment to a clinical empathic-intuitive approach to the analysis of projective test data, selected Rorschach protocols from the Menninger Psychotherapy Research Project and distilled from each record verbatim clusters of "content-fragments" that he considered to be self-representations, object representations, and conflict representations. All patients were evaluated independently on the Health-Sickness Rating Scale, as well as on a wide range of other clinical variables. Mayman examined the extent to which ratings of psychopathology, based exclusively on representational content gleaned from a Rorschach administered before treatment, corresponded to clinical ratings of psychopathology. Editing out all references to traditional Rorschach scores, such as form level or determinants, Mayman asked graduate students and interns to "immerse themselves" in each patient's Rorschach responses, to regard the imagery as a sample of the patient's inner world, and to assign a rating for the degree of psychopathology implicit in the representational content. Mayman found that relatively inexperienced judges could successfully predict ratings based on an independent psychiatric evaluation (r = .86). Beyond demonstrating that an object relations approach to Rorschach content correlates significantly with independent ratings of psychopathology, Mayman also showed that relatively inexperienced, clinically trained raters can make important contributions to research.

Mayman's seminal contributions to Rorschach research have spawned a number of object-representation scales and a host of construct-validity studies that have further refined the concept (Urist, 1973) and have extended the thematic analysis of object representations to manifest dreams (Krohn, 1974), autobiographical data (Urist, 1973), and to studies measuring a person's capacity to enter into and benefit from insight-oriented psychotherapy (Ryan, 1973; Hatcher and Krohn, 1980). Different scales designed to evaluate object-representational levels as specific points on a developmental continuum have been correlated with each other (Urist, 1973) and have been applied and correlated across various data bases, including manifest dreams, the Rorschach test, early memories, and health-sickness ratings (Krohn and Mayman, 1974). These studies reflect Mayman's focal interest in thematic content, his gifted clinical approach to projective data, which emphasizes the value of empathic-intuitive skills of trained clinicians, and his abiding interest in variables related to psychoanalytic theory and treatment.

Following the methodological thrusts of Mayman and integrating the theoretical contributions of Kernberg and Kohut, Urist (1973) examined the multidimensional qualitative aspects of the object-representational concept by correlating several Rorschach scale ratings of 40 adult inpatients, covering a wide spectrum of psychopathology, with independent ratings of written autobiographies. The specific scales developed by Urist were gauged to reflect the developmental ordering of stages in the unfolding of object relations along a number of overlapping dimensions, including mutuality of autonomy, body integrity, aliveness, fusion, thought disorder, richness and complexity, and differentiation and individuation. Urist found significantly high correlations among the various measures of object relations and interpreted this as indicating high consistency among self- and object-representations across a wide range of sampled behavior.

Urist (1973) also demonstrated that object relations are not unidimensional areas of ego functioning. A factor analysis revealed an important distinction between two related but separate structural underpinnings of object representation: an integrity factor, related to issues of self-other differentiation, stability, and consistency (an index of secondary narcissism), and a boundary factor, related to developmental gradations in fusion-merger tendencies and in thought disorder associated with the inability to maintain a cognitive-perceptual sense of the boundary between self and other and between one object and another (an index of primary narcissism).

On the basis of this research, Urist (1977) developed a procedure for systematically evaluating Rorschach responses that expressed interactions between people, animals, and objects—The Mutuality of Autonomy Scale. Utilizing the data from his 1973 study, Urist correlated Rorschach scale ratings with independent measures of the same dimension applied to the written autobiographies and behavioral ratings of ward staff. Urist reported a consistency across all variables and ranges of measures that points to an enduring consistency in patients' representations of relationships. He further demonstrated that the Rorschach can be utilized to systematically assess aspects of mutuality of autonomy within a patient's experiences of self and other. The Mutuality of Autonomy Scale has been validated in several independent studies (Tuber, 1983; Spear and Sugarman, 1984; Ryan, Avery, and Grolnick, 1985; Coates and Tuber, 1988).

In summary, the research findings of Mayman and his colleagues, especially Urist, provide strong support for the importance of assessing object representations in clinical research and practice. These investigators have developed a conceptual model and assessment procedures that have implications for the study of different forms of psychopathology and for the study of the psychotherapeutic process. They have attempted to add a more experiential, phenomenological, and object-relational dimension to theory, assessment, and research. Emphasis is placed on a clinically based methodology, on the development of means for capturing the complexity and unique nature of clinical phenomena, and on a qualitative approach to data collection and analysis that allows the data to maintain their clinical richness.

Research Studies at Yale University

Although Blatt shares with Mayman a commitment to bring into research the more subtle differentiations and observations of experienced clinicians, his research and that of his colleagues at Yale have focused on the assessment of structure as opposed to content. Underlying the research of this group is the assumption that the structural dimensions of object representation can be assessed with acceptable levels of reliability and that they provide valid data that have considerable generalizability for understanding various facets of human functioning.

Blatt's theoretical commitment is to a study of object and self-representations based on an integration of psychoanalytic theory with the cognitive developmental formulations of Piaget and Werner. His contribution to the Rorschach literature has revolved around the study of the development of the concept of an object, both in normal and in various clinical populations.

Building on their initial investigation of boundary disturbances, Blatt and associates (1976) developed a highly comprehensive and sophisticated manual for assessing object representations in Rorschach records. Based on the development theory of Werner (1940) and ego psychoanalytic theory, the system calls for the scoring of human responses along three developmental dimensions: differentiation, articulation, and integration. Within each of these areas, categories were established along a continuum based on developmental levels. Differentiation refers to the type of figure perceived and to whether the figure is quasi-human detail, human detail, a quasi human, or a full human figure. For the dimension of articulation, responses are scored on the basis of the number and types of attributes ascribed to the figure. The integration dimension of the response is scored in three ways: the degree of internality of the action, the degree of integration of the object and its action, and the integration of the interaction with another object. Responses are also scored along a content dimension of benevolence-malevolence.

In an early study (Blatt et al., 1976), the scoring system was applied to the Rorschach protocols of 37 normal subjects on four separate occasions over a 20-year period. Results from this longitudinal study revealed that human responses on the Rorschach test consistently change with development. More specifically, there was a marked and progressive increase in the number of well-differentiated, highly articulated, and integrated human figures. In addition, there was a significant increase in the attribution of activity that was congruent with important characteristics of the figures and an increase in the degree to which human objects were seen in constructive and positive interaction.

Blatt and associates then extended the scale to the human responses of a sample of 48 seriously disturbed borderline and psychotic adolescents and young adults. When compared to the human responses of the normal sample, several interesting findings appeared. First, the seriously disturbed inpatients had a significantly greater number of human responses at lower developmental levels (i.e., responses that were more often quasi-human, distorted, unmotivated, incongruent, passive, and malevolent). These responses at lower developmental levels, however, occurred primarily on accurately perceived responses. Second, and quite surprisingly, patients had a significantly greater number of more developmentally advanced responses than did normals on inaccurately perceived responses. These findings were replicated by Ritzler et al. (1980). According to Blatt, these results indicate that patients, as compared with normals, function at lower developmental levels when in contact with conventional reality, but at higher developmental levels when they give idiosyncratic interpretations of reality. As such, the data indicate that the capacity to perceive reality adequately does not aid psychotic patients to organize their experience more effectively or to function at higher levels. The findings suggest that there are at least two aspects to the psychotic experience. First, the psychotic patient perceives the world as distorted, undifferentiated, fragmented, and destructive. The second aspect involves the psychotic patient's capacity to experience the world unrealistically, but within the unrealistic experience, to function more effectively and to perceive the world less malevolently. These Rorschach findings have implications for the treatment of severely disturbed patients (Blatt, Schimek, and Brenneis, 1980). Specifically, for psychotic patients, introducing and interpreting reality is experienced as painful and disruptive and will engender retreat and withdrawal. Thus, while it is incumbent upon the therapist to maintain a reality orientation, it is equally important that he or she recognize and empathize with the pain that accompanies this stance.

The Concept of the Object Scale has been applied to various types of psychopathology. Blatt and Lerner (1983) applied the instrument to the Rorschach records of several patients, each of whom was independently selected as a prototypic example of a specific clinical disorder. These authors not only found a unique quality of object representation for each of the clinical entities, but their findings, based on Rorschach data, were remarkably congruent with clinical expectations.

In a nonparanoid schizophrenic patient, the object representations in the Rorschach response were found to be inaccurately perceived and at lower developmental levels of differentiation (i.e., quasi-human rather than full human figures). The representations were inappropriately articulated and seen as inert or involved in unmotivated activity. There was relatively little interaction between figures, and the Rorschach content was essentially barren.

In a narcissistic patient organized at a borderline level, the object representations in the Rorschach response were found to gradually deteriorate with stress or simply over time. Intact, accurately perceived full human figures gave way to inaccurate, inappropriately articulated, quasi-human representations. Early responses had a superficially intact quality, and relationships between figures were depicted as benevolent and conventional. Yet action between figures lacked inner definition and there was little meaning attributed to the action. In time, the quality of the concept of the object deteriorated as the representations changed from full to quasi humans or part-objects. As well, the responses became progressively more inaccurately perceived and inappropriately elaborated.

Representatations in a patient diagnosed as an infantile character with anaclitic depressive features were accurately perceived and well-differentiated but minimally articulated. Interaction was perceived between figures, but this typically involved an active-passive transaction in which one figure was seen as vulnerable and in a relationship with a depriving, rejecting, undependable other.

In a seriously suicidal patient with an introjective depression characterized by profound feelings of self-criticism and guilt, there was an oscillation between object representations at a high developmental level and seriously impaired representations in which the activity was destructive and had malevolent intent (Blatt, 1974).

The object representations in the Rorschach record of a delinquent adolescent were conventional full-human figures that were poorly articulated. Figures were accurately perceived but lacked detail, and actions ascribed were purposeless and directionless. In contrast to the narcissistic-borderline patient, responses did not deteriorate in quality nor in developmental level of representation.

Finally, in a patient diagnosed as hysteric, object representations were accurately perceived, well differentiated, and highly articulated. The elaborations, however, involved superficial external and physical details rather than more internal or personal attributes. There was little internal sense of motivation or action between figures; rather, things seemed to simply occur.

Blatt and Lerner (1983) concluded, on the basis of their clinical analysis of these prototypic cases, that there are significant, consistent differences in the structure and content of object representations in patients with different types of psychopathology and that one can validly assess object representations through a systematic appraisal of human responses on the Rorschach. These clinical findings have been substantiated in a number of research studies involving various clinical groups, including borderlines (Spear, 1980; Lerner and St. Peter, 1984), schizophrenics (Johnson, 1980; Spear and Schwager, 1980), depressives (Fibel, 1979), opiate addicts (Blatt et al., 1984), and anorexics (Sugarman, Quinlan, and Devenis, 1982).

Other investigators have related parts of Blatt and associates' (1976) scoring manual to psychological variables conceptually linked to object representations. Johnson (1980) reported significant correlations between two scale measures, degree of articulation of the representation and developmental level of interaction, and an independent measure of field independence. He also found a significant correlation between scale measures of the integration of the object with its action and the portrayal of congruent interactions in a role-playing task. Fibel (1979), in a sample of seriously disturbed adolescent and young adult hospitalized patients, found a significant positive relationship between scale scores and independent clinical ratings of quality of interpersonal relations.

Finally, modified versions of the scale and specific subscales of the scoring system have been employed in research studies. To create a single continuous score, Fritsch and Holmstrom (1990) weighted each response according to its form level. In a sample of 84 adolescent inpatients, the modified score was found to be directly related to measures

of peer relatedness, intelligence, psychological health, and reality testing, and indirectly related to measures of psychosis and unmanageable
behavior. Greco and Cornell (1992) found that adolescents who committed homicides in the context of another crime (e.g., robbery) scored
significantly lower on the differentiation subscale than did a subgroup
of adolescents whose homicides were committed in the context of an
interpersonal conflict.

Throughout his research on psychopathology, Blatt has steadfastly
maintained the significance of assessing impairments in object representations and the role they play in predisposing an individual to a
particular form of psychopathology. Considerable clinical and research
evidence suggests not only that the content and structure of object representations are essential dimensions in specific forms of psychopathology, but, in addition, that changes in the structure of object
representations parallel changes observed in treatment (P. Lerner,
1986). With the development of a Rorschach measure of object representations, this developmental construct is now available for systematic assessment. For Blatt, the assessment of object representation
has involved an integration of psychoanalytic theory with cognitive
developmental psychology. The procedures developed now provide
the means for investigating a wide range of theoretical formulations,
as well as for examining dimensions of the social matrix in which the
developing child evolves. The representational world emerges from the
interaction of cognitive, affective, interpersonal, and social forces. As
such, it may be regarded as a core structure for studying the multitude
of factors that influence normal psychological growth, the impairments
that eventuate in psychopathology, and the changes in the psychotherapeutic process.

◆ ◆ ◆ Conclusion

Whereas instinct theory and, later, ego psychology were once the conceptual centerpieces of analytic theory, psychoanalysis has increasingly
become a developmental theory of self and object relations, with
emphasis on the processes whereby external experiences are internalized and become the basis of personality growth and functioning. With
this shift in theoretical emphasis, new concepts, such as object representation and self-representation, corresponding to a clinical rather
than a metapsychological level, have gained increased currency in the

analytic literature. Because these newer concepts are less removed from the clinical situation and are closer to our clinical data, they lend themselves to operationalizing in a way that the older and more abstract concepts do not.

The research reviewed in this chapter indicates that there are reliable and valid methods and techniques available for the systematic assessment of object representations and internalized object relations. The combined findings further indicate that these constructs are enduring dimensions of personality organization and that they provide meaningful information about the developmental level of personality and the quality of external interpersonal relationships.

Mayman and his colleagues, basing their work on the theoretical formulations of Federn, Jacobson, and Kernberg, have investigated the affective-thematic aspects of human experience. Using such theoretical constructs as "affective states," "experience of self," and "sense of identity," this group has attempted to bring a more phenomenological approach to traditional assessment.

Blatt and his colleagues have also employed concepts and formulations based on ego psychology and object-relations theory; however, they have also integrated these concepts with formulations from cognitive developmental psychology.

Because of different theoretical starting points, each of the two groups has emphasized somewhat different dimensions of object relations. The Michigan group has focused on the contextual and affective aspects of object representations, whereas the Yale group has emphasized the structural and cognitive aspects. Mayman and his colleagues have developed a more experiential approach to assessment, whereby there is a close adherence to clinical data and the judgment of skilled clinicians is maximized by asking them to immerse themselves in the data and then to make ratings in an "intuitive and empathic" manner. The research methodology and theoretical formulations of the Yale group represent a rich synthesis of clinical experience with a developmental perspective. Methods are devised and designed to provide quantitative data anchored in clinically relevant observations.

The findings from each research team overlap and in large measure are mutually supportive. Both groups are interested in how the individual constructs reality and the internal outcome of this process, the nature of mental representations and of their interactions, and the processes whereby experience is transformed into subjective meaning. Each group has contributed significantly to the development of a more phenomenological clinical theory derived directly from test data. Their assessment of the concept of object representation is now providing qualitative and quantitative data that has relevance for a variety of disciplines.

Using various clinical populations, both groups have studied and outlined impairments in object representations among patients differing in severity of psychopathology. More recently, both groups have begun to apply their theoretical concepts and research methodologies to aspects of the psychotherapeutic process. Specifically, research is currently under way in which the construct of object representation is being used to help predict those patients who are more likely to benefit from an insight-oriented psychotherapy. Further, other studies are being conducted in which the construct serves as a criterion measure to assess the effectiveness of long-term intensive treatment.

17

RORSCHACH ASSESSMENT
OF DEFENSE:
1. TRADITIONAL MEASURES

T he concept of defense has been a cornerstone of psychoanalytic theory and a major subject of Rorschach investigation (Schafer, 1954; H. Lerner and P. Lerner, 1990). Until recently, however, the concept has remained relatively immune to the impact of object-relations theory and self theory. As Stolorow and Lachmann (1980) noted, "An examination of the history of the concept of defense indicates that while ideas about what a defense wards off have evolved, the concept of defense itself has remained static" (p. 89). Historically, several writers (A. Freud, 1936; Jacobson, 1971; Gedo and Goldberg, 1973) have attempted to introduce developmental schemes that rank defenses, from archaic or primitive to higher order or advanced, yet these conceptualizations have remained exclusively related to the vicissitudes of psychosexual development and have excluded object-relational and self considerations.

This is now changing. As Cooper (1989) has pointed out, "Within the past 20 years diverse trends have emerged in psychoanalytic understandings of the defense mechanism concept, including elaborations of both the intrapsychic and object-relational contexts" (p. 865). The trends Cooper refers to include theories of complex motivational

properties of the ego (Schafer, 1968; Kris, 1984), a functional theory
of defense (Brenner, 1982), an object representational theory of defense
(Kernberg, 1976), a "two-person" theory of defense (Modell, 1984),
and a self-psychological theory of defense (Kohut, 1984). These newer
conceptualizations differ from each other and from older theories of
defense in any number of ways, including the referent of the defense
(e.g., impulse, affect, environmental failure, self-fragmentation) and
the assumed relationship between internal homeostasis and the external world.

In this chapter I review several of the psychoanalytic theories of
defense, beginning with the conception involved in Freud's drive theory, extending through modifications proposed in structural theory,
and ending with revisions suggested by the work of Modell (1984)
and Kohut (1984). This will be followed by a review of Rorschach
measures of defense based upon drive theory and structure theory. In
the next chapter I review Kernberg's (1976) conception of defense and
discuss more recent Rorschach measures based on object-relations
theory.

♦ ♦ ♦ Freud's Conceptions of Defense

Freud's various and changing views of defense have been reviewed
by several authors (Rapaport, 1958; Madison, 1961; Hoffer, 1968;
Leeuw, 1971). In his earliest writings, prior to 1900, Freud used the
term *defense* to describe the ego's struggles against painful ideas and
affects. In these early papers he outlined the processes of conversion,
displacement of affects, withdrawal from reality, repression, and projection. Freud presented his initial concept of defense within the context of an incomplete conceptualization of the ego; nonetheless, as
Rapaport (1958) has noted, the implicit notions within this early
view—that drives are dammed up and displaced and that the defense,
by preventing the recall or reencountering a reality experience, pre-
vents or delays the experiencing of a painful affect—have remained
cornerstones of most subsequent psychoanalytic conceptions of
defense.

Following a period in which his interest in defense waned, Freud's
interest rekindled in 1923, and with the publication of "The Ego and
the Id" he made explicit his tripartite model of the personality and
accorded the concept of defense a central role. Freud conceived of

defense as an ego function and regarded the defense mechanisms as the executive methods of this ego capacity (Leeuw, 1971). Whereas in his earlier view he conceptualized repression as responsible for the creation of anxiety, he therein posited that it was anxiety that created the need for repression. Freud (1926) further conceived of the ego as having a range of defenses at its disposal. He outlined isolation, undoing, denial, and splitting of the ego, and reconsidered repression.

On the basis of the structural model presented in "The Ego and the Id," authors subsequent to Freud drew attention to the chronology and genesis of the defense mechanisms, as well as to their relation to levels of ego and drive organization. Anna Freud (1936) systematized the concepts of the specific defense mechanisms, clarified the relationship between defense and reality relations, and investigated the role of affects (Rapaport, 1958). Reich (1933) investigated and described the defensive aspects of character formation. He conceived of character as augmenting the primary repression of instincts by way of autoplastic changes.

Schafer (1968) studied the defenses with a particular emphasis on what he referred to as a gap in theory regarding the dynamic properties of the ego as a structure. He suggested that one aspect of this gap related to the neglect in theory of how the defenses, themselves, contain their own hierarchy of motives and wishes. In contrast to earlier views that posited the ego and the id as in opposition to each other, Schafer conceives of a unity between ego and id and argues that defenses are unconscious because of their wish-fulfilling aspects. Schafer's contribution provides a theoretical understanding of the clinical observation that defenses not only regulate drives, but also serve to satisfy drives.

Unlike Schafer, who approached defenses from a motivational perspective, Brenner (1982) emphasizes the functional aspect of defense. He contends that defense is a feature of mental functioning "definable only in terms of its consequence: the reduction of anxiety and/or depressive affect associated with a drive derivative or with superego functions" (p. 73). For Brenner, there are no specific mechanisms of defense; instead, any aspect of psychic life that reduces anxiety or depressive affect constitutes a defense. Brenner argues that by defining defense exclusively by function, one avoids the ambiguity of other definitions, which have included a number of other phenomena such as compromise formations, fantasies, and symptoms.

◆ ◆ ◆   Other Psychoanalytic
Theories of Defense

The contributions of Schafer and Brenner remained exclusively embedded within Freud's intrapsychic model. In suggesting that defenses directly mediate affect between objects, Modell (1984), however, places defense in a new context—a two-person context. He contends that "affects are the mediums through which defenses against objects occur" (p. 41). Once affects are linked to objects, "the process of instinct-defense becomes a process of defense against objects" (p. 41). The individual, as it were, masters affects by controlling the "object carriers" (Brierly, 1937, p. 51).

On the assumption that the communication of affects is "object-seeking," Modell (1975, 1984) describes a tendency among certain borderline and narcissistic patients to withdraw into a cocoon of self-sufficiency and nonrelatedness, so as to defend against a painful piece of reality rather than a wish or a drive. Modell's work is closely linked to Winnicott's (1961) concept of the "false self," and represents an extension of the view of LaPlanche and Pontalis (1973) who define defense as "a group of operations aimed at the reduction and elimination of any change liable to threaten the integrity and stability of the biopsychological individual" (p. 103).

Concerned that classical views of defense tended to obscure considerations of the individual's self-experience, Kohut (1984) reconceptualized defense as referring to any attempt by a person to minimize painful affect associated with the exposure of structural deficits, or what Newman (1980) describes as "experiential deficiencies." According to Cooper (1989), "Kohut speaks of particular defensive structures almost exclusively in the context of maintaining remnants of the self that will preserve the vigor of the self" (p. 882).

Kohut's formulations are close to those of Modell (1975), in that both emphasize the notion of a vulnerable self needing to be safeguarded. Modell's concept of the self's "cocoon state," like Guntrip's (1969) earlier notion of the "schizoid citadel," are terms that have been evoked to describe defensive steps mobilized to protect equivalents of Kohut's (1984) "enfeebled self."

Although conceiving of defense in exclusively intrapsychic terms, Kernberg (1976) too has offered significant revisions. He broadens the notion of intrapsychic conflict to include object representations. Kernberg's effort to integrate structural theory of defense with formulations arising from the British school of object relations is discussed in the next chapter.

◆ ◆ ◆   Rorschach Measures of Defense

The theoretical contributions of Modell and Kohut are just beginning to find their way into the Rorschach literature. In the remainder of this chapter I review two major works that have used the drive and structural models as a basis for translating theoretical formulations regarding defense into Rorschach-related concepts. The two systems for systematically scoring defense, those of Holt (1977) and of Levine and Spivak (1964), have each generated considerable research.

Assessment of Primary-Process Thinking and Its Control

For almost two decades Holt (1977) has been developing and refining a Rorschach scoring manual designed to measure manifestations of primary process thinking and its control. Holt's system calls for the scoring of four sets of variables: content indices of primary process, formal indices of primary process, control and defense, and overall ratings. Because ideation is considered an instinctual derivative—that is, only the idea representing the instinct rather than the instinct itself can achieve consciousness—the section of Holt's manual related to control and defense has relevance in this review of defense and its measurement.

The control and defense scores represent an attempt to assess the manner in which the primary process material is regulated and modulated and how successfully this is accomplished. There are two aspects to this scoring: an identification of the specific defensive operation being employed and a determination as to whether the operation improves or further disrupts the response. Holt devised the following scores to specify the particular defensive operation being used: remoteness, context, postponing strategies, miscellaneous, and overtness.

Remoteness involves several subcategories (e.g., remoteness-ethnic, remoteness-animal, remoteness-geographic) and is based on the principle that when an unacceptable impulse is expressed in a response, it may be rendered more acceptable if the subject distances himself or herself from the response by making the percept distant in time, place, person, or level of reality.

Context refers to the setting in which the response is presented and the extent to which this makes the primary process aspects of the response more acceptable. Four levels of context, comprising the cultural, aesthetic, intellectual, and humorous, are distinguished.

Two types of *postponing strategies*, delay and blocking, are scored. As implied in the name, these refer to processes by which the emergence of primary process is delayed or blocked.

Miscellaneous defenses are a catch-all category that Holt uses to include an array of defensive maneuvers, such as rationalization, vagueness, projection, obsessional defenses, isolation, evasiveness and avoidance, and impotence.

Overtness refers to the distinction between potential and active types of aggression. Four types of overtness are distinguished: overtness in behavior, verbal overtness, experiential overtness, and potential overtness.

In addition to these specific defense scores, the fourth part of the scoring manual, "overall scores," also includes ratings that bear on defense. The *defense demand* rating was devised to evaluate the degree to which either the nature of the idea underlying a response or the way it emerges demands that some defensive and controlling measure be undertaken in order to make the response a socially acceptable communication. This is scored on a six-point scale, ranging from little apparent need for defense to increasingly greater need for defense. A second rating, *defense effectiveness*, was developed in order to evaluate the relative effectiveness of the defensive operation in reducing or preventing anxiety and in permitting a more successful and adaptive response. This score, too, is related on a six-point scale, with positive values indicating good control and negative values indicating more pathological defensive efforts. A final overall rating is *adaptive regression*. This score, which combines the amount of primary process material with the effectiveness of its integration, is obtained by multiplying the defense demand score and the defense effectiveness score, response by response, then summing the products and dividing the summed product by the number of primary process responses.

Reliability

In general, studies involving the reliability of the entire Holt scoring system, including the measures of defense, have investigated the agreement among judges in scoring. Overall, the level of agreement attained with the overall ratings has been satisfactory; the findings regarding the individual categories, however, have been discouraging. One should view the latter conclusion with caution, however, for as Lerner and Lewandowski (1975) have noted, the scoring system has undergone several modifications and revisions, and the degree to which two scorers agree must be considered in light of the edition of the manual used. This becomes especially relevant when one considers that many of the changes were made with the specific intent of enhancing reliability [p. 192].

McMahon (1964) tested his agreement with another experienced scorer on 20 cases randomly selected from a sample of 40 schizophrenic and 40 medical patients in a V.A. hospital. On the mean defense effectiveness score he reported a product-moment correlation of .56.

In a study involving the Rorschach records of psychotherapists in training, Bachrach (1968) reported reliability coefficients greater than .89 between two well-trained graduate students for the ratings of mean defense demand, mean defense effectiveness, and adaptive regression.

Allison (1967) and an independent rater scored the Rorschach protocols of 20 divinity students and obtained the following reliability coefficients: mean defense demand, .99; mean defense effectiveness, .81; and adaptive regression, .67.

Benfari and Calogeras (1968), in a sample of 40 college students, reported reliability coefficients of .95 for mean defense demand and .90 for mean defense effectiveness scores.

Rabkin (1967), together with another experienced scorer, scored 25 records randomly selected from a group of 100 Rorschach records obtained from patients participating in the Menninger Foundation Psychotherapy Research Project. The reliabilities reported by Rabkin were the following: mean defense demand, .86; and mean defense effectiveness, .90.

Russ (1980), in a study involving 20 protocols selected from a group of 51 second graders, obtained inter-rater reliabilities between two experienced scorers of .76 for mean defense demand, .80 for mean defense effectiveness, and .90 for adaptive regression.

As noted previously, findings with respect to the agreement in scoring of the individual categories have been relatively unsatisfactory. Holt (1977), using raw data from two studies, found that scorer agreement was highly related to the frequency with which a specific category was used. Lerner and Lewandowski (1975), using their own scoring of protocols obtained in their clinical practice, reported that "if the content and formal variables were scored accurately, then the control and defense scoring was straightforward and afforded little difficulty" (p. 188). In summary then, while the inter-rater reliability for the overall ratings across several studies is highly adequate, data is inconclusive with respect to the reliability of the individual defense and control scores.

Studies related to the construct validity of the scoring system have involved the following: (1) attempts to link the drive and control measures to behaviors and characteristics theoretically related to primary process thinking; (2) the use of specific scores as criterion measures in studying the effects on thinking and defense of experimentally induced or clinical conditions; and (3) attempts to find differences in the expression and control of primary process thinking among groups differentiated on the basis of other variables, such as diagnosis and level of conscience development. The studies reviewed here are examined exclusively in terms of the specific and overall indices of defense; for a more detailed and comprehensive review of the findings of these studies as they relate to the entire scoring system, refer to Holt (1977) and Lerner and Lewandowski (1975).

Cognitive Studies

Several investigators have attempted to relate aspects of Holt's manual to various cognitive and perceptual variables that are conceptually linked to the expression and control of primary process manifestations. The areas studied include the thought process of individuals who have undergone unusual religious experiences, the capacity to cope with cognitive complexity, the capacity to tolerate unrealistic experiences, conjunctive empathy, tolerance for perceptual deprivation, and creativity.

In a sample of 29 male college students, Maupin (1965) investigated the relationship between responses to a meditation exercise and specific ego capacities, including the capacity to regress adaptively. He reported a correlation (Tau .49, p <.001) between indices of the response to meditation and the measure of adaptive regression. The relative contributions of the various components of the adaptive regression score were explored in a multivariate chi-square analysis. The main contribution to the relationship with response to meditation came from the "defense effectiveness" component ($x^2 = 7.82$, p < .02).

Allison (1967) studied the thought processes of individuals who had undergone a religious conversion experience. The sample consisted of 20 male divinity students who were subdivided into three groups on the basis of an autobiographical statement as to whether or not they had undergone an unusual or mystical experience. Allison found that whereas both the defense demand ($p < .05$) and the adaptive regression ($p < .05$) scores were significantly related to the intensity of the conversion experience, the defense effectiveness score did not discriminate the subgroups.

The most direct test of the relationship between the amount and control of primary process on the Rorschach test and the capacity to deal with cognitive complexity was conducted by Blatt and associates (1969). Fifty male college students were administered the Rorschach test and the John-Rimoldi, an apparatus designed to measure the ability to analyze and synthesize abstract and logical relationships. The authors found that although the ability to handle cognitive complexity, as defined by the John-Rimoldi, was not related to defense demand, it was significantly related to defense effectiveness and adaptive regression.

Similar, but less impressive, results regarding the relationship between adaptive regression and cognitive flexibility were reported by Murray and Russ (1981) in a study of 42 college students. They found a significant relationship between the adaptive regression score and a measure of cognitive flexibility (Mednick's remote association test) for males but not for females.

A third area of investigation that has received considerable attention is that of creativity. Most researchers who have attempted to relate Holt's scores to measures of creativity have been interested in testing Kris's (1952) hypothesis that "regression in the service of the ego" is necessary for the artist. In developing this concept, Kris emphasized the relationship between creativity and adaptive regression.

Pine and Holt (1960) attempted to predict from a triad of scores (the adaptive regression score, effectiveness of defense measure, and demand for defense index) the quality of imaginative productions on a variety of experimental tasks, including a Thematic Apperception Test (TAT) literary quality score, Science Test, and Brick Use Test. In a sample of 27 undergraduate students they found that the adaptive regression score and the effectiveness of defense score were significantly related to a summary imaginative quality measure for the males. For the females the findings were weak and inconclusive.

Support for the above findings was provided by Cohen (1960), who also studied the relationship between creativity and adaptive regression. In his study, which involved college students, gender did not affect the findings.

Using a sample of 56 unemployed actors, Pine (1962) attempted to replicate the findings from the earlier study with Holt (Pine and Holt, 1960). He found, in contrast to the previous investigation, that not one of the correlations between the defense measures and creativity was significant. In explaining this discrepant finding, Pine noted that the variance in the defense effectiveness scores was too small in this sample to permit a meaningful ranking of subjects.

Finally, Dudek and Chamberland-Bouhadana (1982) compared a group of mature, renowned artists with a group of young art students on the various Holt measures. They found that all three overall scores (defense demand, defense effectiveness, and adaptive regression) significantly differentiated the experienced from the inexperienced artists.

Another cognitive perceptual variable that investigators have studied with respect to its relationship to the amount and success of integration of primary process material is the capacity to "tolerate unrealistic experience." Feirstein (1967) tested the hypothesis that subjects who are able to adaptively integrate (high defense effectiveness) drive-related material into their thinking will also be able to perceive their environment in ways that contradict conventional modes of perception. Twenty male graduate students were administered Rorschach tests together with four tests of "tolerance for unrealistic experiences," including Phi phenomena, reversible figures, aniseikonia lenses, and stimulus incongruity. The author reported a significant correlation ($r = .46$, $p < .05$) between the Rorschach defense effectiveness score and a combined measure of tolerance for unrealistic experience. An adaptive regression score, consisting of the defense effectiveness score and an index of the amount of unrealistic thinking, also correlated significantly ($r = .49$, $p < .025$) with the criterion measure.

Another variable that has been related to the various defense measures is empathy. Based on scale ratings derived from tapes of psychotherapy sessions, Bachrach (1968) found that as quality of empathy expressed by the psychotherapist increased, there were significant increases in adaptive regression and defense effectiveness. Defense demand did not significantly relate to the empathy measure, though in reviewing the raw data Bachrach noted a curvilinear relationship with defense demand greater at either extreme of the empathy dimension.

The final factor that investigators have attempted to relate to the expression and control of primary process is the capacity to tolerate perceptual deprivation. Wright and Abbey (1965) found that an index of control score, which consisted of the proportion of defense demand to defense effectiveness, was significantly related to success in tolerating a deprivation situation ($x^2 = 8.04$, $df = 2$, $p < .05$) in a sample of 21 subjects. Because in this study the Rorschach test was administered several months after completion of the isolation experiment, and therefore success or failure in tolerating the deprivation experience might have influenced the Rorschach scores, Wright and Zubek (1969) attempted to replicate the earlier study but used Rorschach tests administered prior to the experiment. The obtained results were quite consistent with those reported in the earlier study. That is to say, the index of control score was again highly related to the capacity to tolerate the perceptual deprivation situation.

Goldberger (1961) employed Holt's manual to predict as well as to study reactions to perceptual isolation. Fourteen college students were isolated for a period of eight hours and encouraged to openly discuss their thoughts and feelings. From a combination of the Rorschach test, a series of cognitive tests, clinical ratings, and overt verbal behavior during the experiment, Goldberger found the following: (1) defense effectiveness was positively related to controlled primary process thinking during isolation and to the experience of positive affect during isolation; (2) defense effectiveness was negatively correlated with poorly controlled primary process thinking during isolation, the experience of negative affects during isolation, and cognitive test impairment in the isolation situation; and (3) defense effectiveness did not predict a tendency to prematurely terminate the isolation experience.

In summary, two summary defense scores from the Holt manual have been found to be related to a host of cognitive-perceptual variables that, on theoretical grounds, are linked to the expression and control of primary process thinking. Across several studies the defense effectiveness score and a measure of adaptive regression have been related to the capacity to tolerate and adaptively cope with situations in which reality contact is temporarily suspended (Zen meditation, religious conversion experiences, perceptual isolation), the ability to tolerate unrealistic experiences, and the capacity to deal with the variety of cognitive tasks. As well, subjects who are able to adaptively regulate drive expressions and integrate logical and illogical thoughts into appropriate Rorschach responses are more empathic in treatment relationships. The findings with respect to creativity were somewhat equivocal; nevertheless, several investigators were able to demonstrate a relationship between the defense scores and indices of creativity.

Clinical Studies

A second area of investigation involves studies in which researchers have used defense scores from the Holt manual to assess the impact on thinking of specific clinical conditions.

Saretsky (1966) investigated the effects of chlorpromazine on the Rorschach records of a group of schizophrenic patients. Forty hospitalized male patients were divided into experimental and control groups with subjects in the experimental group receiving chlorpromazine and those in the control group a placebo. The pre- and post-drug Rorschach protocols for each subject were scored for mean defense effectiveness. For both groups, the author reported significant increases in the defense effectiveness score, thus indicating changes in the patients' attitudes toward disturbing ideation and the manner of controlling it. Furthermore, independent ratings of clinical improvement in both groups correlated significantly with the degree of improvement in the defense-effectiveness score.

A second study employed the Holt scoring system to assess changes in thought processes in a patient diagnosed as having myxedema psychosis. Because treatment of this illness with desiccated thyroid results in rapid clinical improvement, Greenberg and associates (1969) administered three Rorschachs over a seven-month period to a 17-year-old female patient having the disease. The patient was tested three days after thyroxin treatment was initiated, two months later, and during a follow-up period five months after the second testing. Between the first and second testing the patient's clinical condition improved dramatically, whereas between the second and third evaluations the improved state was maintained. Ratings on mean defense effectiveness increased and were consistent with the improved clinical state.

Group Differences

Other studies have investigated differences in the expression and control of primary process manifestations among groups differentiated on the basis of some other psychological variable.

Zimet and Fine (1965) investigated differences in the extent and nature of thought disturbance between subgroups of schizophrenic patients. The Rorschach records of 23 reactive schizophrenics and 36 process schizophrenics were scored using several of the Holt summary ratings. Consistent with clinical expectations, the reactive schizophrenics produced significantly more modulated and controlled primary process responses than did the process group.

Benfari and Calogeras (1968) studied differences in types of thinking between groups distinguished on the basis of conscience development. Forty college students were subdivided into two groups according to their responses to a conscience scale. The members of one subgroup, referred to as having a "nonintegrated conscience," were characterized both by a tendency to hold severe moral principles and strict prohibitions and by a compelling desire to rebel against these severe standards. These subjects revealed inner conflict by presenting such affects as guilt, self-reproach, and ambivalence. The other group, designated "integrated conscience," included subjects who held strong ethical beliefs and a disciplined acceptance of these standards. Conflict regarding values and behavior was not evident in this group. Using scores from the Holt manual, support was found for the proposition that a less well-controlled and defended ego is associated with a more punitive and conflicted conscience.

In conclusion, as part of his attempt to operationalize the concepts of primary and secondary process, Holt devised a number of individual and summary defense scores to evaluate the way in which, as well as how effectively, primary process manifestations are controlled. Unfortunately, the individual scores have received little support in the research literature. Agreement in scoring between raters for the individual categories has not been satisfactory; Lerner and Lewandowski (1975), however, found that scoring was relatively easy if the content and formal expressions of primary process were scored accurately. Although the individual scores, in general, have not been used in studies of validity, H. Lerner and P. Lerner (1982) found negation and minimization to be effective and useful indices of higher level forms of denial. By contrast, research involving several summary scores has been extensive. Highly satisfactory levels of reliability have been reported for the following scores: defense demand, defense effectiveness, and adaptive regression. Measures of defense effectiveness and adaptive regression have been related to the following: (1) a number of conceptually related cognitive and perceptual factors; (2) changes in thought organization associated with improvement in clinical states; and (3) differences between groups distinguished on the basis of either diagnosis or integration of conscience.

Rorschach Index of Repressive Style

Levine and Spivak (1964) devised the Rorschach Index of Repressive Style (RIRS) initially as an attempt to operationalize Freud's concept of repression. In his article "The Unconscious" (1915b), Freud noted that "repression is essentially a process affecting ideas on the border between the systems Ucs and Pcs" (p. 180). Levine and Spivak inferred from Freud's statement that repression works through the cognitive system and has the effect of inhibiting ideational processes.

Were they to have continued conceiving of their scale of repressive style as a measure of the ideational results of repression, their line of reasoning would have been similar to that of Holt. Over time, however, they modified their conceptual basis and came to conceive of their scale as a measure of an ideational style that predisposes one to the use of repression. It is important to keep this conceptual shift in mind, for in the research accompanying the scale the authors do not always make explicit which view of repression they are attempting to assess. As well, this conceptual ambiguity leads to methodological weaknesses in the research itself.

Having shifted their conceptual base from a measure of repression to a measure of repressive style, Levine and Spivak (1964) operationally defined repressive style as "a consistent characteristic of an individual that is manifest in vague, unelaborated language which is lacking in integration and flow" (p. 14). Focusing not as much on the response itself as on the manner in which the response is delivered, the scoring manual represents an attempt to systematically assess the construct of repressive style.

The system calls for the scoring of each response along the following seven dimensions: specificity, elaboration, impulse responses, presence of primary process thinking, self references, presence of movement, and associative flow. Underlying these factors is the thesis that to the extent that the verbalization of a response is impersonal, lacks movement, reflects vague and unelaborated thinking, is unintegrated, and reveals an absence of associative flow, the greater is the degree of repressive functioning. Conversely, the more specific, detailed, reality bound, and logical a response is, and the more it is offered with a free flow of words, the less the degree of repressive functioning.

The scale has been subjected to several types of tests of reliability. Levine and Spivak reported on four separate studies in which inter-rater correlations of .95 to .98 were obtained. The combined results led the authors to conclude that the scale could be scored with considerable consistency by different scorers across various samples.

Because it is assumed that the scale measures an enduring, characterological feature, the authors thought it important to demonstrate the measure's long-term reliability. Data obtained by both Paulsen and Ledwith (Levine and Spivak, 1964) indicate that repressive style is not only an enduring mode of response but, in addition, becomes characteristic of a child at about seven years of age.

Several studies have been conducted to assess the retest reliability of the RIRS. Collectively, these studies found that when the conditions of administration remain constant but different inkblots are used, reliability correlations range from .50 to .67. When the same inkblots are administered under the same conditions within a relatively short interval of time, reliability correlations range between .74 and .82.

Attempts to establish the concurrent validity of the RIRS have involved investigating the relationship between the scale and other Rorschach scores, as well as between the scale and a specific Thematic Apperception Test (TAT) score. In a sample of 68 student nurses, Levine and Spivak (1964) found RIRS scores to be most highly correlated with movement responses (M), color responses (c), and the experience balance. Whereas subjects with high RIRS scores (i.e., less repressive functioning) tended to offer a dilated experience balance, those with low RIRS scores (i.e., higher repressive functioning) produced constricted experience balances. The authors, using as criteria more traditional Rorschach scores, took these findings as indicating that subjects who obtain high RIRS scores tend to produce richer and fuller records. In a second study, which involved 92 college students and used the Holtzman Inkblots, Levine and Spivak (1964) substantiated the earlier findings and also found a positive and significant correlation between RIRS and the number of pure form responses.

Levine and Spivak also studied the relationship between RIRS and TAT "transcendence scores." These scores represent an attempt to assess the extent to which a subject's description of the TAT cards goes beyond the immediate stimulus properties of each card. As predicted, RIRS was found to correlate positively with several indices of transcendence.

From the foregoing studies, then, the authors concluded that subjects who produce high RIRS scores (i.e., less repressive functioning) tend, on other measures, to manifest a richness of intellectual and affective responsiveness, reveal a capacity for reflectiveness, and are able to effect delay of impulse gratification.

Further efforts to demonstrate concurrent validity have included investigations of the relationship between RIRS and questionnaire measures of anxiety and repression. In general, the findings have not been impressive. Correlations between the RIRS and various anxiety scales (Taylor Manifest Anxiety Scale, Saranson Test Anxiety Scale, Cattel IPAT) have been at a borderline level of statistical significance, and none of the relationships has been strong (Levine and Spivak, 1964). With specific regard to repression, little relationship was found in a sample of 155 college students between the RIRS score and the following MMPI scales: the repression scale, the internalization ratio, Hawley's defensive scale, the K scale, and the repression-sensitization scale (Levine and Spivak, 1964).

The construct validity of the scale has been investigated in several studies that have attempted to relate RIRS scores to the ego capacity to tolerate sensory isolation and to various cognitive-perceptual dimensions, including field dependence-independence and leveling-sharpening.

Using the data obtained by Goldberger (1961) in his study of reactions to sensory isolation, Levine and Spivak (1964) rescored the Rorschach protocols employing the RIRS scale. RIRS scores were found to correlate positively and significantly with ratings of the capacity to adapt to sensory isolation ($r = .61$, $p < .05$), as well as with a rating of frequency and vividness of imagery ($r = .73$, $p < .01$). No significant relationship was found between RIRS score and a measure of maladaptive reaction to sensory isolation.

Because Witkin's (1950) description of the personality characteristics of field-dependent and field-independent individuals seemed in keeping with their own understanding of repressive style as assessed by the RIRS, Levine and Spivak (1964) investigated the relationship between the RIRS and measures of field dependence. Using a supplied group of Rorschach protocols obtained from 24 10-year-olds for whom perceptual measures were also available, the authors reported a correlation of $< .25$ between the RIRS score and an index of field dependence. Consistent results were also obtained on data collected by Young (1959), whose sample consisted of college students. In both studies the results, although not strong, indicate that subjects who manifest repressive functioning in the Rorschach, as measured by the RIRS, tend to be field dependent.

Leveling-sharpening, a cognitive dimension investigated by Holtzman and Gardner (1959), refers to the extent to which a subject in solving cognitive tasks is guided more by internal cues (sharpeners) than by immediate, external perceptual properties (levelers). Rorschach protocols previously obtained by Holtzman and Gardner from 10 extreme levelers and 10 extreme sharpeners drawn from a sample of 80 female college students were rescored for RIRS by Levine and Spivak. The authors reported a mean RIRS of 2.25 for levelers and 2.77 for sharpeners, which was significant between the .05 and .10

levels of significance. This result, together with the finding that the RIRS correlated especially well with a measure of ranking accuracy, led the authors to conclude that subjects who score higher on the RIRS tend to perceive stimuli more discretely and then use the discrete impression as an internal frame of reference against which new stimuli are judged.

On the basis of consistent findings across these studies of sensory isolation, field independence-field dependence, and leveling-sharpening, Levine and Spivak (1964) interpreted the results as indicating that subjects who differ on the RIRS dimension also differ with respect to the degree to which they have available and can use their own thoughts and fantasies in interpreting experience, the extent to which they rely on the external properties of the situation, and the extent to which they respond to their surroundings in terms of an internal frame of reference. More specifically, whereas low RIRS subjects (those more globally repressive) tend to be more reliant on immediate perceptual aspects of a situation, look outside of themselves for guiding cues, and have little inner frame of reference, high RIRS subjects (those less globally repressive), by contrast, respond to given situations by interpreting them in terms of their own readily available ideas and memories.

Clinical Groups

Another group of studies was undertaken to compare RIRS scores between clinical groups who, on theoretical grounds, are assumed to differ with respect to their reliance on repression.

Clinical experience shows that the typical patient who relies on repression as a defense is the hysteric, whereas intellectualization and isolation of affect are the defenses one finds in the obsessive-compulsive. Using this clinical impression, Levine and Spivak (1964) reviewed 16 Rorschach records, eight for each syndrome, and scored the protocols using the RIRS scale.

Whereas the mean score for the eight hysterics was 1.97, that for the obsessive compulsives was 3.55 (lower score indicates greater repression). Using the U test, this difference was found to be significant at the .001 level of significance. An investigation of the individual records indicated that the two hysterical cases with the highest RIRS scores were also described as individuals who were tested at a point in which their repressive defenses were failing.

Pursuing this latter finding in a second study, Levine and Spivak

(1964) compared RIRS scores of four patients, each of whom represented a different level of severity of breakdown of repressive defenses. The scores for the respective patients were as follows: well-defended hysteric with repressive trends, 1.47; hysteric with phobic and depressive features presenting precarious defenses, 1.59; hysteric with badly faltering defenses, 2.66; and a borderline psychotic with multiple phobias but with a heavy reliance on repressive defenses, 1.92. In this study of individual cases, then, lower RIRS scores were associated with well-functioning repressive defenses while higher scores seemed to be associated with failing defenses.

Based on the thesis that psychosomatic involvement is associated with a reliance on repression, a third study compared Rorschach records of a group of neurotic patients with somatic complaints with the records of a group of neurotics who presented with other psychological complaints. As predicted, the patients with psychosomatic disorders produced, in general, more repressed Rorschach protocols, as judged by RIRS scores.

In summary, basing their work on Rapaport's pioneering efforts to systematize the ways in which Rorschach responses are delivered, Levine and Spivak creatively quantified this dimension by devising a scale for measuring a specific mode of cognition. Although the scale has considerable face validity and has generated much research, its conceptual base is nonetheless somewhat ambiguous, and many of the supporting studies suffer from methodological weaknesses.

As noted previously, the scale was initially developed to assess the specific defense of repression; however, in time, the authors modified this conceptualization and began to conceive of the scale as measuring a more general cognitive style that predisposed one to the use of repression. As a consequence of this shift, it appears that some studies (i.e., those involving a comparison of different diagnostic groups) were designed and based on the initial conceptualization whereas other studies (i.e., those involving the relationship between the scale and specific cognitive controls) were based on the later conceptualization. Thus, it is not always clear which construct the studies are meant to validate.

Apart from suggesting that ideational style predisposes one to the use of repression, the authors did not develop as fully as possible the more general relationship between cognition and defense, nor did they fully explore and detail the repressive cognitive style. Shapiro (1965) has comprehensively described a cognitive style, which he refers to as the "hysterical style," that is strikingly similar to the one described by

Levine and Spivak. Shapiro carefully delineated the relationship between this style and repression, but he also cautioned that "this mode of functioning or, specifically, of cognition decidedly *favors* the phenomenon we describe as 'repression'" (p. 117). In other words— and consistent with clinical experience—Shapiro is suggesting that there is not a one-to-one relationship between cognitive style and defense, and that cognition is only one aspect of the matrix that determines the specific defense.

Because of the conceptual ambiguities and the contention of Levine and Spivak that the RIRS assesses a unitary dimension, there is much confusion regarding the meaning of higher scale scores. Although higher scores are conceived of as indicating less repressive functioning, in certain studies high scores seem to indicate the use of defenses other than repression, whereas in other studies the higher scores are taken to indicate a breakdown in the defense of repression. Clearly, a preference for other defenses and the faltering of repression are quite different matters.

With respect to methodology, most of the results reported by Levine and Spivak were taken from studies in which the original data were collected by others and, typically, for other purposes; that is to say, Levine and Spivak secured Rorschach protocols from other projects and then rescored these records for RIRS. Thus, not only were the Rorschach records obtained under varying circumstances, but in addition, examiners differing in experience, training, and method of administration initially obtained the records. Levine and Spivak themselves found that although the correlation between RIRS scores is high when the conditions of reexamination are constant, changes in certain conditions of administration affect the scores.

Despite the above-noted conceptual difficulties and methodological weaknesses, the scale does represent an attempt to systematize an important component of Rorschach testing (the delivery of the response) within an overall theoretical framework. Several of the component dimensions identified by Levine and Spivak (specificity, elaboration, impulsivity, and associative flow) are similar to indices Schafer (1954) also used as indicators of a reliance on repression. This, together with the consideration that studies involving the scale have yielded positive findings, suggests that if the conceptual ambiguities can be clarified, especially in the light of later works on repression (Shapiro, 1965; Horowitz, 1972; Krohn, 1978), then the scoring system could serve as a basis for constructing a Rorschach measure of repression. With the more recent growth of interest in primitive

defenses (H. Lerner and P. Lerner, 1982), especially as they contrast
with repression, the need for a valid measure of repression is particularly pressing at the time.

◆ ◆ ◆ Summary

In parallel with shifts in psychoanalytic theory, concepts of defense
have shifted; yet, the notion of defense has remained a cornerstone of
the theory. As part of an overall review of the construct and the ways
it has been operationalized in Rorschach terms, in this chapter I have
reviewed Freud's notions of defense, as conceived first within drive theory and then as reconceptualized within the structural model. I then
discussed two comprehensive Rorschach scoring systems based on
Freud's respective formulations.

Although both scoring systems have generated a considerable
amount of research, many of the studies have suffered from methodological weaknesses. In addition, both scales have proved too cum-
bersome for clinical application.

Overall, the scales have attempted to operationalize a concept of
defense that was abstract and somewhat elusive, couched in mechanistic terms, and embedded in a system of hypothetical energic forces.
Then too, because both drive theory and structural theory have been
pitched at a metapsychological level, their constituent concepts, such
as defense, have been defined in ways far removed from the clinical
situation and the patient's experience. It is this "experience-distant"
quality that has proved troublesome to researchers and has resulted in
a variety of methodological difficulties.

More recently, interest has shifted away from drive theory and
structural theory and toward object-relations theory and self psychology. Accordingly, the concept of defense has been reformulated in
important and refreshingly new ways. These reformulations and the
research they have spawned are the subject matter of the next chapter.

18

RORSCHACH ASSESSMENT
OF DEFENSE:
2. RECENT MEASURES

As noted in the previous chapter, important and innovative changes are arising in the concept of defense. These modifications, in part, have been stimulated by the British school of object relations, beginning with the writings of Melanie Klein. While anchoring her views in several of Freud's specific formulations, Klein nonetheless fundamentally reconceptualized defense by suggesting that such mechanisms not only regulate affects and drives, but are also related to the effects on intimacy and cognition of the experience, organization, and internalization of object relations. For Klein, defenses not only protect the ego from overwhelming sensations, but are also nondefensive organizing principles of infantile mental life.

Two such organizing principles stand out in Klein's portrait of infantile mentation: splitting and projection. Klein's view of splitting derives from Freud's (1915) use of the concept in "Instincts and Their Vicissitudes," in which he proposes the idea of an early developmental distinction between a purified pleasure ego and a collection of excessively negative object impressions (Grala, 1980). Whereas the pleasure ego represents an internalization of gratifying object relations, the latter results from a projection of feelings associated with nongratifying, frustrating object relations.

A special form of projection detailed by Klein is projective identification. Here, unwanted parts of the self and internal object are split off and projected onto an external object. Because the object is not felt to be separate, but rather is identified with the projected parts, the process affords possession of and control over the object. Bion (1967) extended the concept of projective identification in terms of the metaphor of the container and the contained. He suggested that projective identification not only allows the disavowal and projection of unwanted parts of the self but also permits the containment of such parts within the object.

An attempt to integrate the two streams of psychoanalytic formulations of defense—the ego psychological and that evolving from the British school of object relations—is represented by the work of Kernberg (1975), particularly by his structural concept of levels of defensive organization. Kernberg proposes a hierarchical organization of levels of character pathology linked to type of defensive functioning and developmental level of internalized object relation. For Kernberg, internalized object relations are organized on the basis of specific defensive structures. As part of this model, he systematically defines and coordinates the more primitive defenses described by Klein and clarifies the distinction between splitting and repression. Accordingly, while splitting is a developmental precursor of repression, it continues to function pathologically in those patients who are preoedipally fixated, as indicated by an inability to form whole object relations and by a disturbance in object constancy.

Kernberg has identified two overall levels of defensive organization of the ego, one associated with preoedipal and the other with oedipal pathology. At the lower level, splitting or primitive dissociation is the basic defensive operation, with a concomitant impairment of the ego's synthetic function. Splitting is bolstered through the related defenses of low-level denial, primitive idealization, primitive devaluation, and projective identification. At a higher developmental level, associated with oedipal pathology, repression supplants splitting as a major defense and is accompanied by the related defensive operations of intellectualization, rationalization, undoing, and higher-level forms of denial and projection.

◆ ◆ ◆ Lerner Defense Scale

On the basis of Kernberg's theoretical conceptualizations of defense and the clinical test work of Mayman (1967), Pruitt and Spilka (1964),

Holt (1970), and Peebles (1975), P. Lerner and H. Lerner (1980) devised a Rorschach scoring manual designed to evaluate the specific defensive operations presumed to characterize the developmentally lower level of defensive functioning.

The scoring manual is divided into sections on the basis of the specific defenses of splitting, devaluation, idealization, projective identification, and denial. Within each section the defense is defined, Rorschach indices of the defense are presented, and clinical illustrations are offered. The sections on devaluation, idealization, and denial call for an identification of the defense and a ranking of the defense on a continuum of high versus low order. In keeping both with Kernberg's contention that these defenses organize and reflect the internal object world and with the empirical relationship found between human responses on the Rorschach test and quality of object relations (Blatt and Lerner, 1983), the system involves a systematic appraisal of the human-figure response. In assessing the human percept, attention is accorded the precise figure seen (e.g., clowns, warriors, magicians), the way in which the figure is described, and the action ascribed to the figure.

Scoring System

Rationale

Our emphasis on the structural concept of defense was prompted by several considerations. These defenses are considered intrinsic to the nature and quality of the borderline patient's object relations. In addition, because these structures have been well described and illustrated in a clinical context, they lend themselves to operationalization and, eventually, quantification. Finally, if these defenses can be reliably and validly assessed, then not only the clinical researcher but also the clinical practitioner would be furnished a tool of much explanatory and predictive worth.

General Scoring Considerations

1. In general, the basic unit to be scored is the response containing an entire human figure, either static or in movement (H response). There are two exceptions to this principle. Several of the indices for splitting involve two responses. In these instances, only one score is

awarded. Also, one of the scores for projective identification involves the scoring of human-detail responses.

2. Before applying the system, all responses should be scored for form level using a system devised by Mayman (1970).

3. The sections on devaluation, idealization, and denial call for an identification of these defenses, as well as a ranking of the defense on a continuum of high versus low order.

4. Any response may receive more than one score.

5. In assessing the human percept, attention should be paid to the following aspects of the response: the action ascribed to the figure, the way in which the figure is described, and the exact figure seen.

Specific Defenses and Their Scoring

Splitting

Splitting involves an admixture of separations of drives, affects, internal object representations, external object relations, and introjective mechanisms (Robbins, 1976). With regard to object relations, splitting refers to what a person does to and with his inner and outer objects. More specifically, it involves a division of internal and external into (1) parts, as distinct from wholes, and (2) good and bad part-objects (Pruyser, 1975). Behaviorally, splitting is manifest in a tendency to perceive and describe others in terms of overruling polarities (Pruyser, 1975). While these polarities convey the division of good versus bad, they may take several forms, including frustrating versus satisfying, dangerous versus benign, and friendly versus hostile. The tendency to polarize affective descriptions of objects underlies the indices considered indicative of splitting. To denote splitting, use the letter S.

Score splitting in the following cases.

(A) In a sequence of responses, a human percept described in terms of a specific, nonambivalent, nonambiguous affective dimension is immediately followed by another human response in which the affective description is opposite that used to describe the preceding responses: for example, "looks like an ugly criminal with a gun" immediately followed by "couples sitting together cheek to cheek."

(B) In the description of one total human figure a clear distinction of parts is made, so that one part of the figure is seen as opposite another part: for example, "A giant. His lower part here conveys danger, but his top half looks benign."

(C) Included in one response are two clearly distinguished figures, and these figures are described in opposite ways: for example, "Two figures, a man and a woman. He is mean and shouting at her. Being rather angelic, she's standing there and taking it."

(D) An implicitly idealized figure is tarnished or spoiled by the addition of one or more features, or an implicitly devalued figure is enhanced by the addition of one or more features: for example, "a headless angel."

Devaluation

Devaluation refers to a tendency to depreciate, tarnish, and lessen the importance of one's inner and outer objects. It is considered a muted form of spoiling and, as such, is closely linked to envy. Specifically, devaluation is conceptualized as an aim of envy as well as a defense against it. Envy aims at being as good as the object; when this is felt as unattainable, however, it then seeks to spoil that goodness in the object and thus remove the source of the envious feelings (Segal, 1973). In addition to identifying the defense, devaluation is also rated on a five-point continuum. Underlying the continuum are three dimensions. The first dimension involves the degree to which the humanness of the figure is retained. For example, such percepts as waiters or clowns are accorded a higher score than are more distorted forms, such as monsters and mythological objects. A temporal-spatial consideration determines the second dimension. Contemporary human percepts set in a current and close locale are scored higher than are those percepts from either the past or future and set in a distant setting. The final dimension involves the severity of depreciation as conveyed in the affective description. Figures described in more primitive, blatant, socially unacceptable ways are scored lower than are those that are described in negatively tinged but more civilized and socially acceptable ways. To denote devaluation, use the symbol DV. Add to this score the number below that corresponds to the appropriate level of devaluation. For example, "an angry man" is scored DV1.

(1) The humanness dimension is retained, there is no distancing of the figure in time or space, and the figure is described in negatively tinged but socially acceptable terms: for example, "two people fighting"; "a girl in a funny costume."

(2) The humanness dimension is retained, there may or may not be distancing of the figure in time or space, and the figure is described in

blatantly negative and socially unacceptable negative terms. This score would also include human figures with parts missing: for example, "a diseased African child"; "a woman defecating"; "sinister-looking male figure"; "a disjointed figure with the head missing."

(3) The humanness dimension is retained, but involved in the percept is a distortion of human form; there may or may not be distancing of the figure in time or space; and if the figure is described negatively, it is in socially acceptable terms. This rating includes such figures as clowns, elves, savages, witches, devils, and figures of the occult: for example, "sad looking clowns"; "cannibal standing over a pot"; "the bad witch."

(4) The humanness dimension is retained, but implied in the percept is a distortion of human form. There may or may not be distancing of the figure in time or space, and the figure is described in blatantly negative and socially unacceptable terms. This rating involves the same types of figures as in (3); however, the negative description is more severe: for example, "a couple of evil witches"; "two people from Mars who look very scary"; "a sinister Ku Klux Klansman."

(5) The humanness dimension is lost, there may or may not be distancing of the distorted form in time or space, and the figure is described in either neutral or negative terms. This rating includes puppets, mannequins, robots, creatures with some human characteristics, part-human–part-animal responses, and human responses with one or more animal features: for example, "Mannequins with dresses but missing a head"; "two people but half-male and half-animal from outer space"; "a woman with breasts, high-heeled shoes, and bird's beak for a mouth."

Idealization

Idealization involves a denial of unwanted characteristics of an object and then an enhancing of the object by projecting one's own libido or omnipotence onto it. It aims at keeping an object completely separate from persecutory objects, which preserves the object from harm and destruction. This defensive aspect of idealization—that is, its aim is to protect the object from inner harm—is precarious, for the more ideal the object becomes, the more likely it is to arouse envy. As in the case of devaluation, idealization is also rated on a five-point continuum. Underlying the continuum are the same three dimensions. For scoring, denote idealization with the letter I. Add to this score the number below that corresponds with the appropriate level of idealization. Thus, "a person with a big smile" is scored I1.

(1) The humanness dimension is retained, there is no distancing of the figure in time or space, and the figure is described in a positive but not excessively flattering way: for example, "two nice people looking over a fence"; "a person with a happy smile."

(2) The humanness dimension is retained, there may or may not be distancing of the person in time or space, and the figure is described in blatantly and excessively positive terms: for example, "two handsome, muscular Russians doing that famous dance"; "What an angelic figure; long hair, a flowing gown, and a look of complete serenity."

(3) The humanness dimension is retained, but implied in the percept is a distortion of human form. There may or may not be distancing of the figure in time or space, and if the figure is described positively, it is in moderate terms. This rating includes such objects of fame, adoration, or strength as civic leaders, officials, and famous people: for example, "Charles de Gaulle"; "an astronaut, one of those fellows who landed on the moon."

(4) The humanness dimension is retained, but implied in the percept is a distortion of human form. There may or may not be distancing of the figure in time or space, and the figure is described in blatantly and excessively positive terms. This rating includes the same types of figures as in (3); however, the positive description is more excessive: for example, "a warrior; not just any warrior but the tallest, strongest, and bravest"; "Attila the Hun, but with the largest genitals I have ever seen."

(5) The humanness dimension is lost, but implied in the distortion is an enhancement of identity. There may or may not be distancing of the distorted form in time or space, and the figure is described in either neutral or positive terms. This rating includes statues of famous figures, giants, supermen or superwomen, space figures with supernatural powers, angels, and idols. Also included are half-humans in which the nonhuman aspect nonetheless adds to the figure's appearance or power: for example, "a bust of Queen Victoria"; "powerful beings from another planet ruling over these softer creatures."

Projective Identification

This refers to a process in which parts of the self are split off and projected onto an external object or part-object. It differs from projection proper in that what is projected onto the object is not experienced as ego alien. Rather, the self "empathizes" (Kernberg, 1975) with the object and tries to control the object by means of the projection. A close examination of the concept of projective identification suggests the operation of at least three subprocesses: an externalization of parts of the self with a disregard of real characteristics of the external object, a capacity to blur boundaries between self and other, and an overriding need to control the other. The two indices of projective identification represent an attempt to assess these subprocesses. To denote this score, use the letters PI.

Score projective identification in the following cases.

(A) Confabulatory responses involving human figures in which the form level[1] is Fw− or F− and the percept is overly embellished with associative elaboration to the point that real properties of the blot are disregarded and replaced by fantasies and affects. More typically, the associative elaboration involves material with aggressive or sexual meaning, as in the following example: "A huge man coming to get me. I can see his huge teeth. He's staring straight at me. His hands are up as if he will strike me."

(B) Those human or detail responses in which the location is Dr, the determinant is Fc, and the figure is described as either aggressive or having been aggressed against[2]: for example, "an ugly face" (with forehead and features seen in reference to the inner portion of Card IV); "an injured man" (Card VI upper, center area).

Denial

Denial in this system refers to a broad group of defenses arranged on a continuum based on the degree of reality distortion involved in the response. Higher-level forms of denial involve a minimum of reality

---

1. These scores are taken from Mayman's (1970) manual for form level scoring. The Fw− score is assigned to unconvincing, weak form responses in which only one blot detail is accurately perceived. The F− score refers to arbitrary form responses in which there is little resemblance between the percept and the area of the blot being responded to.

2. Dr is a location score used when the area chosen is small, rarely used, and arbitrarily delimited (Rapaport, Gill, and Schafer, 1945). Fc is a determinant used when the subject makes out forms within a heavily shaded area without using shading as shading or uses the nuances of shading within a colored area (Rapaport, Gill, and Schafer, 1945).

distortion, whereas middle- and lower-level manifestations of denial include increasingly greater degrees of reality distortion. Examples of denial at the highest level include several defensive processes observed by Holt (1970) and presented in his manual for the scoring of manifestations of primary process thinking. Middle-level denial includes responses in which there is a major contradiction between the human figure perceived and the actions or characteristics ascribed to that figure. Lower-level manifestations of denial involve significant distortions of reality, to the point that a segment of subjective experience or of the external world is not integrated with the rest of the experience. There is a striking loss of reality testing, and the individual acts as if he were unaware of an urgent, pressing aspect of reality. To score denial, use the symbol DN. Add to this score the number below that corresponds to the level of denial. Thus, the response "I know they are not fighting" would be scored DN1.

(1) *Higher-level denial:* Denial at this level consists of several subsidiary defenses manifested in responses in which the form level of the percept is F+, Fo, or Fw+.

   (a) *Negation:* Negation involves a disavowal of impulse. The disavowal may be manifested in two ways. In one, the disavowal is smoothly blended into the response itself, whereas in the other the response, or aspects of the response, are couched in negative terms: for example, "virgin"; "angel"; "these figures are not angry."

   (b) *Intellectualization:* In this process, the response is stripped of its drive and affective charge by its being presented in an overly technical, scientific, literate, or intellectual way: for example, "two homo sapiens"; "two Kafkaesque figures."

   (c) *Minimization:* With minimization, drive-laden material is included in the response, but in a reduced and nonthreatening way. This includes changing a human figure into a caricature or cartoon figure: for example, "a shadow cast by an evil person"; "a child with his hand clenched in a fist"; "a funny man, more like a caricature."

   (d) *Repudiation:* With repudiation, a response is retracted or the individual denies having even given the response.

(2) *Middle-level denial:* Denial at this level involves responses in which the form level is F+, Fo, or Fw+, and involved in the response is a basic contradiction. The contradiction may be on affective, logical, or reality grounds: for example, "a sexy Santa Claus"; "two nuns fighting"; "a man reading while asleep."

(3) *Lower-level denial:* At this level, reality adherence is abrogated, but in a particular way. Specifically, an acceptable response is rendered unacceptable either by adding something that is not there or by failing to take into account an aspect of the blot that is clearly to be seen. This corresponds to Mayman's (1970) form spoil (Fs) response.[3] In addition, this level *also* includes responses in which incompatible descriptions are given to the percept: for example, "two people, but their top half is the female and bottom half male; each has breasts and a penis"; "a person, but instead of a mouth there is a bird's beak"; "a person sitting on its huge tail."

Reliability

The reliability of the scoring system has been reported in various studies. Commonly, independent judges trained in scoring rate a series of Rorschach protocols and then the level of agreement among the judges for each of the defenses is determined.

In the initial investigation (P. Lerner and H. Lerner, 1980) 10 Rorschach records (of five borderline and five neurotic patients) were scored independently by two well-trained raters. The percentage of perfect agreement between the raters for the major defense categories was as follows: splitting, 100%; devaluation, 91%; idealization, 87%; projective identification, 100%; and denial, 83%. For the subcategories, percentages of perfect agreement ranged from 76% to 95%.

In a second study (Lerner, Sugarman, and Gaughran, 1981) of borderline and schizophrenic groups, high levels of inter-rater reliability were also obtained. Correlation coefficients ranging from .94 to .99 were obtained for the major defense categories, and coefficients between .74 and .95 for the continuum variables. Collapsing the continuum variables into composite scores yielded reliability coefficients ranging from .94 to .96.

Subsequent authors have also reported high levels of reliability as determined by inter-rater agreement. Van-Der Keshet (1988), in a study involving anorexic subjects, reported Cronbach alpha coefficients ranging from 1.00 to .80, and Gacono (1988), in an investiga-

---

3. The form spoil response differs from the F− response in that a basically acceptable response is spoiled by a perceptual oversight or distortion. In the F− response the percept is totally unacceptable.

tion of several subgroups of psychopaths, obtained the following percentages of agreement between raters: projective identification, 100%; idealization, 100%; denial, 100%; and devaluation, 88%. Among the protocols selected for determining reliability, Gacono noted that there were no scoreable responses for splitting.

In summary, results from various studies indicate that the reliability of the scoring system for the Lerner Defense Scale, as judged by level of inter-rater agreement, is particularly high for an inkblot measure.

Validity and Findings

Kernberg (1975, 1977, 1979) has repeatedly asserted that the constellation of lower-level primitive defenses distinguishes borderline and psychotic patients, on the one hand, from neurotic patients, on the other. Thus, to evaluate the construct validity of the scoring system, as well as the utility of Kernberg's proposals, the initial validating studies involved comparing the Rorschach records of borderline patients with the protocols of other clinical groups with respect to manifestations of primitive defenses.

P. Lerner and H. Lerner (1980) compared the Rorschach protocols of 15 outpatient borderline patients with 15 outpatient neurotics with regard to indices of primitive defense. The 30 Rorschach protocols were selected from the private files of one of the authors and scored using the proposed system. Because the testing had initially been conducted for research purposes, the test protocols had not been used in formulating the final diagnoses on which the selections were based. In this way, the selection procedures were guaranteed to be unconfounded by psychological test data. The full assessments included independently obtained mental status examinations and social-developmental histories. As each of the patients subsequently entered either psychotherapy or psychoanalysis, the initial diagnosis was confirmed in discussions with the patient's therapist or analyst. The two original groups (of borderlines and neurotics) were matched on the variables of age, sex, and socioeconomic status. The Rorschach records obtained from the two groups did not differ significantly with regard to the total number of responses.

Several significant findings emerged from this study. The borderline patients manifested test indices of splitting, low-level devaluation, projective identification, and low-level denial significantly more often than did the neurotic patients. The measures of splitting and projective identification, which were observed exclusively in the borderline group, proved especially significant in discriminating the two groups. By contrast, indices of high-level devaluation and high-level denial were found more often in the protocols of the neurotic group. In general, and irrespective of level of severity, measures of idealization occurred more frequently in the records of the neurotic group. With devaluation, the reverse was found. That is, borderline patients tended to depreciate their human figures more often than did the neurotic patients. A review of the individual Rorschach records highlighted the importance of high-level denial. When neurotic patients used low-level devaluation or low-level idealization, it was typically accompanied by manifestations of high-level denial. Such was not the case with the protocols of borderline patients. Their expressions of blatant depreciation and excessive idealization were not mitigated by forms of higher-level denial.

The results of this study not only support theoretical propositions, they coincide with clinical experience as well. Those of us who work with borderline patients are familiar with these patients' intense rage, seeming imperviousness to their impact on others, and tendency to rapidly fluctuate between overvaluing their therapist and regarding their therapist with disdain and contempt. Indeed, with borderline patients, the therapist pays particular attention to how he or she is treated by the patient. The obtained findings shed light on these clinical occurrences. Specifically, it would appear that structures available to better-organized patients—in this instance, high-level denial and idealization—are not available to the borderline patient. Therapeutically, this suggests that because such controlling structures cannot be employed for containing affects and urges, control and regulation need to be provided by the environment. This suggested stance is in accord with Winnicott, who goes so far as to suggest that with certain patients the aggressive and destructive actions may be viewed as unconscious attempts to elicit specific responses from the environment.

In a companion study, H. Lerner, Sugarman, and Gaughran (1981) compared the Rorschach records of a group of hospitalized borderline patients with those of a hospitalized schizophrenic group. In this study, Rorschach protocols were obtained from patient files at a university teaching hospital. Patients at the facility received psychological testing as a standard procedure within the first several weeks of admissions. The sample of borderline patients (N = 21) was selected according to criteria set out in DSM-III. The criteria were applied to information gleaned from a preadmission report that included a history of the present illness, past history, a mental-status examination, and a tentative diagnostic formulation. The sample of schizophrenic patients (N = 19) was selected using the Research Diagnostic Criteria (RDC) of Spitzer, Endicott, and Robbins (1975). The RDC was applied to information obtained from the preadmission summaries in the same manner as DSM-III was used for the borderline sample. In this study, as in the Lerner and Lerner (1980) study cited earlier, the Rorschach records for the two groups did not differ significantly with regard to the total number of responses.

Several significant findings emerged when the defense scores of the borderline and schizophrenic patients were compared. The borderline patients manifested indices of splitting significantly more often than did the schizophrenic patients, and four of the five scale measures of devaluation also were observed significantly more frequently in the borderline group. Indices of projective identification occurred exclusively in the borderline group. With regard to denial, the borderline patients gave significantly more responses at the middle and low levels, and when denial was treated as a composite score, it especially distinguished the two groups.

While the results of the Lerner and Lerner (1980) study supported Kernberg's (1975) formulation of two overall levels of defense organization that differentiate borderline and neurotic patients, the findings of Lerner, Sugarman, and Gaughran (1981) questioned his contention that borderline and schizophrenic patients share a common primitive defensive constellation. In contrast with Kernberg, Lerner and Lerner (1982) have suggested that the results of this study indicate that the defensive organization of the schizophrenic patient is different in kind, along a number of developmental and structural parameters, from the defensive structure of the borderline patient. Splitting, denial, projective identification, and various levels of devaluation were found to discriminate significantly between the two groups. Because the Rorschach measures of the defenses were based on an appraisal of the full human response, it seemed to Lerner and Lerner (1982) that "differences in the level of object representation underlying the specific defenses" (p. 99) accounted for the group differences. Further support for their inference came from the additional finding that the schizophrenics offered far fewer human responses than did the borderline patients.

Although the Lerner, Sugarman, and Gaughran (1981) study was designed to compare defensive structure between groups differing in severity of psychopathology, the study also yielded findings relevant to our understanding of the schizophrenic process. Of particular note were differences between the groups in their capacity to internally represent objects. Whereas the internal world of the borderline patient consists of highly charged—either highly depreciated or highly idealized—representations, that of the schizophrenic patient is devoid of internal representations. If inner representations arise from the internalization of object relations that were invested, then one might conjecture that schizophrenics never invested in external relations and that this accounts for their empty and barren inner object world.

Cross validation for several of the findings reported by Lerner and Lerner (1980) and Lerner, Sugarman, and Gaughran (1981) is provided in a study by Collins (1983). Employing Gunderson's Diagnostic Interview for Borderlines and DSM-III criteria, Collins selected 15 adult subjects from each of three samples (borderline, neurotic, and schizophrenic) from several inpatient and outpatient facilities and administered the Rorschach test. The 45 protocols were then scored using the Rorschach Defense Scale. The differences among all three groups were highly significant, supporting the general hypothesis that borderline patients exhibit a defensive structure significantly different from that of schizophrenics and neurotics. With respect to specific pairings, the borderline patients differed from the schizophrenics on the defenses of splitting, projective identification, low-level idealization, and mid-level devaluation. Although not statistically significant because of the relatively low frequency of scores, the records of the borderline group as compared with the neurotic group did offer more splitting scores and more projective identification scores.

Based on the hypothesis that borderline personality disorders would manifest greater disturbance in defensive organization than narcissistic personality disorders, Farris (1988) applied the Lerner Defense Scale to the Rorschach records of nine matched pairs of borderline and narcissistic patients. A comparison of the two groups revealed that the borderline patients produced a significantly greater number of responses reflecting the use of primitive defenses than did narcissistic subjects. Each of the defense categories was submitted to a chi-square analysis. Significant differences were found regarding the defenses of splitting and projective identification. In both categories the borderline subjects produced a significantly greater number of primitive defense responses than did the narcissistic subjects.

Further Clinical Studies

Other studies have used the Lerner Defense Scale scoring system to investigate the defensive structure of specific clinical populations assumed to have a borderline personality organization. The groups studied have included anorexic patients (Van-Der Keshet, 1988; Piran and Lerner, 1988; Brouillete, 1987), antisocial offenders (Gacono, 1988, 1990), and gender-disturbed children (Kolers, 1986).

Van-Der Keshet (1988) applied the defense scale to the Rorschach records of clinical anorexics, anoretic ballet students, nonanoretic ballet students, and a normal control group. The clinical anoretic group was further subdivided into those patients who manifested solely restrictive characteristics (i.e., restricting food intake) and those who exhibited bulimic symptoms (i.e., binging and purging). A comparison of the various groups on the defense scale revealed several interesting findings. As predicted, the two clinical anoretic groups and the anoretic ballet students used splitting and devaluation significantly more often than did the nonanoretic ballet students and the controls. The restricting anorexics were found to employ denial significantly more often than any of the other groups. The normal control group employed idealization significantly more often than any of the other groups. While the anoretic ballet students did not differ from the nonanoretic ballet students with respect to idealization, both groups used the defense significantly more often than the bulimic anorexics.

Another important finding in Van-Der Keshet's study involves the differential use of denial between the two eating disordered groups. Those treating restrictive anorexics have often employed more extreme types of intervention (e.g., forcing the patient to look in a mirror) as a way of confronting the patient's distorted body image. The obtained findings suggest that accompanying the distortion in body image is a strong reliance on denial and that such therapeutic interventions confront that denial.

In a series of studies (Piran and Lerner, 1987; Piran et al., 1988) using nonprojective instruments, Piran and Lerner found that although restrictive anorexic and bulimic anorexic patients both display a borderline level of personality organization, they differ with respect to impulse control. Whereas bulimics discharge impulses and conflicts directly through action, restrictive anorexics appear as overcontrolled, with massive inhibition and ego restriction. This consistent finding led Piran and Lerner to investigate the defensive structure of both groups more closely, through the use of the Lerner Defense Scale. The sample consisted of 65 eating-disordered patients (bulimics, n = 34; restricters, n = 31) admitted or placed on a waiting list for admission to two large general hospitals specializing in the treatment of eating disorders. All subjects were female, aged 16 to 35, and fulfilled DSM-III criteria for anorexia nervosa. The authors found, in keeping with the respective nature of the symptomatology, that the bulimic anorexics tended to use test indices of projective identification and low-level devaluation, whereas restrictive anorexics relied more often on denial and high-level idealization.

Thus, although restrictive and bulimic anorexics both use primitive defenses, the respective patterning of defenses differs. As indicated, the differing patterns are related to presenting symptoms and, indeed, might account for expression of symptoms; however, defenses have not explicitly been related to treatment planning. The obtained results suggest that in planning treatment, defensive structure should be considered. For example, the role of denial in restrictive anorexics should be confronted, whereas with bulimics one might choose to focus on their tendency to depreciate.

Brouillette (1987), in a unique and important study, assessed the personality organization, including the defense structure, both of women suffering from eating disorders and of their mothers. The three groups of daughters, between 18 and 40 years of age, consisted of 11 women with anorexia nervosa, 10 women with bulimia, and 10 normal control women. Rorschach records were obtained from all daughters and their mothers and assessed using scales devised to measure level of object representation, level of boundary disturbance, quality of reality testing, and nature of defenses. Impressive results were found in the comparison of mothers and daughters. First, no significant differences were found between daughters and mothers in all three groups on all measures of psychological functioning. Second, significant differences were found between the eating-disorder groups and the normal control group for both the mothers and daughters on all of the same measures. Finally, neither the mothers nor the daughters in the anorexia nervosa group differed significantly on any measure from the mothers and daughters in the bulimic group. With respect to the defense scores, evidence of splitting, low-level devaluation, projective identification, and low-level denial occurred with significantly greater frequency in the protocols of anorexia nervosa patients and their mothers and bulimic patients and their mothers than in the records of the normal controls and their mothers. Although not statistically significant, there was a tendency within the bulimic pairing (daughter and mother) to use splitting more frequently than the anorexia nervosa pairing.

A second major clinical group that the Rorschach Defense Scale has been extended to is the antisocial personality. On the basis of Kernberg's (1975) contention that severe character disorders, including patients with an antisocial personality structure, are organized at a borderline level of personality organization, Gacono (1988) compared highly psychopathic males with low to moderately psychopathic males with respect to the proportion of borderline object relations and borderline defenses revealed on their Rorschach protocols. Thirty-three subjects who met the DSM-III-R criteria for Antisocial Personality Disorder participated in a semistructured interview and completed the Rorschach test. On the basis of a review of their records and information obtained in the interview, each subject was rated on the Hare Psychopathy Checklist. Using a score of 30 as a cutoff, 14 subjects were included in the high-psychopathy group and 19 placed in the low- to moderate-psychopathy group.

A between-group comparison revealed that none of the individual defense scores significantly distinguished the two groups. Indeed, quite unexpectedly, the low- to moderate-psychopathy group produced a total of 40 defense scores whereas the high-psychopathy group produced only 24 such scores. A review of the individual categories revealed that the high-psychopathy group, as compared to the low to moderate group, tended to use devaluation, whereas the low to moderate group by comparison made more frequent use of projective identification and higher-level denial. The Rorschach protocols of both groups showed a predominant use of lower levels of denial, and all levels of devaluation were found.

The results of Gacono's (1988) study are somewhat difficult to understand, especially in the light of the absence of a control group. Had a control group been included, one could first have determined if the psychopathy sample as a whole employed primitive defenses more than the controls did. One could then proceed as Gacono did and investigate differences within the psychopathy group. Further, Gacono did not account for the capacity of each of his subgroups to internally represent objects. It is possible that the low- to moderate-psychopathy group produced more defensive scores because they had more potentially scoreable responses, that is, responses with human content.

In accord with Hammond (1984), Gacono (1988) interpreted his findings in terms of limitations in the scoring system:

First, borderline individuals often have difficulty experiencing objects as whole and may respond to the Rorschach by producing the kind of part human responses not scoreable by the system; secondly, human movement responses (M) symbolize an advanced human percept in motion. Children and some developmentally immature individuals may express movement responses in terms of animal content (FM), considered to be developmentally less mature. Lerner and Lerner's (1980) system prohibits the scoring of animal movement, thereby eliminating important data that reveal a subject's defensive functioning [pp. 120–121].

Collins (1983), also registered similar concerns.

Kolers (1986) extended the assessment of primitive defenses to gender-disturbed children. Various ego functions, including defense, as manifested on the Rorschach records of a group of feminine boys, their siblings, and a normal control group were evaluated and compared. The subjects, all age 5 to 12 years, consisted of 37 feminine boys diagnosed as having cross-gender disturbance, 19 siblings with no history of cross-gender behavior, and 23 normal controls. The investigator found that although the normal controls produced significantly more human figure responses, that is, more potentially scoreable responses, the gender-disturbed children and their siblings offered significantly more projective identification scores. Of the other defense scores, higher-level devaluation was found to occur significantly more often among the controls.

Of interest in Kolers' study was the finding that the projective identification score, while differentiating the normal controls from both the feminine boys and their siblings, failed to discriminate between the latter two groups. The meaning of this finding has been amplified by Ipp (1986). Ipp investigated the object relations and object representations of this same sample by applying to their Rorschach protocols the scale of Blatt and associates (1976) for assessing object representations, Blatt and Ritzler's (1974) instrument for evaluating boundary disturbances, and her own Developmental Object Relations Scale (DORS) devised to measure developmental object relations. Using her own findings, especially those related to levels of boundary disturbance, and P. Lerner's (1985) notion of various levels of projective identification depending on the aim (i.e., defense, control, or communication) and the degree to which self-boundaries are blurred and diffused, Ipp (1986) concluded that projective identification operates somewhat differently in the two groups.

Ipp (1986) found that the confabulation score on the Boundary Disturbance Scale occurred with significantly greater frequency in the protocols of the feminine boys than in the records of their siblings. Relating this finding to projective identification allowed her to conclude that in feminine boys, projective identification is at a lower level, in which its aim is control, and there is a severe blurring of self-other boundaries. By contrast, the siblings engage in a higher-level projective identification in which self-boundaries are not blurred and the defense is employed to empathize with potential sources of danger and to communicate through preverbal modalities.

A Note on Idealization

In several of the reviewed studies the findings regarding idealization have stood out like the proverbial bad thumb. Indices from the scale rarely appear in the protocols of individuals with a borderline or assumed borderline personality organization (Gacono, 1988; Gacono and Meloy, 1994), appear more frequently in the records of less disturbed groups and normal controls (Lerner and Lerner, 1980; Kolers, 1986; Van-Der Keshet, 1988), and are independent of the measures of other primitive defenses (Lerner, Albert, and Walsh, 1987). Taken as a whole, these findings suggest that the Idealization subscale is measuring something other than idealization as conceptualized as a primitive defense.

The most extensive discussion of idealization, in both its defensive and adaptive (i.e., nondefensive) aspects, is provided by Kernberg (1980). He posited a developmental line in which idealization is conceptualized as falling on a continuum from pathological to normal. Three levels of idealization were proposed:

(1) A primitive level of ego states that reflect a predominance of splitting mechanisms; this is found in the borderline personality organization. . . . (2) An idealization linked to the establishment of the capacity for mourning and concern (the depressive position), with a more realistic awareness of and empathy for the object, but still devoid of genital features. This level is characteristic of states of falling in love of the usual neurotic patient. . . . (3) A normal idealization achieved toward the end of adolescence or in young adulthood, which is based upon a stable sexual identity and a realistic awareness of the love object [p. 221].

For Kernberg, at the lower, more primitive end of the continuum the defensive aspects of idealization are emphasized, with particular focus on its role in bolstering splitting. At this lower level, idealization is associated with borderline pathology. Toward the upper, more normal pole on the continuum, the adaptive, nondefensive aspects of idealization are highlighted, including its role as a necessary precondition for feelings of mature love. Idealization at this upper level is associated with the absence of severe psychopathology.

In her study, Van-Der Keshet (1988) reviewed individual protocols with respect to the specific idealization scores. Her inspection of the test records indicated that the normal controls had a strong tendency to offer idealization responses at the upper end of the Idealization Scale (scale points 1 and 2). In terms of Kernberg's model of idealization, then, these data suggest that the upper end of the Idealization Scale is more sensitive to the adaptive aspects of idealization than to the defensive ones.

The data are clearly more suggestive than conclusive, however, there is a line of Rorschach research that is relevant here. Exner (1991) developed a special score, designated COP, for assessing cooperative movement. The score is assigned to any movement response (M, FM, or m) involving two or more objects in which the interaction is unequivocally positive or cooperative. Despite differences in the basic unit of analysis (human response versus all movement responses), to judge from Exner's definitions and the examples he offers ("Two people leaning toward each other, sharing a secret" and "Three people doing a dance together"; pp. 18–19), there seems to be some overlap between his cooperative movement response and scale points 1 and 2 on the Idealization Scale. In both instances there is clear positive affect.

Exner (1991) found that COP responses appeared at least once in 80% of the Rorschachs of a sample of 700 adult nonpatients. He also found that third-year high school students and college freshmen who had more than two COP responses on their Rorschach protocols were identified by peers, at a rate five times greater than other subjects, as being the one who "Is easiest to be with."

In several studies (Gacono and Meloy, 1994; Lerner and Lerner, 1980), including Van-Der Keshet's (1988), there was a relative absence of idealization in the more disturbed groups. Although it is unclear what to make of this consistent finding, it seems likely, on the basis of theory and clinical experience, that such individuals (i.e., borderline patients, antisocial males, bulimic anorexics) do not have access to higher levels of idealization.

Additional findings of Exner (1991) are consistent with this hunch. In contrast with his sample of adult nonpatients, COP responses appeared at least once in only 65% of the test records of an outpatient group, 50% of the protocols of a sample of inpatient depressive and schizophrenic patients, and 40% of the Rorschachs of patients diagnosed with character disorders.

Because of the foregoing, and in terms of Kernberg's (1980) formulations, it would appear that the upper ratings (scale points 1 and 2) on the Idealization Scale are more reflective of idealization as an adaptive capacity than of idealization as a primitive defense. With respect to the lower three ratings, those in which there is a progressive distortion of the humanness of the human figure, it is unclear from the data reviewed here what these scores may be assessing.

A second conceptual vantage point for understanding the role of idealization, somewhat different from that of Kernberg, is represented in the writings of Kohut (1971, 1977). For Kohut, the child has "two chances" as he or she moves toward consolidation of the self. The first opportunity to establish a cohesive grandiose-exhibitionistic self depends on the child's early relationship to an empathically responding, merging-mirroring-approving selfobject, usually the mother. If the mother frustrates or prohibits this need of merging and mirroring, the child has a second chance for self-cohesion. The second opportunity is provided by the father and his capacity to empathize with and accept the child's need, first to idealize him and then to merge with him as an idealized object. When this process is successful, self-cohesion is advanced, and the resultant structure that emerges is referred to as a "compensatory structure."

Kohut (1977) described the process this way: "A failure experienced at the first way station can be remedied by a success at the second one" (p. 180). If, however, the success of one of these opportunities for the development of healthy self-functioning is insufficient to compensate for the failure of the other, than the compensatory structure does not function reliably.

For Kohut, then, idealization, or more specifically, the capacity to idealize, is intimately related to the development of compensatory structures along a developmental line of self-consolidation.

From a Kohutian perspective, Van-Der Keshet's (1988) finding regarding the differential use of idealization between the symptomatic ballet students and the bulimic anorexics takes on a particular meaning. Although the two groups did not differ with respect to their use of splitting and devaluation, they did differ in regard to idealization.

Specifically, the symptomatic ballet students manifested expressions of idealization significantly more frequently than did the bulimic anorexics. In reviewing the individual protocols of the symptomatic ballet students, it was found that like the controls, but not to the same extent, they too tended to use higher levels of idealization.

From this viewpoint, one might speculate that the presence of higher level idealization among the ballet students indicates that although symptomatic, they have been able to develop compensatory structures and that these structures have enabled them to function more effectively and adaptively than the bulimic patient group.

Summary

Because of the conceptual roots of the Lerner Defense Scale, initial studies using the scale were designed to evaluate the scoring system's efficacy in distinguishing groups of borderline patients from groups of other diagnostic entities. The combined findings of both initial studies (P. Lerner and H. Lerner, 1980; H. Lerner, Sugarman, and Gaughran, 1981) strongly support the contention that borderline patients present an identifiable constellation of defenses, different from that of neurotic and schizophrenic patients, and that the scoring system is a valid means of identifying these defenses. Subsequent studies extended the use of the scale to various clinical groups assumed to have an underlying borderline structure. In a series of studies (Brouillette, 1987; Piran and Lerner, 1988; Van-Der Keshet, 1988) scale scores distinguished eating-disordered patients from normal controls. Van-Der Keshet's (1988) investigation highlighted the role of idealization and added to its conceptual meaning. Brouillette's (1987) study was unique in that it dealt not only with anorexic patients, but with their mothers as well. Results involving different defensive patterning between subtypes of eating-disorder patients were equivocal and tended to be sample specific. Although the scale was effective in identifying specific defenses (devaluation and low-level denial) employed by a large sample of antisocial personalities, it was not useful in distinguishing between subgroups of such personalities. The scale has been extended to children. Kolers (1986) found that the projective identification score significantly discriminated gender-disturbed children and their siblings from a normal control group. Ipp (1986), in combining her own findings with those of Kolers, was able to add to our understanding of the concept of projective identification.

◆ ◆ ◆ Other Rorschach Measures of Primitive Defense

Cooper and his colleagues (Cooper and Arnow, 1986; Cooper, Perry, and Arnow, 1988) have also developed a Rorschach scale designed, in part, to assess primitive defenses. Based on a somewhat different theoretical perspective and broader in scope than the Lerner and Lerner scale, Cooper's system was initially conceived as part of a complex approach to evaluating defenses in general, rather than specific borderline defenses in particular. Nonetheless, Cooper has identified the following five defenses, which he considers borderline defenses: splitting, devaluation, idealization, projective identification, and omnipotence (Lerner, Albert, and Walsh, 1987).

Drawn on the theoretical propositions of Winnicott (1953), Kohut (1977), and Stolorow and Lachmann (1980), Cooper's scale seeks to integrate object-relations theory, Kohut's notions of narcissism, and Stolorow and Lachmann's concepts of developmental arrest and structural deficiency. In keeping with a position of developmental arrest, the scale takes into account Ames's (1966) empirical finding that with increased development there is an increased frequency of the human-figure response on the Rorschach test and that this parallels and eventually supplants animal responses. This line of reasoning, begun by Ames and conceptually expanded in terms of defensive functioning by Stolorow and Lachmann (1980), leads to the formulation of "prestages" of defense, that is, stages that are considered predecessors of defenses proper: "Prestages are those initial precursors to a defense occurring prior to the consolidation of self and object representation, while a defense proper is the end point in a series of developmental achievements" (Lerner, Albert, and Walsh, 1987, p. 338).

In keeping with the notion of defense precursors, Cooper and Arnow (1986), in contrast to Lerner and Lerner (1980), did not limit their scores to the human figure response.

> Lerner and Lerner (1980) . . . restrict their analysis to percepts that include human figures, static or in motion. In agreement with Smith (1980), we find this circumscription unduly limiting for interpreting protocols in which there is a relative or absolute absence of human figures. More important, however, borderline defenses are more profitably examined with a broader data base regardless of the number of human responses [p. 144].

In addition to different theoretical starting points and varying definitions of what type of Rorschach content constitutes the primary object-relations unit of analysis, the scoring systems differ in other ways as well. Scoring criteria for operationalizing certain defenses differ between systems. Cooper's scale includes the scoring of omnipotence,[4] and the Lerner and Lerner scale provides for the scoring of denial on a graded continuum.

Collins (1983), also concerned with the restrictive nature of the Lerner and Lerner (1980) scale, prior to Cooper, modified the Lerners' scale by extending the categories of percepts to be scored to include animal as well as human percepts. In comparison with the original scale, Collins found that his modified scale markedly increased the power of splitting and marginally increased the power of projective identification to discriminate borderline from schizophrenic patients.

Cooper, Perry, and Arnow (1988) investigated the relationship between defenses and specific dimensions of psychopathology in borderline, antisocial, and bipolar type II adults. They found that borderline psychopathology was positively associated with manifestations of devaluation, projection, splitting, and hypomanic denial, but was negatively associated with intellectualization and isolation. Indices of splitting on the Rorschach correlated significantly with clinical ratings of splitting from independently obtained diagnostic interviews.

Cooper, Perry, and O'Connell (1991) evaluated the ability of Cooper's scale to longitudinally predict global functioning. The authors noted that two defenses in particular—devaluation and projection—were highly predictive of impaired global functioning, whereas intellectualization and isolation of affect were predictive of higher levels of global functioning.

In a series of studies, Gacono (Gacono, 1988, 1990; Gacono, Meloy, and Berg, 1992) used Cooper's scale to assess the defensive structure of subgroups of antisocial offenders, narcissistic personality disorders, and borderline personality disorders. Although not statistically significant, a high-psychopathy group had more responses in the categories of prestage splitting, total splitting, omnipotence, and devaluation as compared with a group of low to moderate psychopaths. By contrast, the low- to moderate-psychopathy group had more responses

---

4. Cooper defines omnipotence as an idealization of the self in which there is the conviction that one is entitled to admiration and privileged treatment. On the Rorschach test, omnipotence is seen in direct descriptions of self in blatantly positive and adulating terms; for example, "I think you are going to hear some exceptional responses. My vocabulary is exceptional."

in the categories of projective identification and idealization. The group comprising narcissistic personality disorder produced more primitive idealization responses than did any of the other groups.

As part of a broad attempt to study ego functions in borderline and narcissistic patients, Berg (1990) used Cooper's scale to compare the preferred defenses of each group. As predicted, the borderline sample produced more instances of splitting and the narcissistic sample more instances of grandiosity.

The most comprehensive comparison of the two defense scales is represented in the work of Lerner et al. (1987). Rorschach protocols used in two previous studies (Lerner and Lerner, 1980; Lerner et al., 1981) and scored using the Lerners' system, were recoded and scored according to the criteria set out by Cooper. Statistical analyses of differences between the four psychiatric groups (neurotics, outpatient borderlines, inpatient borderlines, schizophrenics) were completed separately, in order to assess the power of each scale to discriminate between diagnostic groups and to evaluate the discriminatory capacity of specific defenses within each scale to differentiate among groups.

A profile analysis was conducted to assess the relative capacity of each scale to distinguish among groups. A parallelism of profiles test was run, and the results indicated that the two scales were not parallel. That is, subjects from the four clinical groups were responding somewhat differently to the two scales.

To assess statistical differences between scales in predicting group membership, a discriminant function was conducted. A review of this analysis revealed the following: (1) the Cooper Scale significantly differentiated neurotics from inpatient borderlines ($p < .01$), outpatient from inpatient borderlines ($p < .05$), and inpatient borderlines from schizophrenics ($p < .002$); (2) the Cooper Scale failed to statistically discriminate neurotics from outpatient borderlines, neurotics from schizophrenics, and outpatient borderlines from schizophrenics; (3) the Lerner Defense Scale significantly differentiated neurotics from inpatient borderlines ($p < .001$), neurotics from schizophrenics ($p < .001$), outpatient borderlines from schizophrenics ($p < .001$), and inpatient borderlines from schizophrenics ($p < .001$); (4) the Lerner Defense Scale was unable to statistically distinguish between the two outpatient samples and the two borderline groups. While both scales validly discriminated between groups, in general these results suggest that the Cooper Scale is more effective in distinguishing between healthier outpatients, whereas the Lerners' scale better discriminates more seriously disturbed inpatients.

To assess the discriminatory power of each defense, an analysis of differences among the four experimental groups was conducted separately for each scale. For the Cooper Scale, three specific defense scores distinguished among groups. Splitting distinguished inpatient borderlines from both neurotics and schizophrenics; devaluation differentiated both borderline groups from schizophrenics and neurotics from outpatient borderlines; and omnipotence separated the outpatient borderlines from neurotics and schizophrenics. Scale measures of idealization and projective identification failed to significantly differentiate among groups.

With respect to the Lerner Defense Scale, all five defenses distinguished among groups to a statistically significant degree. Splitting differentiated both borderline groups from neurotics and schizophrenics, as did devaluation and idealization. Projective identification occurred exclusively within the two borderline groups; thus, although it differentiated these groups from neurotics and schizophrenics, it did not separate the two borderline groups from each other. Finally, denial as well distinguished the borderline groups from the other two, but not from each other.

One purpose of the study was to discern the relative discriminatory power of omnipotence, a score exclusive to Cooper's scale, and denial, a category exclusive to the Lerner Defense Scale. While both indices distinguished among groups, measures of omnipotence differentiated both outpatient groups from inpatient borderlines, whereas denial distinguished neurotics from both inpatient groups and inpatient borderlines from schizophrenics. These findings are in accord with the overall pattern of results, indicating the Cooper Scale's greater effectiveness distinguishing outpatient groups and the Lerner Defense Scale's greater effectiveness distinguishing inpatient groups.

To assess the overlap and distinctive features of each scoring system, the scales were intercorrelated. Significant correlations were obtained between subscale measures of splitting (.49) and devaluation (.64), but not between indices idealization (.13) and projective identification (.30). Within-scale correlations were derived and revealed differences in the structure of each test. For the Lerner Defense Scale, measures of splitting, devaluation, denial, and projective identification were all intercorrelated, whereas for the Cooper Scale, the defense measures correlated substantially less strongly. Whereas the findings regarding the Lerner Defense Scale are consistent with theoretical formulations related to defense (Kernberg, 1975; Grotstein, 1981), the results also argue for the superior psychometric properties of the Cooper Scale.

In summary, a second approach to the assessment of primitive defenses is found in the work of Cooper (Cooper and Arnow, 1986). Broader in purpose and scope than the Lerner Defense Scale, the Cooper Scale includes five subscores developed to assess defenses associated with borderline functioning. Like the Lerners' system, Cooper's instrument relies heavily on the analysis of Rorschach content, but in contradistinction to it, the basic unit of analysis in the Cooper Scale extends beyond the human figure response to encompass a broad array of contents (e.g., animal responses, inanimate objects). In a comprehensive concurrent validity study, both scales were found useful in distinguishing borderline patients from other diagnostic entities. At the same time, however, perhaps owing to their different conceptual starting points and their somewhat differing ways of operationally defining specific defenses, scores on the Cooper Scale seemed more effective in distinguishing among higher-functioning outpatients, whereas scores on the Lerner Defense Scale appeared more effective in differentiating poorer functioning inpatients.

A comparison of both scales highlights the issue of restricting the basic unit of analysis to the human figure response. Cooper has cogently argued that extending the unit of analysis to other contents broadens the data base. Collins (1983) and Gacono (1988) empirically found this to be the case, but at the same time, they also found that broadening the data base did not appreciably increase the predictive power of the defense scores. To this point, Lerner et al. (1987) have noted the following:

> While both scales validly discriminated between groups . . . the relative magnitude of group differences highlight the significance of borderline defensive functioning based upon operationalized criteria involving human responses or object representational capacity. It appears that primary process content is most pathogenically indicative of borderline defensive functioning when it effects relationships; that is, when it is embellished in human responses. This finding is important from the point of view of efficiency and theory. That an assessment of defenses only in terms of human responses can adequately predict the borderline diagnostic group as effectively as the full gamut of responses is cost efficient [p. 352].

Beyond psychometric issues and the matter of cost efficiency, the differing stances of Cooper and the Lerners on the question of restricting the analysis to full human figures reflect genuine attempts to remain as close to their respective theoretical underpinnings as possible. Broadening the unit of analysis permitted Cooper to better operationlize such cornerstone concepts as prestages of defense, part-object relations, and levels of integrative failure. Central for the Lerners is the theoretical proposition that defenses and object relations are inextricably related. Thus, restricting the unit of analysis permits them to infer not only defensive structure, but level of object representational capacity as well.

❖ ❖ ❖ Conclusion

In this chapter I have reviewed the current status of a scale devised by Lerner and Lerner to assess primitive defenses. Early studies employing the scale demonstrated its efficacy in accord with theoretical formulations in distinguishing borderline patients from other diagnostic entities. Later studies used the scale to evaluate the defensive structure among other types of clinical groups assumed to have a borderline personality structure.

Despite the consistency of results obtained, the reviewed studies should be regarded as simply a first step in our attempts to investigate and understand the complexities involved in the borderline concept. Much controversy surrounds the borderline diagnosis—and what constitutes the borders of the borderline entity. Thus, comparing groups of diagnosed borderline patients with other types of patients is necessary but insufficient.

Focusing on defense is important, in that defense represents a structural variable (Kernberg, 1975); therefore this permits us to move beyond descriptive considerations. Defense, however, has typically been studied in isolation and has not been studied in terms of its relationship with other structural variables (e.g., reality testing, internalized object relations). An exception is represented in the work of Lerner and Lerner (1982), who attempted to relate defense to level of object representation. With the development of various Rorschach scales designed to assess other structural variables, such as developmental object relations (Kwawer, 1980; Coonerty, 1986; Ipp, 1986), boundary disturbances (Blatt and Ritzler, 1974), and object representation (Blatt et al., 1976), we are now in a position to examine the dynamic interplay among structural factors and approximate more closely the richness of Kernberg's theory and the clinical complexity represented in the individual borderline patient.

19

DISSOCIATION: THEORETICAL AND ASSESSMENT CONSIDERATIONS

$\mathbf{B}$oth clinical work and research in assessment, in a variety of ways, are intimately related to prevailing theories of personality and theories of psychopathology. Thus, in concert with more recent views of psychopathology, it is not surprising that many in assessment are increasingly turning their attention to the concept of dissociation and its psychopathological manifestations—the dissociative disorders. Interest in the dissociative disorders has increased so dramatically that it threatens to supplant our earlier interest of a decade ago in the borderline disorder and borderline phenomena.

Seventeen years ago, Sugarman and H. Lerner (1980), in discussing the popularity of the borderline concept, noted "that like the hysteric of Freud's time, the borderline patient is the problem of our time" (p. 12). These authors went on to add that "Oedipus had been replaced by Hamlet as the mythical prototype of our period" (p. 12). Were one to extend this metaphor, it might be suggested that just as Hamlet replaced Oedipus in 1980, now, in 1997, Hamlet is being replaced by Eve and Sybil as the mythical prototypes of our period.

Dissociation, as a concept, has a long but uneven history within psychiatry. The term was first introduced by Janet in 1907 to describe the mysterious physical ailments and alternate personalities observed in a subgroup of hysterical patients. According to Janet, such symptoms were expressions of unknown fixed ideas that had been dissociated or split off from consciousness but continued to exist in another region—the unconscious.

In the 1890s, with the publication of Breuer and Freud's *Studies in Hysteria* (1893–1895) the concept fell by the wayside, replaced by Freud's concept of repression. In the 1980s, however, the concept has resurfaced, stimulated largely by renewed interest in the phenomenon of trauma.

This resurgence of interest represents the convergence of several contemporary trends: the elaboration of the posttraumatic stress disorder prompted by the symptom picture of returning Vietnam combat veterans, the growing awareness of the high incidence of child abuse, and exciting findings that emerge from both hypnosis and neurophysiology.

Attempts to define "dissociation" abound in the literature; many of these, however, are shrouded in conceptual confusion, especially in the failure to distinguish between dissociation as a defense and dissociation as a clinical disorder. A notable exception here is represented in the work of Brenner (1994), who considers dissociation a defensive altered ego state and places the various disorders on a continuum of character pathology, depending on the degree of integration (or disintegration) of the ego.

In DSM-III-R (American Psychiatric Association, 1987), dissociation is defined as a "disturbance or alteration in the normally integrative functions of identity, memory or consciousness" (p. 269). Spiegel, in several articles (e.g., Spiegel and Cardena, 1991; Jashke and Spiegel, 1992), describes dissociation as some kind of divided or parallel access to awareness. He and his colleagues suggest further that it entails "the ability to compartmentalize experience and break the usual ribbon of continual consciousness that connects one thought with another" (Jashke and Spiegel, 1992, p. 250). Allen (1993), along similar conceptual lines, refers to dissociation as a discontinuity in experience in which the self is separated from its own experience.

Putnam (1989) defines dissociation as a psychodynamically triggered psychophysiological process that produces alternations in consciousness. As part of this process, an individual's thoughts, feelings, and experiences are not integrated into awareness or memory in the normal way. Allen (1993) refers to this process as one in which "realms of experience are relegated to the 'not-me' domain" (p. 289).

Although the work of contemporary theorists (Young, 1988; Marmer, 1991; Kluft, 1992) in the field of dissociation and the dissociative disorders draws heavily upon psychoanalytic concepts, historically the field has grown up outside of psychoanalytic theory. The schism between psychoanalysts and proponents of modern dissociative theory, with specific reference to patients with multiple personality disorder (MPD), is well captured by Armstrong (1994): "To the experienced psychoanalyst who has never seen an MPD patient or who is concerned that the expression of self-dividedness will encourage self-fragmentation, MPD may appear as a perplexingly retrograde phenomenon" (p. 350).

Despite the historical division, there has been a movement afoot to integrate modern concepts of dissociation with psychoanalytic theory. Brenner (1994), for example, defines dissociation narrowly as a defensive altered state based on autohypnosis; however, he then conceives of dissociation as serving to bolster repression or splitting. Smith (1990) and Reis (1993) each contend that the clinical phenomenology of multiple personality disorder can be understood from a developmental psychoanalytic framework based on object-relations theory. Smith (1990), for instance, evokes Winnicott's (1971) concept of "potential space" and conceptualizes the dissociative disorders as representing an instance of collapsed potential space, in which reality and fantasy are experienced as parallel but disconnected realities. Reis (1993) too makes use of Winnicottian concepts, specifically Winnicott's (1960) notion of containment. Reis suggests that with trauma comes a failure in containment, and that the alter personalities in MPD serve to contain affect.

The broad purposes of this chapter are to provide a theoretical overview, from a psychoanalytic perspective, of the concept of dissociation, and then to review attempts to assess dissociation and the dissociative disorders with the Rorschach. The chapter is organized in the following way. I first discuss the relationship between dissociation and trauma. I then describe dissociation, comparatively, as a defense, and using Allen's (1993) notion of discontinuity of experience, discuss the relationships among dissociation, memory, consciousness, and then self. A review of Rorschach attempts to assess dissociation is presented. Finally, I discuss the clinical assessment of the dissociative patient, and then suggest ways of approaching dissociation for research purposes.

✦ ✦ ✦ Dissociation and Trauma

Kluft (1984, 1988) has identified four etiological factors as involved in the dissociative disorders: (1) a biological predisposition to dissociation; (2) an exposure to overwhelming trauma; (3) the role of mediating "shaping factors"; and (4) an inability to soothe, an absence of protection from retraumatization, and a failure to process and integrate the traumatic material.

The close tie that has been observed between the dissociative disorders, especially MPD, and early trauma is clearly stated by Loewenstein and Ross (1992). These authors write:

> The new paradigm of MPD states that it is a complex, chronic form of developmental dissociative disorder, primarily related to severe repetitive childhood abuse or trauma, usually beginning before the age of five. In MPD, it is thought that dissociative defenses are used to protect the child from the full psychological impact of severe trauma, usually extreme, repetitive child abuse [p. 7].

This particularly powerful statement should be tempered with Allen's (1993) caution that dissociation "is not invariably linked to trauma . . . and this form of self-protection is not available to all" (p. 290).

Psychoanalytic writers, without diminishing the importance of external traumatic events, have attempted to place those events in a broader context that includes internal factors as well. Reis (1993), for example, underlines the importance of the specific early developmental stage during which the actual traumatic insult began. He notes that for many individuals the actual trauma began at an infantile stage, during which core psychic boundaries, such as that between reality and fantasy, had not yet been fully formed.

P. Lerner and H. Lerner (1996) point out that it does indeed make a difference whether something traumatic actually happened; however, that does not lessen the importance of the power of fantasy. Years of cumulative psychoanalytic knowledge, the authors contend, have taught us that each individual processes events to give them unique meaning and mental representation.

Abuse, according to P. Lerner and H. Lerner (1996), is important, but should also be viewed as symptomatic of a pathological parent-child relationship. They suggest that "such disturbed relationships all involve trauma and all center around issues of power; that is, they are sadomasochistic" (p. 408). A particular form of parental abuse the authors identify, one less dramatic than physical or sexual abuse but equally devastating, is parental externalization. This involves the parents projecting into the child devalued and disowned aspects of themselves and regarding the child as something he or she is not. Children who are the objects of parental externalization reveal a severe narcissistic disturbance, with psychic pain and conflict rooted in the acceptance of a devalued self and in an inability to integrate positive aspects with their conscious self-representation. They suffer various ego impairments and are unable to maintain self-esteem.

To briefly recap, there is ample empirical and clinical evidence to suggest that dissociation and altered ego states are a basic reaction to trauma, and as Armstrong (1994) puts it, "akin to the freezing response to danger" (p. 351). As compelling and deplorable as the trauma often is, it should not be viewed in isolation from the matrix of a pathological, typically sadomasochistic, parent-child relationship.

✦ ✦ ✦ Dissociation as a Defense

As noted in chapter 17, Freud evoked the term "defense" to describe the ego's struggle to ward off forbidden desires and painful ideas and affects. Anna Freud (1936) broadened this conceptualization by distinguishing between defenses against inner dangers and those against outer dangers.

Dissociation, as conceptualized by most writers (Allen, 1993; Armstrong, 1994; Spiegel, 1988), serves to protect the individual from both internal and external dangers. On the one side, and as Armstrong (1994) explains, in cases of multiple personality disorder, dissociation "acts as a type of stimulus barrier to overwhelming experiences, memories, and conflicts serving as a defense against internal disorganization and chaos" (p. 351). On the other side, as Spiegel (1988) has noted, dissociation also occurs in the immediacy of a situation as a way of removing the individual from the situation and avoiding overwhelming affects. For example, we are familiar with those victims of physical and sexual abuse who, in reporting the event, often describe the experience as if it were happening to someone else or they were located outside of and above their bodies, watching the event from afar. The process, then, seems to involve removing or disconnecting oneself from an experience both at the time and in the remembering of it. The question as to whether it is biologically triggered (Kluft, 1988) or self-induced (Brenner, 1994) remains unclear.

As a defense, it is conceptually useful to distinguish dissociation from other defenses, most notably from repression and splitting. Let us begin with repression. In both repression and dissociation, mental contents are barred from awareness; the processes differ, however, with respect to what happens to the material held out of awareness. With repression, by definition, the material is relegated to the unconscious, that is, to that area of mental life that cannot be brought to conscious awareness by voluntary choice.

Repression, then, is part of a model that assumes a horizontal split in which there is a division between above and below. That is, that which is conscious is placed above and that which is unconscious is placed below, with a repressive barrier separating the two.

Dissociation, by contrast, does not include the implication that unintegrated contents are maintained in the unconscious. Instead, it is suggested that such contents may exist in parallel in a type of co-consciousness, or they may be so accessible to consciousness that one could consider their being located in the preconscious. In any event, the division here is not a horizontal one as with repression, but rather a vertical one, even between sectors of conscious experience, separated by what Hillgard (1977) refers to as a dissociative barrier.

In positing a vertical rather than a horizontal split, and in suggesting that split-off contents are not relegated to the unconscious, dissociation is similar to splitting. Kernberg (1975) defines splitting as the prolonged defensive division of internalized object relations into all "good" and all "bad" part units, in order to prevent the generalization of anxiety and to protect the positive introjections. He further suggests that contradictory ego states are alternatively activated, but are kept separate from each other, and that this underlies identity diffusion.

Splitting and dissociation share several common features. Both involve an active maintaining apart of mental contents; in neither is the division of conscious-unconscious of issue; each is used defensively to ward off anxiety; and both give rise to a disturbance in sense of self or sense of identity.

There are differences between the concepts too, especially in terms of what it is that is split off or kept apart. Splitting, as used by Kernberg, is considerably narrower and refers in a limited sense to the process of maintaining apart object and self-representations of opposite affective quality. Dissociation, by contrast, is far broader and is used to denote a variety of divisions wherein the separations themselves are not typically polarized into good versus bad. For example, the term has become an umbrella concept to cover such diverse phenomena such as the splitting off of memories in amnesia, the splitting off of awareness in fugue states, and the division of roles in multiple personality.

The concepts also differ with respect to the ego functions that each is implicated in disrupting. For instance, according to Kernberg, concomitant with splitting are specific ego weaknesses, including impaired reality testing, poor impulse control, lowered anxiety tolerance, and limited frustration tolerance. With respect to dissociation, authors sometimes describe, without specifically labeling, impaired reality testing; more commonly, however, they draw more attention to associated impairments in memory and consciousness.

Splitting is conceived as involving disruptions to both self and object representations; therefore, attention is accorded its impact not only on the self, but on quality of object relations as well. As to dissociation, although much has been written of its impact upon the self (Beahrs, 1982; Spiegel, 1988; Putnam, 1989), comparatively little has been provided with respect to its effect on object relations, both internal relations and external relations.

Let us not overlook the similarities between splitting and dissociation. In describing splitting, Kernberg (1975) referred to the activating and maintaining apart of contradictory ego states. Unlike Rapaport (Gill, 1967), who used the term "ego states" to denote state of consciousness, Kernberg seems to be using the concept more broadly to include patterns of awareness, action, and relating; ways of experiencing the self and others; and expressions and control of affectivity. As such, his use of the concept appears similar to Horowitz's (1992) notion of states of mind. In addition, Brenner (1994), who conceives of dissociation in terms of an autohypnotically induced altered state, also seems to be using the concept of altered state in this broader way.

Another defense that has been related to dissociation, but has received less attention, is denial. Vaillant (1977) has proposed a hierarchy of defenses, ranging from high-level "mature" mechanisms, such as humor and sublimation, to low-level "psychotic" mechanisms, such as distortion and delusional projection. He considers dissociation to be a "neurotic" defense, places it at the level just below mature mechanisms, and equates it with neurotic denial—the "temporary but drastic modification of one's character or of one's sense of personal identity to avoid emotional distress" (p. 385).

Following Kernberg (1975), P. Lerner and H. Lerner (1980), by contrast, emphasize the reality-distorting aspects of denial. They view denial as consisting of a group of defenses that can be arranged on a continuum based on degree of reality distortion. At the upper end of the continuum are defenses such as minimization and repudiation, in which there is comparatively little reality distortion. At the lower end is low-level denial, which involves significant distortions of reality to the point that a segment of subjective experience, or of the external world, is not integrated with the rest of the experience. From this perspective, dissociation would correspond with low-level denial rather than with a neurotic-level denial.

Finally, dissociation and denial share another common feature. In both, omnipotence plays a major role. Klein (1946), in particular, has discussed the place of omnipotence in denial. Dissociation too, as P. Lerner and H. Lerner (1996) point out, also has an omnipotent quality. It permits an individual to live out his or her fantasies, to behave and feel as if past traumas have not occurred, and to remove oneself magically from any unpleasant situation.

In summary, unlike Brenner (1994), who defines dissociation narrowly and views it as augmenting repression and splitting, I conceive of dissociation as different from repression and splitting. In this section I have attempted to compare and contrast the three defenses. The relationship between dissociation and denial, particularly more reality-distorting forms of denial, has been underexplored, as has the role of omnipotence in dissociation.

✦ ✦ ✦ Discontinuity of Experience

Several authors (Spiegel, 1988; Allen, 1993; Armstrong, 1994) have noted and described the relationship between dissociation and discontinuity of experience. One of the effects of dissociation is a discontinuity in the individual's experience. Allen (1993) contends that consequent to dissociation, the self becomes separated from its own experience and that parts of experience are exiled to a "not-me" region (Sullivan, 1956). At the same time, the need to cut the ribbon of experience serves as a motive prompting dissociation. When experiences become intolerable or are felt to be overwhelming, one learns to disconnect oneself from those experiences for relief and protection.

To better understand the concept of discontinuity of experience, Allen (1993) has identified three components of experience that are implicated in, disrupted by, and inextricably interwoven with dissociation—memory/affect, consciousness, and self-organization. Interestingly, P. Lerner and H. Lerner (1996), independently, have cited these same components as representing an area of psychoanalytic inquiry that has remained untouched by contemporary contributors to modern dissociation theory. In what follows, and in the spirit of integration, I discuss each of these topics from a psychoanalytic perspective.

Memory

For psychoanalysts, as well as for investigators studying the dissociative disorders, the problem of memory has centered around a concern with forgetting—with forgetting narrowly viewed as a consequence of either repression or dissociation. The equating of forgetting with either repression or dissociation has its basis in the early assumption that certain psychological disturbances involve the memory of actual events and that residues from the experience are isolated or split off, yet acquire preemptive power over behavior.

Not all instances of forgetting are the result of repression or dissociation. To understand the types and nature of memory loss consequent to dissociation, I start with the work of George Klein (1970). In contradistinction to others, Klein approached memory, not from the perspective of forgetting, but rather from the point of view of remembering. This then led him to view memory, not as a unitary function, but as a composite of various subfunctions.

Klein identified four subaspects of the overall memory function—registration, storage or retention, coding or categorization within schemata, and retrieval or reconstruction. By allowing that memory consists of various subfunctions, one may then suggest that the effects of dissociation on memory will vary according to the particular function or functions involved.

Horowitz (1992), for example, in noting the effects of psychic trauma on the mind, has suggested that memories of the trauma are registered and retained but are difficult to integrate with existing meaning schemas, including the self-schema. In terms of Klein's model, then, Horowitz is not implicating memory as a whole, but rather the specific categorization function.

Rapaport (1952) drew a distinction between states of consciousness and the ways of experiencing consciousness. By state of consciousness he was referring to the dimension of wakefulness/sleep. Ways of experiencing consciousness, by contrast, refer to the modes by which the contents of consciousness are experienced. For instance, such contents may be experienced as memories, as illusions, as facts, or as wishes. Underlying this mode of experiencing consciousness is the dimension of attributed qualities of realness.

Klein applied this distinction to memory, suggesting that one could look at each stage of memory in terms of both state of consciousness and the mode of experiencing the memory. Whereas the state of consciousness, at each stage, provides the context, the experiential mode determines the way in which the memory is registered, stored, organized, and retrieved, including most importantly, its subjective sense of realness.

For example, on occasion what is considered loss of memory, forgetting or a failure in retrieval, is not that, but rather is a distortion in mode of experiencing. One may respond to the stored representation of an actual event as something not real but as imagined. Or, conversely, a vividly imagined event can be misexperienced as an actual happening and not as a wish.

A 43-year-old, highly impaired, female patient reported vague residues of experiences as a child of having been sexually molested by several adult males, including her father. She was confused as to whether the residues were remembrances of actual events, vestiges of stories told to her by an older sister, or simply unfounded fears based on other instances of exploitation; therefore, she had little sense of their realness.

In a general way, she exemplifies how, in the service of defense, events can be stripped of their realness, not through a loss of the contents of memory, but rather by an altering or clouding of the experiential mode through which they are remembered. Her therapist, too, was unclear as to the authenticity of the events, a counterreaction common in treating dissociative patients. To pursue this case a step further, the therapist's sense with this patient, metaphorically, was of attempting to "put a cloud into a pail." That is, he experienced her as insubstantial, undefined, and lacking coherence—unreal, if you will. One wonders, then, about the relationship between her tendency to defend herself against the realization of painful events in her life by rendering them unreal, her sense of herself, and her therapist's sense of her as unreal.

This case also touches on another aspect of memory, its relationship to identity. Several authors have commented on the reciprocal relationship between memory and identity. In one direction, Beahrs (1982) and Hillgard (1977) have each noted that memory is an essential prerequisite for maintaining a sense of identity over time—the element of continuity.

In the other direction, Rapaport and Gill (1942) have emphasized the importance of personal identity in memory. They suggest that without a sense of me-ness, memories become either logically deductible knowledge or unavailable for recall. According to these authors, personal identity provides the context that allows a memory to enter consciousness. Hence, when a memory conflicts with personal identity it is excluded from consciousness; however, because the memory includes a sense of me-ness, that sense of me-ness is excluded as well. In essence, implicit in memory loss is a loss of personal identity as well.

Interestingly, although written more than 50 years ago in this domain of inquiry, Rapaport and Gill's (1942) work has a remarkably contemporary cast. Their sense of me-ness in memories is consistent with Brewer's (1986) concept of "autobiographical memory," Edelman's (1992) notion of "value-category memory," and the role Reiser (1990) assigns to affect in binding memory elements.

Consciousness

Like memory, consciousness too is a highly complex process that is best viewed, not as a global phenomenon, but instead as a composite of various subprocesses and subaspects. Here I will simply identify and clarify several of these subprocesses.

Psychoanalysis has traditionally considered consciousness an ego function—an apparatus in the service of the ego. It was viewed as a superordinate sense organ that is both organized and selective. Rapaport (1951) went further and conceived of consciousness as distinguishable from states of consciousness and as having several characteristics, including awareness, reflectiveness (aware of being aware), thoughts, forms of thoughts, and ways of experiencing contents (e.g., perceptions, hallucinations, wishes). Both conceptually and empirically "he demonstrated that there is a continuum of states of consciousness between waking and dreaming and that they differ from each other in the kind and extent of reflective awareness, voluntary effort, and forms of thought organization prevailing in them" (Gill and Klein, 1967, p. 26).

Descriptions of dissociative patients often include references to the patient's state of consciousness, as for instance, comments about the dreamlike or hypnotic-like quality of the patient's experience. Such descriptions, however, usually do not elucidate the other aspects of the patient's consciousness elaborated by Rapaport.

Several of the characteristics of consciousness are related to other ego functions as well. Rapaport (1951), for example, has noted that both awareness and reflectiveness (reflexive awareness) are related to effectiveness of control over impulses. Maximal awareness correlates with optimal control of impulses, whereas lack of, or excessive and rigid, impulse control correlates with limited awareness.

Because the way in which the content of consciousness is experienced affects how the content is acted upon, the experiential mode is related to reality testing and judgment. Failures in reality testing and judgment may issue from an inappropriateness of mode of experience. For instance, if a wish is experienced as a fact, or a fantasy is experienced as a reality event, then the ensuing behavior is likely not to fit the situation, and the individual's reality testing and judgment are called into question.

As with memory, here too the experiential modes may be ordered along a dimension of attributed realness. Thus, the level of realness attributed to an experience can be altered through an alteration of the experiential mode.

To say, then, that dissociation involves an alteration in consciousness may be accurate, but it is also imprecise and incomplete. More useful would be a further elaboration of the alteration in terms of the specific characteristics of consciousness involved.

Self

Without exception, every author who writes on dissociation and the dissociative disorders relates the process to the self and self-cohesion. Spiegel (1988) suggests that dissociation results in a loss of self or self-fragmentation. Beahrs (1982) defines the dissociative disorders in terms of personality splitting, meaning, splits in the self. Putnam (1989) has identified two overriding features characteristic of all dissociative disorders, one of which is a disturbance in the individual's sense of self.

Recent years have witnessed the emergence of the concept of self as a preoccupying concern in psychoanalysis. Not withstanding the contributions of Erikson (1950), Klein (1976), and Gedo (1979), there are currently three lines of psychoanalytic theorizing about the self.

One line, represented by the work of Grossman (1982), regards the self as simply a fantasy; a compromise of drive and defense forces that has meaning for the individual, in that it provides a point of reference for organizing inner experience.

A second line regards the self as a subpart of the ego and as an integrated structure of self-representations, with particular reference to introjections. Illustrative of this view is Kernberg (1975), who describes the self as "an intra psychic structure consisting of multiple self representations and their related affect dispositions" (p. 315). Self-representations are understood here as "cognitive affective structures reflecting the person's perception of himself in real and fantasized interactions with others" (p. 316).

The third view, that of Kohut (1977), conceives of the self as a superordinate, unified, coherent constellation, with drives and defenses, that evolves out of a developmental line of narcissism. Kohut's self is superordinate, in that it subsumes the id, ego, and superego. It is also personal, in that he conceives of it as the active and originative source of personal activity, the experiencer of complex experiential states, and the possessor of qualities and capacities that involve an integration of various substructures of the personality.

Typically, investigators studying dissociation do not write from a psychoanalytic perspective. Therefore, although they raise the issue of the self, they often fail to elaborate what they mean by the self or which conception of the self they are using.

If one were to transpose their writings onto the various psychoanalytic conceptions, it would appear that some writers view the self as an aggregate of self-representations, whereas others subscribe to Kohut's notion of the self as a coherent constellation. Thus, when authors describe the convening of multiple selves in the multiple personality disorder, they seem to be implying that a poorly integrated or unintegrated self-structure has become further unglued, resulting in a loose federation of fully developed part-selfs. That is different, both structurally and phenomenologically, from references to a coherent self that fragments. This latter view implies a shattering or breaking apart.

One can approach the self from three perspectives—its structure, its contents, and its functions. Whereas the issue of coherence relates to structure, the notions of self-concept and self-image refer to content.

The impact of dissociation on both the structure and content of the self has been addressed (Beahrs, 1982; Putnam, 1989); what has received less attention is the effect of dissociation on the self's functions. An exception here is the work of Spiegel (1988) and his attempt to examine the relationship between dissociation and the self-functions of regulation and mediating experiences. According to Spiegel, because of dissociation the self loses its awareness of its mediating function.

Two other functions of the self which have been found to be impaired in dissociative patients are the function of immediate experiencing and the function of self-observation. During trauma, for example, when the individual experiences the painful event as happening to a different self, the participating self seems especially separate and estranged from the observing self. Conversely, when an individual looses himself or herself in a special state, such as a hypnoticlike trance, to protect the self from memories of a traumatic experience, the observing self seems to all but diminish with the experiencing self's growing absorption.

The functions of the self usually operate in a harmonious and integrated manner. With dissociation, however, the experiencing and observing functions split and operate quite separately. Most commonly, the experiencing self becomes distant and estranged, whereas there is an accentuation of the observing self. This alteration in the self between the experiencing function and the observing function is precisely what Arlow (1966) noted in his analysis of depersonalization and derealization. For Arlow, depersonalization and derealization were states that reflect a breakdown in the ego's integrative function, resulting in a split between the experiencing self and the observing self.

Interestingly, in his article, Arlow used the term "dissociation"; he did not use it, however, in the conceptual sense being used here. Rather, Arlow employed the term as a transitive verb to simply refer to the process of splitting or separating. As well, the functions of experiencing and observing which we attribute to the self, he attributed to the ego.

In terms of the perspective taken here, that is, conceiving of dissociation as a complex defensive process, it makes conceptual sense to consider depersonalization and derealization affective concomitants associated with alterations in the self.

Summary

To briefly recap, virtually all discussions of dissociation take into account its relationship to memory, consciousness, and the self. Even though each of these topics has been thoughtfully considered and discussed from a psychoanalytic perspective, those discussions have tended to remain outside of contemporary writings on dissociation.

The review offered here, admittedly incomplete, has involved a review of the concepts of memory, consciousness, and self from a psychoanalytic vantage point. Conclusions to be drawn include the following: (1) underlying the various experiential modes of both memory and consciousness is a dimension of attributed realness; (2) experiences can be rendered unreal, not only through a loss of memory contents, but also through an altering of the experiential mode through which they are remembered; (3) memory and identity are intimately related; and (4) concomitant with the split between the self-functions of experiencing and observing are feelings of depersonalization and derealization.

❖ ❖ ❖ Dissociation and the Rorschach: Review

Despite the increased interest that has been accorded dissociation and the dissociative-disordered patient, except for the more recent work of Armstrong (1991, 1994), there is little in the Rorschach literature in regard to the assessment of dissociation. Then too, in most instances, the assessment of dissociation has been intimately linked with the evaluation of multiple-personality disordered patients.

In several studies, investigators adopted the strategy of testing the alter personalities separately and sequentially. In the 1940s, Erickson and Rapaport (1980) tested two patients, each suffering from "dual personality." The authors reported that each patient revealed introversion, intellectualization, and a "compulsive-obsessional" personality.

Wagner and Heise (1974), after reviewing the Rorschach records of three MPD patients, reported two salient features—a large number of diversified movement responses and labile and conflicting color responses. Working from these initial findings and theoretical considerations, Wagner, Allison, and Wagner (1983) developed the following indices for diagnosing multiple personality disorder: (1) a large number of movement responses; (2) at least two qualitatively diverse human-movement responses; (3) a projection of oppression (e.g., attack, subjugation, constraint) onto at least one of the movement responses; (4) at least three color responses with the sum of CF+C exceeding the sum of FC, and (5) At least one color percept having positive connotations and another negative connotations. The indices were then applied to the Rorschach record of a fourth MPD patient, and confirmation was obtained for each sign.

In the initial study, Wagner and Heise (1974) also compared the protocols of the primary personalities with those of the secondary personalities. They reported a "simplification" tendency, meaning that the records of the secondary personalities tended to be less complex and more affectively driven than those of the first.

Lovitt and Lefkof (1985) applied Exner's Comprehensive System to the protocols of three MPD patients and to their alter personalities. With regard to the primary personalities, they found that all three had intact reality testing, but lacked a clear and consistent approach to coping with life's demands, and that two manifested poor affect control. The personality structures of the secondary personalities, as determined by Rorschach scores, were remarkably different from those of the main personalities. More specifically, the authors found wide variability in several of the scoring categories. Scores and ratios, such as number of populars, lambda, color ratios, and F+%, which Exner (1986a) has demonstrated to be stable over time, varied between individual personalities. The authors interpreted their Rorschach findings as indicating that "these patients struggle and vacillate between overcontrol and undercontrol or constructive and destructive forces within their personality" (p. 293). In contrast with Wagner and Heise (1974), then, who reported a tendency toward "simplification" in the secondary personality, Lovitt and Lefkof (1985) noted great variability.

It is sometimes argued that sexual abuse is a major factor of dissociative disorders, an assertion that raises the question whether a similar relation between trauma and defensive reaction can be found in other disturbances. As a result of recent findings that indicate there is a high incidence of childhood sexual abuse and incest among female patients diagnosed as borderline personality disorder, Saunders (1991) employed a constellation of Rorschach scores with the intent of distinguishing those borderline patients who had been sexually victimized from those female borderline patients who had not. Included among her group of Rorschach scores were two new ones related to dissociative symptoms. One involved subcategorizing all movement responses as active, passive, or atypical. Atypical movement was defined as "the temporal disruption of an action, so that it is perceived and described as either having occurred in the past, being about to occur in the future, or being frozen or in a state of suspension" (p. 55).

A second feature of atypical movement involves an implied reference to an agent of the action, without the agent appearing in the perceptual data of the inkblot (i.e., "somebody splattered paint").

The second score, referred to as a "dissociative score," involved translating descriptions of dissociative experiences into Rorschach terms. The following six Rorschach indices comprised the dissociative score:

> (1) extreme and unusual shifts of the scale of percepts within one card; (2) unusual and often arbitrary responses in which distances seem exaggerated or spacial arrangements seem inconsistent; (3) references to forms as 'upside down' or identification of percepts that are upside down in relation to the actual orientation of the inkblot without the subject needing to shift the position of the card to identify these inverted percepts; (4) forms seen through obscuring media such as veils or mists; (5) oddly fragmented modes of seeing that go beyond unusual human detail or animal detail; and (6) frequent memory lapses that suggest psychogenic amnesia between the response and inquiry segments of test administration, or else phasic shifts between florid, flashbacklike percepts and blandly conventional responses either within or between cards [Saunders, 1991, p. 56].

Using Pearson's product-moment correlation, an inter-rater reliability of r = .82 was obtained for atypical movement and r = .90 for the dissociation score. Whereas the atypical-movement score appeared significantly more frequently in the Rorschachs of the sexually abused borderline patients, the dissociation score failed to produce significant results, although the group mean dissociation score was higher for the sexually abused group. Berstein and Putnam's (1986) Dissociative Experiences Scale, a questionnaire instrument, was administered to a subset of the entire sample, and that measure produced significant between-group differences. If that scale had been given to all subjects, it may have been possible to explore its relationship to the Rorschach atypical-movement score and dissociation score.

In a study conducted in Rome, Italy, Ferracuti, Sacco, and Lazzari (1996) administered Rorschachs to 10 subjects (seven females and three males) undergoing exorcisms for devil trance possession state. On the basis of a psychiatric interview, each individual was diagnosed as Dissociative Trance Disorder, a category proposed for further study (DSM-IV), but one that shares common features with Dissociative

Identity Disorder. The Rorschachs were scored with the Comprehensive System and the group means were compared with Exner's standard database means. Rorschach findings indicated that the 10 subjects had a complex personality organization, had severe impairment of reality testing, and had little capacity for self-observation.

In an investigation designed to study the personality structure of MPD patients, and the relationship between that structure and the use of the defense dissociation, Armstrong (Armstrong, 1991; Armstrong and Lowenstein, 1990) administered Rorschachs to 14 patients, each of whom met DSM-III-R criteria for MPD or DD (dissociative disorder) and research criteria for dissociative disorders. Rorschachs were scored according to the Comprehensive System and group means were compared with Exner's standard database means for schizophrenics, major depressives, and normal controls. In general, the group of MPD and DD patients revealed a more obsessive-compulsive coping style with a tendency to internalize, a vulnerability to lapses in reality testing, psychological complexity defined in terms of numerous Rorschach blend responses, human relatedness, and a heightened capacity for self-observation. Armstrong identified several personality features that predisposed and allowed these individuals to use dissociation. These individuals react to situations in a complex manner and are able to become both overinvolved in, and detached from, their own experience. They are highly ideational, readily take distance from themselves, elevate fantasy above logical external constraints, and often are overwhelmed by traumatic imagery stimulated by the inkblot.

A review of these studies leads to the following conclusions. First, authors have been primarily interested in studying the personality structure of specific groups of patients (MPD, DTD, sexually abused female borderlines) and identifying Rorschach indices indicative of the specific diagnosis. Apart from the writings of Armstrong, the assessment of dissociation itself has been of secondary or of no importance. Second, except for the study by Lovitt and Lefkof (1985), patients who employ dissociation offer Rorschach protocols with many and varied movement responses. This suggests that such individuals are highly ideational and have ready access to fantasy. Third, assessing dissociative patients, especially those with alter personalities, presents unique methodological problems. Fourth, only Armstrong and Lowenstein (1990) have attempted to describe, more descriptively and phenomenologically, the experience, both for the testee and the examiner, of assessing a dissociative patient.

◆ ◆ ◆ Assessing the Dissociative Patient

Test Administration

For both clinical and research purposes, there is no established testing protocol for assessing dissociating patients, including those who present rapidly shifting ego states or a divided self-organization. Earlier investigators, as noted, with MPD patients, tested the alter personalities separately and sequentially. In contradistinction, and in keeping with modern dissociation theory, Armstrong (1991) adopted the strategy of attempting to assess the entire individual, regardless of the degree of dividedness. She describes her procedure this way:

> In a pretest interview, using the patient's own terminology for his or her phenomenologic experience of dividedness, all divergent self-aspects . . . [are] invited to participate in the assessment. Attempts . . . [are] made to minimize trauma-related fears and MPD-related confusion by familiarizing the patient with test procedures and surroundings and inviting questions [pp. 535–536].

Armstrong's approach is not only thoughtful and humane, it is also consistent with sound testing practices. That is, she takes into consideration the unique needs of the patient and adjusts her procedure accordingly, and without compromising the integrity of the test. She introduces a carefully considered parameter—a pretest interview—and offers a follow-up feedback session. One need not adopt Armstrong's specific format, however, in deciding upon an approach, one should take into account the distinctive aspects of these patients, one's own conceptualization of dissociation and the dissociative individual, and the effect on test data of the frame used.

Test Behavior and the Patient–Examiner Relationship

Armstrong and Lowenstein (1990) have identified several test behaviors commonly observed in patients who dissociate, including abrupt changes in voice and posture, spontaneous trances, amnesia, eye-roll, and eyelid flutter. Saunders (1991), in devising her dissociative score, attempted to find Rorschach parallels of descriptions of dissociative experiences. If one were to retranslate her score into test behaviors, then one could add to Armstrong and Lowenstein's list changing ego states, vacillations between interpersonal closeness and distance, and memory lapses regarding test administration and test instructions. In addition, I would add that one may also observe periods during which the individual spaces out, episodes of shutting down, and heightened compliance and seeming suggestibility.

Almost nothing has appeared in the Rorschach literature regarding the nature of the patient–examiner relationship in the assessment of dissociative individuals. P. Lerner and H. Lerner (1996) recently reported on the psychoanalytic treatment of a dissociative patient, and several of the transference-countertransference paradigms they described likely have assessment implications.

The major configuration noted involved a transferential enactment of the patient's earlier sadomasochistic relationship with her parents. In varying ways, her therapist became the powerful, abusive, neglectful, and exploitive parent of childhood, and the patient, reciprocally, experienced herself as powerless, abused, neglected, and exploited. At other times, there was a total reversal of these roles when part of the patient seemed identified with the powerful and exploitive parents. With respect to assessment, this suggests that issues of power and victimization will be at the forefront of the patient–examiner relationship.

A second, more subtle paradigm involved the patient, at times, assigning her own high-level ego capacities to the therapist. This operation left the patient feeling like a helpless, needy child. This relational pattern was manifest in several ways, ranging from losing her train of thought, expecting her therapist to maintain it for her to refusing work assignments and demanding that the therapist lower his fee. In dramatic contrast to her stance of helplessness, there were other occasions when the patient was able to access her full capacities and function effectively and autonomously.

The pattern described here occurs frequently in assessing dissociative patients. These patients forget or distort test directions, lose the reality of the test situation, and have amnesia for past sessions. All of these testing phenomena are understood, correctly so, as expressions of dissociation. Nonetheless, it is also important to view these behaviors from a relational and transferential perspective.

Debate abounds in the literature of multiple personality disorder (Benner and Joscelyne, 1984; Buck, 1983; Clary, Burstin, and Carpenter, 1984; Fast, 1974; Armstrong, 1990) as to whether the disorder is a variant of the borderline personality disorder or, instead, is a separate and distinct entity. Aside from this question, it is clear that dissociative patients stir different countertransference feelings than do borderline patients. In treating or assessing borderline patients, several authors (Green, 1975; Boyer, 1977; Gorney and Weinstock, 1980) have pointed to the borderline's capacity to evoke confusion, despair, massive anxiety, and intense rage. By contrast, dissociative patients arouse very different feelings, such as compassion, tolerance, and even admiration. More so than with other types of patients, theorists emphasize the adaptive aspects of the dissociative patient's symptoms and struggles.

For purposes of assessment, then, with this group of patients it is especially important that the examiner pay careful attention to his or her own countertransference reactions. Not only can such feelings be used in determining a differential diagnosis, they can also lead to a deeper understanding of the individual.

Test Performance

At a recent conference, I (P. Lerner, 1996b), together with several others, presented our blind analyses of the Rorschach protocol of a 26-year-old woman who had been involved in a traumatic experience. About two years earlier, while driving, she was involved in an automobile accident in which her husband was badly maimed and died. She felt responsible for his death. Since the accident, she had been hospitalized twice for psychotic-like symptoms, prolonged periods of shutting down, and episodes of dissociating. During the second hospitalization the question arose as to whether the patient was schizophrenic or suffered from a chronic posttraumatic stress disorder. That diagnostic issue, together with assisting in treatment planning, prompted the request for psychological testing.

Of her 22 responses, more than one-third (8) were directly referable to the traumatic incident. That is, each of these percepts reflected the intrusion into the response process of nonintegrated, nonmetabolized traces of the trauma. For example, on Card II she depicted a pleasurable, recreational activity (i.e., "dancing"), which became infused with blood, gore, violence, and ultimately death. On Card III she described a scene in which "tribesmen" were engaged in a ritualistic activity consisting of the attainment of manhood through the "spillage of blood." Looking beyond the secondary refinements and intellectualizing activity, the response was eerily close to the bloodbath that had resulted in the loss, not attainment, of a man and his manhood.

Most compelling was her response on Card VIII. She first offered the morbid and peculiar idea of a "sad skull" (a skull cannot be sad), but quickly changed it to a "sad dog." During inquiry, when the examiner asked about the "skull" response, she dissociated and denied having seen it ("did I say that?"), became confused, suggested the "skull" percept be disregarded ("scratch it"), and then elaborated on the "sad dog" percept.

Armstrong (1991) and Saunders (1991) have also observed that patients who have suffered trauma and employ dissociation offer Rorschach responses in which fantasy material related to traumatic memories emerges with rawness. The frequency of traumatic associations appearing in her MPD sample prompted Armstrong (1991) to develop a simple measure of traumatic content, consisting of the sum of aggressive, morbid, sex, anatomy, and blood responses divided by total number of responses.

As evidenced in the above case material, as raw and blatant as the response may be, it is still a step removed from the actual trauma. Thus, the percept reflects both traces of the trauma and attempts to defend against it. This is consistent with Freud's (1896) early concept of the "return of the repressed," in which defenses weaken and affects and contents related to trauma, previously maintained in repression (in this instance dissociation), intrude into awareness.

Then too, and from an adaptive perspective, such responses may also involve a restitutive function. Implicit in trauma is the need to repeat—in action, in symptoms, and perhaps even in a Rorschach response—the distressing experiences, including the full range of painful affects. The need to repeat has several goals, including the desire to symbolize and find words for events that were rendered unspeakable, the need to master what has threatened and disrupted equilibrium, and the need to confront actively what had been experienced passively.

Primitive and raw as the Rorschach content may be, however, it differs from the content offered by schizophrenic patients in two basic ways. First, with the dissociative patient, in contrast to the schizophrenic, the content can be related to trauma or traumatic memories. Second, the content produced by the dissociative individual is drenched with affect.

Also reflected in the case material was the patient's effort to defend against traumatic Rorschach content by disowning the response. Thus, with these patients, accompanying raw content are various defensive maneuvers, such as lapses in memory and a retreat into a trancelike state, as ways of removing themselves, in the immediacy, from the material.

My own experience is consistent with that of Armstrong's (1991), in that the traumatic content may or may not be accompanied by formal indications of impaired reality testing, thought disturbance, and boundary disturbances. In any case, I agree with Armstrong that "it is the form of the response that carries information about the defensive organization of the traumatic perception" (p. 541).

With the dissociative individual, it is mandatory that one pay close attention to specific words and the wording of phrases. For instance, Armstrong (1991) understood the word "we" used in a response of a MPD patient as indicating that the percept had been given by "combined alters" (p. 541). In the case I have reported, the patient described "two people as dancing, engaged in a death struggle, but their arms are locked together." The phrase "their arms are locked together" signaled to me that the patient continued to deny the actual loss of her husband.

Finally, I have not found any specific conventional Rorschach scores, in and of themselves, that are indicative of dissociation. Even though individuals who dissociate tend to produce an abundance and variety of movement responses, and may be overwhelmed by color, such formal features should not be taken separately from the accompanying content.

✦ ✦ ✦ Implications for Research

As previously noted, the Rorschach study of dissociation has been confounded by an interest in the personality structure of specific groups who assumedly dissociate. This has led investigators to compare these target groups with nondissociating groups on formal Rorschach scores, including those featured in the Comprehensive System. Because these scores are more related to enduring structures than to dynamic processes, except for Armstrong's (1991) attempt to relate these structures directly to dissociation, these studies have not contributed to the systematic assessment of dissociation.

More directly related to dissociation are two innovative scores developed by Saunders (1991)—atypical movement and a dissociation score. In its attunement to movement, the atypical-movement response is consistent with the findings of Wagner and Heise (1974) and

Armstrong and Lowenstein (1990) that movement abounds in the protocols of dissociative patients. In addition, by including in the score a
temporal dimension and reference to an agent that is not seen,
Saunders (1991) attempts to capture some of the complexity involved
in dissociation. The dissociation score represented an attempt to find
Rorschach equivalents of clinical descriptions of dissociation. The
score failed to distinguish a group of sexually abused female borderline patients from a group of nonabused female borderlines. Saunders
took the results as indicating that the score was too eclectic. It is my
impression that the design of her study did not permit a true evaluation of the efficacy of the score.

In any event, I believe that to assess dissociation for research purposes, like Saunders (1991), investigators will have to develop innovative measures that begin to reflect adequately the complexity of the
concept. To judge from the usefulness of Armstrong's (1991) trau-
matic-content score, such measures should combine content with formal features. Investigators must first grasp the phenomenology of the
dissociative experience as expressed on the Rorschach and in the context of the patient–examiner relationship. As mentioned previously,
dissociation appears as more of a process than a structure and finds
expression in any number of ways, including test behavior, word usage,
sequence of responses, and raw content encased in acceptable
responses. To devise scores that make use of various aspects of the
Rorschach, capture the phenomenology of the dissociative experience,
and recognize the complexity of the concept, constitutes a formidable
challenge.

✦ ✦ ✦ Conclusion

I began this chapter by reviewing the concept of dissociation. After
describing the relationship between dissociation and trauma, I discussed dissociation as a defense, distinguishing it from repression and
splitting, and emphasizing the role of omnipotence. Under the topic
of discontinuity of experience, I reviewed the relationship between dissociation and memory, consciousness, and the self. Turning from the
theoretical to the applied, in the second half of the chapter I discussed
the Rorschach assessment of dissociation. A review of the research literature indicates that the study of dissociation has been interwoven
with and complicated by a stronger interest in the personality structure

of individuals who assumedly dissociate. It is suggested that attempts to operationalize the concept should focus on process rather than structure, make use of various aspects of a Rorschach record and not just formal scores, build upon the phenomenology of the dissociative experience, and appreciate the complexity of the concept. Finally, I also discussed the clinical assessment of the dissociative individual.

20

DEVELOPMENTAL
OBJECT RELATIONS

1n 1975, I observed that although Pruitt and Spilka (1964) had developed a promising scale for assessing object relations, investigators still regarded the human-movement response (M) and the human-figure response (H) as the most appropriate indices for assessing object relations.

With a shift in emphasis in psychoanalytic theory toward a view of object relations from a developmental perspective, the past 20 years have witnessed the emergence of a host of psychoanalytically informed Rorschach scales devised to assess quality of object relations along a developmental continuum.

To varying degrees, these scales have been conceptually rooted in Mahler's (Mahler et al., 1975) theory of separation-individuation. Mahler observed and described the steps in the separation-individuation process, which begins with the earliest signs of the infant's differentiation or hatching from a symbiotic fusion with the mother; proceeds through the period of the infant's absorption in its own autonomous functioning, to the near exclusion of the mother; continues through the all-important period of rapprochement, in which the child, precisely because of a more clearly perceived state of separateness from mother, is prompted to redirect attention back to mother;

and finally culminates in a feeling of an early sense of self, of individual identity, and of constancy of the object.

In this chapter I review several of these newer, conceptually based
scales, including the work of Urist (1977), Kwawer (1980), Coonerty
(1986), and Ipp (1986). Representative research employing the scales
is discussed. H. Lerner and P. Lerner (1986) proposed an object-relations model of thinking that integrated Piaget's theory of early cognitive development with Mahler's theory of separation-individuation.
That conceptual model has been extended to the Rorschach (P. Lerner,
1996c), and is also included in this chapter.

✦ ✦ ✦   Research Scales

Mutuality of Autonomy (MOA)

The first scale to be reviewed is Urist's (1977) Mutuality of Autonomy
Scale. Urist developed a measure based solely on Rorschach imagery
to assess stages in the child's shifting sense of self in relation to the
mother. The series of scale points are not seen as discrete categories,
but rather as differentiations along a continuous and coherent line of
development. At the lower, more primitive end of the scale, one finds
Rorschach imagery that reflects themes of an undifferentiated, symbiotic fusion of body parts. At the next higher stage, themes relate to the
child's experience of self and mother as each having physical propri-
etorship over his or her respective body; the body of one, however, can
be sensed as under the control of the other. Themes of mirroring represent the third stage; herein, the child's relatedness involves the other
being regarded as an extension of the child's own need state. In the
fourth stage there are signs of differentiation, but the prevailing anaclitic imagery reflects object relations on a predominantly need-satisfying basis. Higher scale points reflect an approach to object constancy,
in which others are viewed as separate and valued in their own right.
The most advanced stage involves the capacity for empathy, the ability to invest in the subjective world of another while maintaining
mutual autonomy.

Based on the foregoing, the scale consists of the following seven
ascending points: envelopment-incorporation, magical control-coer-
cion, reflection-mirroring, anaclitic-dependent, simple interaction, col-
laboration-cooperation, reciprocity-mutuality. The scale is applied to

all relationships manifested in Rorschach content, that is, relationships between humans, animals, natural forces, and so forth.

In the original study, the scale was applied to the Rorschach records of 60 patients representing a broad spectrum of levels of psychopathology. Using therapist ratings and clinical ratings as independent measures of object relations, Urist (1977) found the scale to correlate significantly with these ratings.

Whereas in the first study the scale was applied to the entire Rorschach protocol, in a second study (Urist and Shill, 1982) the scale was applied exclusively to excerpted Rorschach responses, including responses in which a relationship was implied (e.g., "squashed bug"). In this study, involving 60 adolescent inpatients and outpatients with various diagnoses, independent ratings of object relations were obtained by applying a clinical version of the Mutuality of Autonomy Scale to the patient's confidential records. Here again, significant correlations were found between the Rorschach scale scores and independent clinical ratings.

Harder et al. (1984) found that the Mutuality of Autonomy Scale correlated significantly with ratings of psychopathology as assessed by complex symptom-dimension checklists and independent diagnostic assessments according to DSM-III (American Psychiatric Association, 1980) criteria. A mean MOA score based on only four Rorschach cards distinguished among schizophrenic, affective, and nonpsychotic conditions. More severe psychiatric disorders were associated with a more disrupted mean MOA score. Spear and Sugarman (1984) found that a modified version of the MOA score differentiated among two groups of borderline patients (i.e., infantile borderline and obsessive-paranoid borderline) and a group of schizophrenic patients.

In a sample of acutely disturbed adolescent and young-adult patients admitted to a long-term, intensive, but open residential treatment facility, Blatt, Tuber, and Averbach (1990) reported that the mean MOA score correlated significantly with severity of clinical symptoms and the presence of thought disorder, but not with independent ratings of social behavior and interpersonal relations. The authors concluded that although the MOA scale was designed to assess object relations, their findings suggest that the scale primarily assesses psychopathology, and only secondarily the quality of object relations.

Kavanagh (1985) compared pre- and posttreatment Rorschach protocols of 33 patients selected from the Menninger Psychotherapy Project. He found no differences between admission and termination protocols for the mean MOA score, the single most disrupted score, or the most adaptive score. However, employing an independent clinical judgment of patients' MOA level, Kavanagh did find significant improvement at the end of treatment.

In a number of studies, the Mutuality of Autonomy Scale has been extended to evaluate the protocols of various groups of children. In an early study, Tuber (1983) found a statistically significant relationship between scale ratings based on Rorschach protocols administered at time of admission to a residential treatment center and the incidence of rehospitalization upon follow-up 5 to 20 years later.

Other studies have involved children with varying psychiatric disturbances. Here, the MOA scale has been found useful in distinguishing between clinical and control populations, and in helping to clarify the nature of the pathology within a specific clinical group. Coates and Tuber (1988) used MOA scores to describe the internal object world of 14 children, all diagnosed gender-identity disorder (GID). Each child had at least one MOA scale score that indicated significant imbalance or destruction among interactive percepts on the Rorschach. In this group there was a total of 11 responses that suggested mutual, benign interaction, and of these, 9 of the percepts involved women. By contrast, of the 34 responses scored as malevolent, only 1 involved a female, and the other 33 involved males. The authors interpreted this pattern of idealization of the female and attribution of malevolence to the male as indicating the GID child's need to maintain "his internal tie to his mother and protect her from his rage" (p. 654).

In a second study, Tuber and Coates (1989) compared 26 gender-identity disturbed boys with a control group of 18 subjects. In this study, the GID subjects produced significantly more malevolent interactions as judged by the MOA scale than did the control subjects; had a median MOA score in the malevolent range in contrast to the benign median MOA score of the control group; and had a distribution of MOA scale scores that was significantly more disturbed than the control subjects.

Leifer et al. (1991) compared the Rorschachs of 79 sexually abused black females between the ages of 5 and 16 years with a control group of nonabused girls. The protocols were assessed using several scores and scales, including the Mutuality of Autonomy Scale. Differences in median MOA scores between the two groups indicated that the abused girls perceived interpersonal contact as more disturbed.

Goddard and Tuber (1989) found that a group of boys meeting the DSM-III-R criteria for separation anxiety disorder (SAD) had a significantly more disturbed mean MOA scale score than did a demographically matched control group. Importantly, there was a "notable congruence between the SAD child's clinging behavioral symptomatology and their clinging, leaning MOA responses . . . [providing] an important link between inner representation and manifest behavior" (Tuber, 1992, p. 185).

Thomas (1987) studied and compared the MOA scale scores of the following three clinical groups: children with a DSM-III diagnosis of attention-deficit disorder with hyperactivity, children diagnosed as having both a DSM-III diagnosis of attention-deficit disorder with hyperactivity and borderline personality disorder; and children solely with borderline personality disorder. Children in all three groups produced a wide distribution of scores; for all three groups the modal MOA scale scores were in the more disturbed range. Interestingly, the two groups of children with attention-deficit disorder with hyperactivity produced a higher proportion of scores in the disturbed range than did the borderline group.

Other researchers have related the Mutuality of Autonomy Scale to psychological variables conceptually related to developmental object relations in children. Goldberg (1989) reported a positive correlation between more pathological MOA scale scores and severity of depression, as measured by the Children's Depressive Inventory, in a sample of 100 inner-city girls between the ages of 8 and 16. Ryan et al. (1985) obtained significant correlations between MOA scores and teacher ratings of interpersonal functioning, academic grades, and the child's perceived sense of control (internal versus external). Brown-Cheatham (1993) studied the utility of the MOA scale in the assessment of two groups of father-absent, black male children aged 6 to 12 years. As predicted, children whose fathers left involuntarily revealed less adaptive object relations, as assessed by the MOA, than children whose fathers left voluntarily and had negotiated their leaving.

Meyer and Tuber (1989) examined the MOA scale scores of a group of 4- and 5-year-old children who each had an imaginary companion. Because the phenomenon of imaginary companion serves simultaneously two functions, as a fantasized representation and a "real" companion, it is of considerable interest to those studying object representations and object relations. The authors first compared the Rorschachs of these children with norms for similar aged children provided by Ames et al. (1974). Rorschachs of the imaginary-companion group contained five times as many human-movement responses, four and one half times as many animal-movement responses, and eight times as many inanimate movement responses as the group provided

by Ames and colleagues. Applying the MOA scale to the various movement responses of the imaginary-companion group provided insight
into the nature of their object relations. Important differences in the
quality of MOA scores were found, depending upon whether the rating involved human, animal, or inanimate movement. Those scores
involving human content were largely of a benign, reciprocal nature.
Responses reflective of controlling or menacing interaction were far
more prevalent in the animal movement responses. MOA responses
expressing attacking or catastrophically violent interactions were
exclusively associated with inanimate-movement responses. To judge
from their pattern of MOA scores, in their relationships these children
distance, displace, and disown highly charged conflictual feelings. In
keeping with the writings of Nagera (1969), Sperling (1954), and
Fraiberg (1959), the glaring dichotomy between "good" human and
"bad" animal and inanimate, as revealed on the MOA, indicates "that
the imaginary companions serve simultaneously as the means of disowning 'bad' self representations while sustaining 'good' ones" (Meyer
and Tuber, 1989, p. 166).

Finally, Tuber, Frank, and Santostefano (1989) explored the Mutuality
of Autonomy Scale's sensitivity to short-term shifts in object-representational experience in children facing surgery. Fifteen children, ages
7 to 11, were administered the Rorschach on three separate occasions:
one week prior to elective hernia surgery, the day before the surgery,
and three weeks following hospitalization. These children were compared with a nonsurgical group of 13 children matched for age and
IQ and tested at the same time intervals. Within the surgical group,
the youngsters' MOA scale scores were significantly more disturbed
at Time 2 (the day before surgery) than the scores obtained at Time 1
or Time 3. A similar within-group comparison for the nonsurgical
group revealed no significant differences among the MOA scale scores
across the three administrations. Intergroup comparisons revealed significant differences between the surgical and control groups at Time 2
but not at Time 1 or Time 3. At Time 2, the surgical group had a significantly more malignant MOA scale score.

In summary, research involving both adult samples and child samples indicates that the Mutuality of Autonomy Scale can be reliably
scored. With adults, the scale has been demonstrated to be effective in
distinguishing among different psychiatric diagnostic entities. Scale
scores have also been related to independent ratings of psychopathology, clinical symptoms, and object relations. A question has been
raised as to whether the scale primarily assesses object relations or

severity of psychopathology. With children, the scale has proven useful in depicting significant features of both normative and pathological aspects of child personality. It differentiates between psychiatric and control samples in a predictable way and clarifies important features of the internal experience of children diagnosed with gender-identity disturbance, separation-anxiety disorder, and attention-deficit disorder. It has also been demonstrated to be useful in articulating meaningful features in the inner experience of children who have been sexually abused, have imaginary companions, and have been left by their fathers. Lastly, the scale has proven sensitive to shifts in object representations in children facing the trauma of surgery.

Borderline Interpersonal Relations Scale

As part of an attempt to study early disturbances in the object relations of borderline patients, Kwawer (1980) devised a Rorschach scale consisting of various points that represent stages of level of relatedness in the unfolding of selfhood through differentiation from a primary mothering figure. Underlying the scale is the notion that borderline pathology recapitulates stages of symbiotic relatedness and other primitive modes of unity and disunity. Narrower in scope than the Mutuality of Autonomy Scale because of its emphasis on more primitive modes of object relating, Kwawer's scale also relies exclusively on Rorschach content.

An initial stage, referred to as narcissistic mirroring, includes responses in which mirrors or reflections play a prominent role. Responses at this level are understood as indicating a heightened state of self-absorption, in which the other is experienced solely as an extension of the self and is used for the exclusive purpose of mirroring or enhancing the self. A second stage, entitled "symbiotic merger," consists of responses that reflect a powerful push toward merger, fusion, and reuniting. A third stage of interpersonal differentiation is found in separation and division responses. The Rorschach imagery here is reminiscent of the biology of cell division reflected in the following response: "These two things appear to have been once connected but broke apart." The fourth and final stage, "metamorphosis and transformation," is reflective of the experience of a very early and rudimentary sense of self. Here, incipient selfhood is manifest in themes of one-celled organisms, fetuses, and embryos.

In pilot work, Kwawer (1980) found that Rorschach records of borderline patients could be significantly distinguished from those of a matched control group on the basis of the scoring categories. More specifically, each of the borderline patients offered at least one scoreable response, and this was not the case with the controls.

The most extensive application of Kwawer's scale is found in the work of Gacono and Meloy (1994). In an attempt to describe the inner workings of the aggressive and psychopathic personalities, the authors collected Rorschach data on several different antisocial groups: conduct-disordered children and adolescents; antisocial-personality disordered males, with and without schizophrenia; antisocial adult females; and male and female sexual homicide perpetrators. Findings related to Kwawer's scale will be presented separately for each group, with the exception of the child-conduct disorders. The scale was not applied to the Rorschachs of this group.

The adolescent sample consisted of 100 subjects: 79 males and 21 females, ranging in age from 13 to 17 years, all of whom met criteria for conduct disorder (DSM-III-R; American Psychiatric Association, 1987) as determined by records review, and, in some cases, by clinical interview too. For the males, 81% produced at least one primitive mode of relating response based on Kwawer's indices. The most commonly used scoring category was narcissistic mirroring (37%), followed by boundary disturbance (29%), and violent symbiosis (28%). The pattern and the frequencies are similar to those found in a group of antisocial-personality disordered males. With the females, a slightly lower 76% offered at least one primitive relating response. The order of frequency of categories was different for the females—violent symbiosis (29%), boundary disturbance (24%), and birth-rebirth (24%).

The male antisocial-personality disorder sample included 82 subjects, all incarcerated in forensic hospitals and prisons in the State of California. Ranging in age from 18 to 48 years, all had been diagnosed antisocial-personality disorder (DSM-III-R; American Psychiatric Association, 1987) by two researchers, based on interview and record data. Ninety-four percent of the sample produced at least one primitive mode of relatedness response, the most common being violent symbiosis (50%), narcissistic mirroring (35%), and boundary disturbance (33%). Based on the Hare Psychopathy Checklist (Hare, 1991), a subgroup of 33 primary psychopaths was extracted from the ASPD sample. For this subgroup, 91% offered at least one primitive relatedness response, with narcissistic mirroring (45%) the most frequently scored category, followed by violent symbiosis (42%) and boundary disturbance (39%).

A third group consisted of 80 males, all of whom had been diagnosed both schizophrenic and antisocial-personality disorder (DSM-III-R). Ages of this group ranged from 18 to 65 years. Eighty-nine percent of this group produced at least one Kwawer score, and for the sample as a whole, the mean number of responses per subject averaged almost four. Category usage in descending order of frequency was violent symbiosis (53%), boundary disturbance (35%), malignant internal processes (34%), symbiotic merging (30%), and narcissistic mirroring (29%). In contrast with the nonschizophrenic ASPD sample and the subgroup of primary psychopaths, most striking was the decrease in narcissistic mirroring responses and the increase in malignant internal-process responses. The authors suggest that the category "malignant internal process," as reflected in this group, "may represent a psychotic reality sense of the deterioration of internal organs or a somatic preoccupation" (p. 203).

Among a sample of 38 antisocial women, all of whom were convicted felons and achieved scores on the Hare Psychopathy Checklist placing them in the moderate to severe range of psychopathy, 79% offered at least one Kwawer score. In contrast with the other groups, including the female adolescent conduct-disorder subjects, the most common used category by this group was malignant internal processes (40%). In keeping with other data, the authors understood this finding as indicating the subjects' tendency to somatize. Other frequently used categories for this group included violent symbiosis (37%) and narcissistic mirroring (26%).

The final sample consisted of 20 individuals (18 males and 2 females), each of whom had committed a sexual homicide. Ninety percent of the subjects in this group offered at least one primitive object-relations score. For this sample, the most commonly employed categories were boundary disturbance (56%), narcissistic mirroring (50%), and violent symbiosis (45%).

Overall, the combined results of the entire project indicate that these individuals relate themselves to others in primitive ways and that Kwawer's (1980) scale is sensitive to these more primitive modes. One can interpret these findings along diagnostic lines, for example, in that they support Kernberg's (1976) contention that antisocial disorders are a subvariant of the borderline personality organization. More importantly, however, I believe the nature of the specific categories and the patterning of use of categories provides an up-close look at the dynamic functioning of specific types of individuals, such as those considered here. For instance, the prevalence, across all groups, of the use of the category of narcissistic mirroring, indicates that these individuals not only relate themselves to others in a narcissistic way, but that they are self-absorbed and have been insufficiently mirrored. The correspondence in category order and usage between the adolescent conduct-disordered males and the adult antisocial-personality disordered males have important prognostic and developmental implications. Among those who commit sexual homicide, the most frequently used of the Kwawer categories was boundary disturbance. This means that in addition to five other factors identified by Meloy, Gacano, and Kenney (1994) as implicated in the act of sexual homicide, one should also add disturbances in maintaining ego boundaries. In summary, Kwawer's (1980) scale is useful in assessing more primitive modes of relating; even more, however, the patterning of category usage provides meaning in terms of the structure and functioning of personality.

Coonerty's Scale of Separation-Individuation

The most direct application of Mahler's theory to the Rorschach is represented in the work of Coonerty (1986). Using the descriptions of Mahler, Pine, and Bergman (1975) as a guideline, Coonerty developed a scale for identifying and categorizing Rorschach responses reflective of concerns and issues associated with the preseparation stage and each of the phases of the separation-individuation process. Referable to the preseparation phase are internal responses (e.g., blood, heart, lungs) and responses lacking boundaries (e.g., fabulized combination). Rorschach imagery reflective of merging, engulfment, and hatching is taken as indicative of concerns arising from the early differentiation subphase of separation-individuation. Themes related to the practicing subphase involve narcissistic issues; thus, reflective Rorschach content includes mirroring responses, pairing responses, omnipotent responses, and insignificant creative responses. Responses indicative of rapprochement issues include figures separating or coming together with resulting damage to one or both, figures engaged in a push-pull struggle, figures whose form changes, figures whose affect changes, and figures enmeshed and unable to separate.

Coonerty (1986) applied the scale to the Rorschach protocols of 50 borderline patients and 50 schizophrenic patients drawn from the testing files of a large teaching hospital. Subjects were all adult patients, 18 to 65 years of age, who met DSM-III criteria based upon initial screening evaluations, including a detailed psychological, medical, developmental, social, and psychiatric history. Reliability of the scale was found to be 96% agreement between two raters. As predicted, the borderline group verbalized more separation-individuation themes than did the schizophrenic group, whereas the schizophrenics showed more preseparation-individuation themes.

Van-Der Keshet (1988), in a study referred to in an earlier chapter, applied the separation-individuation scale as well to the Rorschach records of clinical anorexics, anorexic ballet students, nonanorexic ballet students, and a normal control group. As described, the clinical anorexic group was further subdivided into those patients manifesting restrictive characteristics and those exhibiting bulimic symptoms. A comparison of the various groups on the scale revealed several interesting findings. Although no main effect was found among the groups on the preseparation scale, several significant findings were obtained on the separation-individuation scores. Bulimic anorexics produced significantly more engulfment responses than did any of the other groups. Mirroring responses distinguished the anorexic ballet students from each of the other groups. Finally, the controls had significantly fewer rapprochement responses than the other four groups. The overall pattern of results not only lent construct validity to Coonerty's scale, but also revealed the scale's usefulness in highlighting significant dynamic configurations associated with specific clinical groups.

Support for Van-Der Keshet's (1988) findings, specifically those related to the bulimic anorexics, is provided in a study by Parmer (1991). The Rorschachs of 13 bulimic, female undergraduate students, ranging in age from 18 to 21 years, were compared with the protocols of a matched group of nonbulimics on several measures, including Coonerty's scale. The bulimics offered significantly more differentiation subphase responses involving merging, engulfment, and hatching themes than did the controls.

The Separation-Individuation Scale has also been applied to various aspects of treatment. Horner and Diamond (1996) found that in a group of borderline outpatients, scale scores distinguished between those patients who prematurely terminated psychotherapy and those who continued. Those who dropped out offered a predominance of responses with a narcissism theme. Indeed, such responses outnumbered responses with a rapprochement theme four to one. By contrast, the patients who continued in treatment provided a relatively even distribution of scores across all themes, with an even ratio of narcissism to higher level rapprochement themes.

Diamond et al. (1990) used a modified version of Coonerty's original scale to evaluate changes in self- and object-representations concomitant with long-term psychodynamic inpatient treatment. The authors added two higher developmental levels of the separation-individuation process (object constancy and intersubjectivity) and also elaborated existing scale points. The revised scale was applied to the Rorschachs of four patients assessed both at admission and discharge. Shifts toward higher levels of separation-individuation and intersubjectivity were observed in each case, and the changes noted paralleled those obtained on the Object Representation Inventory—a 10-point scale for rating descriptions of self and significant others.

Although it has received limited currency, Coonerty's (1986) Scale of Separation-Individuation has proven effective in differentiating borderline and schizophrenic patients and in highlighting prevailing developmental issues in bulimic individuals. It has also been shown to identify borderline patients who prematurely leave treatment and to reflect internal changes associated with long-term treatment. Van-Der Keshet (1988) used several Rorschach scales in her study, including Coonerty's (1986) scale and P. Lerner and H. Lerner's (1980) measure of primitive defenses. The convergence of findings between these two scales (note chapter 23) not only adds to our understanding of the eating-disordered patient, but also supports the construct validity of the individual scales. Studies such as Van-Der Keschet's, in which several conceptually linked measures are employed, are especially important; it is now necessary, however, to take the additional step of interrelating the scales.

Developmental Object–Relations Scale

Following the earlier work of Urist (1977) and Tuber (1983), Ipp (1986) also attempted to translate Mahler's formulations into Rorschach-related terms. The scale is limited to the assessment of animate (human and animal) movement responses. Like Urist's scale, underlying this scale is the assumption that the manner in which an individual portrays relationships between animate figures on the Rorschach test reflects his or her experience and representation of human relationships.

The scale consists of five basic categories and two subcategories, each category conceptualized as representing a developmentally significant gradient in the individual's emerging sense of self and sense of the other. At the lower end of the scale is the category Catastrophic Disintegration. Included here are responses in which there is a sense of annihilation by external forces greater than the self. Inanimate movement and strong agitation typically accompany these percepts. The category Symbiosis includes percepts that either are undifferentiated or merge with each other. These responses are often vague and amorphous and are accompanied by a strong positive or negative affective component. The category Separation-Individuation is subdivided into the subcategories Rapprochement and Differentiating/Practicing. Included under rapprochement are responses that reflect active efforts toward separation and autonomy. These efforts are often accompanied by separation anxiety, as expressed in implicit threats to the self or to the individual's independence.

Somewhat lower than rapprochement is the subcategory Differentiation/Practicing. Here, percepts reflect an awareness of separateness, but at a more primitive level. Failures in separating are anticipated or stated. False Autonomy refers to a pseudo form of individuation. Beneath superficial, higher-level functioning are feelings of emptiness and low self-esteem, and this is reflected in the Rorschach imagery. Mirroring responses are included here. The highest category, Toward Object Constancy, includes responses in which fully differentiated figures are interacting with each other. A distinction is drawn between figures engaged in a more dependent relationship and figures engaged in activity in which there is no compromise of each other's autonomy. Cutting across all categories is a benevolent-malevolent dimension wherein neutral responses are considered as benevolent.

As part of her attempt to study the personality structures of a group of gender-disturbed children (see chapter 18), Ipp (1986) applied the scale to the Rorschach protocols of 37 feminine boys diagnosed as having cross-gender disturbance, 19 siblings with no history of cross-gender behavior, and 23 normal controls. A comparison of scale scores for the three groups revealed the following: the subcategory Autonomy significantly distinguished the controls from both the feminine boys and their siblings, with the normal controls achieving the higher scores. The feminine boys and their siblings scored significantly more responses at the Differentiation/Practicing substage than the normal controls. None of the categories significantly distinguished the feminine boys from their siblings. And both the feminine boys and their siblings offered significantly more malevolent responses than the normal controls.

In summary, the scale revealed similarities between the feminine boys and their siblings and differences between both groups and the normal controls. As predicted, the Rorschach responses of both the feminine boys and the siblings fell mainly within the Differentiating/Practicing category, whereas the responses of the controls were at a higher level.

✦ ✦ ✦ Object Relations and Thinking

In recent years, basic psychoanalytic concepts that had been understood in exclusively structural and economic terms have been reformulated to take into account the decisive impact of early object relations. As part of this conceptual thrust, H. Lerner and P. Lerner (1986) applied object-relations theory to the more classical psychoanalytic theory of thinking.

Specifically, they attempted to integrate Piaget's theory of cognitive structure formation with Mahler's observations and theory of separation-individuation. Within that integrative effort they outlined the role of the caregiving object in facilitating cognitive development as well as in impeding such development.

A summary of that integration is presented in Table 20-1. Included in the summary is a schematic review of Piaget's early stages of cognitive development and of Mahler's phases of separation-individuation, a statement of the major cognitive task for each of the interdigitated developmental periods, a note on the necessary role and function of the caregiving object, and a review of likely cognitive impairments that may result from the object failing to fulfill its function.

Herein, I attempt to extend this object-relations model of thinking and cognitive impairment to the Rorschach. In what follows, I discuss each of the three interdigitated stages, present Rorschach indices reflective of difficulties at each stage, and apply the conceptual model and Rorschach indices to case material. This extension should be regarded as a beginning effort to integrate several existing and innovative Rorschach scores and indices into a new conceptual framework, which, in time, could serve as a broad theoretical basis for research. For instance, this type of conceptual model could be used to explore the broad area of learning disabilities from a developmental- dynamic perspective.

Table 20-1. Integration of Piaget and Mahler

Interdigitated stages	Piaget's stages of cognitive development	Mahler's periods of separation and individuation	Major cognitive tasks	Role of the object	Potential cognitive impairments
Stage I (early sensorimotor)	Sensorimotor period (Stages 1 & 2)	Normal autism and symbiosis	Beginning awareness of external objects	Holding behavior	Lack of affective relatedness to the environment
Stage II (mid-sensorimotor)	Sensorimotor period (Stages 3 & 4)	Differentiation and practicing	Differentiating objects from their contextual surroundings	Supporting strivings toward separation and mirroring autonomous functioning	Overdependence on the environment and stimulus-boundness
Stage III (early preoperational)	Preoperational period	Rapprochement subphase and consolidation of individuality and the beginnings of object constancy	Internalization and representation	Maintenance of emotional availability in the wake of the child's fluctuations between closeness and distance	Impairment in evocative object constancy and failure in the interiorization of learning skills

Interdigitated Stages

Stage 1: Early sensorimotor

The first interdigitated stage includes the first two phases (exercising the ready-made sensorimotor schema and primary circular responses) of Piaget's sensorimotor period. According to Piaget, a major shift occurs during these stages, which involves the infant's incipient awareness of external objects. This shift noted by Piaget coincides with the infant's entrance into the phase of normal symbiosis in Mahler's theory.

In the second month, the beginning awareness of the need-satisfying object marks the onset of the symbiotic phase. Herein, the infant behaves and functions as though infant and mother were an omnipotent system—a dual unity encircled by one common boundary. The inborn stimulus barrier begins to crack, and with a cathectic shift toward the sensoriperceptive periphery, a protective shield begins to form around and to envelop the symbiotic orbit of the mother-child dual unity. The infant begins to perceive need-satisfaction as coming from some part-object and begins turning toward that source.

Within the symbiotic orbit, the two partners or poles are regarded by Mahler as "polarizing the organizational and structural processes. The structures that derive from this double frame of reference represent a framework to which all experiences have to be related before they are clear whole representations in the ego of the self and the object world" (Mahler et al. 1975, p. 57). Whereas the capacity of the infant to invest in the mother serves as a precursor to all subsequent relationships, the holding and containing behavior of the mother functions as a "symbiotic organizer—the midwife of separation and individuation" (p. 57).

Evidence from various sources (Graham, 1978; Kilchenstein and Schuerholz, 1995; Klein, 1930; Mahler, 1960; Ribble, 1943) suggests that the depth and quality of the infant's interest in external objects is a function of the adequacy of the mother's holding behavior. The combined findings indicate that failures in maternal holding and containing during this early sensorimotor-symbiotic stage result in a lack of affective relatedness to the environment and a reliance on autistic defenses (Ogden, 1989). This state becomes evident in various cognitive deficits, including a limited amount of information about and interest in the external world, difficulty learning, and an inability to conceptualize and interpret the world in human terms.

According to this model, individuals whose symbiotic phase has been disrupted by failures in maternal holding will be severely impaired in their capacity to relate to others; will be unable to experience, modulate, and express affects; and will use autistic defenses. In addition, and as reported by Coonerty (1986), they will express experiential themes referable to the preseparation-individuation phase.

Using the theoretical formulations of Tustin (1984, 1990) and Ogden (1989) and the clinical work of Coonerty (1986), P. Lerner (1991a), and Kilchenstein and Schuerholz (1995), the following Rorschach indices were devised:

1. The protocol has no human content or human detail (i.e., H and/or Hd responses) or has a paucity of human content restricted to distorted human forms or distorted human details (i.e., [H] and/or [Hd] responses).

2. The protocol has no color scores or is restrictively limited to the pure color response (C).

3. Content is related to hard, protective, external surfaces and barriers (e.g., armor, shell, shield, helmet, steel).

4. Reference is made to stimulus properties of the cards, which indicates that the stimuli have made a sensory impression. The reference may appear anywhere in the protocol—as part of the response, during inquiry, or as a spontaneous comment (e.g., "jagged edges," "sharp angles," "soft colors," "harsh lines").

5. Internal responses—internal body parts are completely isolated from a larger response involving a whole being (e.g., "blood," "heart," "lung").

6. Boundaryless response—two or more percepts typically and appropriately seen as separate are combined and seen as one. There is no recognition of the incongruity and no ambivalence. This response includes contaminations and Exner's (1993) Level 2 fabulized combinations.

Stage II: Mid-sensorimotor

In the early sensorimotor period, the major cognitive achievement is the infant's progressive interest in the environment. In the mid-sensorimotor period—Piaget's third, fourth, and fifth stages—the main cognitive task is differentiating objects from their environmental surroundings. According to Piaget, as objects are differentiated, they begin to be represented by internal symbols. Differentiation, then, is a precursor of representation as well as being intimately and reciprocally related to it.

For Mahler, at about six months of age tentative experimentation begins. Manually, tactilely, and visually, the infant begins to explore the mother—her face, body, and attire. The infant literally pulls back from her so as to see her. This visual pattern of checking the mother is the most significant indicator of the beginning of somatopsychic differentiation.

The second subphase of separation-individuation, practicing, has two parts: an early phase marked by the infant's attempts to move physically away from the mother, by means of crawling, climbing, and so on, and the practicing subphase proper, characterized by free locomotion. These early explorations enable the infant to establish familiarity with a broader segment of the world and also permit the recognition of the mother from a distance. With the increased investment in autonomous activity is the continual need for the mother as a "home base," a center for "refueling."

Juxtaposing Piaget's observations with those of Mahler suggests those advances in cognitive development associated with this period occur within the context of the infant's hatching from the symbiotic relationship with the mother and progressing to the point of taking distance from her through various forms of locomotion. Of crucial importance here is the mother's capacity to recognize, tolerate, and allow the infant's need for optimal distance.

It is held that if the mother does not permit differentiation, fails to mirror the infant's efforts at autonomous behavior, or does not serve as a predictable and continuously available "home base," then cognitive difficulties involving an overdependence on the environment with attendant failures in representation, including representation of the self, will ensue.

On the basis of the clinical test work by Coonerty (1986), Exner (1993), Hilsenroth et al. (1996), and P. Lerner (1991a), six scores—three related to overdependence on the environment and three to failures in maternal mirroring—are employed in the scoring system. The first three indices, those related to overdependence on the environment, all reflect a tendency to comply with external demands while relinquishing a more objective, critical attitude:

1. Form-Color arbitrary response (FCarb.)—use of color is incompatible with the content of the response (e.g., "red beavers," "blue spiders").

2. Fabulized combination, Level 1 (Exner, 1993)—two or more accurately seen percepts are combined in a modestly unrealistic and illogical way. Here, the individual is aware of the incongruence.

3. Stimulus-bound score—a perceptual detail is included in the response, resulting in a Level 1 deviant verbalization or a Level 1 incongruous combination (e.g., "a woman with her hands up and there is no head" [DV1], "two men with breasts" [INCON1]).

4. Mirroring response—response includes mention of a mirror or the phenomenon of reflecting.

5. Pairing response—restricted to pairs not differentiated and engaged in a mirrorlike task (e.g., "twins gazing at each other").

6. Idealization response—distortion of human form through an enhancement of the figure's identity. This corresponds to P. Lerner and H. Lerner's (1980) idealization score, ratings III, IV, and V. This response includes such objects of fame as civic leaders, officials, or famous people.

Stage III: Early preoperational

Piaget's (1937) sixth and final stage—"invention of new means through mental combinations"—is a transitional stage to the next period, the preoperational period. In the sensorimotor period, the child is relatively restricted to direct interactions with his or her environment. In the preoperational period, internalization and the representation of external experiences by means of internal symbols become significantly more important. The emerging ability for evocative recall and the greater capacity for manipulating symbols that represent the environment permit a mental life relatively autonomous from the environment.

These advances in cognition coincide in Mahler's theory with the rapprochement subphase and her final subphase, movement toward emotional object constancy. Herein, the child's increased awareness of being separate from the mother leads him or her to attempt to reestablish contact with her, but in a new and different way.

Because the child is caught between competing currents, desiring closeness yet wanting to preserve a precarious autonomy, his or her behavior is marked by vexing oscillations between pulls toward closeness and pushes toward distance. Mahler's observations confirm the critical importance of the mother's capacity to maintain continual

libidinal availability while recognizing and accepting the child's fluctuating behavior.

Findings from both the testing and the broader clinical literature,
especially from those studies related to borderline pathology (Kernberg,
1975; Kwawer et al., 1980), suggest that when the mother is unable
to maintain her emotional availability, impairments in internalization
and representation ensue. Specifically, there is an arrest at a sensorimotor level of object representation, with an impairment in evocative
object constancy and a consequent vulnerability to separation and loss.
The rent in the internalized object world between good and bad part-
objects is not mended. There are massive inhibitions in learning based
on failures in the interiorization of learning skills, and emotional
and gestural behavior, not language, remains as the basic mode of
communication.

Several Rorschach items, individually selected and slightly refined
from the scales of P. Lerner and H. Lerner (1980), Urist (1977), and
Coonerty (1986), are used to assess impairments associated with this
stage. Specific indices include the following:

1. In a sequence of responses, a human percept described in terms of
   a specific, nonambivalent, nonambiguous dimension is followed by
   another human response in which the affective description is
   opposite that used to describe the preceding human response (e.g.,
   "an angry Mafia boss" followed by "two kind older women
   rocking").

2. An implicitly idealized human figure is tarnished by the addition of
   one or more features, or an implicitly devaluated human figure is
   enhanced by the addition of one or more features (e.g., "headless
   angels," "a benevolent savage").

3. There is a marked imbalance in the mutuality of relations between
   human or animal figures, with one exercising malevolent control
   over the other. Themes of influencing, controlling, and casting spells
   are present (e.g., "a witch casting a spell over these helpless babies,"
   "a spider with an insect in its web").

4. Human and animal figures whose form changes (e.g., "it's a man
   turning into a werewolf," "two people, no, no, a couple of birds").

5. Human or animal figures whose affect changes (e.g., "an angry boar
   . . . no, he's sadder and lost").

6. Shading as form response (Fc)—the response is based on form, and
   the nuances of shading are used to articulate and outline the response.

The entire scale, including all Rorschach indices, is presented and summarized in Table 20-2. Included in the table are the three interdigitated stages, the potential cognitive impairments associated with each stage, and the Rorschach scores designed to assess the impairments.

Clinical Examples

To first explore the clinical utility of the scale, not its psychometric properties, I applied the measure to the Rorschach records of several child cases, each of whom was selected as a prototypical example of a clinical disorder. Three of those cases are described here.

Despite suspicions of mild retardation and an assigned diagnosis of ADHD, from a developmental perspective, M.B., a seven-year-old male, was considered illustrative of a youngster who had not resolved the rapprochement crisis of separation-individuation. In line with guidelines provided by Mahler et al. (1975), he evidenced heightened separation anxiety, manifest disturbances in sleep, was overly concerned with his mother's whereabouts, and engaged in dramatic fights with her. The battles and enmeshments that characterized his and his mother's daily relationship seemed strikingly similar to the rapprochement child's alternating desire to push the mother away and to cling to her.

Since beginning school, M.B. and his mother have had intense struggles separating. She acknowledges she is "overprotective," fears she will "lose him," and boasts she will "die if anything happens to him." Before becoming pregnant with M.B., his mother lost a set of Siamese twins. They died soon after birth. M.B. was born prematurely and his mother did not expect him to live. In her mind, his mother tends to merge M.B. with the lost twins.

In terms of the conceptual model, M.B.'s learning problems were understood as expressions of Stage III failures in internalization, including the interiorization of learning skills. Of his 15 Rorschach responses, four met the criteria for scoring at Stage III. One response included a figure whose form changed ("A bat, no, it's a pumpkin"), a second involved an idealized figure that was tarnished ("Batman, but he has little legs"), and two responses were scored shading as form (Fc). Indices from the other two stages did not appear in his record.

J.S., a 9-year-old male, was selected as an example of a narcissistically impaired youngster whose difficulties seemed directly related to

Table 20-2. Rorschach indices

Interdigitated stages	Potential cognitive impairment	Rorschach indices
Stage I	Lack of affective relatedness to the environment	Little human content, limited to (H) and (Hd) Little color, limited to pure C Content related to hard, protective external surfaces Indications that stimulus properties have made a sensory impression Internal response Boundaryless response
Stage II	Overdependence on the environment	Fcarb score Fabulized combination—Level 1 Stimulus-bound score Reflection response Pairing response Idealization response
Stage III	Impairment in evocative object constancy and failures in the interiorization of learning skills	Polar opposite affective descriptions in two human responses to the same card Tarnished idealized figure and/or enhanced devalued figure Imbalance in relationship, with one figure exercising malevolent control over the other Figures whose form changes Figures whose affect changes Fc score

his mother's physical and emotional unavailability during the early phases of separation-individuation.

Beneath a veneer of grandiosity he sensed himself as ghostlike. He did not experience others as separate and distinct, but instead, as extensions of himself. His sense of self lacked substance, coherence, and vitality. Owing to an absence of internal structures, including cognitive ones, he was constantly at the mercy of internal and external forces.

When J.S. was 7 months old, his maternal grandparents died tragically in an automobile accident. His mother, devastated by the loss, became seriously depressed and required psychiatric hospitalization. She has yet to fully recover from the trauma. It is likely that his separation from her was severe and sudden and she was unavailable for him throughout most of the separation-individuation period.

In keeping with the conceptual model, his cognitive and learning difficulties were considered reflective of Stage II failures in representation. Rorschach scores devised to assess Stage II impairments appeared in more than one-third (8) of his 21 responses. He produced two pairing responses ("Two ladies looking in a mirror," "Two ladies acting like each other"), two fabulized combinations, level 1 ("There are two werewolves carrying money bags," "Two mice playing a violin"), two form color arbitrary responses ("A blue bat," "A green moth"), one stimulus-bound score ("Two ladies fighting, they are all black, have no heads, banging hands together"), and a response involving both pairing and idealization ("Two angels praying to each other"). His record also included a response scored Stage I, boundaryless ("Looks like a butterfly ghost"), and another response scored Stage III, a figure whose form changes ("Looks like a cat, no, a ghost, its head is long, it's a crab").

Case study: R.V.

R.V., a male 7½ years old, was selected as representative of a higher level autistic-functioning child whose difficulties were referable to the preseparation-early differentiation phase of development. He is described by his current teacher as "inattentive, detached, isolated, unusual, and weird." His academic performance is substandard and he is rapidly falling behind the rest of his second grade class.

His parents were not married when he was born because his mother insisted that she did not want to get married just because she was pregnant. She changed her mind after being hospitalized for several months when R.V. was four months old. Her hospitalization was prompted by a postpartum manic episode. During his mother's hospitalization, R.V. was placed in a foster home and remained there until he was 18 months of age.

The foster parents describe him as a difficult infant who often banged his head against the sides of his crib or against the walls. The head banging gradually lessened but lasted until he was about 3 years old. He is described by his parents as "oblivious," and they note that he is so unaware of others and of physical boundaries that he often bumps into them. He is also difficult to manage, highly ritualistic, and resistant to change.

According to the conceptual model, R.V.'s learning problems were considered a reflection of Stage I failures in developing an affective relatedness to the environment. R.V. gave 20 Rorschach responses, five of which met the criteria for Stage I scoring. Four of his responses were scored as boundaryless responses and one was rated as content related to hard, protective external surface ("The castle with worms coming out of the top. The castle is made of rock"). In addition, he offered no human content and his two color responses were scored pure C. His record also included two responses referable to Stage II.

Findings from the case studies provide promising but limited support for the efficacy of the scoring system. The scale needs to be subjected to more rigorous empirical investigation involving target groups of children and adults. Only with further data collection can reliability in scoring be determined and refinements in quantification made.

In applying the scale, a note of caution needs to be sounded. In developing the scoring system, the three interdigitated stages were treated as discrete points and specific impairments were associated with each stage, as if there is a one-to-one relationship between stage and impairment. Such a one-to-one relationship, indeed, does not exist. Implicit in both Mahler's and Piaget's models is the notion of a developmental continuum. This implies that stages overlap and that impairments and difficulties at an earlier stage will impact upon later stages. In evaluating data yielded from the scoring system, the concept of a developmental continuum should be held in mind.

◆ ◆ ◆ Conclusion

In this chapter I have reviewed several Rorschach Scales that were developed to assess level of object relations from a psychoanalytically informed developmental perspective. Based in varying degrees on

Mahler's theory of separation-individuation, each scale makes generous use of thematic content.

In 1991, I (P. Lerner, 1991a) noted that because of their relative recency, several of the scales had not received broad currency in the Rorschach literature. That is no longer the case. Owing to the work of Tuber (1992), the Mutuality of Autonomy Scale has been meaningfully extended to the study of different groups of children, and Gacono and Meloy (1994) have made considerable use of Kwawer's (1980) scale in investigating various antisocial samples. Whereas my earlier book (P. Lerner, 1991a) served to acquaint readers with these scales, this book may be regarded as more of an updating and progress report of these scales.

The conceptual work of H. Lerner and P. Lerner (1986), together with the clinical findings on three cases reported here, touches on thorny issues currently facing Rorschach and developmental theorists. For instance, the test findings suggest that children may represent in Rorschach content experiences and developmental deficits that themselves are referrable to prerepresentational stages. How, then, do such experiences and deficits get translated into representation? We know from the trauma literature that in instances of severe trauma aspects of the trauma resist being encoded in verbal-representational thought, but are encoded in other ways, such as visually. Does this mean, then, that a test of visual representational capacity, such as the Rorschach, can access experiences that occurred before verbal representation was available? The reader interested in these issues should refer to Leichtman (1996) and Dorpat and Miller (1993). As noted in the introduction, Rapaport and colleagues (1945–1946) considered the Rorschach test a potential means for operationalizing psychoanalytic concepts whose operational definitions could then be used for testing basic formulations. Creative investigators have done just this; that is, they have devised innovative scales for operationalizing concepts that heretofore were overly abstract and elusive. We have reached a point where what is now called for is an interrelating of these scales across different clinical and normal populations. In this way, the Rorschach test can truly add to the evolving scope of psychoanalytic theory.

21

RAPAPORT'S DEVIANT VERBALIZATION SCORES AND RESEARCH

As noted in chapters 6 and 9, the analysis of deviant verbalizations represents an exceptionally valuable and lasting contribution of Rapaport et al. (1945–1946) to Rorschach theory and practice. From a clinical perspective, these scores have typically been considered and used as cardinal indicators of disturbances in thinking. From a research perspective, these scores have been conceptualized and applied in any number of ways, including as measures of thought disturbance, boundary disturbance, and primitive modes of object relating. Furthermore, specific indices, such as fabulized combinations, confabulations, and contaminations, have been included in scales devised to assess defense (P. Lerner and H. Lerner, 1980) and developmental object relations (Coonerty, 1986). Significantly, regardless of how these indices are conceptualized, investigators have found them to be remarkably useful in assessing the variable (e.g., thinking, boundaries, defense) being studied. In addition, the yield from these indices is rich. It is important and reasonable, then, to ask two related questions: first, what accounts for the robustness of these scores? and second, what is it they are measuring?

In this chapter I discuss the several ways in which researchers have conceptualized these scores. With each conceptualization, I review Rorschach scales that apply the scores in that specific way. I then use the reviews as a basis for addressing the issue of what these scores might be assessing.

◆ ◆ ◆   Disturbed Thinking

Accepting Rapaport and colleagues' (1945–1946) theoretical formulations, early researchers considered these scores as indicators of disturbed thinking, and set about quantifying the specific categories. The first systematic use of these scores for research purposes is represented in the work of Watkins and Stauffacher (1952). They selected from Rapaport et al. (1945–1946) 15 types of verbalizations most markedly deviant or most frequent in appearance. They assigned tentative weights to these, representing what they considered the degree and significance of psychopathology.

Modifications of the index, termed the Delta Index, were proposed by Powers and Hamlin (1955) and Pope and Jensen (1957). The former, in their revision, abstracted 10 categories from Rapaport's initial group of deviant verbalizations. These were then combined into four classes designated intellectual disorganization, socially deviant content, inappropriate increase or loss of distance, and affective response. The categories were placed on a continuum ranging in value from 10 to 50 with intervals of 5. Pope and Jensen suggested the use of a 5-point rating for each response with the following values in the order of increasing pathology: .00, .25, .75, and 1.00. The authors also developed a manual that included detailed scoring instructions and an extensive list of sample responses taken largely from Rapaport.

Studies involving validity have attempted to use the Index for discriminating among groups that represent varying degrees of psychopathology. Implicit in these studies is the proposition that if the Delta score is a valid measure of thought disorder, it should be related to levels of psychological disorganization.

As held in a number of studies (Watkins and Stauffacher, 1952; Powers and Hamlin, 1955; Pope and Jensen, 1957; Kataguchi, 1959; Quirk et al., 1962), the Index, or one of its modifications, was found effective in discriminating groups of schizophrenics from other clinical groups and this extended across certain cultures. Furthermore, the Delta percentages for different clinical groups were noted to be strikingly similar (psychotics, over 17%, neurotics, less than 11%). Not unexpectedly, the scale's efficacy in discriminating "normals" from less disturbed, nonpsychotic groups was less satisfactory.

Much broader in scope than the Index of Watkins and Stauffacher's, is Holt's (1956) manual for assessing primary process manifestations and their control. Holt's instrument encompasses an appraisal of the drive domination of thought, a measure of the degree to which formal aspects of primary process are reflected in the response, a rating of the degree to which the underlying idea embedded in the response demands that some defensive and controlling efforts be evoked to make the response a socially acceptable communication, and an assessment of the effectiveness of the controlling and defensive efforts.

The system calls for the scoring of four sets of variables: content indices of primary process, formal indices of primary process, control and defense, and overall ratings. It is in the section on formal indices of primary process that Holt includes several of Rapaport's categories of deviant verbalizations. Cutting across these categories is a level-1–level-2 distinction indicating two degrees of closeness to the primary process pole.

In the manual a number of summary scores are used, several of which include the formal indices of primary process. Percentage of primary process, or "total percent pripro," for example, indicates the number of responses in a record that have been scored for either a formal or content expression of primary process. Applied to responses scored primary process is a demand for defense score. This six-point rating scale assesses the degree to which the idea intrinsic to a percept or the way it emerges (formal aspect of primary process) requires that some defensive and controlling measure be instituted so as to make the response a socially acceptable communication. A mean defense demand score is the sum of all the defense demand ratings divided by the number of pripo responses.

Several of these summary scores have proven useful in assessing changes in thinking associated with selected experimental and clinical conditions. In one series of studies (Silverman, 1966; Silverman and Goldwebber, 1966; Silverman and Candell, 1970) it was found that following the presentation at a subliminal level of aggressive-related stimuli there was an increase in disturbed thinking, as evidenced by an increase in total formal manifestations of primary process. In another study (Saretsky, 1966), the mean defense effectiveness score (sum of all the defense effectiveness scores divided by the number of pripro responses) was found to increase following the use of chlorpromazine, and this increase was significantly related to an independent measure of clinical improvement. Finally, three scores taken from the formal part of the manual, the mean defense demand score, and the mean defense effectiveness score, were all found to change in expected directions in a patient whose clinical condition improved following treatment for myxedema psychosis (Greenberg et al. 1969).

The most recent system for quantifying disturbed thinking that includes several of Rapaport's initial categories is the Thought Disorder Index developed by Johnston and Holtzman (1976). Herein, four distinct levels of disturbed thinking are identified and conceived of as representing qualitative differences in "pathology of verbal responses." The levels are considered as manifestations of "reality contact and the ability to maintain an appropriate cognitive focus" (p. 1).

The first level, which is defined in greater detail than the other levels, represents an extension of Rapaport's category "peculiar responses." This level consists of "moderate idiosyncrasies which are probably only rarely noticed in ordinary conversation, although an accumulation of them might result in a lack of clarity. . . . there is some slight intrusion of an idiosyncratic set, . . . some difficulty in maintaining a clear unambiguous focus" (p. 5). Patients who offer responses at this level are described as "on the fringe," but still "in tune with [their] surroundings" (p. 22).

Categories at the second level include confusion, impossible or bizarre fabulized combinations, looseness, more pronounced idiosyncratic symbolism, and queer responses. Categories at the third level center around confabulation, but also include absurd responses, autistic logic, and fluidity. Finally, the most severe thought-disordered categories comprise level four, and these include contaminations, incoherence, and neologisms.

◆ ◆ ◆ Boundary Disturbance

One of the first theorists to broaden the conceptual basis of several of Rapaport's deviant verbalization scores was Blatt (Blatt and Ritzler, 1974; Blatt, Wild, and Ritzler, 1975; Blatt and Lerner, 1983). In an attempt to bridge thought organization with object relations, he evoked the superordinate concept of "boundary disturbance," and then applied it to several of Rapaport's categories. Boundaries are conceived of as early cognitive structures that are fundamental to both cognitive development and, as part of the internalization process, to the formation of the representational world.

In development, at first, representations of independent objects (including self and nonself) are merged and fused. Thus, the earliest boundary or differentiation is that between independent objects. Once the distinction between independent objects has been established, the developing child must then differentiate the actual object from his or her internal representation of the object. A third boundary to be established is the differentiation between the external object and one's own associations and reactions to it; that is, between inside and outside and between fantasy and reality. As noted, each of these boundaries or differentiations is viewed as a critical step in the development of mental representations, including representations of the self and of others.

Blatt and Ritzler (1974) operationally defined the concept of boundary disturbances in terms of three of Rapaport's deviant verbalization scores—contamination, confabulation, and fabulized combination. Accordingly, disturbances in maintaining the boundary between independent objects are reflected in the Rorschach contamination score, a response in which there is a fusing of separate percepts and concepts. Disturbances in maintaining the boundary between inside and outside are reflected in the confabulation response. Here, there is a loss of the distinction between an external perception and personal associations and reactions to the perception. What initially may have been an accurate perception becomes compromised by, and lost in, excessive personal elaborations and associations. A third and less severe type of boundary disturbance is found in the fabulized combination response. In these responses, independent percepts maintain their separateness but are illogically and unrealistically combined, usually on the basis of their spacial contiguity. Although each image maintains its individuality and integrity, the boundary disturbance is reflected in the drawing of the inappropriate relationship.

Lerner, Sugarman, and Barbour (1985) devised a Boundary Disturbance Scale based on the work of Blatt and Ritzler (1974). The six-point weighted scale consists of three developmentally ordered types of boundary disturbances and six Rorschach indices for assessing the disturbances. The least severe of the boundary disturbances is termed "boundary laxness" and is indicated by the fabulized combination response. More severe is the inner-outer boundary disturbance, which is indicated by a confabulation tendency and a confabulation response. The third and most severe of the boundary disturbances is the self–other boundary. Rorschach indices of this disturbance include a contamination tendency, the incongruous combination (i.e., fabu-lized combination serious), and the contamination response. The scale is summarized in Figure 21-1.

Boundary Disturbance Scale

Boundary Laxness
    Fabulized Combination
Inner–Outer Boundary
    Confabulation Tendency
    Confabulation
Self–Other Boundary
    Contamination Tendency
    Incongruous Combination
    Contamination

Figure 21-1

In their initial study, Blatt and Ritzler (1974) found that the various levels of boundary disturbances, as measured by Rapaport's deviant ver-balization scores, were related to several conceptually related variables, including capacity for reality testing, quality of interpersonal relations, and the nature of object representations. For instance, "poorly articu-lated boundaries occurred primarily in more disturbed, chronic patients who have poor or impoverished personal relationships, seriously impaired ego functions, and a lifelong history of estrangement, isola-tion, and generally poor adjustment" (Blatt and Lerner, 1983, p. 216). The authors also found that severity of boundary disturbance was related to level of object representation. Patients with more severe boundary disturbances produced significantly more Rorschach responses in which human and inanimate features were blended.

Lerner, Sugarman, and Barbour (1985) applied the Boundary Disturbance Scale to the Rorschach records of the following groups of patients: outpatient neurotics, outpatient borderlines, inpatient bor-derlines, and inpatient schizophrenics. The authors first inspected dif-ferences between groups on the total and weighted scores. They found that the inpatient sample as a whole (inpatient borderlines and schiz-ophrenics) offered significantly more total boundary-disturbed responses and more severely disturbed responses (weighted scores) than did either the outpatient neurotics or outpatient borderlines. Although these quantitative scores clearly distinguished inpatients from outpatients, they failed to distinguish the two inpatient groups.

The authors also examined qualitative distinctions in specific boundary disturbances across groups. Here, several important findings emerged. First, the categories boundary laxness (fabulized combinations), mild inner-outer boundary disturbance (confabulation tendency), and mild self-other boundary disturbance (incongruous combination) failed to distinguish any of the groups. Second, the inpatient borderlines offered significantly more confabulatory responses, indicative of inner-outer boundary disturbances, than all other groups. Finally, the contamination response, reflective of self-other boundary disturbances, appeared significantly more frequently in the protocols of the schizophrenic patients. Overall, then, this study demonstrated the following: (1) there is a direct relationship between severity of psychopathology and severity of boundary disturbance, (2) specific types of psychopathology are characterized by specific types of boundary disturbances, and (3) the confabulation response and the contamination response are reliable and useful indicators of specific types of boundary disturbances.

As reported in chapter 23, more recently, authors have extended the boundary-disturbance concept to the Rorschach records of eating-disorder patients and young gender-identity disturbed males.

❖ ❖ ❖ Organization of Regressive Experience

A third way of conceptualizing the deviant verbalization scores is represented in the work of Athey (1974, 1986). Like Blatt, his interest too is in the general relationship between thought organization and object relations. While noting similarities between his own conceptualizations and Blatt's, Athey (1986) also points out limitations of the boundary-disturbance hypothesis, suggesting that the model "cannot account for differences which may emerge in individual patients' thinking and object representation, explicate the meaning of different types or degrees of boundary loss, or offer any explanation of how boundaries become 'lost'" (p. 20).

Athey (1974) takes as his point of departure Shevrin and Schectman's (1973) definition of mental disorder: "the disturbance of certain psychological functions bearing on specific personal relationships" (p. 474). Explicit in this definition, Athey notes, is the notion that psychological functions, such as attention, memory, affect, comprise the formal features of mental life, while object relations comprise the content and are organized by these functions.

On the basis of this definition, Athey (1974) then suggests that three of the deviant verbalization scores (fabulized combinations, confabulations, contaminations) indicate qualitatively different levels of organization of regressed psychological processes. Noting that thought disorder may be considered an active process of regressing to an earlier, more urgent point, Athey goes on to add, "the regression may involve a full rekindling of a mode of organization of psychological processes appropriate to the age of the person when the infantile conflict was taking shape" (p. 421).

On the basis of a clinical study in which the Rorschach records of two schizophrenic patients were compared with their subsequent treatment records, Athey identified and described two levels of organization of regressive experience. The first, termed the "confabulatory mode," involved "unalloyed affect-laden fantasy relationships" (p. 423). Here, the reality basis for representing a relationship is lost and is replaced with affect and fantasy. The second, referred to as the "contaminatory mode," involves a loss of conceptual distinctions among fundamental frames of reference. By frames of reference, Athey means "the conceptual dimensions by which reality experience is vertically represented internally and which exist as superordinate structures" (p. 424). The concept "frames of reference" is broader than that of "boundaries" and includes conceptions of time (e.g., memory, anticipation) and of space (e.g., here and there, events versus symbolic representation, self versus other). Finally, Athey cogently points out that schizophrenia—and I would add any major disorder—may be conceived of in terms of regressed object relations; however, one must also attend to the psychological processes that provide the psychological substrata for the regressed object relation.

In a recent presentation, Steinberg (1997) described the work of the Boyer Research Institute and their attempt to develop a content-based Rorschach scale to assess primitive object relations and early affects. I mention their work here because, from a conceptual perspective, their ideas are very similar to those of Athey. Like Athey, Steinberg and her research group use the concept "regressive experience," view serious psychopathology or "primitive mental states" as more than thought disorder, place major emphasis on the process of regression, and attend to regressed object relations.

In describing levels of organization of regressive experience, Athey sticks close to the Rorschach and uses the terms "confabulatory mode" and "contaminatory mode." Steinberg, by contrast, views these levels in terms of Klein's (1957) and Ogden's (1989) concept of "positions." Klein's concept of positions is considerably broader than that of levels or stages, and includes, all at once, forms and content of thought, specific affects, certain defenses, select modes of object relating, and focal core conflicts.

From a methodological standpoint, Steinberg's work is complimentary to Athey's. Athey, as noted, began with the distinction Shevrin and Schectman (1973) drew between psychological functions and object relations. Athey suggested that psychological functions comprise the formal features that organize the content, which consist of object relations. Because Athey employed Rapaport's formal categories, his emphasis was on the formal features of the regressive experience. Steinberg, on the other hand, is more interested in the content or substance of the regressive experience. It is this emphasis that has led Steinberg and her colleagues to develop content-based scales designed to assess the substance, not the form, of affect experience and internalized object relations. Steinberg (1997) put it this way: "Through an analysis of the content of the patient's psychosis rather than its form, the 'what' of their distorted thinking rather than the 'how,' we become more familiar with the patient's inner world" (p. 7).

❖ ❖ ❖ Other Conceptualizations

Investigators have used several of the deviant verbalization responses to assess processes far removed from their initial meaning as indicators of thought disorder. P. Lerner and H. Lerner (1980), for example, as part of their attempt to operationalize Kernberg's (1975) concept of primitive defenses, employed the confabulation response involving human figures as one index of projective identification, and the incongruous-combination response as an indicator of lower-level denial. In the former instance, they reasoned that one aspect of projective identification was the capacity to blur the distinction between self and other, and that the confabulatory response assessed this capacity. With the latter, they noted that lower-level denial consisted of significant reality distortions, to the point that a segment of external reality is not integrated into experience, and that the incongruous-combination response reflected this process.

As noted in chapter 20, Coonerty (1986) devised a scale, based on the work of Mahler, Pine, and Bergman (1975), for identifying and categorizing Rorschach responses reflective of concerns and issues associated with the preseparation stage and each of the phases of the separation-individuation process. Although hers is essentially a content-based scale, Coonerty used the contamination response and the fabulized combination response as indicators of issues referable to the preseparation stage. Coonerty considered the scores as examples of boundaryless responses.

P. Lerner (1996c), also as reported in chapter 20, developed a Rorschach scale rooted in an object-relations model of thinking. The model, based on an integration of Piaget's theory of cognitive development with Mahler's theory of separation-individuation, included a statement of the major cognitive task associated with each of three interdigitated developmental periods, a note of the necessary role and function of the caregiving object at each period, and a review of likely cognitive impairments that may ensue from the object failing to fulfill its stage-specific function. The Rorschach scale represented an attempt to operationalize the stage-specific cognitive impairments. Several of the deviant-verbalization responses were included in the scale. For example, contamination responses were used as an indicator of Stage I (lack of affective relatedness to the environment) and the incongruous-combination response and fabulized combination responses were employed as reflections of Stage II (overdependence on the environment).

◆ ◆ ◆ Discussion

As indicated in this brief review, several of Rapaport's original deviant-verbalization responses, especially contaminations, confabulations, incongruous combinations, and fabulized combinations, have been included in Rorschach scales designed to assess various concepts, including thought disorder, boundary disturbance, organization of regressive experience, defense, and developmental object relations. Regardless of how the scores have been conceptualized, they have proven useful to the researcher and in most instances have yielded positive findings.

On the basis of repeated positive yield, one could suggest that the scores are tapping a general factor that can be referred to as "level of psychopathology." Even though this may be accurate, I find the concept level of psychopathology too broad and nonspecific. It does little to clarify and specify the meaning of these scores. In an attempt to better understand these scores, particularly in light of the advances in psychoanalytic theory, from this review I submit the following conclusions.

First, there is general agreement that these scores can be ordered along a development continuum of severity of psychopathology. For example, whether they are considered an indication of thought disorder or of boundary disturbance, contaminations reflect a more severe disturbance than do the other scores. At the same time, these scores also reflect important qualitative differences. The work of Lerner, Sugarman, and Barbour (1985) and Athey (1974) convincingly demonstrates that the scores reflect distinct and different ways of thinking, relating, and experiencing.

Second, as a corollary of the above, Athey's (1974) clinical study indicates that for a specific score, such as confabulation, there are qualitative similarities across modes. That is, individuals who think in a confabulatory way also relate in a confabulatory way.

Third, theorists are gradually expanding the conceptual basis of these scores from an initial narrow focus on thought disorder to include a number of other concepts, such as boundaries, object relations, and defense. Despite this broadening, theorists still anchor these scores in cognition. For instance, boundaries are defined as cognitive-affective structures, and although Athey (1974) refers to levels of organization of regressed psychological processes, he clearly includes cognition among these processes. From a theoretical perspective, this research raises the question of the relationship between cognition, on one hand, and object relating, experiencing, and defense on the other hand. Or to ask this question slightly differently, what is the role of cognition in these other processes?

Fourth, implicit in all of these conceptualizations is the notion of regression or deficit. That is, whether they are considered as indications of disordered thinking, disturbed boundaries, disturbed object relations, or primitive defenses, the meaning ascribed to these scores includes the consideration that they reflect developmentally earlier, more primitive forms. The specific idea of regression, as opposed to deficit or fixation, is captured by Athey (1974), who suggests that thought disorder is an active process of regressing, that it is part of a broader regression (i.e., organization of psychological processes), and that the regression has a specific temporal dimension (i.e., when the infantile conflict took shape).

One may glean from these conclusions that our current research cannot yet answer the question of what these scores assess. It seems likely that conceptualizing these responses narrowly in terms of thought disorder is unnecessarily restrictive and limiting. Nonetheless, regardless of how these scores are eventually formulated, the place of cognitive processes must be accounted for. Then too, the notion of regression or deficit must be included.

◆ ◆ ◆ Summary

In this chapter I have reviewed, from a research perspective, ways in which several of the deviant-verbalization responses have been conceptualized and applied. In keeping with Rapaport, these scores were initially considered indicators of thought disorder; later theorists, however, expanded their conceptual base, so that they may also be viewed as expressions of boundary disturbance and levels of organization of regressive experiences. In addition, select scores have been included in measures of defense and developmental object relations. Regardless of how they are conceptualized, the yield from these scores has been impressive. At this time it is not clear precisely what these scores measure. Nonetheless, theorists anchor these scores, totally or in part, in cognitive processes and include in their formulations the principle of regression or deficit. Theoretically, the meaning of these scores is intimately tied to the issue of the relationship between cognition, on one hand, and object relations, experience, and defense on the other.

22

THE BORDERLINE CONCEPT
AND THE RORSCHACH TEST

The borderline concept, as Sugarman and Lerner (1980) have noted, "has a long, uneven and particularly controversial history in both psychiatry and psychoanalysis" (p. 11). The term *borderline*, as these authors point out,

> has been referred to as a "wastebasket" diagnosis for patients who could not be classified as neurotic or psychotic (Knight, 1953), as an "unwanted category" traceable to Bleuler's (1924) attempts to classify patients whose conventional behavior masked an underlying schizophrenia (Gunderson and Singer, 1975), and more recently as a "star work"—seeming to illuminate a great deal [Pruyser, 1975, p. 11].

The concept of borderline, as well as its designation as a pathological entity, has arisen from the convergence of two streams of conceptual development within psychiatry—descriptive psychiatry, with its emphasis on discrete and observable phenomena and exclusive nosological categories, and psychoanalysis, with its focus on attempting to establish structural, dynamic, and developmental roots of the disorder.

Contemporary contributions of the descriptive stream come from three major areas: empirical research and reviews (Grinker, Werble, and Drye, 1968; Gunderson and Singer, 1975; Carpenter, Gunderson, and Strauss, 1977; Perry and Klerman, 1978), genetic and adoption studies (Kety et al., 1968; Rosenthal, 1975; Wender, 1977), and psychopharmacological studies (D. Klein, 1973, 1975). The combined findings indicate that borderline disorders are (1) psychologically similar to, but distinguishable from, the neuroses and schizophrenia, (2) linked genetically to schizophrenia, and (3) related psychopharmacologically to affect disorders.

It should be noted that the term "borderline disorders" is being used in a particular way. More specifically, the above authors place borderline on a psychopathological continuum midway between neurotic at one pole and psychotic at the other. The term is meant to include a number of different subgroups of patients, such as schizoptypal, latent schizophrenia, borderline personality. Others, as noted in earlier chapters, use the designation differently. For example, some authors refer to the "borderline character," a specific kind of patient who differs in important ways from others, including the schizoptypal patient. Yet others, most notably Kernberg (1970), consider borderline a level of personality organization.

The second stream, the psychoanalytic, originated in early explorations of character development and character pathology. Beginning with Reich's pioneering work on character analysis, particularly in "The Impulsive Character" (1933), this stream extends through Alexander's (1930) description of the "neurotic character," Stern's (1938) extension of the "neurotic character" to the "ambulatory schizophrenic," Deutsch's (1942) important contributions regarding the "as if" personality, and Schmideberg's (1947, 1959) writings regarding a group of patients who were "stable in their instability."

The movement within psychoanalysis from a more descriptive and dynamic perspective to a more structural one is represented in the work of Knight (1953) and his emphasis on the severe ego weaknesses underlying the borderline patient's superficial object relations and seeming adaption to environmental demands. For Knight, these patients were more disturbed than they appeared, and he outlined three basic aspects of the syndrome to be considered in establishing a differential diagnosis: (1) the use of compensatory defenses and symptoms to cover over the underlying defects, (2) the patient's lack of awareness of his or her psychotic-like manifestations, and (3) an inability to maintain anchoring in reality in unstructured situations, such as projective tests.

Beginning in 1966 with a reexamination of the borderline concept and the range of disorders of character from the perspective of structural derivatives, the work of Kernberg (1975, 1976) has had an enormous impact on the field. In integrating contributions from the British school of object relations with more classical formulations from structural theory, he has been able to develop a unitary-process conceptualization of psychopathology and to demonstrate that a descriptive classification of borderline disturbances is insufficient, in that it includes only "presumptive diagnostic elements" (Kernberg, 1975, p. 8).

Kernberg (1970) conceptualized a hierarchical organization of levels of character pathology based on instinctual, ego, superego, defense, and object-relations considerations. For Kernberg, from a structural perspective, patients organized at a borderline level exhibit the following: (1) nonspecific manifestations of ego weaknesses (deficits in anxiety tolerance, impulse control, and subliminatory potential); (2) shifts toward primary process modes of thinking; (3) a reliance on specific primitive defensive operations; (4) disruptions in superego development; (5) a disturbance of internalized object relations; and (6) identity diffusion.

Using the conceptual groundwork laid by Kernberg and the increasing number of empirical studies emerging from descriptive psychiatry, and beginning with the publication of *Borderline Phenomena and the Rorschach Test* (Kwawer et al., 1980), a host of empirical investigations that have sought to bring greater clarity and precision to the borderline concept have appeared in the Rorschach literature in the past decade. In general, these studies have focused on the quality of reality testing, the nature of thought disorder, the type of boundary disturbance, the level of defensive operation, and the quality of object relations of the borderline patient. In virtually every study, the experimental design has involved comparing, with respect to a specific variable, a group of borderline patients with a group of assumably more or less disturbed patients. On balance and collectively, these studies have provided information and clarified findings. More recently, individual case studies integrating nomothetic and idiographic Rorschach data have appeared in the assessment literature, and these too have served to clarify the borderline concept (Meloy and Gacono, 1993; Murray, 1993; Peterson, 1993).

Even though no single diagnostic concept has received more attention from theorists and clinicians alike, as Acklin (1993) reminds us, the borderline diagnosis still abounds with debate and controversy. One especially contentious issue is that of diagnosis, or what exactly constitutes the borders of the borderline concept. A second issue, prompted by the question of the relationship between the borderline personality and the schizoptypal personality disorder, involves the matter of subtypes of borderline patients. A third issue, sparked by the recent interest in child abuse, involves the question of the role of chronic childhood abuse, especially sexual abuse, in the etiology of borderline pathology.

In this chapter I review Rorschach investigations related to the borderline concept and patient. The studies are organized in terms of the following topics: reality testing, thought disorder, boundary disturbances, defense, object relations, and development. I then discuss several of the contentious issues that have surrounded and continue to surround the borderline concept.

◆ ◆ ◆ Reality Testing

Of the three major structural variables associated with borderline pathology (identity diffusion, level of defensive operation, and reality testing), Kernberg (1975) considered reality testing the crucial factor in distinguishing the borderline level of organization from the psychotic level and the neurotic level. At the lower level, he indicated that borderlines maintain some capacity for reality testing, whereas psychotics do not. At the upper level, he suggested that borderline patients do reveal impaired reality testing and that this is not the case with neurotics.

These propositions have been investigated in several studies. Hymowitz and associates (1983) compared the Rorschach test and Weschler Adult Intelligence Scale (WAIS) records of two groups of psychiatric inpatients diagnosed as having either a borderline or a psychotic personality organization on the combined basis of Kernberg's (1981) structured interview and the Diagnostic Interview for Borderlines (Kolb and Gunderson, 1980). Reality testing was operationally defined in terms of Mayman's (1970) system for rating the form quality of Rorschach responses. As predicted, the borderline subjects achieved higher scores than the psychotic subjects, with the differences in F+ percentage attaining statistical significance. A closer inspection of the data revealed that only the borderline patients could produce the more original and better-conceived form responses (F+). The attempts of the psychotic subjects to go beyond the ordinary form response faltered and resulted in serious reality departures.

On the basis of DSM-III criteria, Exner (1986b) distinguished a group of borderline personality disorders from a group of schizotypal personality disorders, and then compared the Rorschach records of the two groups with each other, as well as with two sets of Rorschach protocols obtained from first-admission schizophrenic patients. The first set of records was collected soon after admission and the second obtained shortly before discharge. Using the F+ percentage as an index of reality testing, Exner found that there was little difference in reality testing between the schizophrenic and schizotypal patients but that both groups scored significantly lower (indicating greater impairment) than the borderline patients.

Gartner, Hurt, and Gartner (1989) found that in the typical borderline patient's Rorschach, about 65% to 70% of the responses are of good form quality. They also noted that the borderlines' weak or unusual form quality responses indicated idiosyncratic and not distorted reality perception as found in protocols of psychotic patients. My own experience is consistent with the authors' finding, in that I have found that borderline patients maintain lax standards of reality testing and take liberties with reality, whereas psychotic individuals lose reality.

At the upper level of the borderline range, Rorschach records of borderlines have also been shown to be distinguishable from those of neurotically organized individuals with respect to perceptual accuracy and reality testing (Singer and Larson, 1981). Berg (1990) employed the Rorschach to investigate differences in ego functions between borderline and narcissistic personalities. As predicted, the borderlines produced significantly more unusual responses, indicating a greater distortion in reality testing, than did the narcissists. Berg's findings are consistent with earlier ones reported by Farris (1988). Using Friedman's (1953) system for scoring developmental level, Farris found that borderline patients, as compared with narcissistic patients, revealed transient disturbances in reality testing.

◆ ◆ ◆ Thought Disorder

Beginning with Rapaport and colleagues' (1945–1946) formulations regarding overideational and coarctated preschizophrenics, it has long been held that borderline patients require external structure to compensate for defects in internal structure. Singer (1977) extended this notion into a nearly axiomatic rule for the diagnosis of borderline pathology: individuals with such pathology exhibit thought disorder on unstructured tests, such as the Rorschach test, yet manifest relatively normal performance on more structured tests, such as the WAIS.

To examine the role of structure on the thinking of borderline patients, Edell (1987) compared Rorschach protocols and scores with a more structured test of cognitive slippage in patients with borderline personality disorders and schizophrenic disorders and in normal controls. The borderline group included patients diagnosed as schizotypal personality disorder and mixed borderline-schizotypal disorder. All Rorschach records were scored for thought disorder on the basis of a measure developed by Johnston and Holtzman (1979), The Thought Disorder Index (TDI). The TDI is a revision of Watkins and Stauffacher's (1952) Delta Index, which quantifies categories of deviant verbalizations initially described by Rapaport et al. (1945–1946). The TDI includes 21 categories of thought disorder, with each instance in each category weighted for severity at one of four levels (.25, .50, .75, and 1.0). To assess milder forms of thought disorder or cognitive slippage, a structured multiple-choice vocabulary test developed by Chapman and Chapman (1982) was employed. This measure includes two subtests, one requiring discrimination between subtle nuances of meaning and the other involving a knowledge of more obscure words. Edell's findings supported his hypothesis that borderline patients do manifest thought disorder but that such manifestations are limited to more unstructured tasks. More specifically, he found that the borderline and schizophrenic groups did not differ from one another on total TDI score but that each differed significantly from the control group. He also found that the borderlines were indistinguishable from the normal controls on the more structured test of cognitive slippage and that each group differed significantly from the schizophrenic patients. Edell reported two other findings that are of importance. First, he noted that the borderlines, schizotypals, and mixed borderline-schizotypals were indistinguishable from one another in both quantity and quality of thought disorder. Second, he noted that although the borderline and schizophrenic groups did not differ on total TDI, there was a significant tendency among the schizophrenics to offer responses at the more severe levels of thought disorder.

Edell's (1987) study touches upon several issues in this area that remain contentious and unresolved. First, and as Acklin (1993) has pointed out, "Observations about the role of structure in testing borderline patients . . . [and its relationship to thought disorder] . . .

has been subject to considerable debate and attempts at replication" (p. 336).

For example, findings at variance with Edell (1987) have been reported by Hymowitz and his colleagues (1983). The authors applied the Thought Disorder Index to both the Rorschach and the WAIS records of their sample of borderline and psychotic patients. They found that the TDI scores on each of the tests distinguished the two groups. They reported that minor disruptions in the WAIS were equally frequent in both groups, but that more severe disruptions were twice as prevalent among the psychotics, and that only the psychotic patients offered impaired responses at the .75 and 1.0 levels.

By contrast, Skelton, Boik, and Madero (1995) reported that adolescents with a diagnosis of Identity Disorder (the diagnosis of Identity Disorder is given to children and adolescents who exhibit borderline-like identity disturbance) revealed a significantly larger discrepancy between TDI scores on the WAIS or WAIS-R and TDI scores on the Rorschach than did adolescents diagnosed as Conduct Disorder, Oppositional Defiant Disorder, and Schizophreniform Disorder.

Harris (1993) also found that borderline patients exhibit thought-disordered responses on unstructured tests, but not on more structured tests. The Thought Disorder Index was applied to the Rorschach and Wechsler Adult Intelligence Scale-Revised (WAIS-R) protocols of two outpatient groups; one group consisted of patients diagnosed Borderline Personality Disorder (BPD) and the other group consisted of patients with other personality disorders (OPD). As predicted, the BPD group produced a significantly greater number of thought-disordered responses on the Rorschach but not on the WAIS-R compared to the OPD group. For a more complete discussion of this controversial issue, refer to excellent reviews by Widiger (1982) and Berg (1983).

Second, Edell (1987) reported no differences in quantity and quality of thought disorder among borderlines, schizotypals, and mixed borderline-schizotypals. Contradictory findings are reported by Exner (1986b). He found marked differences in the presence of thought disorder between a group of patients with borderline personality disorders and a group with schizotypal personality disorders. Whereas the borderline patients showed comparatively little evidence of thought disorder on the Rorschach test, the schizotypals, much like the schizophrenics, offered responses that were strange and distorted and revealed considerable slippage.

The third issue raised in Edell's (1987) investigation relates to the question of quality or nature of thought disorder. This issue has been most directly addressed by H. Lerner et al. (1985). Speaking from an object-relations perspective, these authors argue that differences in thought disorder between borderlines and schizophrenics are essentially qualitative, not a matter of quantity or even the degree of structure. Groups of outpatient neurotics, outpatient borderlines, inpatient borderlines, and inpatient schizophrenics were compared with respect to classic Rorschach expressions of thought disorder as originally developed by Rapaport et al. (1945–1946). Although Lerner and associates (1985) had reconceptualized the scores in terms of the concept of boundary disturbances, nonetheless they found that the inpatient borderline group offered significantly more confabulatory responses than the other groups and that the inpatient schizophrenics were distinguishable by their offering of contaminations.

The findings of Lerner and associates (1985) are important, in that they help to explain the seemingly disparate findings reported by Edell (1987) and Hymowitz and associates (1983) and to account for the observation reported by these investigators that schizophrenics offer the most severe instances of thought disorder. Clearly, viewing thought disorder as a unitary dimension and investigating it purely quantitatively is insufficient. Following Watkins and Stauffacher (1952) and their attempts to arrange thought disorders along a single continuum of severity, subsequent investigators have continued these efforts and in the process have obscured possible qualitative differences among various types of thought disorders. It should be remembered that Rapaport's indices of deviant verbalizations represented an attempt to find Rorschach counterparts to what Freud (1900) had initially described as the mechanisms of dream work. Therefore, while Rapaport's indices may vary in level of severity and may be collectively grouped under the broad umbrella of "primary process," at the same time they may possibly be tapping quite different processes. If this is the case, then differences in thought disorder between borderline patients and schizophrenic patients is not one of amount, but rather one of kind. This issue, together with the question of the relationship between thinking and other aspects of personality functioning (e.g., object relations, defense), is examined in subsequent sections in this chapter.

The questions raised by Exner's (1986b) findings are diagnostic in nature and relate to the relationship between the diagnoses of borderline personality disorder and schizotypal personality disorder. Exner viewed the two as quite distinct and considered the schizotypal disorder closer to the schizophrenic disorder than to the borderline disorder. Where to place and how to conceptualize the schizotypal disorder is important, and this issue too is discussed later in this chapter.

✦ ✦ ✦ Boundary Disturbances

Ego boundaries are hypothetical constructs that refer to the capacity to create particular cognitive and affective distinctions along some bipolar coordinate of experience where previously no distinction was possible. The establishment of boundaries between self and nonself and between fantasy and reality (inside and outside) is considered the earliest and most fundamental stage in the development of object representations.

Using three of Rapaport's indices of thought disorder (contamination, confabulation, fabulized combination) as measures of various levels of severity of boundary disturbances, Blatt and Ritzler (1974) found such indices to be related to disturbances in a variety of ego functions (capacity for reality testing, quality of interpersonal relations, nature of object representations) in a mixed schizophrenic and borderline sample. The authors further found that poorly articulated boundaries occurred most frequently in the more disturbed, chronic patients, who had impoverished object relations, impaired ego functions, and a lifelong pattern of isolation and estrangement.

Because different forms of psychopathology can be understood in terms of an impairment of the capacity to sustain specific boundaries, several authors have attempted to identify the boundary disturbance particular to the borderline patient.

H. Lerner et al. (1985) found that independently diagnosed borderline patients could be distinguished from both schizophrenics and neurotics on the basis of level of boundary disturbance. Borderline patients were found to experience difficulty maintaining the inner-outer boundary as assessed through the confabulation response of the Rorschach; that is, these patients had difficulty discriminating between an external object and their own affective reaction to that object. By contrast, the schizophrenic patients experienced difficulty in maintaining the developmentally earlier boundary between self and other, as reflected in the contamination response.

In a study involving boundary disturbances in depressive, borderline, and schizophrenic hospitalized inpatients, Wilson (1985) obtained findings strikingly similar to those of Lerner and associates

(1985). He too found that the borderline group scored significantly higher on the Rorschach indices of laxness and (moderately severe) inner-outer boundary disturbance. The schizophrenic group, by comparison, scored significantly higher on measures of self-other boundary disturbance.

Thus, findings from the studies of both Wilson (1985) and Lerner and associates (1985) are consistent in indicating that whereas the developmental structural impairment of the borderline patient is at the point of the inner-outer boundary, for the schizophrenic patient it is at the earlier point of self-other boundary formation.

◆ ◆ ◆ Defense

Kernberg has identified two overall levels of defense organization, one associated with neurotic pathology and the other with borderline and psychotic pathology. At the lower level of organization (borderline and psychotic) splitting, or primitive dissociation, is the basic defense, which is augmented through the related mechanisms of low-level denial, primitive idealization, primitive devaluation, and projective identification. At the higher developmental level, repression replaces splitting as the major defense and is bolstered by the related operations of intellectualization, rationalization, undoing, and higher-level forms of denial and projection.

Two comprehensive Rorschach scoring systems (P. Lerner and H. Lerner, 1980; Cooper et al., 1988) were developed to assess the more primitive defenses. These scales, together with the research each has generated, are discussed in chapter 14. Here I briefly review those findings directly related to the defensive structure of the borderline patient.

In an initial study, Lerner and Lerner (1980) applied their defense scale to the Rorschach protocols of 15 outpatient borderlines and 15 outpatient neurotics. As predicted, the borderline subjects used test indices of splitting, low-level devaluation, projective identification, and low-level denial significantly more often than did the neurotic subjects. The measures of splitting and projective identification appeared exclusively in the borderline group. Indices of high-level devaluation and high-level denial were found more frequently in the records of the neurotic group.

H. Lerner et al. (1981) extended the defense scale to a comparison of the Rorschach records of a group of hospitalized borderline patients with those of a hospitalized schizophrenic group. Here too, the borderline patients were found to have a unique and distinctive defensive structure. Indices of splitting and four of the five scale measures of devaluation were observed significantly more often in the borderline group, and scores reflective of projective identification occurred exclusively in the borderline group. Denial, when treated as a composite score, also distinguished the two groups, with borderlines scoring higher.

Collins (1983), in a cross-validating study, obtained findings supportive of those reported by Lerner and Lerner (1980) and Lerner et al. (1981). Rorschach protocols were collected from a sample of 15 borderline patients, 15 neurotic patients, and 15 schizophrenic patients, and scored using the Lerner Defense Scale. Overall differences among the three groups were highly significant, supporting the general hypothesis that borderline patients reveal a defensive structure significantly different from that of neurotics and schizophrenics. Major differences were found between the borderline and schizophrenic patients. The borderlines offered significantly more responses reflective of splitting, projective identification, low-level idealization, and mid-level devaluation. Although not statistically significant, the borderline patients, as compared with the neurotic group, used indices of splitting and projective identification more frequently.

Using the hypothesis that borderline personality disorders would manifest greater disturbance in defensive organization than narcissistic personality disorders, Farris (1988) applied the Lerner Defense Scale to the Rorschach records of nine matched pairs of borderline and narcissistic patients. A comparison of the two groups revealed that the borderline patients produced a significantly greater number of responses reflecting the use of primitive defenses than did narcissistic subjects. Each of the defense categories was submitted to a chi-square analysis. Significant differences were found regarding the defenses of splitting and projective identification. In both categories, the borderline subjects produced a significantly greater number of primitive defense responses than did the narcissistic subjects.

Rooted in the theoretical contributions of Kernberg (1975) and Stolorow and Lachmann (1980) and in the test work of Schafer (1954), Holt (1970), and Lerner and Lerner (1980), Cooper et al. (1988) devised a content-based scoring system for assessing 15 defenses, including the designated borderline defenses of devaluation, omnipotence, primitive idealization, projection, projective identification, and splitting. Rorschach protocols were obtained from 68 subjects, including 21 diagnosed as borderline personality disorder, 14 diagnosed as having borderline traits, 17 diagnosed as antisocial personality disorder, and 16 diagnosed as bipolar II affective disorder. All borderline personality disorders met DSM-III criteria and scored above 150 on the Borderline Personality Scale. Those diagnosed as having borderline traits met four (rather than five) of the eight DSM-III criteria and obtained a lower cutoff score on the Borderline Personality Scale. The antisocial personalities were diagnosed according to DSM-III criteria, and the affective disorders were diagnosed on the basis of the Research Diagnostic Criteria. These diagnostic variables, together with two continuous measures (a subset of 36 items of the Borderline Personality Scale and the weighted Antisocial Personality Scale), were used for data analysis.

To examine the discriminant validity of the defense scale, correlations were obtained between subject diagnostic variables and the individual defense scores. The Borderline Personality Disorder Scale was found to correlate positively with the defense scores of devaluation, projection, splitting, and hypomanic denial, and negatively with intellectualization. The number of positive DSM-III borderline criteria correlated positively with each of the same defenses, except for projection. The dichotomous and continuous antisocial personality variables and the affective disorder variable did not correlate with any of the borderline defenses. The relationship between defense mechanisms and specific aspects of borderline pathology was examined by calculating correlations between the defenses and each of the nine subscales of the Borderline Personality Disorder Scale. As predicted, splitting correlated positively with Subscale VI (splitting of other images) and Subscale VII (unstable identity, including splitting of self-images) as well as with a greater number of the BPD subscales than did the other defenses.

In a study comparing borderline and narcissistic patients described previously, one of the ego functions studied by Berg (1990) was defense. Using the scoring system developed by Cooper and Arnow (1986), Berg found that the borderline sample offered more signs of splitting, whereas the protocols of the narcissistic patients revealed a greater use of grandiosity.

In a follow-up study, Gacono et al. (1992) selected a subgroup of male subjects from each of Berg's (1990) samples of borderline and narcissistic patients, and then compared them on the Cooper and Arnow (1986) defense scale with two groups of antisocial personalities—a psychopathic group (P-APD) and a nonpsychopathic group (NP-APD). A significant main effect was found for the defense of primitive idealization. Pairwise comparisons revealed that the narcissistic personality disorders and the borderline personality disorders produced significantly more primitive idealization responses than the NP-APDs.

In a study reviewed in chapter 18, Lerner, Albert, and Walsh (1987) applied the borderline defense measures of the scale of Cooper et al. (1988) to the Rorschach protocols collected in two previous studies (Lerner and Lerner, 1980; H. Lerner et al., 1981). In a discriminant function analysis the borderline defense scores significantly distinguished inpatient borderlines from neurotics, outpatient borderlines from inpatient borderlines, and inpatient borderlines from schizophrenics. Three defense scores—splitting, devaluation, and omnipotence—were found especially effective in discriminating among groups.

In summary, in a variety of studies it has been demonstrated that patients organized at a borderline level manifest a discernable defensive structure different in kind from those of neurotic patients, schizophrenic patients, and patients with narcissistic personality disorders. Characterizing this defensive structure are the operations of splitting, projective identification, primitive devaluation, and low-level denial. Findings regarding grandiosity and primitive idealization are rather mixed, and these are discussed in chapter 24.

◆ ◆ ◆ Object Relations

A concept basic to Kernberg's work that has received considerable examination is that of "internalized object relation." Attempts to assess this concept have involved the study of impairments in object representations found in patients with various forms of pathology, including those with borderline levels of personality organization. Although several authors (Modell, 1963; Krohn, 1974; Kernberg, 1975) have described the borderline patient's object hunger, desperate search for direct contact, and intense fear of object loss, only recently have investigators been able to relate these observations to such underlying factors as level of internal object representation.

Using the scoring system of Blatt and associates (1976), Blatt and Lerner (1983) applied the scale to the Rorschach records of several patients, each of whom was independently selected as a prototypic example of a specific clinical disorder. In reviewing the protocol of a borderline patient the authors found that the object representations progressively deteriorated both over time and with stress. Initially, the representations were accurate, well-differentiated, and appropriately articulated; this gave way, however, to representations that were inaccurately perceived, inappropriately articulated, and seen as part, rather than whole, figures. The latter finding, the shift from whole to part figures, is consistent with Kernberg's proposition that under the pressure of intense anxiety, the borderline patient defensively attempts to manage the anxiety by splitting the object into more tolerable good- and bad-part units.

Farris (1988), in his comparative study of borderline and narcissistic patients, also applied the scale of Blatt and associates (1976) to the subjects' Rorschach protocols. Using a summary score, he found, as predicted, that the narcissistic subjects showed a significantly higher level of object differentiation, articulation, and integration than did borderline subjects.

Stuart et al. (1990) employed the Blatt et al. (1976) scale to compare the object relations of borderline inpatients with those of inpatient depressives and normal controls. The parts of the Blatt measure that assess the subjects' experience of human action and interaction distinguished among the three groups. Distinguishing the cognitive from the affective component of object relations, the authors found that the borderlines displayed a greater object-relational sophistication, saw human action as highly motivated, and had an overwhelming tendency to construe interpersonal relations as malevolent.

Spear (1980) differentiated two subtypes of borderline personalities and then compared their Rorschach records with one another and with the records of a group of schizophrenic patients on the basis of both the structural measure of Blatt and associates (1976) and Krohn and Mayman's (1974) thematic measure of object representations. One subgroup of borderline patients included more infantile personalities, characterized by emotional lability, intense dependency, concerns regarding object loss, and proclivity for anaclitic depression. The other group consisted of obsessive/paranoid personalities, characterized by intellectualization, isolation of affect, and a proneness for introjective depression. Two major findings were obtained. First, although the structural measure significantly distinguished the combined borderline group from the schizophrenic group, it did not differentiate the two borderline groups. Second, the thematic measure distinguished the two borderline groups and differentiated the infantile borderlines from the schizophrenics; it failed, however, to differentiate the obsessive/paranoid borderlines from the schizophrenic group.

Although the scale of Blatt and associates (1976) consists of six developmental dimensions, in his initial study Spear (1980) used one summary developmental score. Further, the thematic scale was originally devised to assess object representations as manifested in dream material. To rectify these methodological shortcomings, Spear and Sugarman (1984) replicated the earlier study; in their study the six developmental dimensions of Blatt's scale were treated separately, and the thematic aspect was evaluated using a modified version of Urist's (1977) Mutuality of Autonomy Scale. An examination of the Rorschach protocols of a sample consisting of 22 obsessive/paranoid borderline patients, 17 infantile/hysterical borderline patients, and 15 schizophrenic patients yielded the following results: (1) four of the six developmental dimensions distinguished the combined borderline group from the schizophrenic group; (2) only the differentiation subscale differentiated each of the three groups; (3) the differentiation subscale also differentiated the infantile/hysterical borderline group from the combined obsessive/paranoid borderline group and schizophrenic group; (4) three scores on the thematic measure distinguished the two borderline groups; (5) none of the thematic measures distinguished the obsessive/paranoid borderlines from the schizophrenics; and (6) the infantile/hysterical borderlines were significantly more developmentally advanced than the schizophrenics on two of the thematic scores. From these findings the authors concluded that from a structural perspective, the borderline groups were relatively homogeneous, but from a thematic perspective, the infantile/hysterical borderline patients functioned at a higher object-relations level and the obsessive/paranoid borderline patients functioned at a lower level, closer to that of the schizophrenic patients.

The most comprehensive study of impairments in level of object representation among groups differing in severity of psychopathology is the work of H. Lerner and St. Peter (1984). These authors applied the Blatt scale to a sample of four groups, including outpatient neurotic patients, outpatient borderline patients, hospitalized borderline patients, and hospitalized schizophrenic patients. Overall, strong support was found for the general proposition that impairments in level of object representation, as indicated by the assessment of the developmental-structural properties of human responses given to the Rorschach test, show distinct patterns in groups differing in type and severity of psychopathology. Several other informative and unexpected findings were also obtained. Subdividing the responses into those accurately perceived and those inaccurately perceived, the investigators found an inverse relationship between developmental level of the concept of the object and degree of psychopathology. That is, the less severe the psychopathology the higher the developmental level of the patient's object concept. This inverse relationship, however, did not hold for the inaccurately perceived responses. Here, quite surprisingly, the hospitalized borderline group achieved the highest levels of human differentiation, articulation, and integration (i.e., for inaccurately perceived responses). Because response accuracy is taken as an indicator of quality of reality testing, this finding prompted H. Lerner and St. Peter to question the relationship between reality testing and object relations and led them to compare the protocols of the two borderline groups.

It was found that although the outpatient borderlines produced more accurate and less inaccurate human responses than did their hospitalized counterparts, their responses tended to involve quasi-human rather than whole-human figures. In other words, although the outpatient borderlines were able to perceive objects accurately (intact reality testing), the perception was accompanied by a distancing and dehumanizing of the object. The hospitalized borderlines, by contrast, were unable to distance their objects, and as a consequence, their reality testing suffered. If one conceptualizes the ability to distance and devalue objects as reflective of the defenses of splitting and primitive devaluation, and the inability to distance and devalue objects as indicative of the absence or failure of these defenses, then the findings may be interpreted as supporting Kernberg's (1975) contention regarding the intimate relationship between quality of reality testing, nature of the defensive structure, and the organization of internalized object relations.

Finally, in reviewing the thematic content of the human responses, the investigators found that the hospitalized borderline patients, in comparison with the three other groups, offered the most malevolent content and were the only group to produce inaccurately perceived malevolent responses. Conceptually, these patients may be understood in terms of their inability to defend against or escape from internal malevolent objects.

A review of the above findings leads to several interesting conclusions: (1) there is consistent evidence to suggest that the object representations of borderline patients are significantly more impaired and less developmentally advanced than are those of neurotic and narcissistic patients; (2) when a sample of borderline patients is subdivided on the basis of character types and the object-representation concept is viewed in terms of its constituent components, the borderline subgroups differ significantly on select components; (3) from a structural perspective, the object representations of various borderline patients are relatively homogenous and different from, and more advanced than, those of schizophrenic patients; (4) from a thematic perspective, the object representations of infantile/hysterical borderline patients are significantly more advanced than those of schizophrenic patients, and the representations of obsessive/paranoid borderline patients are indistinguishable from those of schizophrenics; and (5) object representations, and hence object relations, are intimately related to reality testing and defense organization and are most profitably investigated and understood in that context.

❖ ❖ ❖ Development

This section includes a heterogenous group of studies that have all approached the investigation of the borderline patient from a developmental perspective. The studies differ in the targeted area of investigation (e.g., cognitive-perceptual, object relations) as well as in their conceptual roots.

Farris (1988), in a study that has been referred to often in this work, also investigated differences in cognitive-perceptual functioning between borderline and narcissistic patients. Applying Friedman's (1953) developmental-level scoring system to the subjects' Rorschach protocols, Farris found that the narcissistic subjects achieved significantly higher scores than did the borderline subjects. He interpreted the finding as indicating that borderline patients, as compared with narcissistic patients, are fixated or arrested at an earlier developmental point, are more prone to transient disruptions in reality testing, and have stronger regressive tendencies.

Farris's finding that the borderline subjects tended to produce more poorly structured, amorphous, and more fabulized combinations was consistent with findings obtained by Singer and Larson (1981) in an earlier study. These investigators had used a scoring system derived from Becker's (1956) modification of Friedman's (1953) developmental scoring system to investigate ego functioning and had applied it to the Rorschach protocols of a sample of 114 subjects, including borderline patients. In addition to finding that borderline patients produce developmentally poorer responses, Singer and Larson found that a discriminant function analysis involving 11 variables correctly classified 20 of the 25 borderline subjects.

Coonerty (1986), as discussed in chapter 15, using Mahler's theory of separation and individuation, devised a developmental object-relations scale for identifying and scoring Rorschach responses reflective of concerns and issues associated with the preseparation stage and with each of the subphases of the separation-individuation process. The scale was applied to the Rorschach records of 50 borderline subjects and 50 schizophrenic subjects. Coonerty found that while the borderline group produced significantly more responses indicative of separation-individuation concerns, the schizophrenic group, by contrast, offered significantly more responses indicative of preseparation concerns.

Despite different methodologies and different conceptual underpinnings, there is a consistent thread that runs through these studies. The combined findings of Farris (1988) and Singer and Larson (1981) suggest that the level of cognitive-perceptual functioning of borderline patients is higher than that of schizophrenic patients, but lower than that of narcissistic patients. In both investigations the authors used measures for scoring developmental level. P. Lerner (1975), in his review of developmental-level scoring systems, noted that implicit in the underlying theory is the assumption that "level of maturation is a unitary dimension underlying several diverse aspects of human functioning and that a study of any one aspect has predictive import for other aspects" (p. 27). He further suggested that "if this assumption is tenable, then one should be able to predict from Rorschach indices other areas of psychological functioning which lend themselves to developmental ordering" (pp. 27–28). Because Mahler's theory lends itself to developmental ordering (i.e., development of an autonomous sense of self and of constancy of the object), Coonerty's (1986) finding that borderline patients expressed themes referable to a later developmental stage than did schizophrenic patients is consistent with developmental theory and, hence, with the other findings.

Beyond this, Coonerty's results are especially important in that they lend support to those writers (Masterson and Rinsley, 1975; Settlage, 1977) who locate the occurrence of developmental arrest in borderline patients during the separation-individuation phases.

♦ ♦ ♦   Controversial Issues

Although the borderline concept has spawned a substantial number of empirical Rorschach-based studies focused on the borderline patient and specific borderline processes, and the results from these studies have been consistent and impressive, controversy still abounds regarding the validity of the borderline diagnosis and the inner and outer boundaries of the borderline category.

A review of the psychoanalytic literature reveals that there are two overarching alternative understandings of the diagnosis borderline. One, the position represented in this chapter, views the borderline diagnosis as a clearly delineated category, distinguishable from neurotic organizations and psychotic organizations. The other position understands borderline as a vague, approximately defined location on a continuum of psychopathology. Representative of the latter position are the writings of Abend, Ponder, and Willick (1983) and Rosegrant (1995).

Rosegrant reanalyzed several of the studies reviewed in this chapter. From his analysis of the size of group differences reported in these studies, he concludes:

> The borderline diagnosis does not appear to be internally homogeneous; differences between different types of borderlines may be as great as or greater than differences between borderlines on the one hand and neurotics and schizophrenics on the other. The most judicious conclusion is that the borderline diagnosis does not represent a discrete group of patients identifiable by particular psychic structure and dynamics, as Kernberg and others have stated. Rather, the borderline diagnosis names a vaguely defined and internally diverse group of patients on the continuum from neurosis to psychosis, as Abend et al. (1983) suggested [p. 422].

For those who conceptualize the borderline diagnosis as a discrete and identifiable entity, qualitatively, not just quantitatively, different from neurosis and psychosis, a separate but related issue involves clearly articulating the boundaries of the borderline category. Over the past two decades such boundaries had progressively become firmer. More recently, however, stimulated largely by the strong interest accorded the dissociative patient and patients experiencing posttraumatic stress disorder (PTSD), these boundaries have again become hazier and more elusive.

Several earlier authors (Benner and Joscelyne, 1984; Buck, 1983; Clary et al., 1984; Fast, 1974; Horevitz and Braun, 1984) not only reported similarities between patients with multiple personality disorder and those with borderline personality disorder, but saw the former as a subtype of the latter. Saunders (1991) has pointed out Rorschach features common to both multiple personality and borderline patients. She suggested that in the protocols of each group one sees a relative dominance of color over form, suggesting problems of affect regulation, signs of formal thought disorder indicative of boundary disturbances, specific lapses in reality testing, and polarization of self and object representations as reflected in human-movement responses.

Links between multiple personality disorder and borderline personality disorder have also been forged on the basis of an assumedly common etiology—sexual abuse trauma. Several studies have reported a high incidence of sex-abuse histories in individuals diagnosed as borderline (Brown and Anderson, 1991; Bryer et al., 1987; Herman, Perry, and van der Volk, 1987; Ludolph et. al., 1990; Ogata et al., 1990). Multiple personality disorder has also been related to a history of childhood sex abuse (Putnam et al., 1986; Schultz, Braun, and Kluft, 1987).

Despite recognizing similarities between the MPD patient and the borderline patient, Armstrong (1991) argues compellingly that "the borderline personality concept gives us too broad and blurred a view of the MPD/DD terrain" (p. 544). She points out, on the basis of Rorschach findings, that unlike the borderline, the MPD has an introversive personality style that allows for internalization, is able to view and relate to others in an empathic manner, and deals with anxiety ideationally.

Parallels between the borderline personality disorder and post-traumatic stress disorder (PTSD) initially appeared in reports on Vietnam veterans (Brende, 1983; Parson, 1984) and were subsequently more fully elaborated by Herman and van der Kolk (1987). These authors argued that both disturbances are characterized by similar impairments in five basic areas: affect regulation, impulse control, reality testing, object relations, and identity formation.

Rorschach findings indicative of dysfunctions in affect regulation, impulse control, and reality testing have been reported for PTSD groups including Vietnam Veterans (Hartman et al., 1991; Swanson, Blount, and Bruno, 1990), Persian Gulf Veterans (Sloan et al., 1995), women who commit homicide (Kaser-Boyd, 1993), and women with a history of sexual abuse (Saunders, 1991). Nevertheless, it should be noted that several of these studies have methodological shortcomings (Frank, 1992), and in their follow-up of the Persian Gulf Veterans, Sloan et al. (1996) reported that scores associated with acute distress, capacity for control and coping, and feeling overwhelmed all significantly decreased over time. Armstrong (1991) takes issue with including PTSD patients and MPD/DD patients under the borderline rubric and presents Rorschach data that highlight important differences among the three groups.

Whereas defining the outer boundaries of the borderline category has been difficult and at times contentious, so too has been the matter of articulating the inner parameters—the issues of subtypes of borderline patients. Especially thorny is the question of the nosological placement of the schizotypal personality disorder. Several authors (Serban, Conte, and Plutchic, 1987; Edell, 1987) view the schizotypal personality as a subvariant of, and as indistinguishable from, the borderline personality, whereas others (Exner, 1986b; Carr, 1987) conceive of the schizotypal disorder and the borderline disorder as separate and distinct entities, with the schizotypal patient more closely approximating the schizophrenic disorder. This specific issue is important because it prompts one to consider from what perspective the borderline patient can most profitably be viewed.

Edell (1987), as noted previously, found that borderline patients, schizotypal patients, and patients with a mixed diagnosis of the two were indistinguishable from each other on a measure of thought disorder, but were significantly different from a group of schizophrenics and a group of normal controls.

In contrast, Exner (1986b) found marked and pervasive differences between the Rorschach records of a group of borderline patients and those of a group of schizotypal patients. He reported significant differences in quality of thinking, intactness of reality testing, degree of self-absorption, and effectiveness of affect control. Specifically, whereas the schizotypal patients revealed more disturbed thinking, greater disruptions in reality testing, and higher levels of self-absorption than the borderlines, the borderline patients showed greater disturbance with regard to affect control. Furthermore, when both groups were compared with a group of schizophrenic patients, three distinct patterns of psychological organization and functioning emerged. Although there was much overlap between the schizotypal group and the schizophrenic group regarding their organizational characteristics, the groups differed significantly with respect to their level of functioning. The borderline group differed from the others both in organization and in functioning. According to Exner, both the schizotypals and schizophrenics presented as introversive, detached, somewhat affectless, and highly ideational. Not surprisingly, their disruptions and symptoms appeared in the realm of ideation. By contrast, the borderline patients appeared as affect-oriented and their impairments centered around affect-oriented modulation and regulation. Because of the similarities

noted in organization and style between the schizotypals and schizophrenics, Exner suggested that one might refer to the schizotypals more
accurately by the older term "borderline schizophrenics."

The distinction Exner (1986b) drew between the borderlines and
schizotypals is very similar to the distinction between two subtypes of
borderline patients made by Spear (1980) and Spear and Sugarman
(1984). Like Exner's borderline group, Spear's infantile/hysterical borderlines were characterized by emotional lability, heightened dependency, and vulnerability to object loss. Similarly, the obsessive/paranoid
borderlines, like Exner's schizotypals, were depicted as hyperideational
and as manifesting an isolation of affects. Spear and Sugarman (1984)
found that although both subgroups achieved the same level of object
representation on a structural measure, on a thematic measure they
differed significantly; these researchers also found that the obses-
sive/paranoid subgroup more closely resembled the schizophrenic
patients. Like Exner, yet quite independently, these authors suggested
that one might judiciously reserve the term "borderline schizophrenic"
for the obsessive/paranoid borderline patient.

Despite the consistency and impressiveness of their findings, the
conclusions reached by Exner (1986b) and Spear and Sugarman
(1984) may be interpreted differently, especially in light of the work
of H. Lerner and St. Peter (1984). Both in conception and in design,
Exner's study was pitched at a descriptive level. The variables studied
and the Rorschach measures used were stylistic in nature, and the conclusions reached related to characterological features. That descriptive or characterological differences appear among borderline patients
is not unexpected; indeed, it was this observation that led Kernberg
(1975) to argue that an exclusive emphasis on descriptive features was
necessary but insufficient and that one should also consider underlying structural factors. Spear and Sugarman (1984) focused on a structural variable, level of object representation, but they studied this
factor in isolation, and conceptually they stopped short of consider-
ing the interrelationships among various structural variables.

Lerner and St. Peter (1984) also investigated level of object representation, but in recognizing differences that appeared between outpatient and hospitalized borderline groups, they also considered
defense and reality testing. This permitted them to interpret their findings in terms of the dynamic interplay between various structural variables and thereby remain closer to the richness of Kernberg's theory
and the clinical complexity of the individual borderline patient.

The results of the Lerner and St. Peter study—in particular, the observed differences between the borderline groups on the structural variables of level of object representations, quality of reality testing, and effectiveness of defenses—lend themselves to the notion of a psychopathological continuum with a spectrum of borderline disorders. From a developmental perspective, Rinsley (1979) and Stone (1980) have both advanced the concept of a "spectrum" for understanding the pathogenesis of the various borderline disorders. These authors proposed a "diathesis-stress" model, with the role of genetic loading and constitutional factors assuming increased weight toward the more severe, psychotic-like end of the continuum and intrafamilial, interpersonal, and experiential factors assuming greater importance with the less severe borderline disorders. Placing issues of etiology aside and assuming a structural perspective, Lerner and St. Peter conclude that "points on this . . . continuum appear to be a function of levels of internalization and concomitant cognitive and affective development, all within an interpersonal matrix involving the progressive differentiation, articulation, and integration of the representational world" (p. 18).

❖ ❖ ❖ Conclusion

The past two decades have witnessed an increasing number of empirical Rorschach studies intended to add to our understanding of the borderline patient and borderline phenomena. Rooted in either descriptive psychiatry or psychoanalytic theory, these investigations have sought to clarify and define more rigorously the borderline patient's type of thought disturbance, disruption in reality testing, level of boundary disturbance, defensive structure, and quality of object relations.

The borderline concept, although well established, has been and continues to be beset by various conceptual ambiguities, including whether an exclusively descriptive diagnostic schema, such as represented in DSM-IV, is sufficient, whether the borderline patient reveals a stable and identifiable personality disturbance, qualitatively and quantitatively distinguishable from neurosis and psychosis, and what precisely constitutes the inner and outer borders of the borderline category.

The studies reviewed in this chapter, collectively, suggest that a purely descriptive approach is necessary but not sufficient; a dynamic-structural approach is needed as well. For example, from a purely descriptive perspective, the schizotypal and borderline patient are distinctly different, yet when looked at from a structural perspective in terms of underlying personality variables (e.g., defensive structure, level of internalized object relations), one sees similarities.

Various lines of evidence, group studies and individual case studies, indicate that borderline patients are qualitatively different from psychotic and neurotic patients; to simply place them on a quantitative continuum of severity of psychopathology obscures these differences. Unlike neurotic patients, borderline patients exhibit ego weaknesses, impaired reality testing, thought impairment, boundary disturbances, primitive defenses, and highly disturbed object relations. Yet, their disruptions in reality testing, the nature of their thought disorder, their type of boundary disturbance, and their quality of object relations are all very different from those of psychotic patients.

The relationship between posttraumatic stress disorders and dissociative disorders on the one hand, and the borderline category on the other, is unclear. Both diagnostic categories, PTSD and DD, arise from descriptive psychiatry, not psychoanalysis, thus, how they fit into Kernberg's schema is yet to be determined. With PTSD, select ego weaknesses, such as poor affect control, impaired reality testing, and disturbed thinking, have all been demonstrated; however, how enduring these dysfunctions are is not yet known. Then too, and as Frank (1992) has noted, little has been written of the pretrauma personality structure.

There is much evidence to suggest that patients diagnosed dissociative disorder are, in Kernberg's (1976) terms, organized at a borderline level. Such individuals manifest significant ego weaknesses, employ primitive defenses, and evidence massive identity diffusion. Rather than emphasizing trauma as others have, I suggest that the dissociative patient, like others organized at a borderline level, was raised in a pathological family milieu. From a descriptive perspective, as Armstrong (1991) has persuasively noted, there are important differences between dissociative disorder and borderline personality disorder. In using the term borderline as Kernberg does, as a level of personality organization, I believe that these differences are not obscured.

More than 15 years ago, the question was asked as to whether the borderline disturbance is primarily a disorder of ego functioning or of object relations (Sugarman and Lerner, 1980). Given the current status of research and the measures now available, this question requires reformulation. We are now at a point in our understanding of borderline patients where we can instead ask in what ways the disturbances in ego functioning are related to the disturbances in object relations, and how we might understand these impairments from a developmental perspective.

Two recent studies addressed this reformulated issue. Berg, Packer, and Nunno (1993) investigated the relationship between a measure of thought disorder (Special Scorings from the Comprehensive System) and a measure of developmental object relations (Mutuality of Autonomy Scale) in a sample consisting of borderline, narcissistic, and schizophrenic patients. As predicted, the authors found a highly significant relationship between severity of thought disorder and severity of imbalance in internalized object relations.

In a non-Rorschach study, Greene (1996) examined the relationship between specific defense mechanisms and object relations in borderline personality disorder and the role of each in predicting symptomatic expression. A canonical correlation analysis was performed on self-report questionnaires obtained from 53 borderline patients. The findings supported Kernberg's (1975) formulation of a reciprocal relation between the defense of splitting and pathological object relations. A second finding indicated that borderline defenses (i.e., splitting) could be distinguished from narcissistic defenses (i.e., idealization, omnipotence).

Finally, because the borderline concept has stirred intense debate and controversy, the studies in this chapter, as a whole, clearly demonstrate how the Rorschach can be used to investigate contentious conceptual issues, clarify ambiguities, and furnish new understandings. In this regard these studies bear out Rapaport's initial vision; namely, that the Rorschach is an excellent means for not only applying psychoanalytic theory, but also for clarifying and refining it.

23

VARIANTS OF THE BORDERLINE CONCEPT AND THE RORSCHACH TEST

Paralleling the increased interest in and investigation of the borderline patient, greater research attention has been accorded specific groups of patients that clinicians and researchers have come to associate with what they call "primitive mental states." Despite presenting various symptoms, these patients appear to share archaic personality elements that become evident in profound regressions, especially in treatment. Their disturbances reflect a variety of etiologies whose common denominator would appear to be a history of frustrating, rather than satisfying, early object relations. On the assumption that there is a commonly shared borderline personality organization underlying the clinical presentation and the expression of symptoms, many of the Rorschach scoring systems devised to assess borderline patients have been extended to the protocols of these patients as well. In this chapter I review those studies that have applied these Rorschach scales to the following clinical populations: eating-disorder patients, patients manifesting gender-identity disturbances, antisocial personalities, and sexually abused females. Several of these studies have been described and discussed previously (in general, from the point of view of the measures employed). Here I emphasize the obtained findings, in part to demonstrate the contribution of Rorschach studies to our understanding of specific forms of psychopathology.

◆ ◆ ◆ Eating Disorder Patients

Many of the early Rorschach studies involved clinical, impressionistic appraisals of the protocols of anoretic patients; despite limitations inherent in this methodology, the findings reported have often been substantiated in more rigorous and systematic investigations.

Roland (1970) studied the Rorschach protocols of 23 anoretic patients. On the basis of content analysis, he reported strong depressive trends, feelings of rejection, suicidal ideation, body image distortions, difficulties in reality testing, and tenuous controls.

From a review of the Rorschach records of 40 anoretic patients, Selvini-Palazzoli (1974) concluded that no specific test pattern characterized these patients. She did find, however, that her sample could be subdivided into two groups on the basis of the presence or absence of thought disorder.

Wagner and Wagner (1978) presented and reviewed the Rorschach records of three cases of anorexia (two females and one male). As a result of the patterning of scores, they suggested that each case could be diagnosed as conversion hysteria with repressed orality. Although their diagnosis is questionable, a review of the actual protocols reveals the subjects' attunement to oral imagery (e.g., food, eating) and the prevalence of responses reflective of a somatic preoccupation (e.g., body parts and organs).

Small and associates (1982) compared the Wechsler records and Rorschach protocols of a group of 27 hospitalized anorexics with those of a group of schizophrenic females. On the basis of a combination of findings related to the differential use of conventional Rorschach scores (i.e., location, determinants, form level) and varying responses to structure (i.e., quality of test performance on the more structured WAIS versus the less structured Rorschach test), the authors concluded that the anoretic patients were organized at a higher level than the schizophrenic patients but that they shared features in common with borderline personalities. These similarities included a proclivity toward disturbed thinking on unstructured tests and a sensitivity to depression and affective needs. The authors also compared the

Rorschach protocols on the Delta index, a measure of thought disorder devised by Watkins and Stauffacher (1952); these results are reported under the section on thought disorder.

Weisberg, Norman, and Herzog (1987) compared the Rorschach protocols of 57 normal-weight bulimic women, a group of outpatient depressed women, and a group of nonpatient controls. With a variety of scores developed by Exner (1974), the groups were compared with respect to the following areas of personality functioning: depression, suicidal ideation, emotional lability and impulsivity, egocentricity and narcissism, thought disorder, anger and negativity, and copying and organizational style. The authors found that in contrast to the nonpatient controls, the bulimic and depressed groups were similar in their overall high level of dysphoric affect, emotional lability and impulsivity, avoidance of affective stimulation, state of emotional overload, relatively poor perceptual accuracy, lower interest in other people, and lack of a set coping style. Compared with both other groups, however, the bulimic patients displayed greater egocentricity and anger and negativity. In contrast to the depressives, who appeared more introspective, the bulimics presented as "underincorporative," meaning that they often failed to attend to important information in their environment.

Findings consistent with those of Weisberg et al. (1987), also using Comprehensive System (Exner, 1986) variables, have been reported by Parmer (1991) and Smith et al. (1991). Parmer compared the Rorschachs of 13 bulimic, female undergraduate students with a matched group of female undergraduate students who were nonbulimic. The bulimics offered a significantly higher percent of unusual/minus human-movement responses, indicating serious cognitive slippage and poor perceptual accuracy.

Smith et al. (1991) employed the Rorschach to distinguish between purging and nonpurging bulimics and controls. Comprehensive System scores failed to distinguish between the two bulimia groups. However, when the bulimia groups were combined and compared with the controls, the bulimics revealed perceptual inaccuracies, disturbed thinking, a vulnerability to interpersonal problems, a sense of self as damaged, and a pessimistic outlook.

In contrast with the above studies, which have either been impressionistic and anecdotal or associated with conventional Rorschach scores, the group of studies reviewed in the following paragraphs all employed conceptually based scoring systems. As in the previous chapter, these studies are discussed under the general headings of reality testing, thought disorder, boundary disturbances, defense, and object relations.

Reality Testing

To assess level of reality testing, each of the studies reviewed here employed the form-level scoring manual developed by Mayman (1970). Based on the earlier work of Rapaport, Mayman's system consists of seven distinct and graded scores that range from "reality adherence" at one extreme to "reality abrogation" at the other extreme. Numerical values have been assigned to each of the form-level ratings by Holt (1977).

Van-Der Keshet (1988) applied the scoring system to the Rorschach records of groups of anoretic ballet students, nonanoretic ballet students, restricting anorexics, bulimic anoretics, and normal controls. In accord with her predictions, the author found that the nonanoretic ballet students and the controls attained a significantly higher level of reality testing than the anoretic ballet students. No differences were found between the restrictive anorexics, the bulimic anorexics, and the anoretic ballet students. The nonanoretic ballet students and the controls demonstrated a significantly higher level of reality testing than the restrictive anorexics and the bulimic anorexics. The author noted that although the three eating-disorder groups manifested a lower level of reality testing, their perception of reality was still accurate.

In a study involving not only patients with eating disorders, but their mothers as well, Brouillette (1987) compared form-level ratings of groups of restricting anorexics, bulimic anorexics, normal controls, and, for all three groups, their mothers. The author reported several interesting findings. First, in all three groups, no significant differences were found between the daughters and mothers (generation factor) regarding level of reality testing. Second, the normal controls and their mothers, both separately and paired together, achieved significantly higher levels of reality testing than did either group of eating-disorder patients and their mothers. Third, no significant differences were reported between the restricting anorexics and the bulimic anorexics, nor between their mothers. As with Van-Der Keshet's (1988) findings, a closer review of Brouillette's results indicates that although the eating-disorder patients and their mothers attained lower reality testing ratings, their perception of reality could be characterized as accurate.

Finally, Piran (1988) compared the form-level ratings of a group of restricting anoretic patients with those of a group of bulimic patients. Although no significant differences between the groups were reported, there was a tendency for the bulimic patients to display a lower level of reality testing.

In summary, when compared with normal controls, eating-disorder patients have been found to present a lower level of reality testing, yet in each instance their reality testing overall has been judged as adequate. Nonetheless, it should be noted that in each of these studies, numerical values have been assigned to each of the form-level ratings, means have been calculated, and then the means have been compared. Theory and clinical experience suggest that the reality testing of eating-disorder patients, especially bulimics, is highly variable. Therefore, in future research it would be important to focus on the range of form-level ratings.

Thought Disorder

In a study referred to earlier, Small and associates (1982) compared the Rorschach protocols of a group of anorexics with those of a comparable group of schizophrenics on an index of thought disorder (Delta Index) developed by Watkins and Stauffacher (1952). Interestingly, no significant differences were found between the two groups, and the mean scores for both groups fell into what Watkins and Stauffacher refer to as the "pathological range."

Piran (1988) reported comparable results: restricting and bulimic anorexics did not differ from each other regarding the degree of thought disorder, but both groups scored within the pathological range. Analyzing specific measures, Piran also reported that whereas bulimics offered a greater number of fabulized combinations, the restricting anorexics produced more overelaborate symbolism responses.

Although both studies reported Delta Indexes that fall within the pathological range of thought disorder, the results are difficult to interpret because of the nature of the Delta Index. In earlier chapters it was noted that Watkins and Stauffacher (1952) assigned weights to various types of disordered thinking on the assumption that thought disorder was a unitary dimension. But, as noted, that assumption may be in error. What is called for are studies, like Piran's (1988), that examine qualitative aspects of disturbed thinking in separate samples of restrictive and bulimic anorexics and that also include a control group in the experimental design.

Boundary Disturbance

Strober and Goldenberg (1981) examined boundary disturbances in a group of anoretic patients and in a group of depressed patients. To assess the concept of boundary disturbance five indices were used, including affect elaboration, overspecificity, incongruous-fabulized combinations, barrier, and penetration. As predicted, the researchers reported that the anoretic group experienced a greater loss of internal-external boundaries and more difficulties with conceptual boundaries than did the depressed group.

Kaufer and Katz (1983) also found evidence of serious self-other and reality-fantasy boundary disturbances in a group of anoretic women as compared to a matched control group of normal women. The breakthrough of primary process material was taken as an indication of severe disruption in the boundary between reality and unconscious processes (i.e., the repressive barrier).

Other studies employed a scale for assessing boundary disturbances devised by Blatt and Ritzler (1974). As discussed in the previous chapter, these authors selected three of Rapaport's indices of thought disorder (contamination, confabulation, fabulized combination) and reconceptualized the scores as indicating various levels of severity of boundary disturbances.

Sugarman, Quinlan, and Devenis (1982) applied the Boundary Disturbance Scale to the Rorschach protocols of 12 anoretic patients and 12 normal controls. The anoretic patients produced significantly more contamination responses, which the authors interpreted as indicating disturbances in maintaining the boundary between self and other.

Van-Der Keshet (1988) also found significant boundary disturbances among eating-disorder patients and anoretic ballet students, though the level of disturbance noted was less severe than that previously reported by Sugarman and associates (1982). Van-Der Keshet reported no main effect for the contamination test index. By contrast, major effects were obtained for both the confabulatory and fabulized combination responses. With respect to the confabulation response she found the following: anoretic ballet students produced significantly more confabulatory responses than the nonanoretic ballet students and the controls; no differences were found between the anoretic ballet students, the restricting anorexics, and the bulimic anorexics; and bulimic anorexics offered significantly more confabulations than the restricting anorexics. With regard to the fabulized combination score, the bulimic anorexics produced more of these responses than any of the other groups. Finally, using an overall summary boundary disturbance score, Van-Der Keshet found that the anoretic ballet students and the bulimic anorexics demonstrated a significantly higher level of impairment in maintaining boundaries compared to the other groups, but did not differ from each other. In summary, Van-Der Keshet's results indicate that there are important differences in level of boundary disturbance between restricting and bulimic anorexics and that with bulimic anorexics and anoretic ballet students the boundary implicated is that between inner and outer (fantasy and reality).

Boundary disturbances in eating-disorder patients and their mothers have been studied by Brouillette (1987). No significant differences were found between restricting anorexics and bulimic anorexics nor between their mothers; however, when both patient groups were combined and both mother groups were combined, these joint groups revealed significantly greater boundary impairment than did a group of normal controls and their mothers. Further, no significant differences were noted between daughters and mothers in any of the three groups. Because Brouillette used a summary score, the specific level of boundary disturbance was not determined.

In summary, consistent findings from several studies indicate that individuals with eating disorders manifest significant boundary disturbances. Although the particular level of boundary disturbance involved appears to be sample specific, in general the findings suggest that the impairment includes the developmentally earlier and more fundamental boundaries of self-other and reality-fantasy. It is unclear whether there are differences in severity in boundary disturbances between subtypes of eating-disorder patients though there is some suggestion that bulimic patients exhibit more severe impairments.

Defense

Because applications of the Lerner Defense Scale for assessing primitive defenses were reviewed in chapter 18, the following paragraphs are only a summary of those findings related to eating-disorder subjects. Van-Der Keshet (1988), in general, found similarities in defensive patterning among restricting anoretic patients, bulimic anoretic patients, and anoretic ballet students and found differences from normal controls and nonanoretic ballet students. Both clinical anoretic groups and the anoretic ballet students used splitting and devaluation significantly more often than the control group, and the restricting anorexics were further distinguishable by their frequent use of denial.

Brouillette (1987) found that splitting, low-level devaluation, projective identification, and low-level denial occurred with significantly greater frequency in the protocols of restricting anoretic patients and their mothers and of bulimic patients and their mothers than in the records of normal controls and their mothers.

Piran and Lerner (1988) compared the defensive structure of restricting anorexics with that of bulimic anorexics. Consistent with the respective nature of their presenting symptoms, the bulimic anorexics tended to use projective identification and low-level devaluation whereas restricting anorexics, by contrast, relied on denial and high-level idealization.

The overall findings from these studies indicate that eating disorder patients tend to use more primitive defenses. Test measures of splitting, low-level devaluation, and projective identification consistently distinguish these patients from controls. There is also evidence to suggest that while both restricting anorexics and bulimic anorexics utilize primitive defenses, the specific defenses they use are somewhat different and are consistent with their symptomatology.

Object Relations

Attempts to study the object relations of eating-disorder patients have typically involved an application of Blatt and associates' (1976) scale for assessing the concept of the object to the subjects' Rorschach records.

On the basis of a comparison of the Rorschach protocols of a group of 12 anoretic patients and 12 controls, Sugarman, Quinlan, and Devenis (1982) reported that the anoretic patients did not differ significantly from the controls in level of object representation.

Brouillette (1987), in contrast, found that the level of object representation in a group of restricting anorexics and their mothers and in a group of bulimics and their mothers was significantly lower than that of a control group consisting of nonpatients and their mothers. No significant differences were found between mothers and daughters in any of the three groups, between restricting anorexics and bulimic anorexics, or between mothers.

Piran (1988) investigated and found significant differences in object representations between restricting and bulimic anorexics. Whereas the two groups did not differ on the scale dimensions of differentiation and articulation, significant differences were obtained on the frequency of action responses and the content of the action. The bulimics not only incorporated action in their responses significantly more often than did the restrictors, but in addition, the action incorporated was of a malevolent nature. Intrigued by this finding, Piran looked at the quality of malevolent action more closely. Subdividing the malevolent content into sadistic ("attack"), masochistic ("victim"), and sadistic-masochistic categories, she found that sadistic responses appeared exclusively among the bulimics.

In general, findings regarding impairment in level of object representation among eating-disorder patients are inconclusive and somewhat inconsistent; however, it should be noted that there is a paucity of research in this area and that the studies that are available have all used the same scale (Blatt et al.'s [1976] Concept of the Object Scale). Of particular interest is Piran's finding that malevolence is more characteristic of the interaction of bulimic patients than of restricting anoretic patients. This specific result is consistent with findings from the studies of defense in which several investigators noted that the bulimic patients employed primitive devaluation significantly more often than did the restrictive anorexics. The combined findings suggest that bulimic patients, as compared with the restricting anorexics, are actively involved in a struggle with internal "bad objects." From the perspective of internal object relations, the bulimics are quite similar to the inpatient borderlines described by H. Lerner and St. Peter (1984), whereas the restrictive anorexics are closer to the outpatient borderlines (see chapter 22).

Development

Two developmental object relations scales have been applied to the Rorschach records of eating-disorder patients. Van-Der Keshet (1991) and Parmer (1988) each used Coonerty's (1986) scale (refer to chapter 20) to assess separation-individuation themes, and Piran (1988) employed Kwawer's (1980) measure to investigate primitiveness of interpersonal relations.

Van-Der Keshet (1988), in her often-mentioned study, reported several important findings regarding the prevalence of separation-individuation themes in the following five groups: restrictive anorexics, bulimic anorexics, anoretic ballet students, nonanoretic ballet students, and normal controls. First, the bulimic patients produced significantly more responses involving the theme of engulfment than did any of the other groups. Second, the mirror response, regarded as an index of narcissism, was observed significantly more often in the records of the anoretic ballet students than in any of the other groups. Finally, the normal controls obtained a significantly lower mean score than any of the other four groups on the rapprochement measure, indicating that they alone had achieved a level of nonconflicted autonomy.

Parmer (1991), in his study of 13 bulimics, found that the bulimics, as compared with a control group, gave significantly more responses indicative of developmentally primitive ideations. Specifically, the bulimics gave more differentiation subphase responses involving themes of merging, engulfment, and hatching.

Using Kwawer's (1980) scale, Piran (1988) also found themes of engulfment particularly prominent in the responses of bulimic patients. Piran compared the Rorschach records of a group of bulimia patients with a group of restricting anoretic patients with respect to primitive interpersonal themes. She noted that the percentage of protocols with responses displaying primitive themes was significantly higher in the bulimic group.

In summary, in an attempt to determine if eating-disorder patients are organized at a borderline level, several investigators have extended scales initially developed to assess borderline phenomena to the Rorschach records of these patients. In general, the findings do indicate that eating-disorder patients are organized at a borderline level, if one uses Kernberg's (1975) concept and criteria of borderline; this conclusion, however, should be regarded cautiously. It is important to recognize that the term *borderline* constitutes a diagnosis and that the various studies reported here involve levels of personality functioning and development that are defined by different criteria. To be sure, eating-disorder patients have been found to manifest low reality testing, impaired thinking, serious boundary disturbances, primitive defenses, and unresolved conflicts regarding separation-individuation; but, as with the borderline concept generally, it is quite possible that eating-disorder patients too may be viewed from the perspective of a spectrum. Finally, whereas earlier studies regarded anorexia as a homogeneous entity, more recent investigations have subdivided anoretic patients according to presenting symptoms (restrictive versus bulimic) and have found important differences between these subgroups.

♦ ♦ ♦ Gender Identity Disturbances

A second group of patients assumed to have a borderline personality organization that has been studied with the Rorschach test are those individuals who present gender-identity disturbances. The specific groups investigated have included extremely feminine boys and male transsexuals.

Having observed the chaotic regressions in psychotherapy and the caricatured feminine behavior and mannerisms of extremely feminine boys, Tuber and Coates (1989) examined the self and object representations of a group of 14 such subjects. All were between the ages of 5 and 12 years, were of at least average intelligence, and had met the DSM-III criteria for gender-identity disorder of childhood. Normative Rorschach data published by Ames et al. (1974) were used for comparative purposes. Results of the investigation revealed several significant findings, especially those related to the representation of human figures. While the percentage of whole human responses given by the gender disorder boys was approximately equal to that of the normative sample of Ames et al. (1974), their records contained eight times as many quasi-human responses (H). The quasi-human responses often took the form of monstrous, aggressive creatures. Moreover, the content of the fully human responses was significantly different from the content of the quasi-human responses. Subdividing the content of all responses into the categories benevolent, neutral, and malevolent, the authors found that fully human responses were equally represented in the benevolent and malevolent categories. By contrast, more than 80% of the quasi-human responses involved malevolent content, such as creatures and monsters imbued with menacing or threatening intent or action.

Impairment in self and object representations was further manifested in the fluidity and fusion that characterized many of these youngsters' responses. On the basis of Blatt and Ritzler's (1974) concept of a hierarchy of "boundary disturbances" to categorize and conceptualize the fluid and fused percepts, 18 instances of contamination and fabulized combination responses were found. Responses in which the overelaboration of affect signaled a disturbance in the boundary between reality and fantasy were also observed with significant frequency. Quite startling and significant was the finding that each of the 14 subjects produced at least one response of either the fused or overelaborated type.

Paralleling the behavioral phenomenology of these boys, the study also revealed overt gender confusion and stereotypical feminine responses. Caricatured female representations, elaborate depiction of stereotypical female objects (e.g., jewelry), and female clothing were the types of responses frequently found in the records of this group. Gender confusion was evident in responses in which the gender of a percept was changed during the response from one sex to another and in responses in which male and female body parts were arbitrarily combined into a single response.

Mindful of the core role of separation anxiety in the dynamic life of these children, Coates and Tuber (1988) examined the concept of autonomy of self in a second study. They applied a modified version of Urist's (1977) Mutuality of Autonomy Scale to the Rorschach records of the original sample of 14 feminine boys. Like Urist's original scale, the modified version consists of seven points along a progressive continuum, including mutual, reciprocal, empathic, malevolent, overwhelming, engulfing, and destructive relatedness.

Strong evidence of the disturbed quality of these youngsters' object relations and object representations was obtained. Of the 14 subjects, 12 had at least one response in the seriously disturbed range—that is, a range characterized by an experience of the object as controlling or dominating at best, and as parasitic-attacking or engulfing at worst. Seven of the boys' records had at lest one response in which one figure was actively destroying another. The remaining five included at least one response in which domination or control of one figure by the other was paramount.

The nature of the data also permitted the investigators to examine the notion of the idealization of the maternal figure, a dynamic frequently associated with gender dysphoric males. To do this, responses indicative of benign, reciprocal relatedness were reviewed. Eleven such responses were identified. Of these, nine involved women, whereas the other two involved animals of an unspecified sex. Thus, interactive depictions of benign relatedness were associated virtually exclusively with female representations. By contrast, an inspection of the responses involving malevolent content or parasitic interaction was noteworthy for the glaring absence of female representations. The authors (Coates and Tuber, 1988) concluded from this analysis:

> This haven of positive female reciprocity is further safeguarded by their ability to avoid seeing women in responses characterized by malevolence or destruction. Instead, malevolence is ascribed to

more regressed quasi-human male figures, thereby preserving the maternal figure [p. 654].

Ipp (1986) also studied the quality of object relations and object representations of extremely feminine boys and of their siblings as well. Using somewhat more rigorous methodology, she reported findings strikingly similar to those of Tuber and Coates (1989). Ipp's subjects, all age 5 to 12 years, included 37 feminine boys diagnosed as having cross-gender disturbance, 19 siblings with no history of cross-gender behavior, and 23 normal controls. Rorschach records were obtained from all subjects and scored for level of object representation (Blatt et al., 1976), severity of boundary disturbance (Blatt and Ritzler, 1974), and developmental level of object relations (Ipp, 1986). Results from the Scale of Blatt and associates (1976) indicated that the feminine boys and their siblings, as compared with the normal controls, achieved less differentiated, articulated, and integrated responses and produced significantly more inaccurately perceived fully human responses and significantly more quasi-human responses, both accurate and inaccurate. Furthermore, while the controls had significantly more benevolent interaction in their human responses than did the feminine boys, the siblings displayed greater malevolence in their responses than did the feminine boys.

In further support of the findings of Tuber and Coates (1989), Ipp (1986) also found serious boundary disturbances in the records of the feminine boys. Whereas the feminine boys differed from the controls on all three levels of boundary disturbances, the differences were especially prominent on the more severe levels of self-other and fantasy-reality. At these more severe levels, the feminine boys also produced significantly more responses than did their siblings.

Ipp's (1986) Developmental Object Relations Scale differs in emphasis from Urist's (1977) Mutuality of Autonomy Scale. Although both focus on more primitive modes of relating, Urist's scale highlights the nature of interaction whereas Ipp's scale categorizes responses into developmental stages based on Mahler's theory of separation-individuation. Two points on Ipp's scale significantly distinguished the groups. The controls offered significantly more responses referable to the autonomy stage than did either the feminine boys or the siblings. By contrast, both the feminine boys and their siblings had significantly more responses scored at the differentiation/practicing stage than did the controls. Cutting across all categories in the Ipp scale is a benevolence-malevolence dimension. On this measure the feminine boys offered significantly more malevolent content than the controls.

Using several conceptually based scales and several scores devised by Exner (1974), Murray (1985) investigated borderline manifestations in the Rorschach records of male transsexuals. The sample consisted of a group of 25 male transsexuals, a group of 25 male borderlines, and a control group of 25 male college students. Rorschach protocols were obtained from all subjects and scored for intensity of aggression (Holt's defense demand score), quality of object relations (Mutuality of Autonomy Scale), level of reality testing (Exner's x+ percentage), and degree of self-object differentiation (Exner's special scores). Highly significant results were reported. Compared to the normal controls, both the transsexuals and the borderlines displayed significantly more intense levels of aggression, highly impaired object relations, poorer reality testing, and greater boundary disturbances. Further, the transsexuals and the borderlines did not differ significantly on any of these variables. A measure of egocentricity failed to distinguish the three groups.

Collectively, the results of all four studies strongly suggest that males, both adults and children, manifesting gender dysphoric behavior and attitudes present a borderline personality organization. Their self and object representations are impaired; they present severe boundary disturbances; their object relations are on a more primitive level; they have not successfully negotiated all the phases of separation-individuation; and they struggle with aggression and malevolent objects. The studies of Coates and Tuber (1988) and Ipp (1986) indicate that conceptually based Rorschach scales designed for adults, either directly or with modifications, can be extended to the protocols of children. Further, the work of Coates and Tuber (1988) illustrates how clinical observations can be translated into Rorschach-related terms and then evaluated using quantifiable measures.

♦ ♦ ♦ Antisocial Personality

More recently, investigators have been extending conceptually based scales to the Rorschach records of a third group of individuals assumed to have a borderline personality organization: the antisocial personality. Authors of the DSM II–IV series subscribe to the notion that to describe the behavior of these individuals is sufficient. I agree with Gacono and Meloy (1994) that this, indeed, is not the case, and what is required is a conceptual model that can provide a clinical understanding of the disorder. Gacono and Meloy put it this way: "A search for clinical knowledge leads to questions of motivation and meaning, prompting further inquiry into the thought organization, affective life, defensive operations, impulses, and object relations of psychopaths and other aggressive individuals" (p. 3).

Psychoanalytic theorists (Kernberg, 1977; Rinsley, 1979) have recognized the antisocial (including psychopathic) individual's inability to tolerate boredom, anxiety, or frustration, lack of empathy, chronically impaired object relations, absence of subliminatory channels, and typical manner of regulating self-esteem. It is these characteristics that have led theorists to view the antisocial personality as a more pathological variant of narcissistic disorder organized at a borderline level of personality functioning (Kernberg, 1976; 1977).

Viewing the antisocial individual through this psychoanalytic lens—as a form of pathological narcissism organized at a borderline level—Gacono and Meloy (1994) present an extraordinary, comprehensive, and in-depth account of the personality structure and functioning of these difficult individuals. Culminating a decade of programmed clinical research, the authors use the Rorschach to chart the internal life of these individuals, and of the lives of select children and adolescents who are at risk for the later development of an antisocial orientation.

Their approach to the Rorschach involves an attempt to integrate psychoanalytic theory and methodology with Exner's (1986a) more empirical Comprehensive System. With respect to psychoanalytic methodology, Urist's (1977) Mutuality of Autonomy Scale, Kwawer's (1980) measure for assessing primitive modes of object relations, the Lerner Defense Scale (P. Lerner and H. Lerner, 1980), and Cooper and Arnow's (1986) Defense Scale were applied to various antisocial groups, ranging from conduct-disordered children to highly psychopathic antisocial males. Findings involving these measures have been reported elsewhere in this book (note chapter 18 and chapter 20). In general, the combined results indicate that antisocial individuals relate themselves to others in pathological ways and employ primitive defenses centered around splitting and devaluation. The authors also found that Kernberg's (1976) notion of levels of personality organization proved a useful model for conceptualizing these individuals. Conceiving of these individuals as organized at a borderline level enables one to go beyond their actions and begin to understand them both structurally and dynamically.

✦ ✦ ✦   Sexually Abused Females

Because of the relationship that has been drawn between childhood sexual abuse and borderline personality disorder (Arnold and Saunders, 1989; Barnard and Hirsch, 1985; Goodwin, Cheeves, and Connell, 1990), a fourth group I have included in this section is that of females who experienced childhood sexual abuse. A growing body of research indicates that there are multiple and significant effects on personality of child sexual abuse, most of these studies, however, have been anecdotal (Shengold, 1989) or have relied on self-report measures (Cohen and Mannarino, 1988; Tong, Oakes, and McDowell, 1987; Tufts New England Medical Center, 1984). In the Rorschach literature, there are only two studies that have used conceptually-based measures to investigate the effects of childhood sexual abuse.

Leifer et al. (1991) compared a group of 79 black females between the ages of 5 and 16, all of whom had a documented history of sexual abuse, with a comparison group of nonabused girls. In addition to Exner's (1986a) Comprehensive System, all Rorschachs were scored using the Mutuality of Autonomy Scale (Urist, 1977), the Barrier and Penetration Scales (Fisher and Cleveland, 1968), and Elizur's (1949) Rorschach Content Test Scale. The sexually abused girls were found to show greater disturbances in ego functioning, to experience greater distress, to describe human relationships as more primitive and hostile, and to reveal more preoccupation with sexuality than the comparison group.

In a study referred to in chapter 19, Saunders (1991) compared a group of female borderline patients with a history of extended sexual victimization with a group of female borderline patients who had not been sexually victimized. All subjects were between the ages of 21 and 60 years. All Rorschach protocols were scored using the system of Rapaport et al. (1945–1946) as well as Holt's (1977) aggression score and Wilson's (1985) refinement of several deviant verbalization scores from Rapaport et al. The patients with histories of sexual abuse revealed significantly more primary-process breakthroughs of thoughts connected with sexual and aggressive content and of confabulatory thinking.

Conclusion

In this chapter I have reviewed a host of studies that have applied conceptually based Rorschach scoring systems to the protocols of clinical populations assumed to have a borderline personality organization. The groups investigated have included eating-disorder individuals, gender-dysphoric children and adults, antisocial offenders, and sexually abused females. In several studies, eating-disorder patients were found to manifest poor reality testing, impaired thinking, serious boundary disturbances, lower level defenses, and a failure to separate and attain full autonomy. Differences have been reported between eating-disorder patients subdivided into restricting and bulimic groups. The differences noted in defensive patterning, quality of object relations, and dealing with malevolent objects roughly parallel those observed between hospitalized and outpatient borderline patients (H. Lerner and St. Peter, 1984). As such, the eating-disorder patient, like the borderline patient, may be most profitably viewed as being represented on a spectrum or continuum.

Evidence regarding borderline-level processes in gender dysphoric adults and children is compelling. Both groups across several studies manifested impaired self and object representations, severe boundary disturbances, lower level object relations, and significant difficulties in separating and individuating. Gender differences have provided an especially useful arena for displaying the Rorschach test's efficacy in highlighting the interplay between aberrant behavior and underlying dynamics.

Using several psychoanalytically based, innovative Rorschach scales, across several different populations, Gacono and Mcloy (1994) have demonstrated that antisocial individuals engage in primitive modes of object relating and employ primitive defenses, especially splitting and devaluation. Their research indicates that narcissistic and borderline processes interface with the antisocial personality. In two studies involving young girls and adult women who have been sexually abused, it has been shown that victimized females have impaired ego functioning, are more vulnerable to primary-process breakthroughs, and see relationships as more hostile.

24

RORSCHACH MEASURES
OF NARCISSISM AND THE
NARCISSISTIC PATIENT

With the emergence of new models of personality development in psychoanalysis have come new formulations regarding the nature and genesis of psychopathology. Whereas earlier formulations emphasized the role of conflict between relatively well-developed structures in giving rise to symptom formation, more recent formulations stress the pathology of the structures themselves, understanding them as a consequence of incomplete or arrested development.

A foremost example of psychopathology based on impaired structure formation is the narcissistic disturbances. The theoretical and clinical literatures abound with discussions of narcissism; however, it has only been in the last decade that the concept has found its way into the research literature. In this chapter I review the concept of narcissism, report descriptions of the narcissistic patient advanced by Kernberg (1975) and Kohut (1971, 1977), describe attempts to use the Rorschach test to assess the narcissistic patient for clinical purposes, and finally, review the growing Rorschach research on this topic.

◆ ◆ ◆   Concept of Narcissism

With his publication of the paper "On Narcissism," Freud (1914) laid the conceptual groundwork from which all subsequent theoretical developments of the concept have arisen. In that paper he defined secondary narcissism as a withdrawal of libido from the external world with a redirection of the libido onto the ego, designated the ego ideal as the "heir" or adult version of infantile narcissism, recognized the intimate relationship between self-esteem and narcissistic libido, and observed that a particular type of object choice and object relation was referred to as "narcissistic" on the basis of the quality of need for the object and the psychic function served by the object.

Authors subsequent to Freud have replaced the term "ego" with that of "self," have redefined narcissism as the "libidinal investment of the self" (Hartmann, 1950), and have extended the concept of self along several lines by (1) redefining it as part of the structure ego, understood to mean the conscious, preconscious, and unconscious representations of the total person; (2) elaborating the role of internalization in the structuring of self-representations; (3) elaborating the processes by which self and object representations become differentiated and then internalized as stable, enduring, internal structures; and (4) distinguishing between self as structure and self as experience (Teicholtz, 1978).

◆ ◆ ◆   The Narcissistic Patient

Despite major advances in our understanding of and capacity to treat narcissistic patients, the field, historically and presently, has been beset by a lack of agreement as to what constitutes a "narcissistic patient." Two major, but quite different, clinical descriptions have emerged.

Kernberg (1975), from a more structural perspective, reserved the designation for those patients "in whom the main problem appears to be the disturbance of their self-regard in connection with specific disturbances in their object relations" (p. 227). Maintaining that most narcissistic patients are a subvariant of the borderline level of personality organization, he describes these patients as manifesting a heightened degree of self-absorption, an inordinate need to be loved and admired, and an overinflated sense of themselves amid a desperate desire for adoration. He further suggests that their emotional life is shallow, they exhibit little genuine empathy for the motives and feelings of others, and they feel restless and bored unless their self-regard is being nourished. Potential providers of narcissistic supplies are idealized, whereas those from whom these patients expect little are depreciated and treated with contempt. Beneath a veneer of warmth and charm, in Kernberg's view, such persons are cold, arrogant, ruthless, and exploitive. From this perspective, the psychopath or sociopath would be considered a subtype of narcissistic disorder.

Kohut (1971) too provided a comprehensive clinical description of the narcissistic patient, but he viewed these disturbances from a different perspective (self psychology) and characterized the narcissistic patient quite differently from Kernberg. He did not conceive of the narcissistic patient as organized at a borderline level, but rather, placed the disturbance closer to the neurotic end of the psychopathological continuum.

Kohut identified a specific symptom complex (i.e., lack of enthusiasm and zest, perverse activity, subjective feelings of deadness) as characteristic of the narcissistic patient; however, he saw such a cluster of symptoms as diagnostically insufficient. Instead, he evoked the concept of the "cohesive self" and suggested that it is the instability or propensity for regression of this structure that constitutes the critical diagnostic sign of a narcissistic personality. Kohut also identified and described a set of atypical transference patterns that characterize the narcissistic patient and unfold in treatment. Referred to overall as self-object transferences, specific subtypes include the mirroring transference and the idealizing transference. Although Kohut was less definitive in his description of the narcissistic patient than Kernberg is, from his case descriptions one distills a picture of a group of people who are excessively self-conscious and self-preoccupied, who experience continuous feelings of vulnerability, who defend against lowered feelings of self-esteem with grandiosity, and who experience a particular type of depressive affect involving feeling of depletion, emptiness, and nonexistence.

✦ ✦ ✦ The Narcissistic Patient and the Rorschach Test: Clinical Contributions

The conceptual and clinical contributions of Kernberg (1975) and Kohut (1971) have been extended to the Rorschach by H. Lerner

(1988) and Arnow and Cooper (1988). Both applications are extensive and comprehensive, and although each is geared toward clinical assessment, rich formulations are provided in each and could conceivably furnish a basis for more empirical study.

On the basis of Kernberg's (1975) structural analysis, H. Lerner (1988) intensively reviewed the test records of 10 patients, all of whom met DSM-III criteria for narcissistic personality disorder. The five females and five males comprising the sample were all single, from middle-class or upper-middle-class families, and ranged in age from 16 to 26 years.

Lerner suggests that in assessing narcissistic patients the test features to be looked for include:

> A social facade characterized by egocentricity and self-references; an extreme personalizing of experience and discourse coupled with an almost rigid tendency to avoid anxiety and anxiety-arousing situations; and a solicitation of the examiner's affection, assistance, and admiration, often juxtaposed with subtle and not so subtle devaluations of the test and the examiner. Representations of the grandiose self, of its constituent elements (a "shadowy" real self, an ideal self, and an ideal other), and of what this structure masks—intense narcissistic rage and a deep conviction of unworthiness and frightening images of barrenness, emptiness, and void—can be discerned on the Rorschach. Further, test representations of borderline defenses, boundary disturbances, and a preponderance of malevolent objects are frequently exhibited by these patients [p. 264].

Using formal scores, thematic content, and test behavior, Lerner outlines Rorschach indices of these features under the broad headings of specific and nonspecific manifestations of ego weakness, affect organization, pathology of internal object relations, defensive structure, and treatment considerations.

Kohut's (1971, 1977) formulations have been applied to the Rorschach testing situation by Arnow and Cooper (1988). Viewing the testing experience as a context for the expression of primary needs for selfobjects as well as for the arousal of feelings when such needs are not met, these authors suggest that test responses can be thought of as containing three referents or interpretive dimensions: the state of the self, the role of archaic selfobjects, and anticipations regarding new objects.

Arnow and Cooper also describe Rorschach indices associated with certain syndromes of self-pathology initially identified by Kohut and Wolf (1978). The specific syndromes include the understimulated self, the overstimulated self, the fragmented self, and the overburdened self.

The person with an understimulated self craves stimulation in order to ward off feelings of inner deadness associated with an unresponsive selfobject. One sees in such persons either massive attempts to seek stimulation or the empty depression that lies beneath the frantic search. According to Arnow and Cooper (1988), either the search or the underlying depression may be expressed on the Rorschach test. The sought-for stimulation becomes manifest in imagery depicting a high level of sensory input, such as "the Mardi Gras," "colorful sea scene," and "a brilliantly colored galaxy." By contrast, the empty depression that appears when the search fails is evident in themes of barrenness, deadness, and desolation.

The overstimulated self arises from repeated experiences in which the self is required to serve as a selfobject for others. The self, in these instances, feels drawn into the role of maintaining the delicate and precarious narcissistic balance of its selfobjects. Such people typically feel that their selfobjects have selectively responded to their own self's exhibitionistic behavior, emphasizing accomplishments and achievements in isolation from the broader self. Accordingly, Arnow and Cooper suggest that those with an overstimulated self provide Rorschach records in which themes of performance and accomplishment pervade. Not only are themes of performance expressed directly in responses (e.g., "dancing bears"), in addition, ordinary percepts are elevated to special productions through elaborate embellishments. The fantastic creations, for these individuals, are not in the service of self-enhancement; rather, they derive from a need to comply with the imagined expectations of the other.

The fragmented or fragmenting self represents a form of narcissistic disequilibrium consequent to the failure of selfobjects to provide integrating responses. Historically, the selfobject has not responded to the whole self but rather to selected parts of the self that satisfy the needs of the selfobject. For Arnow and Cooper, patients with fears of fragmenting offer Rorschach percepts in which there is concern about the integrity of objects or preoccupations reflecting hypochondriacal worries. These authors further suggest that the experience of a fragmented self may also be expressed in images that are broken or falling apart, such as "a broken glass" or "an exploding bug with parts all scattered."

The overburdened self results from a failure to merge with an omnipotent, soothing selfobject. The early experience of turning to a selfobject for calming typically failed and resulted instead in the intensification of dysphoric affect. As a consequence of the empathic failure, the self does not develop the capacity to soothe itself or protect itself from being traumatized by the spreading of emotions, especially the spreading of anxiety. The object relations of these persons vividly reflect the danger of exposing the self to interactions that threaten its capacity to modulate affects. The ever-present fear of losing emotional control colors the overburdened self's perception of involvement and underlies the characteristic aloofness and preoccupation with control. Rorschach percepts offered by these individuals directly express their apprehension regarding emotional control. For example, on Card IX a patient offered the following response: "A volcano but it's covered with snow so the lava never erupts."

In addition to the broad overviews provided by H. Lerner (1988) and Arnow and Cooper (1988), other authors too (see H. Lerner and P. Lerner, 1988) have identified Rorschach indices for assessing specific aspects of narcissistic pathology. These more specific features include the narcissistic patient's excessive self-absorption, the role of omnipotence, the particular quality of depressive affect, and the mode of object relating.

Self–absorption

Exner (1974) developed an index for assessing egocentricity. Consisting of the proportion of reflection and pair responses to the total number of Rorschach responses, the index was found to relate to intense self-focusing and disturbances in self-esteem (Exner, Wylie, and Bryant, 1974).

H. Lerner (1988) and Arnow and Cooper (1988) also considered mirror and reflection responses as indicative of excessive self-involvement, but they placed this observation in a broader and more object-relational context. Accordingly, while such responses convey self-absorption, they also indicate a need to be mirrored and confirmed. In describing a patient, H. Lerner (1988) put it this way: "Her frequent perception of mirror images on the Rorschach speak quite graphically to . . . her reliance upon the reflection of herself in others in order to know herself (p. 288).

Omnipotence

A second major feature characteristic of the narcissistic patient involves feelings of omnipotence. These patients not only present an overinflated view of themselves (grandiose self) but also cling to omnipotence for defensive purposes, including the maintenance of ego integration. Rorschach expressions of omnipotence have been developed by H. Lerner (1988), P. Lerner (1988), and Arnow and Cooper (1988). Each has noted narcissistic patients' compelling need to be treated as special, their craving for admiration, and their irritating sense of entitlement, as well as the ways in which these factors eventuate in the patients' ongoing assaults on the structure of the testing procedure. For such patients, test responses have a particular purpose. They are not offered with the intent of conveying meaning or of sharing an experience, but rather are given with the desire to impress the examiner and to create a product that they believe will bring confirmation of their overinflated sense of self. Finally, populating the protocols of patients with omnipotence are an abundance of self-aggrandizing percepts, such as kings, goddesses, temples, insignias, crests, and crowns.

Depression

Despite questions regarding the capacity of narcissistic patients to experience genuine feelings of loss for others, there is agreement that the depressive affect they do experience has a distinctive and distinguishing quality. Referred to by Kohut (1977) as "depletion depression," this affect is characterized by unbearable feelings of emptiness, deadness, and nonexistence and reflects a self-perception of weakness, helplessness, and vulnerability.

H. Lerner (1988) has pointed to the role of narcissistic injury as a major source of depressive affect for these patients and has suggested that Rorschach imagery reflective of damage or flaw may be taken as an expression of such injury. For example, such content as "a butterfly with damaged wings," "an alligator coming out of the mud," and a "tired, wet moth" can be interpreted as reflective of a sense of self as damaged, exploited, or victimized.

P. Lerner (1988) developed Rorschach indices reflective of emptiness. Defining emptiness as a sense of deadness together with an inner impoverishment of feelings, fantasies, and wishes, he found that patients experiencing emptiness provide enfeebled records in which there is a sparseness of responses and in which few dimensions other than forms are used. Their responses, in general, tend to be muted and drab, lack in vitality, and make little impact upon the examiner. Their attunement to white areas is thought to reflect a sensitivity to themes of hollowness. The empty patient, according to Lerner, is reality bound, yet the contents perceived typically convey themes of emptiness and deadness. Thus, abundant through their records are such percepts as skeletons, deserts, faceless creatures, and dead trees.

Mode of Object Relating

A fourth dimension involves Rorschach manifestations of the narcissistic patient's mode of object relating. As noted previously, Freud (1914) distinguished between a true object relation and a narcissistic object relation, suggesting that in the latter the object is not regarded as separate and distinct but is seen rather as an extension of the self and is needed to fulfill functions that should, but cannot, be managed intrapsychically.

In chapter 20, several Rorschach developmental object-relations scales are reviewed. Each scale includes reflection and mirror responses and conceptualizes such content as indicating a relatively early phase of relatedness in which the object, whose sole purpose is to mirror the self, is regarded as an extension of the self.

Mayman (1977) identified aspects of the human-movement response that distinguish and typify individuals who tend to relate on a more narcissistic basis. He suggested that such individuals offer M responses in which (1) the response is offered with undue conviction; (2) the action ascribed and the attributes provided are more fabulized than inherent in the percept itself; (3) there is intense absorption and involvement in the behavior of the perceived figures; and (4) the testee infuses himself or herself into the figure as if vicariously sharing in the other's experience. Implicit in Mayman's indices is the notion that the nature of the relationship between the testee and his or her M response reflects and parallels the quality of relationship the testee establishes with his or her objects.

Finally, H. Lerner (1988) has identified test behavior and test responses reflective of narcissistic withdrawal. He suggests that one can observe a withholding or letdown in the patient in response to an empathic failure in the test situation. Because this reaction often has an intimidating quality, it may nudge "the examiner out of a position of neutrality into a more superego-like position of apologizing, being nice to the patient, and, in the process, away from a position of intellectual curiosity and active inquiry" (p. 293). This tendency of the patient to withdraw may also be inferred from Rorschach responses involving quasi-human figures (clowns, witches, caricatures) or human figures distanced in time and space. Here, such figures are taken as self-representations and convey the patient's sense of "a lack of authentic affective relatedness to the environment" (p. 294).

❖ ❖ ❖ The Narcissistic Patient and the Rorschach Test Research Contributions

With the increased interest shown in the concept of narcissism and the growing number of case reports appearing in the clinical literature, the narcissistic personality disorder was finally introduced as a diagnostic category in 1980 in the third edition of the Diagnostic and Statistical Manual of Mental Disorders (DSM-III; American Psychiatric Association, 1980). It was not until the late 1980s, however, that investigators began to describe and systematize the characteristic features of the narcissistic personality disorders. Using various assessment methods, including semistructured interviews, self-report inventories, and the Rorschach, these researchers have sought to identify specific criteria that both characterize the narcissistic personality disorder and distinguish the disturbance from other personality disorders.

Initial studies with the Rorschach attempted to differentiate the narcissistic personality disorder from the borderline personality disorder. Farris (1988) found that narcissistic patients, as compared with borderlines, produce significantly more responses indicative of higher cognitive-perceptual functioning and more advanced levels of psychosexual development (phallic-oedipal). Borderline patients, by contrast, offered significantly more test indices reflective of the lower level defenses of splitting and projective identification and of primitive object relations.

Findings consistent with those of Farris (1988) have been reported by several authors. In her comparison of narcissistic personality disorders and borderline personality disorders, Berg (1990) too found that the borderlines produced more unusual percepts and responses indicative of splitting. In addition, her results highlighted the importance of grandiosity in the defensive structure of the narcissist. Gacono et al. (1992) noted that borderlines relate in more primitive ways and provide more themes suggestive of violent symbiotic separation than do narcissistic patients.

In addition to comparing narcissists with borderlines, Gacono et al. also compared the narcissists with several antisocial groups. Here, the authors found that the narcissists produced as many reflection responses as nonpsychopathic antisocial individuals and as many personalized responses as psychopathic antisocial subjects. Finally, the authors noted that the narcissistic group produced significantly more primitive idealization responses than did any of the antisocial groups. Results supporting the significant role of idealization in narcissistic patients have also been provided by Hilsenroth et al. (1993).

Hilsenroth et al. investigated differences in defensive structure, aggression, and egocentricity among narcissistic personality disorders, borderline personality disorders, and cluster C personality disorders (i.e., avoidant, dependent, obsessive-compulsive, passive-aggressive). The borderlines, in keeping with earlier studies, employed the more primitive defenses of splitting and projective identification and showed greater amounts and more intense expressions of aggression. The narcissists evidenced significantly higher levels of egocentricity than the borderlines and greater use of idealization than the cluster C group.

Building upon earlier research, Hilsenroth et al. (in press) compared a group of narcissistic personality disorders with groups of cluster A personality disorders (i.e., paranoid, schizoid, schizotypal), cluster C personality disorders (see above), and normal controls on the Rorschach variables reflection response, pair response, personalization response, idealization score (indices from the Lerner Defense Scale), and Exner's (1986a) egocentricity index. Two of the variables, the reflection response and the idealization score, proved particularly effective in distinguishing and identifying the narcissistic personality disorders. In addition, the number of reflection responses was positively and significantly related to a narcissistic scale on the MMPI-2, patients' total number of DSM-IV criteria for narcissistic personality disorder, and specific DSM-IV criteria for narcissistic personality disorder, including fantasies of unlimited success, sense of entitlement, and a grandiose sense of self-importance. The idealization score was found to correlate significantly with the MMPI-2 narcissistic scale and with one of the DSM-IV criteria—fantasies of unlimited success.

Finally, Berg et al. (1993) compared the object relations of narcissistic personality disorders with those of borderline personality disorders and schizophrenics. Both the narcissistic and borderline patients produced a significantly greater number of object-relational scores reflecting figures in need of some external source of support than did the schizophrenics. The borderline patients, compared to the narcissistic patients, gave significantly more responses indicative of the object-relational themes of severe imbalance, malevolence, and engulfment. In general, the Rorschach protocols of the narcissistic patients reflected a tendency to relate to others on a need-satisfying basis and a proclivity for viewing others as extensions of the self.

In summary, empirical studies involving the narcissistic patient are increasingly appearing in the Rorschach literature. In general, investigators are seeking to find Rorschach indices that both reflect defining characteristics of the narcissistic patient and distinguish these patients from other personality disorders. Emphases in these studies have been upon the narcissistic patient's core characterlogical features, defensive structure, and quality of object relating. Several important conclusions may be gleaned from these investigations. First, collective evidence reveals that the narcissistic patient is self-absorbed and self-preoccupied; has a defensive structure different from that of the borderline patient, in that grandiosity, omnipotence, and primitive idealization are central; and relates to others less chaotically and primitively than does the borderline patient, but, nonetheless, sees the other as an extension of the self. Second, several Rorschach indices have been developed involving a combination of formal and content features and conventional and nonconventional scores that reliably and validly assess these personality variables. Third, these studies further demonstrate the importance for diagnostic purposes of assessing the defensive structure. Finally, in comparing narcissistic personality disorders with borderline personality disorders, several of these authors are implicitly accepting a descriptive diagnostic scheme. According to Kernberg's (1976) diagnostic system, the narcissistic personality and the borderline level of personality organization lie along different dimensions. As such, one can conceptualize a narcissistic personality organized at a borderline level. Therefore, from this latter perspective, it would appear that several of these studies are sampling a particular type of narcissistic patient—those organized at a neurotic level—and not the full range of narcissistic disturbances.

As noted, the studies above have employed conventional Rorschach scores (e.g., reflection response, pair response) or parts of existing Rorschach scales (e.g., idealization scale from the Lerner Defense Scale) to operationalize specific concepts. Only two innovative

Rorschach scales have been developed to assess aspects of the narcissistic personality structure; each, however, has important limitations. Relying upon Reich's (1933) description of the phallic-narcissistic character, Harder (1979) devised a scoring system to assess the ambitious-narcissistic character style. Unfortunately, although the scale closely parallels Reich's depiction of the phallic-narcissistic character, it differs in significant ways from the narcissistic patients described in the current literature. P. Lerner (1988) is in the process of developing a scale to operationalize Winnicott's (1965) concept of the "false self." He has identified and described Rorschach indices reflective of components of the false self; however, his work has not reached the stage of a refined quantitative system. Despite their respective limitations, both scales are discussed here, because they represent potentially useful starting points for more systematically investigating the narcissistic personality.

Ambitious–Narcissistic Character Style

In keeping with Reich's (1933) characterization of the phallic-narcissistic character and Shapiro's (1965) notion of character style, Harder's (1979) scale consists of the following five component headings: intrusive/thrusting, exhibitionism/ voyeurism, urethral excitation, mastery/competence/power, and self-potency. The categories are applied to Rorschach content, particularly those percepts that involve activity being channeled through specific interpersonal modes. For example, responses reflective of the intrusive/thrusting component include figures exploring new territory, vigorous physical activity, objects propelled through space, and so forth. In addition, cutting across all component categories is an intensity dimension.

In an initial study (Harder, 1979) the scale was applied to the Rorschach records of 40 relatively well-functioning male college students, all of whom intended to pursue a professional program or graduate school. Satisfactory levels of reliability based on percent of inter-rater agreement were reported. Parallel forms of the scale were developed for the Thematic Apperception Test (TAT) and the Early Memories Test; therefore, validity could be determined by the level of relationship between the Rorschach scale and these other measures, as well as by its relationship with an independent criterion measure. The scales were found to intercorrelate, thus indicating that they were measuring a common dimension. With regard to the criterion measure, the Rorschach scale, more so than the other scales, significantly differentiated subjects rated by clinically trained judges as ambitious/narcissistic in style from subjects rated as not ambitious/narcissistic.

In an attempt to identify personality correlates of the concept of defensively high self-esteem (a conscious, exaggerated satisfaction with the self used defensively to ward off feelings of low self-regard), Harder (1979) extended the scale to the Rorschach protocols of 40 male college students subdivided into four groups based upon clinicians' ratings of defensiveness of self-esteem and level of self-regard. As predicted, subjects rated as defensively high on self-esteem scored significantly higher on the Rorschach measure of Ambitious-Narcissistic Character Style than did subjects in the other three groups.

Farris (1988) found that although his narcissistic and borderline subjects did not differ on a summary composite score from Harder's scale, they did differ with respect to two specific categories. For the category Phallic Organ, the narcissistic patients produced a number of ambitious-narcissistic responses reflecting a greater departure from the expected frequency than did the borderline patients. Similarly, narcissistic subjects produced a greater number of Body Narcissism responses than did borderline subjects.

False Self Scale

Winnicott's (1965) concept of the false self is pitched at a different level than is the more abstract and distant concept of narcissism. As to be described, it refers to a defensive structure rather than a diagnosis. I have included the scale in this chapter because the false self is often, although not exclusively, found in certain narcissistic patients. There is good reason for this. Both concepts indicate fundamental disturbances in sense of self.

Using the theoretical formulations of Winnicott (1965), the test writings of Schachtel (1966), and his own clinical experience, P. Lerner (1988) is in the process of developing a scale to assess the concept of the false self.

Winnicott (1961) conceived of the false self as an elaborate defensive structure that serves to hide and protect the true self from the dangers of control, ridicule, and exploitation. The origins of the false self are found in the infant's seduction into a compliant relationship with a nonempathic mother. Accordingly, when the mother substitutes part of herself for the infant's spontaneous gestures, the infant experiences traumatic disruptions of his or her developing sense of self. When these impingements become a core feature of the mother-child relationship, the infant will attempt to defend himself or herself by developing a second, reactive personality organization—the false self. The false self sensitively monitors and adapts to the conscious and unconscious needs of the mother and, in so doing, provides a protective exterior behind which the true self is afforded the privacy it requires to maintain its integrity. The false self, then, becomes a key feature of the personality organization and functions rather as a caretaker, managing life so that an inner self might not experience the threat of annihilation resulting from excessive pressure on it to develop according to another's needs.

A review of the concept indicates that basic to the false self are hyperalertness and heightened sensitivity to the expectations and anticipations of others, with a concomitant tendency to mold one's own feelings, behaviors, and attitudes accordingly. P. Lerner (1988) found a specific test-taking attitude, two formal Rorschach scores, and specific contents especially sensitive to these aspects of the false self.

Test-Taking Attitude

Patients who present with a false self often begin testing under a cloak of vigilance and with a readiness to be distrustful. They are there, but with one foot out the door, as it were. Quickly, various aspects of the examiner, including office furnishings, tone of voice, and testing directions, come under careful scrutiny. For example, if on the Rorschach test the examiner inquires after each card, after the first such series of inquiries these patients often attune at once to what is being asked for and thereafter supply such information during free association, thereby rendering the examiner's role unnecessary. In other words, these patients move toward a compliant self-sufficiency and virtually begin testing themselves. The examiner's experience, paradoxically, is that of being the one examined. Not only is every movement closely monitored, but all comments are carefully scrutinized and regarded as evidence to be weighed and judged before the relationship is allowed to deepen and possibly move toward mutuality. The patient's attitude quite understandably evokes a marked countervigilance and hypercautiousness on the part of the examiner. Recognizing that certain comments meant to be helpful may be taken as an attack, the examiner becomes more careful and inhibited.

Formal Scores

Two formal scores are considered especially sensitive to false-self features. The first, the Fc score, as noted in chapter 7, is applied to responses that are delineated and determined by variations in shading. The variations in shading are subtle; therefore, to achieve such a response one must seek out, discover, and attune to finer nuances, as well as feel one's way into something that is not readily apparent. To do this requires perceptual sensitivity in addition to a searching, articulating, and penetrating type of activity. Individuals with this type of sensitivity—who have their antennae out, if you will—tend to present as hypervigilant, thin-skinned, and excessively vulnerable, and each of these characteristics is consistent with aspects of the false self.

A second formal score reflective of the false self is the color arbitrary score, Carb. This score is accorded to responses in which the use of color is clearly incompatible with the content (blue monkeys, pink dogs); yet the subject clings to its inclusion and makes minimal effort to account for the blend. Schachtel (1966) has noted the role of compliance in this response: the subject relinquishes a more objective, critical, and judging attitude and provides a percept he or she knows is not realistic. In this respect, the score conveys a sense of unreality.

Content

One would expect that individuals who are constantly alert to danger, who are concerned with protection and privacy, who relate themselves to others in a compliant way, and who experience only fleeting feelings of inauthenticity would offer Rorschach imagery reflective of these experiential themes. Indeed, such themes do appear in the Rorschach records of patients who present with a false self: one finds content reflective of hiding and accommodation, such as masks, costumes, camouflage, and chameleons. Further, human or animal figures are often seen as performing or serving (e.g., waiters, clowns, magicians, trained seals, circus bears).

As part of an attempt to assess vulnerability to victimization, Nifakis (1989) has applied these concepts to the Rorschach records of 17 adult women who experienced sexual abuse as children and 16 normal controls. To operationalize the test-taking attitude, Nifakis developed a three-point rating scale in which both the examiner and independent judges rated the subject's "attunement and sensitivity" to the examiner. Although the study is not yet complete, preliminary results indicate the following: (1) the test-taking attitude index significantly distinguished the two groups in the predicted direction, (2) there was a strong but not statistically significant tendency for the sexually abused subjects to use the Fc score more frequently than the controls, and (3) the Carb score and the content did not differentiate the two groups.

✦ ✦ ✦ Conclusion

In this chapter I have briefly reviewed the concept of narcissism and discussed the assessment of the narcissistic patient by means of the Rorschach. On the basis of the theoretical contributions of Kernberg and Kohut, two highly comprehensive Rorschach approaches—one by H. Lerner (1988) and the other by Arnow and Cooper (1988)—have been outlined to assist the clinical examiner in evaluating various aspects of narcissistic pathology. Each approach describes such pathology in several areas of personality functioning and provides Rorschach manifestations and other clinical illustrations. Only since the late 1980s have empirical studies involving the narcissistic patient begun to appear in the Rorschach literature. Overall, investigators have attempted to identify Rorschach indices that both reflect core features of the narcissistic personality disorder and differentiate these patients from other personality disorders. These studies have focused upon the narcissistic patient's character structure, defensive structure, and mode of object relating. Two innovative research scales designed to assess aspects of the narcissistic patient have been developed. Although Harder's (1979) Ambitious-Narcissistic Character Style scale parallels descriptions provides by Reich, it does not capture several of the more contemporary features of the narcissistic patient as described by Kernberg or Kohut. P. Lerner has devised several indices reflective of aspects of the false self; however, at this point his work represents a loose-fitting collection of indices rather than an integrated scale.

25

THE RORSCHACH AND ASSESSING TREATMENT OUTCOME

1n chapter 15, I discussed, from a clinical perspective, several aspects of the assessment situation, such as the frame, the patient–examiner relationship, and test responses that could be used in making treatment recommendations and treatment predictions. I also referred to specific studies in which the Rorschach had been employed to predict particular treatment events, including the capacity to benefit from intensive psychotherapy (Hatcher and Krohn, 1980), prognosis for hospital treatment (Frieswyk and Colson, 1980), premature termination (Hilsenroth and Handler, 1995; Horner and Diamond, 1996), and treatment outcome (Carlsson et al., 1996; Lindfors, 1996; Meyer and Handler, 1996).

In this chapter the emphasis is upon the use of the Rorschach in assessing treatment outcome. Although investigators studying treatment outcome repeatedly insist upon the need for independent assessment, only rarely have psychological tests that include projective instruments been used. As Blatt et al. (1988) have noted, "Despite the fact that projective techniques, especially the Rorschach, could be quite useful for assessing positive and negative symptoms as well as the tendency to have disrupted relationships, these assessment procedures have rarely been utilized in psychotherapy research" (p. 130).

Herein, I selectively review specific studies that have used the Rorschach to assess changes associated with psychological treatment. Several criteria were used in choosing these investigations. First, each of these studies was done under naturalistic clinical conditions rather than laboratory conditions. That is, all of the researchers attempted to study the effects of psychotherapy as it is actually practiced and understood. Second, except for one (Appelbaum, 1977), all of these studies were carried out relatively recently. This means that the investigators were able to learn from and avoid the methodological shortcomings of earlier studies. Third, in most instances I have selected studies that have a psychoanalytic slant. More specifically, in several studies, though not all, the treatment being evaluated was long-term and psychoanalytically informed, and the Rorschach was approached from a psychoanalytic perspective.

✦ ✦ ✦ Review

Over a several year period, Weiner and Exner (1991) collected Rorschach protocols at four stages during and following the treatment of two groups of patients receiving outpatient psychotherapy. All patients were assessed at the beginning of treatment and on three subsequent occasions, including at or following termination. One group, referred to as long-term patients, consisted of 88 individuals who were seen more than once weekly in a dynamic, uncovering therapy for a period of 48 months on average. The second group, termed short-term patients, also consisted of 88 individuals, but these were seen once weekly in a nondynamic therapy for fewer than 16 months.

On an apriori basis, 27 Comprehensive System Rorschach variables, all considered reflective of adjustment difficulties, were selected and then used to assess treatment progress and outcome. Four of the indices were thought to indicate difficulty managing stress, five reflected difficulty dealing with experience attentively and conventionally, five related to problems in affect modulation, four suggested struggles in adaptively using ideation, four indicated problems in self-examination, and five suggested discomforts in interpersonal relationships. Specific Rorschach indices for assessing these dimensions may be found in Weiner and Exner (1991).

An examination of the findings revealed that both groups of patients, as judged by these Rorschach indices, benefited from their treatment experience. The long-term patients revealed a significant decrease in the frequency of 24 of 27 of the Rorschach indices of adjustment difficulties from the baseline assessment over the course of the three retestings to and including the final one posttreatment. As a group, they showed test evidence of a greater capacity to manage stress and modulate affects, to deal with experience more attentively and conventionally, to use ideation more effectively, to be less preoccupied and dissatisfied with themselves, and to experience less discomfort in interpersonal relationships.

The short-term patients also improved with treatment, but to a lesser degree. Using the Rorschachs obtained at the beginning of treatment as a baseline, subsequently administered Rorschachs revealed a significant decrease in 20 of the 27 Rorschach variables. As with the long-term patients, changes toward improvement were noted in each area of adjustment difficulties.

The accuracy with which the Rorschach monitored change over time was taken, by the authors, as evidence of the method's construct validity for this particular purpose.

In a companion study, Exner and Andronikof-Sanglade (1992) used a similar design in evaluating the effects of both short-term therapy and brief therapy. In this study, two groups of 35 patients each, one group treated with brief therapy (average number of sessions was 14.2 and patients were seen on a once-per-week basis) and the other treated with a short-term therapy (average number of sessions was 47 and patients were seen once weekly), were administered the Rorschach and the Katz Adjustment Scales-Form S on three occasions—before entering treatment, at termination, and at follow-up.

Rorschachs were assessed in terms of 27 structural variables. Although the indices were similar to those used in the earlier study (Weiner and Exner, 1991), they were not conceptualized as indicators of adjustment difficulties, but instead, as reflections of psychological organization and/or operations, or both. The variables were organized in terms of the following clusters: capacity for control, stress tolerance, and coping styles; affective features; characteristics of ideation; information processing; cognitive mediation; self perception; and interpersonal perception.

At termination, the brief therapy group revealed signs of improvement on 12 of the 27 variables. Of these 12 variables, four related to affective features, three to self and interpersonal perception, two to processing and mediation, and one each to control, copying style, and ideation. At follow-up, however, several of these gains were not sustained.

On the second retesting, lower frequencies of positive findings were found for only seven of the 27 variables. Changes noted in the short-term therapy group were more impressive. At termination, the first retesting showed a significantly lower frequency for 20 of the 27 variables, and these changes extended across all seven clusters. Unlike the brief therapy group, at follow-up retesting all of these changes maintained.

Diamond et al. (1990) assessed changes in self- and object-repre-sentations among adolescent and young adult patients being seen in psychoanalytically oriented, long-term inpatient treatment. Rorschachs were administered to the patients both at admission and discharge. To evaluate the extent to which the subjects progressed from symbiotic relationships to more differentiated relationships, Rorschach responses were analyzed with an extended version of Coonerty's (1986) Separation-Individuation Scale. Specifically, the authors added two higher developmental categories—object constancy and intersubjec-tivity—and elaborated existing scale points. The revised scale was applied to the Rorschachs of four patients. In each case, changes toward higher levels of separation-individuation and intersubjectivity were observed. In addition, these changes corresponded with those obtained on the Object Representation Inventory, a 10-point scale for rating descriptions of self and significant others. Of importance, data from the Separation-Individuation Scale indicated the unique rate and configuration of change for each of the four patients.

The most extensive and comprehensive study of changes in patients during long-term intensive inpatient treatment is found in the work of Blatt et al. (1988). The sample consisted of 90 seriously disturbed ado-lescents and young adults, aged 18 to 29 years, hospitalized in an inpa-tient facility with a therapeutic community, in which the patients were seen in intensive, psychoanalytically oriented psychotherapy at least four times per week. On the basis of ratings of initial case records, the patients were subdivided into two groups defined by the nature of their psychopathology. One group included patients whose psychopathol-ogy was primarily anaclitic. That is, their preoccupations centered around issues of affection, intimacy, and attempts to establish satisfy-ing interpersonal relationships. The second group consisted of patients who presented with a more introjective psychopathology. These overideational individuals were preoccupied with different concerns, such as anger, aggression, and self-definition.

The research data involved two independent sets of observations, case records, and psychological test protocols, including the Rorschach.

Both types of data were obtained at two points in the treatment process—after the first six weeks of hospitalization and approximately one year later. Rorschachs were scored along a number of lines, including thought disorder; the number of differentiated, articulated, and integrated human forms that are accurately or inaccurately seen (concept of the object); extent of adaptive or regressive fantasy; and mutuality of autonomy.

Several important and interesting findings were obtained. Taken as a whole, the entire sample demonstrated significant improvement in social behavior and a reduction in clinical symptoms as judged by both ratings from the case records and a significant decline in thought disorder on the Rorschach. The decrease in thought disorder essentially involved the more serious types—contamination tendencies, confabulations, and confabulation tendencies. Both groups displayed a significant increase in the amount of adaptive fantasy and a significant decrease in the level of malevolence attributed to interactions as reflected on the Mutuality of Autonomy Scale. Changes observed clinically and found on other Rorschach indices were not found on the developmental index and the mean developmental level of the concept of the object measure.

To determine the configurations of change, the authors intercorrelated the various measures from the two independent sources of data. Here too, several interesting findings emerged. For both groups, but especially for the introjective patients, changes in thought disorder covaried to a significant degree with changes in the assessment of clinical symptoms, particularly a decrease in psychotic and neurotic symptoms and in labile and flattened affect. With the introjective patients, increase in the developmental index for accurately perceived object representations correlated significantly with a decrease in labile affect. For the anaclitic patients, a decrease in inaccurately perceived object representations was significantly related to social and sublimatory effectiveness, superego integration, quality of object relations, and motivation for treatment. In general, the Rorschach variable object representation was a more sensitive indicator of change in anaclitic patients than in introjective patients.

Particularly striking in this study was the strong evidence that changes in patients concomitant with treatment are primarily in terms of features most salient in their personality organization. For example, in the more ideational introjective patients, changes were primarily noted in clinical symptoms as rated from case records and in cognitive functioning as assessed by Rorschach thought disorder indices. By contrast, in the more interpersonally oriented anaclitic patients, changes were primarily found in case record ratings of interpersonal relationships and in a decrease in inaccurately perceived human forms on the Rorschach.

Beginning in the early 1950s, the most intensive and microscopic investigation of the effects of long-term psychotherapy and psychoanalysis is represented in the Psychotherapy Research Project of the Menninger Foundation (Kernberg et al., 1972; Wallerstein, 1968; Appelbaum, 1977). For more than 20 years, the investigators used an array of assessment measures, including a psychological test battery, to evaluate intrapsychic changes associated with long-term treatment.

Using the work of Appelbaum (1977) as a basis, here I report on the findings derived solely from the psychological tests. Using a clinical test battery consisting of the Wechsler-Bellevue Form I, Rorschach Test, Word Association Test, BRL Object Sorting Test, Thematic Apperception Test, and Babcock Story Recall, patients were tested at three different times. Thirty-four patients were tested both pretreatment and at termination, 28 tested at termination and at two years posttermination, and 26 patients at all three points. In general, the patients suffered from neurotic and characterological difficulties (now, 40 years later, many would be considered borderline) and, compared to the general population, they tended to be more intelligent (mean IQ 124) and wealthier.

Research testers, as contrasted with the clinical testers who administered the tests based on their reading of the test protocols, made individual statements about 24 patient variables that lent themselves to test analysis and about changes in those variables across the three testings. A partial list of patient variables includes symptoms, patterning of defenses, core neurotic conflicts, self-concept, psychological mindedness, affect organization, and thought organization. It should be noted that there was variability among the patient variables with respect to their conceptual clarity and ease versus difficulty in being ascertained from psychological tests.

The study yielded several interesting findings. In the broader project (Kernberg et al., 1972), several statistical analyses were done, including a modification of the Fechnerian Method of Paired Comparisons. These paired comparisons, based on nontest clinical information, were compared with the ratings of patient variable change derived from the psychological tests. For the variables symptoms, ego strength, conflict resolution, and global change, the correlations between the psychological test ratings and paired comparison analysis were relatively high; for the other patient variables, however, the correlations were relatively low. There was considerable evidence to suggest that differences in judgments of change were due to different kinds of information yielded by the tests as compared to the nontest sources.

Global ratings as to whether the patient benefitted from treatment and to what degree, based on judgments from the tests, showed high reliability with two other independent assessments.

Changes in patient variables based on test information alone may be summarized as follows. First, the patient variables reflective of structural change ranked high on percentage of patients changing on them. Changes on variables directly related to feelings (i.e., anxiety, depression) and related to specific symptoms also changed in a high percentage of patients. Second, the more that conflicts were resolved through expressive modalities, the more likely there would be structural change. Nonetheless, there were a number of patients who showed structural change without resolution of conflict through expressive means. Third, with respect to these intrapsychic patient variables, patients changed considerably and the change was more often for the better. Fourth, psychotherapy tends to build upon existing capacities rather than creating new ones. For example, those patients who in their pretreatment testing revealed psychological mindedness and insight, changed more on these variables than did patients who initially showed little psychological mindedness and insight. This phenomenon, which Appelbaum (1977) labeled "the rich get richer" (p. 89), characterized many of the patient variables. For a more detailed discussion of the direction and extent of change for each variable, refer to Appelbaum (1977, pp. 79–214).

In addition to assessing treatment outcome, Appelbaum's (1977) portion of the project had other purposes as well. One involved comparing inferences based on test data with inferences based on other psychiatric data with respect to accuracy of diagnosis and accuracy of treatment recommendations and predictions. A second purpose was to determine which variables afforded the most and least accurate predictions and are best suited for analysis through tests.

In a study involving 13 cases, Appelbaum (1977) found that test-based inferences, as compared with nontest-based inferences, were significantly more often in agreement with an external criterion in regard to global diagnostic assessment, treatment recommendations, and specific treatment predictions. The variables, in ascending order, found to be most important in drawing accurate inferences were ego strength, transference paradigms, core neurotic conflicts, quality of interpersonal relations, patterning of defenses, self-concept, and psychological mindedness.

In a second study involving the same 13 cases, Appelbaum (1979) compared inferences based solely on the pretreatment test report with inferences based on nontest psychiatric data with respect to diagnosis and treatment recommendations and predictions. Here again, the test-based inferences were found more accurate. The same variables (e.g., ego strength, transference paradigms), together with the addition of thought organization, were identified as critical in rendering accurate predictions.

In a third study, 26 cases on which there was only an initial clinical test report were added to the 13 cases used in the earlier studies. For these 39 cases, test findings again were found to agree significantly more often with the external criterion than did nontest psychiatric findings on the diagnostic and treatment questions. Interestingly, not only were the same variables implicated in making correct predictions, but they were also the same ones about which the testers and psychiatrists disagreed.

In summary, the three studies, collectively, indicate that test findings are more valid than nontest findings in predicting treatment outcome. The variable ego strength was found to be the major source of difference between the testers and the nontest clinicians. In addition, the initial clinical test report was found as valid as the extensive research analysis of test data in deriving accurate treatment predictions.

◆ ◆ ◆ Discussion

Despite the call for independent assessment in evaluating the effects of psychological treatment, the Rorschach, especially as part of a test-retest design, has been used sparingly. Mistakenly, researchers have been concerned with a "practice effect"; however, as Exner and Adronikof-Sanglade (1992) point out, "Rorschachs of nonpatient adults remain highly stable over both short- and long-term intervals" (p. 60).

The studies reviewed here indicate that the Rorschach, when used by itself or as part of a test battery, is sensitive to changes concomitant with treatment. In employing the Rorschach for this purpose, investigators have used conventional scores and ratios (Weiner and Exner, 1991; Exner and Andronikof-Sanglade, 1992), innovative scales (Diamond et al., 1990; Blatt et al., 1988; Schwager and Spear, 1981; Kavanagh, 1985), and test-based inferences as reported on a clinical psychological testing report (Appelbaum, 1977).

In these studies, the Rorschach has been used to assess treatment outcome; however, in turn, implicit in the Rorschach findings are important implications for psychotherapy research. For example, in two studies (Diamond et al. 1990; Blatt et al., 1988) it was found that patients differ with respect to rate and configuration of change. Both the extent and nature of change, to judge from these studies, are influenced by type of psychopathology and salient features in the patient's personality organization. Unfortunately, much of the research in psychotherapy has assumed that all patients are the same and that they all change along the same dimensions (Blatt et al., 1988). Findings from these studies clearly indicate that future research in psychotherapy, both in design and methodology, must take into account differences among patients.

Also of research and clinical import are several findings reported by Appelbaum (1977). He found that of 24 patient variables, those which were particularly revealing of change were the structural ones. The efficacy of the Rorschach for assessing structural aspects of personality has been well demonstrated (Exner, 1991, 1993; P. Lerner, 1991a). This suggests that not only has the Rorschach been underutilized in psychotherapy research, but, in addition, the instrument is considerably more sensitive to change than has been commonly recognized.

Appelbaum (1977) also found that psychotherapy tends to build upon existing capacities, such as ego strength and psychological mindedness, rather than creating them anew. In a narrow sense, this suggests that what a patient derives from treatment corresponds with his or her "intrapsychic starting points" (p. 289). In a broader clinical sense, it underscores the need for diagnostic assessment before treatment. As Appelbaum (1977) puts it, "Adequate diagnoses would lead to better decisions as to who should get treatment and who should not. . . , what kinds of treatment interventions would benefit one person or another, and what goals and goal-linked strategies would be commensurate with patient capacities" (p. 289).

Finally, two other findings reported by Appelbaum are especially confirming to those of us invested in the Rorschach. First, he found that test results were more valid for predicting treatment outcome than were nontest results. Second, he also found that inferences appearing in the brief clinical test report were as valid in predicting treatment outcome as were inferences derived from an extensive research analysis of the same data. In essence then, Appelbaum has demonstrated that a careful and thoughtful assessment using the Rorschach conducted prior to treatment is both necessary and highly useful.

❖ ❖ ❖ Conclusion

In this chapter I have reviewed several studies that have used the Rorschach, alone and as part of a test battery, to assess changes associated with psychological treatment. Each was conducted under naturalistic clinical conditions, except for one, all were done in the last decade, and the majority were psychoanalytically rooted. Taken together, the studies compellingly demonstrate that the Rorschach is sensitive to changes concomitant with treatment and is a valid measure of these changes. That testing data, as compared with other psychiatric data, are a more valid predictor of treatment outcome is particularly heartwarming.

26

TOWARD AN INTEGRATED
RORSCHACH APPROACH

1n the preface to my 1991 book *Psychoanalytic Theory and the Rorschach,* I noted with pleasure the significant resurgence of interest in and use of the Rorschach for the understanding of people. I suggested that the revival of Rorschach's test was prompted by two forces—the empirical work of John Exner and the development of the Comprehensive System and the important shifts and developments that were occurring in psychoanalytic theory. Although different in important ways, the Rorschach approaches that arose from each force represented a different side of Rorschach's original vision.

Now, in 1997, it is clear that the Rorschach's popularity has not only maintained, but likely has increased. A survey of the present Rorschach landscape, however, indicates that a third force is emerging. In books, articles, and professional presentations, former students of Exner's and younger proponents of psychoanalytic theory—a third generation of Rorschachers, if you will—are creatively and thoughtfully attempting to integrate these approaches.

In this chapter I discuss these integrative endeavors. Before doing so, I provide a backdrop by briefly reviewing the evolution of both

Exner's approach and the psychoanalytic approach. For a more thorough and comprehensive discussion, refer to a review of the history of the Society for Personality Assessment that was prepared by Exner (O'Roark and Exner, 1989) for the Society's 50th anniversary.

❖ ❖ ❖ Development of the Comprehensive System

In the prefaces to his 1991 and 1993 volumes, Exner details the history of the development of the Comprehensive System. He notes that some 20 years earlier, in 1971, he decided "to integrate the empirically defensible components of five major Rorschach Systems into a single, standardized approach to Rorschach's test" (Exner, 1991, p. ix). The seeds for such a project were planted well in advance. In the 1950s, after being introduced to the test, Exner served as a summer intern, first for Samuel Beck and then for Bruno Klopfer. While genuinely liking and admiring each, he was baffled by the animosity between them and their refusal to communicate with each other.

Failing in his attempts as a peace maker, and prompted by a suggestion by Beck, Exner decided to write a paper describing their differences. As he began writing the paper, he quickly discovered that he could not simply compare Beck's ideas with those of Klopfer without including the contributions of Piotrowski, Rapaport, and Hertz. Thus, by 1962, Exner recognized that he needed to expand his original work so as to include all five approaches.

Upon completing this broadened project, Exner shared his work with each of the contributors, except for Rapaport, who had died. Although supportive of the project, each contributor pointed to the absence of conclusions. This stimulated Exner, in 1968, to found the Rorschach Research Foundation, later known as Rorschach Workshops, for the purpose of collecting and studying Rorschach data that would enable him to "find the missing conclusions" (Exner, 1991, p. xi).

Guiding Exner's works were two questions: which system had the soundest empirical sturdiness and which the strongest clinical efficacy? In time, he decided that instead of having to choose any one system, it made more sense to integrate the best of each into one all-inclusive system—the Comprehensive System.

Throughout, Exner's (1993) goal has been "to provide a standardized method of using the test which is easily taught, manifests high interscorer reliability, and for which the interpretive premises will withstand validation demands" (p. vii).

From this cursory review, what is evident is Exner's empirical bent and psychometric emphasis. From the beginning, he focused upon the *empirically defensible* elements of the different systems and his yardsticks have involved *standardization, reliability, and validity*.

✦ ✦ ✦ Psychoanalytic Approach

As noted in the preface to this book, the psychoanalytic approach arose from the pioneering work of David Rapaport (Rapaport et al., 1945–1946) and the intimate relationship he established between the Rorschach method and psychoanalytic theory. Rapaport provided a test rationale steeped in psychoanalytic theory for each of the major determinants, proposed a more clinical manner of conducting testing, identified and systematized categories for studying and understanding deviant verbalizations, outlined the role of cognition and its relationship to perception in the response process, and offered a justification for the place of psychological testing in psychiatric settings.

Colleagues and students of Rapaport's built upon and extended several of his initial contributions. Schafer (1948, 1954), in two major works, provided an in-depth description of the patient–examiner relationship and its importance as a source of clinical information, systematized the analysis of Rorschach content, outlined the steps in the clinical inference process, laid the groundwork for the use of the Rorschach in identifying defensive processes, elaborated criteria for judging the validity of test-based interpretations, and offered idiographic case material to complement Rapaport's nomothetic data.

Rapaport considered the Rorschach a valuable vehicle for operationalizing psychoanalytic concepts that were elusive and overly abstract, and hoped that this would permit the empirical testing of basic formulations. Holt and his students, for more than a quarter of a century, have built upon and contributed to this side of Rapaport's vision. In an attempt to find operational definitions for Freud's concepts of primary and secondary process, Holt developed Rorschach measures for assessing many important psychoanalytic concepts, including aggressive and libidinal urges, defense, and adaptive regression. Using these measures, Holt and his colleagues have then empirically investigated such diverse but significant areas as thinking, motivation, unconscious processes, and creativity.

Another student of Rapaport's who made significant contributions to the psychoanalytic stream was Mayman. In a series of writings (Mayman, 1964a, 1967, 1977), Mayman specified more clearly what was meant by a clinical approach to testing, refined the assessment of form level and related it more directly to reality-adherence/reality-abrogation, teased out the various components of the human-movement response, and provided innovative ways of understanding Rorschach content. In elaborating ways in which the Rorschach could be used to assess self and object representations, Mayman filled in significant gaps in Rapaport's work and provided an experiential dimension to Rorschach assessment.

Paralleling Mayman's contributions were those of Blatt. Conceptually more tied to developmental theory than was Mayman, Blatt too provided a systematic way of evaluating self and object representations. In his examination of the nature of the Rorschach task, Blatt was one of the first to accord representational processes a significant role.

A person who was a prime contributor to the psychoanalytic stream but was outside of the Rapaport tradition was Schachtel. With a less structural focus and a more phenomenological emphasis, Schachtel's psychoanalytic roots were different from Rapaport's. Rapaport took as his point of departure Freud's structural theory and followed a trail blazed by Hartmann. Schachtel's point of departure was interpersonal theory, and the path he followed had been cut by Fromm and Sullivan. Because of their different psychoanalytic leanings, Schachtel's contributions complemented those of Rapaport rather than extending them.

Schachtel's contributions were discussed in chapter 1. As noted, in basing his test rationale on perception rather than cognition, he provided a meaning for the determinants that was more closely tied to phenomenological experience. In addition, he elaborated an experiential approach to interpretation, drew attention to the psychological significance of the test instructions, and highlighted aspects of the patient–examiner relationship not discussed by Schafer.

Beginning in the 1980s, a second generation of Rorschach workers made significant contributions to the psychoanalytic tradition. Prompted by the writings of Kernberg and Kohut and the increased interest in more difficult patients, especially the borderline patient, these writers brought to the Rorschach theoretical formulations derived from object-relations theory, self-theory, and contemporary developmental theory. Out of this work have come new ways of formulating the patient–examiner relationship (Arnow and Cooper, 1988), research scales for assessing object relations (Urist, 1977; Kwawer, 1980; Coonerty, 1986) and primitive defenses (P. Lerner and H. Lerner, 1980), reconceptualizations of the deviant verbalization responses (Blatt and Ritzler, 1974; Athey, 1986), and a reexamination of the nature of the Rorschach task (Leichtman, 1996). In addition, because of the emphasis on object relations and self, these writers have incorporated the contributions of Schachtel and thereby accorded him the importance he merits (P. Lerner, 1991a; Leichtman, 1996).

From this brief review, it is evident that the psychoanalytic approach maintains a primary *theoretical* focus. Further, in contrast with the empirical approach, psychometric issues are accorded lesser importance than are *clinical* ones.

◆ ◆ ◆　Toward Integration

Although not intended for integrative purposes, an article by Weiner (1994) has provided a basis for the integrative attempts of others. As indicated in chapter 1, Weiner highlighted the distinction between the Rorschach as a method, not a test, for generating data and theories of personality that have been brought forward to interpret that data. Weiner further noted that such data could be interpreted from different theoretical perspectives.

An early proponent of an integrated approach to the Rorschach was Erdberg. Schooled in the Comprehensive System but interested in psychoanalytic theory, Erdberg (1993, 1995) has demonstrated how the empirical approaches' insistence upon normative data to provide response baselines can be balanced with the heuristic sweep of psychoanalytic formulations. In particular, Erdberg has focused upon the Axis II component of DSM-III. Drawing upon Kernberg (1975), Erdberg has shown how several of Kernberg's descriptive and dynamic formulations regarding the characterlogically disturbed patient can be translated into the language of the Comprehensive System and then used for clinical and research purposes.

A strategy similar to Erdberg's, but extended in several ways, is represented in the work of Meloy et al. (1997). Fashioning themselves as empiricists who are guided by psychoanalytic theory, these authors provided over a three-year period (1991–1993) a series of presentations to the Society for Personality Assessment in which they used the single case study to demonstrate the sturdiness and power of an integrated Rorschach interpretive approach. The presentations were organized in terms of Kernberg's (1976) three levels of personality organization—psychotic, borderline, and neurotic.

As had Erdberg, Meloy, et al. (1997), collectively and individually, began by finding Comprehensive System scores and ratios that corresponded to Kernberg's structural criteria (i.e., integrity of thought, reality testing, identity integration, self-other differentiation, impulsivity) for establishing a differential diagnosis. For example, a heightened Schizophrenic Index (SCZI), a heavily weighted sum of special scores, a high percent of poor form level, and several human-movement responses with poor form level were all taken as evidence of a psychotic level of personality organization (Peterson, 1992). More specifically, these Rorschach indices were understood as signs of disturbed thinking, impaired reality testing, the presence of a psychotic fantasy, and a preponderance of primary-process manifestations.

Peterson's (1992) approach can be used as a prototypic example. Peterson first established a differential diagnosis and described structural features of the personality on the basis of Comprehensive System variables. He then applied the psychoanalytic work of Urist (1977), Kwawer (1980), Schafer (1954), and Schachtel (1966) to the content of specific responses. In contrast to his earlier structural focus, Peterson's interest here was on the patient's self-experience, object world, and quality of relating to others. The following example illustrates this aspect of interpretation. On Card III the patient saw "Two showgirls on the shoulders of a man wearing a bow tie." The interpreter commented:

> The scoring of this response, namely the M- and the special scores, clearly indicates that this is a psychotic response. Although the interaction is benevolent, it occurs between quasi- (miniature) humans and a partial human. The oral content establishes the psychosexual level as primitive, a view reaffirmed by other contemporary perspectives. Kwawer (1980) referred to this as a 'boundary disturbance response,' addressing the fluidity, weakness, and permeability of the ego boundaries. Urist's (1977) perspective underlies the primitive dependency [Peterson, 1992, p. 469].

A quite similar integrative approach was taken by Gacono and Meloy (1994) in their investigation of the aggressive and psychopathic personalities. In a series of studies involving both large groups (nomothetic data) and individual case studies (idiographic data), these authors too used the Comprehensive System to assess psychostructural features of personality and psychoanalytic methods to assess psychodynamic features. The specific psychodynamic aspects addressed were primitive modes of relating (Kwawer, 1980), defense (Cooper et al., 1988), and aggression. Here, too, the authors tended to apply the Comprehensive System to the formal aspects of a protocol and the psychoanalytic methods to the content aspects.

All of the authors mentioned above have attempted to draw from each approach what they consider best. Their intent has been to combine an empirical methodology with the richness of psychoanalytic theory to generate test-based interpretations that are clinically meaningful and rest on sturdy empirical findings.

Such an integrated approach differs from the approach taken in this book in several ways. It is based on an empirical methodology, not on a clinical one; it draws sharper, and what Smith (1997) refers to as "spurious," distinctions between structure and dynamics and formal features and content, and it provides little room for what Mayman (1964a) termed a "clinical intuitive" and what Schachtel (1966) and I (Lerner, 1994) refer to as an "experiential" interpretive approach to Rorschach data.

A second integrative approach, one different from and less ambitious than the above, is found in the work of Kleiger. In two publications (Kleiger and Peebles-Kleiger, 1993; Kleiger, 1997), Kleiger and his colleagues have attempted to demonstrate how psychoanalytic theory can expand and deepen empirically-based understandings of the psychological meaning of specific Rorschach scores.

In his more recent article, Kleiger (in press) examines each of the Comprehensive System's shading responses through the lenses of all four submodels of psychoanalytic theory—drive theory, structural theory, object-relations theory, and self-theory. The following provides an illustrative example of the direction of Kleiger's integrative effort:

> Of all the shading categories, texture responses have the most direct and clear-cut connection to object relations theory. Attachment needs and object seeking are concepts intrinsic to Rorschach texture responses. Exner's (1986a) normative data show that most nonpatient adults have at least one texture response (usually an FT), a finding which supports the central role of attachment in human experience. However, according to Exner (1986a), more

than one texture response (of any type or quality) suggests the presence of more intense dependency needs. One good texture response may then suggest a more developmentally mature form of attachment or mature dependence (Fairbairn, 1952). In line with this, McFate and Orr (1949) noted that TF and pure T responses occur more in children and adolescents than in adult records. Thus, it seems reasonable to conclude that texture dominated responses (TF or pure T) reflect immature or poorly modulated needs for closeness and contact [p. 16].

In the earlier article, Kleiger and Peebles-Kleiger (1993) applied psychoanalytic theory to Exner's (1986) empirically rooted special scores, again with the intent of enriching the conceptual understanding of these scores. As indicated in chapter 9, they also suggested minor modifications to several of the special score categories. Even though their integrative effort is narrower and is tilted toward the psychoanalytic approach, it nonetheless builds upon empirically based findings and seeks to achieve the balance Erdberg (1993) refers to between normative data and theoretical richness.

A third type of integration, one even more weighted to the psychoanalytic side, is presented by Smith (1997). Smith begins by arguing that for assessment to be meaningful, one needs a theoretical framework within which to fit test-based observations and interpretations. As Sugarman (1991) had noted earlier, a coherent theory of personality allows one to find meaning in a particular response or set of responses, provides a structure for organizing the mass of data, and enables the clinician to derive prognostic and therapeutic inferences from test data. For Smith, only psychoanalytic theory in general, and object-relations theory in particular, "contains propositions capable of linking test results with underlying psychological processes, genetic or developmental . . . , [so that] observable behavior can provide the framework for a comprehensive psychological evaluation" (p. 193).

Smith's methodology is clinical, not empirical. He scores the protocol in terms of the Comprehensive System and makes use of the structural summary. He begins interpretation by examining the structural variables, but then adopts a "more fluid interpretive process" in which he "moves back and forth between structural variables and more narrative data" (p. 195). Unlike Exner (1993), who recommends an interpretive strategy based on key variables, Smith first attends to "the most striking findings, especially those that were noteworthy during the administration" (p. 195). He then examines cognitive factors, affects, defenses, self- and object representations, and dynamics.

◆ ◆ ◆ Discussion

Efforts to integrate the empirical and psychoanalytic approaches rekindle basic questions that have concerned and challenged Rorschach practitioners, researchers, and students since Rorschach introduced his method virtually 75 years ago. Like our forefathers and foremothers, we still ask: What is a test sign? How do we come to attribute meaning to test signs? Is a sign approach sufficient? Are clinically intended, theoretically sound and consistent test-based inferences valid if they are not bolstered by empirical findings? What are acceptable criteria of validity that both meet the needs of the clinician and satisfy the more stringent demands of the researcher? And, how do we come to know and understand another person in his or her complexity, depth, and uniqueness?

The tension that exists between the empiricist, with his or her interest in hard and solid data, numbers that can be crunched with objectivity, and the clinician, with his or her investment in softer narrative data, subjective meanings, and human drama, is not, of course, restricted to our provincial Rorschach realm. Something of the same dynamic may be found in any number of arenas, including baseball.

Baseball loyalists, too, may be divided into two camps: those who are drawn to the numbers and statistics, and those who are prompted by the human-interest side of the game. The former group, much like the Rorschach empiricist, regards traditional baseball statistics, such as batting average, earned-run average, and winning percent, as signs of a player's or team's value and greatness. Such individuals spend endless and pleasurable hours devising innovative and intricate mathematical formulas to explain a team's past success, to suggest who should and who should not be elected to the Hall of Fame, or to forecast next season's pennant winners. Here, one is interested in the box score, not the narrative of the game.

The interests and passions of the latter group are altogether different. Like the psychoanalytically oriented Rorschacher, for these individuals, statistics and records fail to capture the grit, essence, and character (meaning "substance") of a player. The contributions of a player, they insist, who consistently makes the routine play, advances a runner from second to third base, and constantly hustles, cannot be found in a box score. Only by observing that player up close and on a regular basis, can one truly assess the player's mettle and value to his team. Here, one's interest is not in the player's numbers, but rather in his personhood.

Like baseball, the Rorschach is broad, complex, and compelling enough to embrace both empiricists and conceptualists, as well as this newer group of integrationists. Speaking as a psychoanalyst, I believe that the Rorschach approach one subscribes to is not primarily based on rational and pragmatic considerations. Instead, one's training and personality makeup, including one's desires, attitudes, interests, values, and identity, play a more decisive role.

In this chapter and throughout this book I have attempted to present a particular Rorschach point of view as thoughtfully and clearly as possible. To bring this full circle, in the preface I indicated that for Mayman and myself, the psychoanalytic approach has allowed each of us to feel exhilarated, curious, and creative every time we are presented a new protocol. It is not my place to tell another which approach is right for him or her. It is my prerogative, however, to hope that whatever approach one follows, his or her perspective permits similar feelings of excitement and challenge.

❖ ❖ ❖ Summary

I began this chapter by reviewing briefly the evolution of both Exner's empirical approach and the psychoanalytic approach. I then discussed three different ways in which Rorschach authors have attempted to integrate the two perspectives. One, the broadest and most ambitious, begins with an empirical methodology. In general, the Comprehensive System is applied to the formal aspects of a protocol to assess structural features of personality, and psychoanalytic methods are applied to content to assess dynamic features. Typically, the findings are integrated and organized within a psychoanalytic framework. A second effort, considerably narrower than the first, has involved applying each of the psychoanalytic submodels to specific Comprehensive System scores with the intent of deepening the conceptual understanding of the score. A third approach consists of incorporating the Comprehensive System into an essentially psychoanalytic methodology. It was suggested that the tension between empiricists and conceptualists is not unique to the Rorschach. Viewed in broader terms, the division perhaps reflects the differences between those who have a more scientific bent and those who have a more artistic bent.

REFERENCES

Abend, S., Ponder, M. & Willick, M. (1983), *Borderline Patients*. New York: International Universities Press.

Abraham, K. (1921–1925), Psycho-analytic studies on character formation. In: *Selected Papers on Psycho-Analysis*. London: Hogarth Press, 1927, pp. 370–417.

Acklin, M. (1993), Psychodiagnosis of personality structure II: Borderline personality organization. *J. Pers. Assess.*, 61:329–341.

———— (1995), Avoiding Rorschach dichotomies: Integrating Rorschach interpretation. *J. Pers. Assess.*, 64:235–238.

Ainsworth, M., Blehar, M., Waters, E. & Wall, S. (1978), *Patterns of Attachment*. Hillsdale, NJ: Lawrence Erlbaum.

Alexander, F. (1930), The neurotic character. *Internat. J. Psycho-Anal.*, 11:292–311.

Allen, J. (1993), Dissociative processes: Theoretical underpinnings of a working model for clinician and patient. *Bull. Menn. Clin.*, 57:287–308.

Allison, J. (1967), Adaptive regression and intense religious experiences. *J. Nerv. Ment. Dis.*, 145:452–463.

———— Blatt, S. & Zimet, C. (1968), *The Interpretation of Psychological Tests*. New York: Harper & Row.

American Psychiatric Association (1980), Diagnostic and Statistical Manual of Mental Disorders, 3rd ed. Washington, DC: American Psychiatric Association.

———— (1987), Diagnostic and Statistical Manual of Mental Disorders (3rd ed. rev.). Washington, DC: American Psychiatric Association.

Ames, L. (1966), Longitudinal survey of child Rorschach responses: Older subjects aged 10 to 16 years. *Genetic Psychol. Monogr.*, 62:185–229.

———— Metraux, R., Rodell, J. & Walker, R. (1974), *Child Rorschach Responses*, 2nd ed. New York: Brunner/Mazel.

Appelbaum, S. (1959), The effect of altered psychological atmosphere on Rorschach responses. *Bull. Menn. Clin.*, 23:179–189.

—— (1963), The masochistic character as a self-saboteur. *J. Proj. Tech.*, 27:35–45.

—— (1970), Science and persuasion in the psychological test report. *J. Consult. & Clin. Psychol.*, 135:349–355.

—— (1975), Psychotherapy before and after. Unpublished manuscript. Menninger Foundation, Topeka.

—— (1977), *The Anatomy of Change*. New York: Plenum.

—— & Colson, D. (1968), A re-examination of the color-shading Rorschach test response and suicide attempts. *J. Proj. Tech. & Pers. Assess.*, 32:160–164.

—— & Holtzman, P. (1962), The color-shading response and suicide. *J. Pers. Assess.*, 26:155–161.

Arlow, J. (1966), Depersonalization and derealization. In: *Psychoanalysis—A General Psychology,* ed. R. Lowenstein, L. Newman, M. Schur & A. Solnit. New York: International Universities Press, pp. 456–478.

Armstrong, J. (1991), The psychological organization of multiple personality disordered patients as revealed in psychological testing. *Psychiat. Clin. N. Amer.*, 14:533–546.

—— (1994), Reflections on multiple personality disorder as a developmentally complex adaptation. *The Psychoanalytic Study of the Child,* 49:349–370. New Haven, CT: Yale University Press.

—— & Lowenstein, R. (1990), Characteristics of patients with multiple personality and dissociative disorders on psychological testing. *J. Nerv. Ment. Dis.*, 178:448–454.

Arnold, F. & Saunders, E. (1989), Reframing borderline disorder: Etiology, conceptualization, and treatment. Presented at the Harvard Medical School, Cambridge.

Arnow, D. & Cooper, S. (1988), Toward a Rorschach psychology of the self. In: *Primitive Mental States and the Rorschach,* ed. H. Lerner & P. Lerner. Madison, CT: International Universities Press, pp. 53–70.

Aronow, E., Reznikoff, M. & Moreland, K. (1995), The Rorschach: Projective technique or psychometric test? *J. Pers. Assess.*, 64:213–228.

Athey, G. (1974), Schizophrenic thought organization, object relations, and the Rorschach test. *Bull. Menn. Clin.*, 38:406–429.

—— (1986), Rorschach thought organization and transference enactment in the patient–examiner relationship. In: *Asessing Object*

Relations Phenomena, ed. M. Kissen. New York: International Universities Press, pp. 19–50.

Bachrach, H. (1968), Adaptive regression, empathy and psychotherapy: Theory and research study. *Psychotherapy,* 5:203–209.

Barnard, C. & Hirsch, C. (1985), Borderline personality and victims of incest. *Psychol. Reports,* 57:715–718.

Beahrs, J. (1982), *Unity and Multiplicity.* New York: Brunner/Mazel.

Beck, S. (1944–1945), *Rorschach's Test.* New York: Grune & Stratton.

Becker, W. (1956), A genetic approach to the interpretation and evaluation of the process-reactive distinction in schizophrenia. *J. Abnorm. & Soc. Psychol.,* 53:229–336.

Benfari, R., & Calogeras, R. (1968), Levels of cognition and conscience typolgies. *J. Proj. Tech. & Pers. Assess.,* 32:466–474.

Benner, D. & Joscelyne, B. (1984), Multiple personality as a borderline disorder. *J. Nerv. Ment. Dis.,* 172:98–104.

Berg, J. (1990), Differentiating ego functions of borderline and narcissistic personalities. *J. Pers. Assess.,* 55:537–548.

———— Packer, A. & Nunno, V. (1993), A Rorschach analysis: Parallel disturbance in thought and in self/object representation. *J. Pers. Asess.,* 61:311–323.

Berg, M. (1983), Borderline psychopathology as displayed on psychological tests. *J. Pers. Assess.,* 47:120–133.

Berstein, E. & Putnam, F. (1986), Development, reliability, and validity of a dissociation scale. *J. Nerv. Ment. Dis.,* 174:727–735.

Binder, H. (1933), Die Helldunkeldeutungen im psychodiagnostischen Experiment von Rorschach. *Schweiz. Arch. Neurol. Psychiat.,* 30:1–67.

Bion, W. (1956), Development of schizophrenic thought. In: *Second Thoughts.* New York: Aronson, 1967, pp. 36–42.

———— (1967), *Second Thoughts.* London: Heinemann.

Blatt, S. (1974), Levels of object representation in anaclitic and introjective depression. *The Psychoanalytic Study of the Child,* 29:107–157. New Haven, CT: Yale University Press.

———— (1990), The Rorschach: A test of perception or an evaluation of representation. *J. Pers. Assess.,* 55:394–416.

———— & Lerner, H. (1982), Investigations in the psychoanalytic theory of object relations and object representations. *Empirical Studies in Psychoanalytic Theory, Vol. 1,* ed. J. Masling. Hillsdale, NJ: The Analytic Press, pp. 189–249.

———— & Lerner, H. (1983), The psychological assessment of object representation. *J. Pers. Assess.,* 47:7–28.

——— & Ritzler, B. (1974), Thought disorder and boundary disturbances in psychosis. *J. Consult. Clin. Psychol.,* 42:370–381.

——— Allison, J., & Feirstein, A. (1969), The capacity to cope with cognitive complexity. *J. Pers.,* 37:269–288.

——— Schimek, J. & Brenneis, C. (1980), The nature of the psychotic experience and its implications for the therapeutic process. In: *The Psychotherapy of Schizophrenia,* ed. J. Strauss et al. New York: Plenum.

——— Tuber, S. & Averbach, J. (1990), Representation of interpersonal interactions on the Rorschach and level of psychopathology. *J. Pers. Assess.,* 54:711–728.

——— Wild, C. & Ritzler, B. (1975), Disturbances of object representations in schizophrenia. *Psychoanal. & Contemp. Thought,* 4:235–288.

——— Berman, W., Bloom-Feshbach, S., Sugarman, A., Wilber, C. & Kleber, H. (1984), Psychological assessment in opiate addicts. *J. Nerv. Ment. Dis.,* 172:156–165.

——— Brenneis, C., Schimek, J. & Glick, M. (1976), A developmental analysis of the concept of the object on the Rorschach. Unpublished manuscript, Dept. Psychology, Yale University.

——— Ford, R., Berman, W., Cook, B. & Meyer, R. (1988), The assessment of change during the intensive treatment of borderline and schizophrenic young adults. *Psychoanal. Psychol.,* 5:127–158.

Bleger, J. (1967), Psychoanalysis of the psychoanalytic frame. *Internat. J. Psycho-Anal.,* 48:511–519.

Bleuler, E. (1924), *Textbook of Psychiatry.* New York: Dover.

Blum, H. (1981), Object inconstancy and paranoid conspiracy. *J. Amer. Psychoanal. Assn.,* 29:789–814.

Bohm, E. (1959), The Binder Chiaroscuro system and its theoretical basis. In: *Rorschach Psychology,* 2nd ed., ed. M. Rickers-Ovsiankina. Huntington, NY: Krieger, 1977, pp. 303–324.

Boyer, B. (1977), The treatment of a borderline patient. *Psychoanal. Quart.,* 46:386–424.

Brende, J. (1983), A psychodynamic view of character pathology in Vietnam combat veterans. *Bull. Menn. Clin.,* 47:193–216.

Brenner, C. (1982), *The Mind in Conflict.* Madison, CT: International Universities Press.

Brenner, I. (1994), The dissociative character. *J. Amer. Psychoanal. Assn.,* 42:819–846.

Bretherton, I. (1987), New perspectives on attachment relations: Security, communication, and internal working models. In: *Handbook of Infant Development,* 2nd ed., ed. J. Osofsky. New York: Wiley, pp. 1061–1100.

Breuer, J. & Freud, S. (1893–1895), Studies on hysteria. *Standard Edition,* 2:1–306. London: Hogarth Press, 1955.

Brewer, W. (1986), What is autobiographical memory? In: *Autobiographical Memory,* ed. D. Rubin. New York: Cambridge University Press, pp. 25–49.

Brierly, M. (1937), Affects in theory and practice. In: *Trends in Psychoanalysis.* London: Hogarth Press, 1951, pp. 43–56.

Brouillette, C. (1987), A Rorschach assessment of the character structure of anorexia nervosa and bulimia patients and of their mothers. Unpublished doctoral dissertation, Dept. of Applied Psychology, University of Toronto.

Brown, G. & Anderson, B. (1991), Psychiatric morbidity in adult inpatients with childhood histories of sexual and physical abuse. *Amer. J. Psychiat.,* 148: 55–61.

Brown, L. (1996), A proposed demography of the representation world. *Melanie Klein and Object Relations,* 14:21–60.

Brown-Cheatham, M. (1993), The Rorschach mutuality of autonomy scale in the assessment of black father-absent male children. *J. Pers. Assess.,* 61:524–530.

Bryer, J., Nelson, B., Miller, J. & Krol, P. (1987), Childhood sexual and physical abuse as factors in adult psychiatric illness. *Amer. J. Psychiat.,* 144:1426–1430.

Buck, O. (1983), Multiple personality as a borderline state. *J. Nerv. Ment. Dis.,* 171:62–65.

Carlsson, A., Bihlár, B., & Nygren, M. (1996), The Stockholm Comparative Psychotherapy Study (COMPASS): Project presentation and preliminary Rorschach findings. Presented to the International Rorschach Congress, Boston.

Carpenter, W., Gunderson, J. & Strauss, J. (1977), Considerations of the borderline syndrome: A longitudinal comparative study of borderline and schizophrenic patients. In: *Borderline Personality Disorders,* ed. P. Hartocollis. New York: International Universities Press, pp. 231–253.

Carr, A. (1987), Borderline defenses and Rorschach responses: A critique of Lerner, Albert and Walsh. *J. Pers. Assess.,* 51:349–351.

Chapman, L. & Chapman, J. (1982), Subtle cognitive slippage scale. Unpublished manuscript.

Chasseguet-Smirgel, J. (1992), Some thoughts on the psychoanalytic situation. *J. Amer. Psychoanal. Assn.,* 40:3–26.

Clary, W., Burstin, K. & Carpenter, J. (1984), Multiple personality and borderline personality disorder. *Psychiat. Clin. N. Amer.,* 7:89–99.

Coates, S. & Tuber, S. (1988), The representation of object relations in the Rorschachs of extremely feminine boys. In: *Primitive Mental States and the Rorschach,* ed. H. Lerner & P. Lerner. Madison, CT: International Universities Press, pp. 647–664.

Cohen, I. (1960), An investigation of the relationship between adaptive regression, dogmatism, and creativity using the Rorschach and dogmatism scale. Unpublished doctoral dissertation, Dept. of Psychology, Michigan State University.

Cohen, J. & Mannarino, A. (1988), Psychological symptoms in sexually abused girls. *Child Abuse & Neglect,* 12:571–577.

Colligan, S. & Exner, J. (1985), Responses of schizophrenics and nonpatients to a tachistoscopic presentation of the Rorschach. *J. Pers. Assess.,* 49:129–136.

Collins, R. (1983), Rorschach correlates of borderline personality. Unpublished doctoral dissertation, Dept. of Applied Psychology, University of Toronto.

Coonerty, S. (1986), An exploration of separation-individuation themes in the borderline personality disorder. *J. Pers. Assess.,* 50:501–511.

Cooper, S. (1981), An object relations view of the borderline defenses: A Rorschach analysis. Unpublished manuscript.

———— (1989), Recent contributions to the theory of defense mechanisms. *J. Amer. Psychoanal. Assn.,* 37:865–891.

———— & Arnow, D. (1986), An object relations view of the borderline defenses: A review. In: *Assessing Object Relations Phenomena,* ed. M. Kissen. New York: International Universities Press, pp. 143–171.

———— Perry, J. & Arnow, D. (1988), An empirical approach to the study of defense mechanisms: I. Reliability and preliminary validity of the Rorschach defense scale. *J. Pers. Assess.,* 52:187–203.

———— ———— & O'Connell, M. (1991), The Rorschach Defense Scales: II. Longitudinal perspectives. *J. Pers. Assess.,* 56:191–201.

Dana, R. (1968), Six constructs to define Rorschach M. *J. Proj. Tech. and Pers. Assess.,* 32:138–145.

Deutsch, H. (1942), Some forms of emotional disturbance and their relationship to schizophrenia. *Psychoanal. Quart.,* 11:301–321.

Diamond, D., Kaslow, N., Coonerty, S. & Blatt, S. (1990), Changes in separation-individuation and intersubjectivity in long-term treatment. *Psychoanal. Psychol.*, 7:363–398.

Dorpat, T. & Miller, M. (1993), *The Analysis of Meaning.* Hillsdale, NJ: The Analytic Press.

Dudek, S. & Chamberland-Bouhadana, G. (1982), Primary process in creative persons. *J. Pers. Assess.*, 46:239–247.

Easser, R. (1974), Empathic inhibition and psychoanalytic technique. *Psychoanal. Quart.*, 43:557–580.

—— & Lesser, S. (1965), Hysterical personality: A re-evaluation. *Psychoanal. Quart.*, 43:390–405.

—— & —— (1966), Transference resistance in hysterical character neurosis: Technical considerations. *Developments in Psychoanalysis at Columbia University.* New York: Columbia University Press, pp. 69–80.

Edell, W. (1984), The Borderline-Syndrome Index: Clinical validity and utility. *J. Nerv. Ment. Dis.*, 172:254–263.

—— (1987), Role of structure in disordered thinking in borderline and schizophrenic disorders. *J. Pers. Assess.*, 51:23–41.

Edelman, G. (1992), *Bright Air, Bright Fire.* New York: Basic Books.

Elizur, A. (1949), Content analysis of the Rorschach with regard to anxiety and hostility. *J. Proj. Tech.*, 13:247–284.

Epstein, L. (1979), Countertransference with borderline patients. In: *Countertransference,* ed. L. Epstein & A. Feiner. New York: Aronson, pp. 375–406.

Erdberg, P. (1993), The U.S. Rorschach scene: Integration and elaboration. *Rorschachiana,* 18:139–151.

—— (1995), An integrative approach to the Rorschach. Presented to the Society for Personality Assessment, Atlanta.

Erickson, M. & Rapaport, D. (1980), Findings on the nature of the personality structures in two different dual personalities by means of projective and psychometric tests. In: *The Collected Papers of Milton Erickson: Vol. 3.* New York: Irvington.

Erikson, E. (1950), *Childhood and Society.* New York: Norton.

Exner, J. (1974), *The Rorschach, Vol. 1.* New York: Wiley.

—— (1986a), *The Rorschach, Vol. 1,* 2nd ed. New York: Wiley.

—— (1986b), Some Rorschach data comparing schizophrenics with borderline and schizotypal personality disorders. *J. Pers. Assess.*, 50:455–471.

—— (1989), History of the Society. In: *History and Directory,* ed. A. O'Roark & J. Exner. Hillsdale, NJ: Lawrence Erlbaum, pp. 3–54.

———— (1991), *The Rorschach, Vol. 2*, 2nd ed. New York: Wiley.

———— (1993), *The Rorschach, Vol. 1*, 3rd ed. New York: Wiley.

———— (1996), Critical bits and the Rorschach response process. *J. Pers. Assess.*, 67:464–477.

———— & Andronikof-Sanglade, A. (1992), Rorschach changes following brief and short-term therapy. *J. Pers. Assess.*, 59:59–71.

———— & Bryant, E. (1974), Rorschach responses of subjects recently divorced or separated. Unpublished manuscript, Rorschach Workshops, Bayville, NY.

———— Armbruster, G. & Mittman, B. (1978), The Rorschach response process. *J. Pers. Assess.*, 42:27–38.

———— Wylie, J. & Bryant, E. (1974), Peer preference nominations among outpatients in four psychotherapy groups. Unpublished manuscript, Rorschach Workshops, Bayville, NY.

Fairbairn, W. (1952), *Psychoanalytic Studies of the Personality*. London: Tavistock.

Farris, M. (1988), Differential diagnosis of borderline and narcissistic personality disorders. In: *Primitive Mental States and the Rorschach*, ed. H. Lerner & P. Lerner. Madison, CT: International Universities Press, pp. 299–338.

Fast, I. (1974), Multiple identities in borderline personality organization. *Brit. J. Med. Psychol.*, 47:291–300.

Feirstein, A. (1967), Personality correlates for unrealistic experiences. *J. Consult. Psychol.*, 31:387–395.

Fenichel, O. (1945), *Psychoanalytic Theory of Neurosis*. New York: Norton.

Ferracuti, S., Sacco, R. & Lazzari, R. (1996), Dissociative trance disorder: Clinical and Rorschach findings in ten persons reporting demon possession and treated by exorcism. *J. Pers. Assess.*, 66:525–539.

Fibel, B. (1979), Toward a developmental model of depression: Object representation and object loss in adolescent and adult psychiatric patients. Unpublished doctoral dissertation, Dept. of Psychology, University of Massachusetts, Amherst.

Fisher, S. & Cleveland, S. (1968), *Body Image and Personality*. New York: Van Nostrand Reinhold.

Ford, M. (1946), *The Application of the Rorschach Test to Young Children*. Minneapolis: University of Minnesota.

Fraiberg, S. (1959), *The Magic Years*. New York: Scribners.

Frances, A. (1995), A practitioner's guide to DSM-IV. Conference sponsored by Institute for Behavioral Healthcare, Philadelphia, PA, February 18.

Frank, G. (1992), On the use of the Rorschach in the study of PTSD. *J. Pers. Assess.*, 59:641–643.

Freiswyk, S. & Colson, D. (1980), Prognostic considerations in the hospital treatment of borderline states: The perspective of object relations theory and the Rorschach. In: *Borderline Phenomena and the Rorschach Test*, ed. J. Kwawer, H. Lerner, P. Lerner, & A. Sugarman. New York: International Universities Press, pp. 229–256.

Freud, A. (1936), *The Ego and the Mechanisms of Defense*. New York: International Universities Press.

Freud, S. (1896), Further remarks on the neuro-psychoses of defense. *Standard Edition*, 3:159–188. London: Hogarth Press, 1962.

——— (1900), The interpretation of dreams. *Standard Edition*, 4 & 5. London: Hogarth Press, 1953.

——— (1908), Character and anal erotism. *Standard Edition*, 9:167–175. London: Hogarth Press, 1959.

——— (1910), The future prospects of psycho-analytic therapy. *Standard Edition*, 11:139–152. London: Hogarth Press, 1957.

——— (1912), Recommendations for physicians practicing psycho-analysis. *Standard Edition*, 12:109–120. London: Hogarth Press, 1958.

——— (1914), On narcissism: An introduction. *Standard Edition*, 14:73–102. London: Hogarth Press, 1957.

——— (1915a), Instincts and their vicissitudes. *Standard Edition*, 14:109–140. London: Hogarth Press, 1957.

——— (1915), The unconscious. *Standard Edition*, 14:159–216. London: Hogarth Press, 1957.

——— (1917), Mourning and melancholia. *Standard Edition*, 14:237–260. London: Hogarth Press, 1957.

——— (1923), The ego and the id. *Standard Edition*, 19:12–59. London: Hogarth Press, 1961.

——— (1926), Inhibitions, symptoms and anxiety. *Standard Edition*, 20:87–172. London: Hogarth Press, 1959.

——— (1931), Libidinal types. *Standard Edition*, 21:215–220. London: Hogarth Press, 1961.

Friedman, H. (1953), Perceptual regression in schizophrenia. An hypothesis suggested by use of the Rorschach test. *J. Proj. Tech.*, 17:171–185.

Friedman, L. (1990), *Menninger: The Family and the Clinic*. New York: Alfred A. Knopf.

Frieswyk, S. & Colson, D. (1980), Prognostic considerations in the hospital treatment of borderline states: The perspective of object relations theory and the Rorschach. In: *Borderline Phenomena and the Rorschach Test*, ed. J. Kwawer, H. Lerner, P. Lerner, & A. Sugarman. New York: International Universities Press, pp. 229–256.

Fritsch, R. & Holmstrom, R. (1990), Assessing object representations as a continuous variable: A modification of the concept of the object on the Rorschach scale. *J. Pers. Assess., 55*:319–334.

Gabbard, G. (1989), Two subtypes of narcissistic personality disorder. *Bull. Menn. Clin., 53*:527–532.

Gacono, C. (1988), A Rorschach analysis of object relations and defensive structure and their relationship to narcissism and psychopathy in a group of antisocial offenders. Unpublished doctoral dissertation, United States International University.

——— (1990), An empirical study of object relations and defensive operations in antisocial personality. *J. Pers. Assess., 54*:589–600.

——— & Meloy, J. R. (1994), *The Rorschach Assessment of Aggressive and Psychopathic Personalities*. Hillsdale, NJ: Lawrence Erlbaum.

——— ——— & Berg, J. (1992), Object relations, defensive operations, and affective states in narcissistic, borderline, and antisocial personality. *J. Pers. Assess., 59*:32–49.

Gaddini, R. (1975), The concept of transitional object. *J. Amer. Acad. Child Psychiat., 4*:731–736.

Gage, N. (1953), Explorations in the understanding of others. *Educational and Psychological Measurement, 13*:14–26.

Gardiner, M. (1971), *The Wolf Man*. New York: Basic Books.

Gardner, H. (1985), *The Mind's New Science*. New York: Basic Books.

Gartner, J., Hurt, S. & Gartner, A. (1989), Psychological test signs of borderline personality disorder: A review of the empirical literature. *J. Pers. Assess., 53*:423–441.

Gedo, J. (1979), *Beyond Interpretation*. New York: International Universities Press.

——— & Goldberg, A. (1973), *Models of the Mind*. Chicago: University of Chicago Press.

George, C., Kaplan, N. & Main, M. (1985), The attachment interview for adults. Unpublished manuscript, University of California, Berkeley.

Gibson, M. & Shapiro, E. (1993), From the Menninger to Austen Riggs: A circular chronology. *The American Psychoanalyst, 27*:18–20.

Giedt, F. (1955), Comparison of visual, content, and auditory cues in interviewing. *J. Consult. Psychol., 18*:407–416.

Gill, M. (1967), *The Collected Papers of David Rapaport*. New York: Basic Books.

—— & Klein, G. (1967), The structuring of drive and reality: David Rapaport's contributions to psychoanalysis and psychology. In: *The Collected Papers of David Rapaport*, ed. M. Gill. New York: Basic Books, pp. 8–34.

Goddard, R. & Tuber, S. (1989), Boyhood separation anxiety disorder. *J. Pers. Assess.*, 53:239–252.

Goldberg, E. (1989), Severity of depression and developmental levels of psychological functioning in eight sixteen-year old girls. *Amer. J. Orthopsychiat.*, 59:167–178.

Goldberger, L. (1961), Reactions to perceptual isolation and Rorschach manifestations of the primary process. *J. Proj. Tech.*, 25:287–302.

Goodwin, J., Cheeves, K. & Connell, V. (1990), Borderline and other severe symptoms in adult survivors of incestuous abuse. *Psychiat. Annals.*, 20: 22–32.

Gorney, J. & Weinstock, S. (1980), Borderline object relations, therapeutic impasse, and the Rorschach. In: *Borderline Phenomena and the Rorschach Test,* ed. J. Kwawer, H. Lerner, P. Lerner & A. Sugarman. New York: International Universities Press, pp. 167–188.

Graham, I. (1978), Representational and cognitive aspects of a depressive personality. Presented to the Toronto Psychoanalytic Society, Toronto, Ontario.

Grala, C. (1980), The concept of splitting and its manifestations on the Rorschach: *Bull. Menn. Clin.,* 44:253–271.

Greco, C. & Cornell, D. (1992), Rorschach object relations of adolescents who committed homicide. *J. Pers. Assess.*, 59:574–583.

Green, A. (1975), The analyst, symbolization and absence in the psychoanalytic setting. *Internat. J. Psycho-Anal.*, 56:1–22.

Greenberg, N., Ramsay, M., Rakoff, V. & Weiss, A. (1969), Primary process thinking in myxedema psychosis: A case study. *Can. J. Behav. Sci.,* 1:60–67.

Greene, L. (1996), Primitive defenses, object relations, and symptom clusters in borderline psychopathology. *J. Pers. Assess.*, 67:294–304.

Greenson, R. (1967), *The Technique and Practice of Psychoanalysis*. New York: International Universities Press.

Grinker, R., Werble, B. & Drye, R. (1968), *The Borderline Syndrome*. New York: Basic Books.

Grossman, W. (1982), The self as fantasy: Fantasy as theory. *J. Amer. Psychoanal. Assoc.*, 30:919–938.

Grotstein, J. (1981), *Splitting and Projective Identification*. New York: Aronson.

——— (1987), Schizophrenia as a disorder of self-regulation and inter-actional regulation. Presented at the Boyer House Foundation Conference "The Regressed Patient," San Francisco.

——— (1991), An American view of the British psycho-analytic experi-ence: Psychoanalysis in counterpoint. *Melanie Klein and Object Relations,* 9:1–62.

Gunderson, J. & Singer, M. (1975), Defining borderline patients: An overview. *Amer. J. Psychiat.,* 132:1–10.

Guntrip, H. (1952), A study of Fairbairn's theory of schizoid reactions. *Br. J. Med. Psychol.,* 25:86–103.

——— (1961), *Personality Structure and Human Interaction*. New York: International Universities Press.

——— (1969), *Schizoid Phenomena, Object Relations and the Self*. New York: International Universities Press.

Hamilton, N. (1995), Object relations units and the ego. *Bull. Menn. Clin.,* 59:416–426.

Hammond, J. (1984), Object relations and defensive operations in gen-der identity disordered males. Unpublished doctoral dissertation, United States International University.

Harder, D. (1979), The assessment of ambitious-narcissistic character style with three projective tests: The Early Memories, T.A.T., and Rorschach. *J. Pers. Assess.,* 43:23–32.

——— Greenwald, D., Wechsler, S. & Ritzler, B. (1984), The Urist Rorschach mutuality of autonomy scale as an indicator of psy-chopathology. *J. Clin. Psychol.,* 40:1078–1082.

Hardin, H. (1985), On the vicissitudes of early primary surrogate moth-ering. *J. Amer. Psychoanal. Assn.,* 33:609–629.

Hare, R. (1991), *Manual for the Revised Psychopathy Checklist*. Toronto: Multihealth System.

Harris, D. (1993), The prevalence of thought disorder in personality dis-ordered outpatients. *J. Pers. Assess.,* 61:112–120.

Hartman, W., Clark, M., Morgon, M., Dunn, V., Fine, A., Perry, G. & Winsh, D. (1991), Rorschach structure of a hospitalized sample of Vietnam veterans with ptsd. *J. Pers. Assess.,* 54:149–159.

Hartmann, H. (1950), comments on the psychoanalytic theory of the ego. In: *Essays on Ego Psychology*. New York: International Univer-sities Press, 1965, pp. 115–141.

Hatcher, R. & Krohn, A. (1980), Level of object representation and capacity for intensive psychotherapy in neurotics and borderlines. In: *Borderline Phenomena and the Rorschach Test,* ed. J. Kwawer, H. Lerner, P. Lerner & A. Sugarman. New York: International Universities Press, pp. 299–320.

Herman, J. & van der Kolk, B. (1987), Traumatic antecedents of borderline personality disorder. In: *Psychological Trauma,* ed. B. van der Kolk. Washington, DC: American Psychiatric Press, pp. 111–126.

———— Perry, J. and van der Kolk, B. (1986), Childhood trauma in borderline personality disorder. *Amer. J. Psychiat.,* 146:490–495.

Hillgard, E. (1977), *Divided Consciousness.* New York: Wiley.

Hilsenroth, M. & Handler, L. (1995), Bridging the gap between assessment and treatment. Presented to the Society for Personality Assessment, Atlanta.

———— Fowler, C., Padawer, J. & Handler, L. (in press), Narcissism in the Rorschach revisited: Some reflections upon empirical data. *Psychol. Assess.*

———— Hibbard, S., Nash, M. & Handler, L. (1993), A Rorschach study of narcissism, defense, and aggression in borderline, narcissistic, and cluster C personality disorders. *J. Pers. Assess.,* 60:346–361.

Hoffer, W. (1968), Notes on the theory of defense. *The Psychoanalytic Study of the Child,* 23:178–188. New York: International Universities Press.

Holt, R. (1954), Implications of some contemporary personality theories for Rorschach rationale. In: *Developments in the Rorschach Technique, Vol. 1,* ed. B. Klopfer, M. D. Ainsworth, W. G. Klopfer & R. Holt. New York: Harcourt, Brace & World, pp. 501–560.

———— (1956), Gauging primary and secondary processes in Rorschach responses. *J. Proj. Tech.,* 20:14–25.

———— (1958), Clinical and statistical prediction: A reformulation and some new data. *J. Abnorm. and Soc. Psychol.,* 56:1–12.

———— (1970), *Manual for the Scoring of Primary Process Manifestations and Their Controls in Rorschach Responses.* New York: Research Center for Mental Health.

———— (1977), A method for assessing primary process manifestations and their controls in Rorschach responses. In *Rorschach Psychology,* 2nd ed., ed. M. Rickers-Ovsiankina. Huntington, NY: Krieger, pp. 375–420.

———— D. Rapaport, M. Gill & R. Schafer, (1968) *Diagnostic Psychological Testing,* revised ed. New York: International Universities Press.

Holtzman, P. & Gardner, R. (1959), Leveling and repression. *J. Abnorm. & Soc. Psychol.*, 59:151–155.

Horevitz, R. & Braun, B. (1984), Are multiple personalities borderline? An analysis of 33 cases. *Psychiat. Clin. N. Amer.*, 7:69–87.

Horner, M. & Diamond, D. (1996), Object relations development and psychotherapy dropout in borderline outpatients. *Psychoanal. Psychol.*, 13:205–224.

Horowitz, M. (1972), Modes of representation of thought. *J. Amer. Psychoanal. Assn.*, 20:793–819.

——— (1992), The effects of psychic trauma on mind: Structure and processing of meaning. In: *Interface of Psychoanalysis and Psychology*, ed. J. Barron, M. Eagle & D. Wolitzky. Washington, DC: American Psychological Association, pp. 489–500.

Hymowitz, P., Hunt, H., Carr, A., Hurt, S. & Spear, W. (1983), The W.A.I.S. and the Rorschach in diagnosing borderline personality. *J. Pers. Assess.*, 47:588–596.

Ipp, H. (1986), Object relations of feminine boys: A Rorschach assessment. Unpublished doctoral dissertation, York University.

Jacobson, E. (1971), *Depression*. New York: International Universities Press.

Janet, P. (1907), *The Major Symptoms of Hysteria*. New York: Macmillan.

Jaschke, V. & Spiegel, D. (1992), A case of probable dissociative disorder. *Bull. Menn. Clin.*, 56:246–260.

Johnson, D. (1980), Cognitive organization in paranoid and nonparanoid schizophrenia. Unpublished doctoral dissertation, Dept. of Psychology, Yale University.

Johnston, M. & Holtzman, P. (1976), The Thought Disorder Index. Unpublished manuscript.

——— & Holtzman, P. (1979), *The Nature and Measurement of Thought Disorder*. San Francisco: Jossey-Bass.

Karmel, R. (1996), The Eichmann Rorschach and the concept of manic defense. Unpublished manuscript, Montreal General Hospital, Montreal.

Kaser-Boyd, N. (1993), Rorschachs of women who commit homicide. *J. Pers. Assess.*, 60:458–470.

Kataguchi, Y. (1959), Rorschach schizophrenic score. *J. Proj. Tech.*, 23:214–222.

Kaufer, J. & Katz, J. (1983), Rorschach responses in anorectic and nonanorectic women. *Internat. J. Eating Disorders*, 3:65–74.

Kavanagh, G. (1985), Changes in object representations in psychoanalysis and psychoanalytic psychotherapy. *Bull. Menn. Clin.*, 49:546–564.

Kelly, E. & Fiske, D. (1950), The prediction of success in the V.A. training program in clinical psychology. *Amer. Psychol.*, 4:395–406.

Kernberg, O. (1970), A psychoanalytic classification of character pathology. *J. Amer. Psychoanal. Assn.*, 18:800–822.

———— (1975), *Borderline Conditions and Pathological Narcissism*. New York: Aronson.

———— (1976), *Object Relations Theory and Clinical Psychoanalysis*. New York: Aronson.

———— (1977), The structural diagnosis of borderline personality organization. In: *Borderline Personality Disorders*, ed. P. Hartocollis. New York: International Universities Press, pp. 87–121.

———— (1979), Two reviews of the literature on borderlines: An assessment. *Schizophrenia Bull.*, 5:53–58.

———— (1980), *Internal World and External Reality*. New York: Aronson.

———— (1981), Structural interviewing. *Psychiat. Clin. N. Amer.*, 4:1–24.

———— (1982), Self, ego, affects, and drives. *J. Amer. Psychoanal. Assn.*, 30:893–917.

———— Burstein, E., Coyne, L., Appelbaum, A., Horwitz, L. & Voth, H. (1972), Psychotherapy and psychoanalysis: Final report of the Menninger Foundation's psychotherapy research project. *Bull. Menn. Clin.*, 36:3–275.

Kety, S., Rosenthal, D., Wender, P. & Schulsinger, F. (1968), The types and prevalence of mental illness in the biological and adoptive families of adopted schizophrenics. In: *The Transmission of Schizophrenia*, ed. D. Rosenthal & S. Kety. New York: Pergamon, pp. 345–362.

Kilchenstein, M. & Schuerholz, L. (1995), Autistic defenses and the impairment of cognitive development. *Bull. Menn. Clin.*, 59:443–459.

Kleiger, J. (in press), Rorschach shading responses: From a printer's error to an integrated psychoanalytic paradigm. *J. Pers. Assess.*

———— & Peebles-Kleiger, J. (1993), Toward a conceptual understanding of the deviant response in the Comprehensive Rorschach System. *J. Pers. Assess.*, 60:74–90.

Klein, D. (1973), Drug therapy as a means of syndromal identification and nosological revision. In: *Psychopathology and Pharmacology*, ed. J. Cole & A. Friedhoff. Baltimore: Johns Hopkins University Press.

———— (1975), Psychopharmacology and the borderline patient. In: *Borderline States in Psychiatry*, ed. J. Mack. New York: Grune & Stratton.

Klein, G. (1970) *Perception, Motives, and Personality.* New York: Alfred A. Knopf.

——— (1976), *Psychoanalytic Theory.* New York: International Universities Press.

Klein, M. (1926), The psychological principles of early analysis. In: *Love, Guilt, and Reparation.* New York: Delacorte Press, 1975, pp. 128–138.

——— (1927), Symposium on child analysis. In: *Love, Guilt, and Reparation.* New York: Delacorte Press, 1975, pp. 139–169.

——— (1930), The importance of symbol formation in the development of the ego. *Internat. J. Psycho-Anal.,* 11:24–39.

——— (1935), A contribution to the psychogenesis of manic-depressive states. *Contributions to Psycho-Analysis 1921–1945.* London: Hogarth Press, 1948, pp. 282–310.

——— (1946), Notes on some schizoid mechanisms. In: *Envy and Gratitude and Other Works 1946–1963.* New York: Delacorte Press/Seymour Lawrence, 1975, pp. 1–12.

——— (1957), Envy and gratitude. In: *Envy and Gratitude and Other Works 1946–1963.* New York: Delacorte Press/Seymour Lawrence, 1975, pp. 176–235.

Klopfer, B. (1938), The shading response. *Rorschach Res. Exch.,* 2:76–79.

——— & Kelley, D. (1942), *The Rorschach Technique.* Yonkers: World Book.

——— & Margulies, H. (1941), Rorschach reactions in early childhood. *Rorschach Res. Exch.,* 5:1–23.

——— Fox, J. & Troup, E. (1956), Problems in the use of the Rorschach technique with children. In: *Developments in the Rorschach Technique, Vol. 2,* ed. B. Klopfer, New York: Harcourt, Brace & World, pp. 3–21.

——— Spiegelman, M. & Fox, J. (1956), The interpretation of children's records. In: *Developments in the Rorschach Technique, Vol. 2,* ed. B. Klopfer. New York: Harcourt, Brace & World, pp. 22–44.

——— Kirkner, F., Wisham, W. & Baker, G. (1951), A preliminary report on the predictability of the Rorschach. Prognostic Rating Scale. *J. Proj. Tech.,* 15:421–422 (Abstract).

——— Ainsworth, M., Klopfer, W. & Holt, R. (1954), *Developments in the Rorschach Technique, Vol. 1.* New York: Harcourt, Brace & World.

Kluft, R. (1984), Treatment of multiple personality disorder: A study of 33 cases. *Psychiat. Clin. N. Amer.,* 7:9–29.

———— (1988), The dissociative disorders. In: *American Psychiatric Press Textbook of Psychiatry*, ed. J. Talbott, R. Hales & S. Yudofsky. Washington, DC: American Psychiatric Press, pp. 557–585.

———— (1992), Discussion: A specialist's perspective on multiple personality disorder. *Psychoanal. Inq.*, 12:139–171.

Knight, R. (1953), Borderline states. In: *Psychoanalytic Psychiatry and Psychology*, ed. R. Knight & C. Friedman. New York: International Universities Press, pp. 97–109.

Kohut, H. (1959), Introspection, empathy, and psychoanalysis. In: *The Search for the Self, Vol. 1*, ed. P. Ornstein. Madison, CT: International Universities Press, 1978, pp. 205–232.

———— (1971), *The Analysis of the Self*. New York: International Universities Press.

———— (1977), *The Restoration of the Self*. New York: International Universities Press.

———— (1984), *How Does Analysis Cure?* ed. A. Goldberg & P. Stepansky. Chicago: University of Chicago Press.

———— & Wolf, E. (1978), The disorders of the self and their treatment: An outline. *Internat. J. Psycho-Anal.*, 59:413–425.

Kolb, J. & Gunderson, J. (1980), Diagnosing borderlines with a semi-structured interview. *Arch. Gen. Psychiat.*, 37:37–41.

Kolers, N. (1986), Some ego functions in boys with gender identity disturbance. Unpublished doctoral dissertation, York University, Ontario.

Kostlan, A. (1954), A method for the empirical study of psychodiagnostics. *J. Consult. Psychol.*, 18:83–88.

Kris, A. (1982), *Free Association*. New Haven, CT: Yale University Press.

———— (1984), The conflicts of ambivalence. *The Psychoanalytic Study of the Child*, 38:439–458. New Haven, CT: International University Press.

Kris, E. (1952), *Psychoanalytic Explorations in Art*. New York: International Universities Press.

Krohn, A. (1974), Borderline empathy and differentiation of object representations: A contribution to the psychology of object relations. *Internat. J. Psychoanal. Psychother.*, 3:142–165.

———— (1978), Hysteria: The elusive neurosis. *Psychological Issues*, Mongr. 45/46. New York: International Universities Press.

———— & Mayman, M. (1974), Object representations in dreams and protective tests. *Bull. Menn. Clin.*, 38:445–466.

Krystal, H. (1988), *Integration and Self-Healing*. Hillsdale, NJ: The Analytic Press.

Kwawer, J. (1980), Primitive interpersonal modes, borderline phenomena, and Rorschach content. In: *Borderline Phenomena and the Rorschach Test,* ed. J. Kwawer, H. Lerner, P. Lerner, & A. Sugarman. New York: International Universities Press, pp. 89–106.

———— Lerner, H., Lerner, P. & Sugarman, A. (1980), *Borderline Phenomena and the Rorschach Test.* New York: International Universities Press.

LaPlanche, J. & Pontalis, J. (1973), *The Language of Psychoanalysis.* New York: Norton.

Laughlin, H. (1956), *The Neuroses in Clinical Practice.* Philadelphia: Saunders.

Leeuw, P. (1971), On the development of the concept of defense. *Internat. J. Psycho-Anal.,* 52:51–58.

Leichtman, M. (1996), *The Rorschach.* Hillsdale, NJ: The Analytic Press.

Leifer, M., Shapiro, J., Martone, M. & Kassem, L. (1991), Rorschach assessment of psychological functioning in sexually abused girls. *J. Pers. Assess.,* 56:14–28.

Lerner, H. (1988), The narcissistic personality as expressed through psychological tests. In: *Primitive Mental States and the Rorschach,* ed. H. Lerner & P. Lerner. Madison, CT: International Universities Press.

———— (1996), When less is more: Single responses on barren Rorschachs. Presented to the Society for Personality Assessment, Denver, CO.

———— & Lerner, P. (1982), A comparative study of defensive structure in neurotic, borderline, and schizophrenic patients. *Psychoanal. Contemp. Thought,* 5:77–113.

———— & Lerner, P. (1986), Contributions of object relations theory towards a general psychoanalytic theory of thinking. *Psychoanal. Contemp. Thought,* 9:469–513.

———— & Lerner, P. (1988), *Primitive Mental States and the Rorschach.* Madison, CT: International Universities Press.

———— & Lerner, P. (1990), Rorschach measures of psychoanalytic theories of defense, *Advances Pers. Assess.,* 8:121–160.

———— & Lerner, P. (in press), Dissociation: Structure and dynamics. In: *Making Diagnosis Meaningful,* ed. J. Barron. Washington, DC: APA Books.

———— & St. Peter, S. (1984), Patterns of object relations in neurotic, borderline and schizophrenic patients. *Psychiatry,* 47:77–92.

———— Albert, C. & Walsh, M. (1987), The Rorschach assessment of borderline defenses. *J. Pers. Assess.,* 51:344–354.

———— Sugarman, A. & Barbour, C. (1985), Patterns of ego boundary disturbances in neurotic, borderline and schizophrenic patients. *Psychoanal. Psychol.*, 2:47–66.

———— Sugarman, A. & Gaughran, J. (1981), Borderline and schizophrenic patients: A comparative study of defensive structure. *J. Nerv. Ment. Dis.*, 169:705–711.

Lerner, P. (1975), *Handbook of Rorschach Scales*. New York: International Universities Press.

———— (1979), Treatment implications of the (c) response in the Rorschach records of patients with severe character pathology. *Ontario Psychol.*, 11:20–22.

———— (1981), Cognitive aspects of the (c) response in the Rorschach records of patients with severe character pathology. Presented to the International Rorschach Congress, Washington, DC.

———— (1985), Current psychoanalytic perspectives on the borderline and narcissistic concepts. *Clin. Psych. Rev.*, 5:99–114.

———— (1986), Experiential and structural aspects of the (c) Rorschach response in patients with narcissistic personality disorders. In: *Assessing Object Relations Phenomena*, ed. M. Kissen. New York: International Universities Press, pp. 333–348.

———— (1988), Rorschach measures of depression, the false self, and projective identification with narcissistic personality disorders. In: *Primitive Mental States and the Rorschach,* ed. H. Lerner & P. Lerner. Madison, CT: International Universities Press, pp. 71–94.

———— (1991a), *Psychoanalytic Theory and the Rorschach*. Hillsdale, NJ: The Analytic Press.

———— (1991b), The analysis of content revisited. *J. Pers. Assess.*, 56:145–157.

———— (1992), Toward an experiential psychoanalytic approach to the Rorschach. *Bull. Menn. Clin.*, 56:451–464.

———— (1994), Inferring object relational capacities from an assessment of affect. Presented to the Society for Personality Assessment, Chicago.

———— (1996a), Current perspectives on psychoanalytic Rorschach assessment. *J. Pers. Assess.*, 67:450–460.

———— (1996b), Rorschach case study. Presented to the International Rorschach Congress, Boston.

———— (1996c), Rorschach assessment of cognitive impairment from an object relations perspective. *Bull. Menn. Clin.*, 60:351–365.

———— & Lerner, H. (1980), Rorschach assessment of primitive defenses in borderline personality structure. In: *Borderline Phenomena and the Rorschach Test,* ed. J. Kwawer, H. Lerner, P. Lerner & A. Sugarman. New York: International Universities Press, pp. 257–274.

—— & Lerner, H. (1996), Further notes on a case of possible multiple personality disorder: Masochism, omnipotence, and entitlement. *Psychoanal. Psychol.,* 13:403–417.

—— & Lewandowski, A. (1975), The measurement of primary process manifestations: A review. In: *Handbook of Rorschach Scales,* ed. P. Lerner. New York: International Universities Press, pp. 181–214.

Leura, A. & Exner, J. (1976), Rorschach performances of children with a multiple foster home history. Unpublished manuscript, Rorschach Workshops, Bayville, NY.

Levine, L. & Tuber, S. (1993), Measures of mental representation: Clinical and theoretical considerations. *Bull. Menn. Clin.,* 57:64–87.

—— —— Slade, A. & Ward, M. (1991), Mother's mental representations and their relationship to mother-infant attachment. *Bull. Men. Clin.,* 55:454–469.

Levine, M. & Spivak, C. (1964), *The Rorschach Index of Repressive Style.* Springfield, IL: Thomas.

Levine, R. (1988), Contributions of countertransference data from the analysis of the Rorschach: An object relations approach. In: *Primitive Mental States and the Rorschach,* ed. H. Lerner & P. Lerner. Madison, CT: International Universities Press, pp. 95–106.

Lindfors, O. (1996), Rorschach evaluation of psychotherapy outcome: Research plan of the Helsinki psychotherapy study. Presented to the International Rorschach Congress, Boston.

Loewald, H. (1973), On internalization. *Internat. J. Psycho-Anal.,* 54:9–18.

Loewenstein, R. & Ross, D. (1992), Multiple personality and psychoanalysis: An introduction. *Psychoanal. Inq.,* 12:3–48.

Lovitt, R. & Lefkof, G. (1985), Understanding multiple personality with the comprehensive Rorschach system. *J. Pers. Assess.,* 49:289–294.

Luborsky, L. & Holt, R. (1957), The selection of candidates for psychoanalytic training. *J. Clin. & Experiment. Psychopathol.,* 18:166–176.

Ludolph, P., Milden, R. & Lerner, H. (1988), Rorschach profiles of depressives: Clinical case illustrations. In: *Primitive Mental States and the Rorschach,* ed. H. Lerner & P. Lerner. Madison, CT: International Universities Press, pp. 463–494.

—— Westen, D., Misle, B., Jackson, A., Wixom, J. & Wiss, C. (1990), The borderline diagnosis in adolescents: Symptoms and developmental history. *Amer. J. Psychiat.,* 147:470–476.

MacKinnon, D. (1951), The effects of increased observation upon the accuracy of prediction. *Amer. Psychol.*, 6:311 (abstract).

Madison, P. (1961), *Freud's Concept of Repression and Defense.* Minneapolis: University of Minnesota Press.

Mahler, M. (1960), Symposium on psychotic object-relationships: III. Perceptual de-differentiation and psychotic object relationships. *Internat. J. Psycho-Anal.*, 41:548–553.

————— (1968), *On Human Symbiosis and Vicissitudes of Individuation,* Vol. 1. New York: Basic Books.

————— Pine, F. & Bergman, A. (1975), *The Psychological Birth of the Human Infant.* New York: Basic Books.

Main, M., Kaplan, N. & Cassidy, J. (1985), Security in infancy, childhood, and adulthood: A move to the level of representation. In: *Growing Points of Attachment Theory and Research* (Monograph of the Society for Research in Child Development, Vol. 50, Nos. 1–2, Serial No. 209), ed. I. Bretherton & E. Waters. Chicago: University of Chicago Press, pp. 66–104.

Marmer, S. (1991), Multiple personality disorder: A psychoanalytic perspective. *Psychiat. Clin. N. Amer.*, 14:677–693.

Masterson, J. & Rinsley, D. (1975), The borderline syndrome: The role of the mother in the genesis and psychic structure of the borderline personality. *Internat. J. Psycho-Anal.*, 56:163–177.

Maupin, E. (1965), Individual differences in response to a Zen mediation exercise. *J. Consult. Psychol.*, 29:139–145.

Mayman, M. (1963), Psychoanalytic study of the self-organization with psychological tests. In: *Recent Advances in the Study of Behavior Change,* ed. B. Wigdor. Montreal: McGill University Press, pp. 97–117.

————— (1964a), Some general propositions implicit in the clinical application of psychological tests. Unpublished manuscript, Menninger Foundation, Topeka.

————— (1964b), Form quality of Rorschach responses. Unpublished manuscript, Menninger Foundation, Topeka.

————— (1967), Object representations and object relationships in Rorschach responses. *J. Proj. Tech. and Pers. Assess.*, 31:17–24.

————— (1970), Reality contact, defense effectiveness, and psychopathology in Rorschach form level scores. In: *Developments in Rorschach Technique, Vol. 3,* ed. B. Klopfer, M. Meyer & F. Brawer. New York: Harcourt Brace Jovanovich, pp. 11–44.

————— (1976), Psychoanalytic theory in retrospect and prospect. *Bull. Menn. Clin.*, 40:199–210.

—— (1977), A multi-dimensional view of the Rorschach movement response. In: *Rorschach Psychology,* ed. M. Rickers-Ovsiankina. Huntington, NY: Krieger, pp. 229–250.

—— (1996), Rorschach imagery: The reconstruction of an inner object world in psychosexual terms. Presented to the International Rorschach Congress, Boston.

McFate, M. & Orr, F. (1949), Through adolescence with the Rorschach. *Rorschach Res. Exch.,* 13:302–319.

McMahon, J. (1964), The relationship between "overinclusive" and primary process thought in a normal and a schizophrenic population. Unpublished doctoral dissertation, New York University.

McWilliams, N. (in press), Relationship, subjectivity, and inference in diagnosis. In: *Making Diagnosis Meaningful,* ed. J. Barron. Washington, DC: APA Books.

Meloy, J. R. & Gacono, C. (1993), A borderline psychopath: "I was basically maladjusted." *J. Pers. Assess.,* 61:358–373.

—— Gacono, C. & Kenny, L. (1994), A Rorschach investigation of sexual homicide. *J. Pers. Assess.,* 62:58–67.

—— Acklin, M., Gacono, C., Murray, J. & Peterson, C. (1997), *Contemporary Rorschach Interpretation.* Hillsdale, NJ: Lawrence Erlbaum.

Menninger, K. & Holtzman, P. (1973), *Theory of Psychoanalytic Technique,* 2nd ed. New York: Basic Books.

Meyer, G. & Handler, L. (1996), The ability of the Rorschach to predict response to psychotherapy: A metaanalysis. Paper presented to the International Rorschach Congress, Boston.

Meyer, J. & Tuber, S. (1989), Intrapsychic and behavioral correlates of the phenomenon of imaginary companions in young children. *Psychoanal. Psychol.,* 6:151–168.

Michels, R. (1983), Plenary address. Presented at the symposium "Distortions of Personality Development and Their Management," Toronto, Ontario.

Modell, A. (1963), Primitive object relationships and the predisposition to schizophrenia. *Internat. J. Psycho-Anal.,* 44:282–292.

—— (1975), A narcissistic defense against affects and the illusion of self-sufficiency. *Internat. J. Psycho-Anal.,* 44:282–292.

—— (1978), The conceptualization of the therapeutic action of psychoanalysis: The action of the holding environment. *Bull. Menn. Clin.,* 42:493–504.

—— (1984), *Psychoanalysis in a New Context.* Madison, CT: International Universities Press.

Murray, J. (1985), Borderline manifestations in the Rorschachs of male transsexuals. *J. Pers. Assess.*, 49:454–466.

———— (1993), The Rorschach search for the borderline holy grail: Personality style and situation. *J. Pers. Assess.*, 61:342–357.

———— & Russ, S. (1981), Adaptive regression and types of cognitive flexibility. *J. Pers. Assess.*, 45:59–65.

Nagera, H. (1969), The imaginary companion: Its significance for ego development and conflict resolution. *The Psychoanalytic Study of the Child*, 24:165–195. New Haven: Yale University Press.

Newman, K. (1980), Defense analysis in self psychology. In: *Advances in Self Psychology*, ed. A. Goldberg. New York: International Universities Press, pp. 263–278.

Nifakis, D. (1989), Victims of father–daughter incest: An investigation using object relations theory. Unpublished doctoral dissertation, Dept. of Applied Psychology, University of Toronto.

Ogata, S., Silk, K., Goodrich, S., Lohr, N., Westen, D. & Hill, E. (1990), Childhood sexual and physical abuse in adult patients with borderline personality. *Amer. J. Psychiat.*, 147:1008–1013.

Ogden, T. (1983), The concept of internal object relations. *Internat. J. Psycho-Anal.*, 64:227–243.

———— (1989), On the concept of an autistic-contiguous position. *Internat. J. Psycho-Anal.*, 70:127–140.

O'Roark, A. & Exner, J. (1989), *History and Directory*. Hillsdale, NJ: Lawrence Erlbaum Associates.

Parmer, J. (1991), Bulimia and object relations: M.M.P.I. and Rorschach variables. *J. Pers. Assess.*, 56:266–276.

Parson, E. (1984), The reparation of the self: Clinical and theoretical dimensions in the treatment of Vietnam combat veterans. *J. Contemp. Psychother.*, 14:4–56.

Peebles, R. (1975), Rorschach as self-system in the telophasic theory of personality development. In: *Handbook of Rorschach Scales*, ed. P. Lerner. New York: International Universities Press, pp. 71–136.

Perry, J. & Klerman, G. (1978), The borderline patient. *Arch. Gen. Psychiat.*, 35:141–150.

Peterson, C. (1992), A psychotic gyneminmetic: "I just had a pregnant thought." In: *J. Pers. Assess.*, 58:464–479.

———— (1993), A borderline policeman: AKA, A cop with no COP. *J. Pers. Assess.*, 61:374–393.

Piaget, J. (1937), *The Construction of Reality in the Child*. New York: Basic Books, 1954.

———— (1959), *The Language and Thought of the Child*. London: Routledge & Kegan Paul.

Pine, F. (1962), Creativity and primary process: Sample variations. *J. Nerv. Ment. Dis.*, 134:506–511.

———— (1990), *Drive, Ego, Object, and Self*. New York: Basic Books.

———— & Holt, R. (1960), Creativity and primary process: A study of adaptive regression. *J. Abnorm. and Soc. Psychol.*, 61:370–379.

Piotrowski, Z. (1947), *A Rorschach Compendium*. Utica, NY: State Hospital Press.

———— (1957), *Perceptanalysis*. New York: Macmillan.

Piran, N. (1988), Borderline phenomena in anorexia nervosa and bulimia. In: *Primitive Mental States and the Rorschach*, ed. H. Lerner & P. Lerner. Madison, CT: International Universities Press, pp. 363–376.

———— & Lerner, P. (1987), Piagetian cognitive development and ego development: A study of anorexic patients. Unpublished manuscript, Toronto General Hospital, Toronto, Ontario.

———— & ———— (1988), Rorschach assessment of anorexia nervosa and bulimia. *Advances Pers. Assess.*, 7:77–102.

———— ———— Garfinkle, P., Kennedy, S. & Brouillette, C. (1988), Personality disorders in anorexic patients. *Internat. J. Eating Disorders*, 7:589–600.

Pistole, M. (1995), Adult attachment style and narcissistic vulnerability. *Psychoanal. Psychol.*, 12:115–126.

Pope, B. & Jensen, A. (1957), The Rorschach as an index of pathological thinking. *J. Proj. Tech.*, 21:54–62.

Powers, W. & Hamlin, R. (1955), Relationship between diagnostic category and deviant verbalizations on the Rorschach. *J. Consult. Psychol.*, 19:120–129.

Prelinger, E., Zimet, C., Schafer, R. & Levin, M. (1964), *An Ego Psychological Approach to Character Assessment*, Glencoe: Free Press.

Pruitt, W. & Spilka, B. (1964), Rorschach empathy-object relationship scale. In: *Handbook of Rorschach Scales*, ed. P. Lerner. New York: International Universities Press, 1975, pp. 315–323.

Pruyser, P. (1975), What splits in splitting. *Bull. Menn. Clin.*, 39:1–46.

Putnam, F. (1989), *Diagnosis and Treatment of Multiple Personality Disorder*. New York: The Guilford Press.

———— Guroff, J., Silberman, E., Barban, L. & Post, R. (1986), The clinical phenomenology of multiple personality disorder: Review of 100 recent cases. *J. Clin. Psychiat.*, 47:285–293.

Quirk, D., Quarrington, M., Neiger, S. & Slemon, A. (1962), The performance of acute psychotic patients on the Index of Pathological Thinking and on selected signs of idiosyncracy on the Rorschach. *J. Proj. Tech.*, 26:431–441.

Rabkin, J. (1967), Psychoanalytic assessment of change in organization of thought after psychotherapy. Unpublished doctoral dissertation. New York University.

Racker, H. (1968), *Transference and Countertransference*. New York: International Universities Press.

Rapaport, D. (1950), The theoretical implications of diagnostic testing procedures. *Congres International de Psychiatric*, 2:241–271.

——— (1951), States of consciousness: A psychopathological and psychodynamic view. In: *The Collected Papers of David Rapaport*, ed. M. Gill. New York: Basic Books, 1967, pp. 385–404.

——— (1952), Projective techniques and the theory of thinking. *J. Proj. Tech.*, 16:269–275.

——— (1957), The theory of ego autonomy: A generalization. *Bull. Menn. Clin.*, 22:13–35, 1958.

——— (1958), An historical review of psychoanalytic ego psychology. In: *The Collected Papers of David Rapaport*, ed. M. Gill. New York: Basic Books, 1967, pp. 745–757.

——— & Gill, M. (1942), A case of amnesia and its bearing on the theory of memory. In: *Collected Papers of David Rapaport*, ed. M. Gill. New York: Basic Books, 1967, pp. 113–119.

——— ——— & Schafer, R. (1945–1946), *Diagnostic Psychological Testing*, 2 vols. Chicago: Year Book.

Reich, A. (1960), Pathological forms of self-esteem regulation. *The Psychoanalytic Study of the Child*, 15:215–232. New York: International Universities Press.

Reich, W. (1933), *Character Analysis*. New York: Farrar, Straus & Giroux, 1972.

Reis, B. (1993), Toward a psychoanalytic understanding of multiple personality disorder. *Bull. Menn. Clin.*, 57:309–327.

Reiser, M. (1990), *Memory in Mind and Brain.*. New York: Basic Books.

Ribble, M. (1943), *The Rights of Infants*. New York: Columbia University Press.

Rinsley, D. (1979), The developmental etiology of borderline and narcissistic disorders. *Bull. Menn. Clin.*, 44:147–170.

Ritzler, B., Zambianco, D., Harder, D. & Kaskey, M. (1980), Psychotic patterns of the concept of the object on the Rorschach test. *J. Abn. Psychol.*, 89:46–55.

Robbins, M. (1976), Borderline personality organization: The need for a new theory. *J. Amer. Psychoanal. Assn.*, 24:831–854.

Roland, C. (1970), Anorexia nervosa: A survey of the literature and review of 30 cases. In: *Anorexia and Obesity*. Boston: Little, Brown, pp. 45–60.

Rorschach, H. (1921), *Psychodiagnostik*. Berne: Ernest Bircher (trans. *Psychodiagnostics*, 6th ed. New York: Grune & Stratton, 1964).

———— (1942), *Psychodiagnostics*. Berne: Hans Huber.

Rosegrant, J. (1995), Borderline diagnosis in projective assessment. *Psychoanal. Psychol.*, 12:407–428.

Rosenthal, D. (1975), The concept of schizophrenia disorders. In: *Genetic Research in Psychiatry*, ed. R. Fieve, D. Rosenthal & H. Brill. Baltimore: Johns Hopkins University Press, pp. 199–215.

Russ, S. (1980), Primary process integration on the Rorschach and achievement in children. *J. Pers. Assess.*, 44:338–344.

Ryan, E. (1973), The capacity of the patient to enter an elementary therapeutic relationship in the initial psychotherapy interview. Unpublished doctoral dissertation, Dept. of Psychology, University of Michigan.

Ryan, R., Avery, R., & Grolnick, W. (1985), A Rorschach assessment of children's mutuality of autonomy. *J. Pers. Assess.*, 49:6–12.

Sandler, J. (1960), The background of safety. *Internat. J. Psycho-Anal.*, 41:352–356.

———— & Rosenblatt, B. (1962), The concept of the representational world. *The Psychoanalytic Study of the Child*, 15:128–162. New York: International Universities Press.

Sarbin, T. (1943), A contribution to the study of actuarial and individual methods of prediction. *American Journal of Sociology*, 48:593–602.

Saretsky, T. (1966), Effects of chlorpromazine on primary process thought manifestations. *J. Abnorm Psychol.*, 71:247–252.

Saunders, E. (1991), Rorschach indicators of chronic childhood sexual abuse in female borderline inpatients. *Bull. Menn. Clin.*, 55:48–71.

Schachtel, E. (1966), *Experiential Foundations of Rorschach's Test*. New York: Basic Books.

Schafer, R. (1948), *Clinical Application of Psychological Tests*. New York: International Universities Press.

———— (1954), *Psychoanalytic Interpretation in Rorschach Testing*. New York: Grune & Stratton.

———— (1968), The mechanisms of defense. *Internat. J. Psycho-Anal.*, 49:49–62.

———— (1983), *The Analytic Attitude*. New York: Basic Books.

Schlesinger, H. (1973), Interaction of dynamic and reality factors in the diagnostic testing interview. *Bull. Menn. Clin.*, 37:495–518.

Schmideberg, M. (1947), The treatment of psychopathic and borderline patients. *Amer. J. Psychother.*, 1:47–71.

———— (1959), The borderline patient. In: *American Handbook of Psychiatry, Vol. 1*, ed. S. Arieti. New York: Basic Books, pp. 398–416.

Schultz, R., Braun, B. & Kluft, R. (1987), Preliminary findings about abuse in the histories of multiple personality disorders and borderline personality disorder. Unpublished manuscript, St. Louis University, St. Louis.

Schwager, E. & Spear, W. (1981), New perspectives on psychological tests as measures of change. *Bull. Menn. Clin.*, 45:527–541.

Segal, H. (1973), *Introduction to the Work of Melanie Klein*. London: Hogarth Press.

Selvini-Palazzoli, M. (1974), *Self-Starvation*. New York: Aronson.

Serban, G., Conte, H. & Plutchic, R. (1987), Borderline and schizotypal personality disorders: Mutually exclusive or overlapping? *J. Pers. Assess.*, 51:15–22.

Settlage, C. (1977), The psychoanalytic understanding of narcissistic and borderline personality disorders: Advances in developmental theory. *J. Amer. Psychoanal. Assoc.*, 25:805–833.

Shapiro, D. (1965), *Neurotic Styles*. New York: Basic Books.

Sharpe, E. (1940), Psycho-physical problems revealed in language: An examination of metaphor. In: *Collected Papers on Psychoanalysis*, ed. M. Brierly. New York: Brunner/Mazel, 1978, pp. 155–169.

Shengold, L. (1989), *Soul Murder*. New Haven, CT: Yale University Press.

Shevrin, H. & Schectman, F. (1973), The diagnostic practice in psychiatric evaluation. *Bull. Menn. Clin.*, 37:451–494.

Siegman, A. (1954), Emotionality: A hysterical character defense. *Psychoanal. Quart.*, 23:339–354.

Silverman, D. (1991), Attachment patterns and Freudian theory. *Psychoanal. Psychol.*, 8:169–193.

———— (1995), Problems with linking constructs from different domains: Commentary on Pistole's "Adult attachment style and narcissistic vulnerability." *Psychoanal. Psychol.*, 12:151–158.

Silverman, L. (1966), A technique for the study of psychodynamic relationships: The effects of subliminally presented aggressive stimuli on the production of pathological thinking in a schizophrenic population. *J. Consult. Psychol.*, 30:103–111.

——— & Candell, P. (1970), On the relationship between aggressive activation, symbiotic merging, intactness of body boundaries and
manifest pathology in schizophrenics. *J. Nerv. Ment. Dis.*,
150:387–399.

——— & Goldwebber, A. (1966), A further study of the effects of subliminal aggressive stimulation on thinking. *J. Nerv. Ment. Dis.*,
143:463–472.

Singer, J. (1975), *The Inner World of Daydreaming.* New York: Harper
and Row.

Singer, M. (1977), The borderline diagnosis and psychological tests:
Review and research. In: *Borderline Personality Disorders,*
ed. P. Hartocollis. New York: International Universities Press,
pp. 193–212.

——— & Larson, D. (1981), Borderline personality and the Rorschach
test. *Arch. Gen. Psychiat.*, 38:693–698.

Skelton, M., Boik, R. & Madero, J. (1995), Thought disorder on the
WAIS-R relative to the Rorschach: Assessing Identity-Disordered
Adolescents. *J. Pers. Assess.*, 65:533–549.

Slade, A. & Aber, J. (1992), Attachments, drives, and development:
Conflicts and convergences in theory. In: *Interface of Psycho-
analysis and Psychology,* ed. J. Barron, M. Eagle & D. Wolitzsky.
Washington, DC: APA Publications, pp. 154–185.

Sloan, P., Arsenault, L., Hilsenroth, M., Handler, L. & Harvill, L. (1996),
Rorschach measures of posttraumatic stress in Persian Gulf War
Veterans: A three-year follow-up study. *J. Pers. Assess.*, 66:54–64.

——— ——— ——— Harvill, L. & Handler, L. (1995), Rorschach measures of posttraumatic stress in Persian Gulf War veterans. *J. Pers.
Assess.*, 64:379–414.

Small, A., Teango, L., Madero, J., Gross, H. & Ebert, M. (1982), A comparison of anorexics and schizophrenics on psychodiagnostic measures. *Internat. J. Eating Disorders,* 1:49–57.

Smith, B. (1990), Potential space and the Rorschach: An application of
object relations theory. *J. Pers. Assess.*, 55:756–767.

——— (1994), Object relations theory and the integration of empirical
and psychoanalytic approaches to Rorschach interpretation.
Rorschachiana, 19:61–77.

——— (1997), White bird flight from the terror of empty space. In:
Contemporary Rorschach Interpretation, ed. J. R. Meloy, M.
Acklin, C. Gacono, J. Murray & C. Peterson. Hillsdale, NJ:
Lawrence Erlbaum.

Smith, J., Hillard, M., Walsh, R., Kubacki, S. & Morgan, C. (1991),

Rorschach assessment of purging and nonpurging bulimics. *J. Pers. Assess.*, 56:277–288.

Smith, K. (1980), Object relations concepts as applied to the borderline level of ego functioning. In: *Borderline Phenomena and the Rorschach Test,* ed. J. Kwawer, H. Lerner, P. Lerner & A. Sugarman. New York: International Universities Press, pp. 59–88.

Spear, W. (1980), The psychological assessment of structural and thematic object representations in borderline and schizophrenic patients. In: *Borderline Phenomena and the Rorschach Test,* ed. J. Kwawer, H. Lerner, P. Lerner & A. Sugarman. New York: International Universities Press, pp. 321–342.

———— & Schwager, E. (1980), New perspectives on the use of psychological tests as a measure of change over the course of intensive inpatient psychotherapy. Presented at meeting of the Society for Personality Assessment, Tampa, FL.

———— & Sugarman, A. (1984), Dimensions of internalized object relations in borderline and schizophrenic patients. *Psychoanal. Psychol.,* 1:113–130.

Sperling, O. (1954), An imaginary companion representing a pre-stage of the superego. *The Psychoanalytic Study of the Child,* 9:252–258. New Haven, CT: Yale University Press.

Spiegel, D. (1988), Dissociation and hypnosis in post-traumatic stress disorder. *Journal of Traumatic Stress,* 1:17–33.

———— & Cardeña, E. (1991), Disintegrated experience: The dissociative disorders revisited. *J. Abn. Psychol.,* 100:366–378.

Spitzer, R., Endicott, J. & Robbins, E. (1975), Research Diagnostic Criteria (RDC). *Psychopharmacol. Bull.,* 11:22–24.

Steinberg, B. (1997), The Boyer Institute's psychoanalytic interpretive method of assessing psychotic and primitive mental states. Presented to the Society for Personality Assessment, San Diego.

Stern, A. (1938), Psychoanalytic investigation of therapy in the borderline neurosis. *Psychoanal. Quart.,* 7:467–489.

Stolorow, R. & Lachmann, F. (1980), *Psychoanalysis of Developmental Arrest.* New York: International Universities Press.

Stone, M. (1980), *The Borderline Syndromes..* New York: McGraw-Hill.

Strober, M. & Goldenberg, J. (1981), Ego boundary disturbance in juvenile anorexia nervosa. *J. Clin. Psychol.,* 37:433–438.

Stuart, J., Westen, D., Lohr, N., Benjamin, J., Becker, S., Vorus, N. & Silk, K. (1990), Object relations in borderlines, depressives, and normals: An examination of human responses on the Rorschach. *J. Pers. Assess.,* 55:296–318.

Sugarman, A. (1979), The infantile personality: Orality in the hysteric revisited. *Internat. J. Psycho-Anal.,* 60:501–513.

———— (1985), The nature of clinical assessment. Unpublished manuscript. San Diego.

———— (1991), Where's the beef? Putting personality back into personality assessment. *J. Pers. Assess.,* 56:130–144.

———— & Lerner, H. (1980), Reflections on the current state of the borderline concept. In: *Borderline Phenomena and the Rorschach Test,* ed. J. Kwawer, H. Lerner, P. Lerner & A. Sugarman. New York: International Universities Press, pp. 11–38.

———— Quinlan, D. & Devenis, L. (1982), Ego boundary disturbance in juvenile anorexia nervosa. *J. Pers. Assess.,* 46:455–461.

Sullivan, H. S. (1956), *Clinical Studies in Psychiatry.* New York: Norton.

Swanson, G., Blount, J. & Bruno, R. (1990), Comprehensive system Rorschach data on Vietnam combat veterans. *J. Pers. Assess.,* 54:160–169.

Teicholtz, J. (1978), A selected review of the psychoanalytic literature on theoretical conceptualizations of narcissism. *J. Amer. Psychoanal. Assn.,* 26:831–862.

Thomas, T. (1987), A Rorschach investigation of borderline and attention deficit disorder children. Presented to the Society for Personality Assessment, San Francisco.

Thompson, A. (1986), An object relations theory of affect maturity. In: *Assessing Object Relations Phenomena,* ed. M. Kisson. New York: International Universities Press, pp. 207–224.

Tolpin, M. & Kohut, H. (1978), The disorders of the self: The psychopathology of the first year of life. In: *The Course of Life, Vol. 1,* ed. G. Pollock & S. Greenspan. Washington, DC: NIMH, pp. 425–458.

Tong, L., Oakes, K. & McDowell, M. (1987), Personality development following sexual abuse. *Child Abuse and Neglect,* 11:371–383.

Tuber, S. (1983), Children's Rorschach scores as predictors of later adjustment. *J. Consult. and Clin. Psychol.,* 51:379–385.

———— (1992), Empirical and clinical assessments of children's object relations and object representations. *J. Pers. Assess.,* 58:179–197.

———— & Coates, S. (1989), Indices of psychopathology in the Rorschachs of boys with severe gender identity disorder. *J. Pers. Assess.,* 57:100–112.

———— Frank, M. & Santostefano, S. (1989), Children's anticipation of impending surgery. *Bull. Menn. Clin.,* 53:501–511.

Tufts New England Medical Center Division of Child Psychiatry (1984), Sexually Exploited Children: Service and Research Project (Final Rep. No. 80-JN-AX001 for the Office of Juvenile Justice and Delinquency Prevention). Washington, DC: U.S. Department of Justice.

Tustin, F. (1981), *Autistic States in Children*. Boston: Routledge & Kegan Paul.

——— (1984), Autistic shapes. *Internat. Rev. Psycho-Anal.*, 11:279–290.

——— (1990), *The Protective Shell in Children and Adults*. London: Karnac Books.

Urist, J. (1973), The Rorschach test as a multidimensional measure of object relations. Unpublished doctoral dissertation, Dept. of Psychology, University of Michigan.

——— (1977), The Rorschach test and the assessment of object relations. *J. Pers. Assess.*, 41:3–9.

——— & Shill, M. (1982), Validity of the Rorschach Mutuality of Autonomy Scale: A replication using excerpted responses. *J. Pers. Assess.*, 46:451–454.

Vaillant, G. (1977), *Adaption to Life*. Boston: Little, Brown.

Van-Der Keshet, J. (1988), Anorexic patients and ballet students: A Rorschach analysis. Unpublished doctoral dissertation, Dept. of Applied Psychology, University of Toronto.

Vernon, P. (1950), The validation of civil service selection board procedures. *Occupational Psychology*, 24:75–95.

Wagner, E. & Heise, M. (1974), A comparison of Rorschach records of three multiple personalities. *J. Pers. Assess*, 38:308–331.

——— & Wagner, C. (1978), Similar Rorschach patterning in three cases of anorexia nervosa. *J. Pers. Assess.*, 42:426–433.

——— Allison, B. & Wagner, C. (1983), Diagnosing multiple personalities with the Rorschach: A confirmation. *J. Pers. Assess.*, 47:143–144.

Wallerstein, R. (1968), The psychotherapy research project of the Menninger Foundation: A seminal view. In: *Research in Psychotherapy*, Vol. 3, ed. J. Shlien. Washington, DC: American Psychological Association, pp. 584–605.

Watkins, J. & Stauffacher, J. (1952), An index of pathological thinking in the Rorschach. *J. Proj. Tech.*, 16:276–286.

Weiner, I. (1977), Approaches to Rorschach validation. In: *Rorschach Psychology*, 2nd ed., ed. M. Rickers-Ovsiankina. Huntingdon, NY: Krieger, pp. 575–608.

——— (1994), The Rorschach Inkblot Method (RIM) is not a test:

Implications for theory and practice. *J. Pers. Assess.*, 62:498–504.

―――― & Exner, J. (1991), Rorschach changes in long-term and short-term psychotherapy. *J. Pers. Assess.*, 56:453–465.

Weisberg, L., Norman, D. & Herzog, D. (1987), Personality functioning in normal weight bulimia. *Internat. J. Eating Disorders*, 6:615–631.

Wender, P. (1977), The contribution of adoption studies to an understanding of the phenomenology and etiology of borderline schizophrenia. In: *Borderline Personality Disorders*, ed. P. Hartocollis. New York: International Universities Press, pp. 255–269.

Werner, H. (1940), *The Comparative Psychology of Mental Development*. New York: International Universities Press, 1957.

―――― & Kaplan, B. (1963), *Symbol Formation*. New York: Wiley.

Westen, D. (1991), Social cognition and object relations. *Psychol. Bull.*, 109:429–455.

―――― (1993), Social cognition and object relations scale: Q-sort for projective stories. Unpublished manuscript, Cambridge Hospital and Harvard Medical School, Cambridge.

―――― Lohr, N., Silk, K., Kerber, K. & Goodrich, S. (1989), Object relations and social cognition TAT scoring manual 14th ed. Unpublished manuscript, University of Michigan, Ann Arbor.

Widiger, T. (1982), Psychological tests and the borderline diagnosis. *J. Pers. Assess.*, 46:227–238.

Willock, B. (1992), Projection, transitional phenomena, and the Rorschach. *J. Pers. Assess.*, 59:99–116.

Wilson, A. (1985), Boundary disturbance in borderline and psychotic states. *J. Pers. Assess.*, 49:346–355.

―――― (1988), Levels of depression and clinical assessment. In: *Primitive Mental States and the Rorschach*, ed. H. Lerner & P. Lerner. Madison, CT: International Universities Press, pp. 441–462.

Winnicott, D. (1935), The manic defense. In: *Through Paediatrics to Psycho-Analysis*. London: Hogarth Press, 1975, pp. 129–144.

―――― (1953), Transitional objects and transitional phenomena. *Internat. J. Psycho-Anal.*, 34:89–97

―――― (1956), The antisocial tendency. In: *Through Paediatrics to Psycho-Analysis*. London: Hogarth Press, 1975, pp. 306–315.

―――― (1960), The theory of the parent-infant relationship. *Internat. J. Psycho-Anal.*, 41:385–395.

―――― (1961), Ego distortion in terms of true and false self. In: *The Maturational Processes and the Facilitating Environment*. Madison, CT: International Universities Press, 1965, pp. 140–152.

—— (1969), The use of an object. *Internat. J. Psycho-Anal.*, 50:711–716.

—— (1971), *Playing and Reality*. New York: Basic Books.

Witkin, H. (1950), Individual differences in ease of perception of embedded figures. *J. Pers. Assess.*, 19:1–15.

Wright, B. (1986), An approach to parent-infant psychotherapy. *Infant Mental Health J.*, 7:247–263.

Wright, N. & Abbey, D. (1965), Perceptual deprivation tolerance and adequacy of defense. *Percept. Motor. Skills*, 20:35–38.

—— & Zubek, J. (1969), Relationship between perceptual deprivation tolerance and adequacy of defense as measured by the Rorschach. *J. Abnorm Psychol.*, 74:615–617.

Young, H. (1959), A test of the Witkin's field-dependence hypothesis. *J. Abnorm. & Soc. Psychol.*, 59:188–192.

Young, W. (1988), Psychodynamics and dissociation: All that switches is not split. *Dissociation*, 1:33–38.

Zeanah, C. & Barton, M. (1989), Introduction: Internal representations and parent-infant relationships. *Infant Mental Health J.*, 10:135–141.

—— Anders, T., Seifer, R., & Stern, D. (1989), Implications of research on infant development for psychodynamic theory and practice. *J. Amer. Acad. Child & Adolesc. Psychiat.*, 28:657–668.

Zimet, C. & Fine, H. (1965), Primary and secondary process thinking in two types of schizophrenia. *J. Proj. Tech. & Personal. Assess.*, 29:93–99.

INDEX